Dame Eva Turner

'A Life On The High Cs'

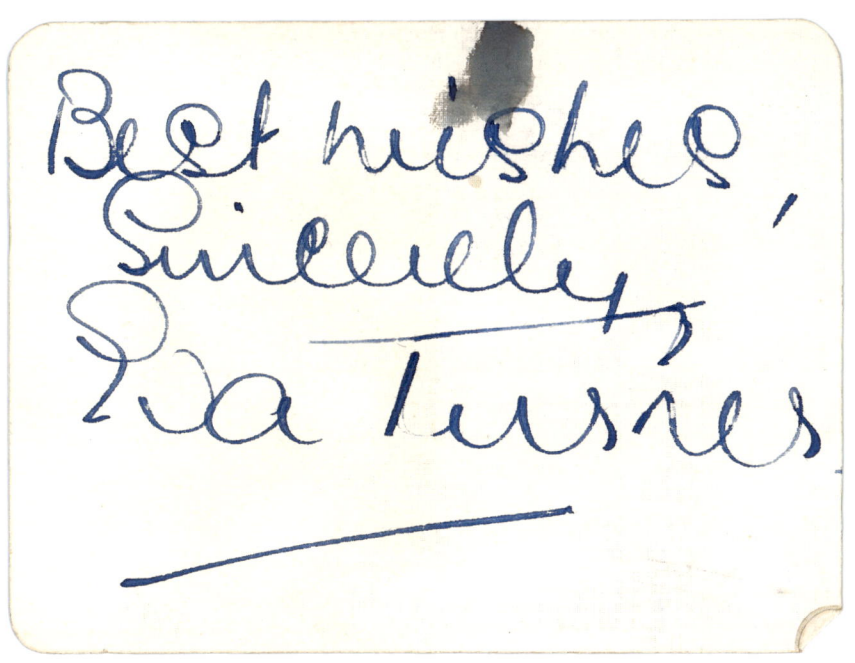

English Prima Donna
1892-1990

DAME EVA TURNER
'A Life on the High Cs'

© LINDA ESTHER GRAY 2011
ALL RIGHTS RESERVED

No part of this publication may be reproduced, stored in a retrievable system or transmitted, in any form or by any means, electronic, mechanical, photocopying, recording or otherwise, without the prior permission in writing of the copyright owner and publisher.

ISBN No 978-0-9555505-2-2

First Published April 2011

Green Oak Publishing
35 Green Lane, New Malden, Surrey, KT3 5BX
www.singbelcanto.com

Designed by Justin Spain

Printed in Great Britain by MPG Books Limited
Victoria Square, Bodmin, Cornwall PL31 1EB

DAME EVA TURNER
A SINGER

*'How many things by season, seasoned are to
their right praise and true perfection!'*

WILLIAM SHAKESPEARE

Researched and Written by
LINDA ESTHER GRAY

FINANCED AND SPONSORED BY ROBERT HENDRA

Published by Green Oak Publishing

Forward

Dame Eva Turner is a beacon of light in my life.

I met her in 1970, when she was 78 years of age and I was 21 and thereafter the light burned. She was a force for good and after the end of her long life, lived on in the hearts of those who knew her. Eva Turner's message was a strong one: work hard at whatever talent you have and it will bear fruit.

Many of her contemporaries wrote their autobiographies but she rejected this idea saying: 'You are mistress of the unspoken word but the spoken word is mistress of you.' Neither did she invite anyone to write her story, nor when asked by many if they might write it, did she consent, shaking her head saying: 'There are only 24 hours in a day dear and I do not have enough time to give you the information you would need.'

Nevertheless, she carefully saved many documents and memorabilia and left them in the care of her relative Katherine Morgan who in turn, at Eva's request, donated them to the archives of the Royal Opera House. Dame Eva did not destroy any evidence of her life; that would not have been her style, although some things were lost when her house was hit by a bomb and later demolished during the war. It is thanks to the kindness of both Katherine Morgan and the Royal Opera House Collections Department, with Francesca Franchi at its helm, that I was able to sift through this personal material and, over the period of a year, gather information to begin Eva Turner's story. Nearing the completion of the book, Dame Gwyneth Jones very kindly brought, from Switzerland, memorabilia which she had housed for Dame Eva after helping her clear out Villa Junesca before selling it and so I was able to ascertain certain facts and fill in a few gaps in her Italian years.

Many others helped me on the way, including her Alma Mater, the Royal Academy of Music, where Janet Snowman was particularly encouraging and helpful, and John Streets, one of Eva's colleagues from her teaching days there, was a tower of strength during the initial writing stage of the book. Angela Arratoon very kindly made the tapes of Dame Eva's 90th Birthday Celebration at the Coliseum available to me and other information was gleaned from; interviewing people who knew her, listening to private interviews which she had given, notably to Daniel Snowman and Catherine David and interviews from the archives of British Broadcasting Corporation Radio and Television: 'This is Your Life', 'Kaleidoscope', Sue MacGregor, Teleri Bevin, Roy Plomley and

London Broadcasting Company, and from words which others have written about her. Rosemary Owens, one of her American friends, interviewed colleagues and students from Eva Turner's Oklahoma days for her doctorate, the subject of which was Eva Turner. The notes from these interviews were among Dame Eva's papers and I have used information from them.

Dame Eva was focused on her life's journey of singing, with few distracting interests, but she loved people and included many in her life, some of whom are now part of her story. The sections telling details of her more distant friends and associates, or the social history of Eva Turner's times, have been placed across the margin. If the reader already knows the information in those little cameos, they can be missed out and Eva's own story can be read without distractions but I would hope that rather than being ignored, the insets could be treated like photos and looked at in that way, thus adding background interest and flavour to her story.

All who knew Eva Turner cheered me on and willingly helped in any way they could because they wanted the world to share and remember her. She was a pioneer in the world of singing and as such, not only a great singer, but part of the history of the developments in singing in the 20th century.

'Thank you'

To all who helped this book into life and most importantly,
to Eva Turner herself for all she gave to all of us.

Filling the Bill

1.	1892-1915	Lifestyle and Family	1
2.	1915-1924	The Royal Carl Rosa Opera Company	31
3.	1924-1927	Italian Beginnings	75
4.	1928-1933	Eva Turner Triumphs	113
5.	1933-1939	Day to Day Life and Performances	163
6.	1940-1948	War Years and Final Performances	219
7.	1949-1959	Oklahoma	243
8.	1959-1982	London	273
9.	1982-1984	Celebrations	319
10.	1985-1990	And Draw her Home with Music	333
Appendix			347
Index			385

CHAPTER ONE

1892-1915 Lifestyle and Family

Wednesday 21st January 1976 Bayswater, London

'God speed! God speed!' says Dame Eva Turner in projected tones to her television, whilst clasping her hands under her chin. She is exactly seven weeks away from her eighty-fourth birthday. Dame Eva always gets a little bit over-excited and nervous as her next birthday approaches and when it does eventually come, there is relief and celebration in the air. The very next day she will announce that she is in her eighty-fifth year and so she goes forward with hope and confidence towards the next number.

Her confidence this year had been a little dented, the previous week, by the death of Dame Agatha Christie (a year older than our Dame), who died aged eighty five and for whom music had been: 'the essence of the being'. Dame Agatha loved singing and playing the piano and had even dreamt of being a performer as a young person but when she was told by an associate of the Metropolitan Opera House that her voice was essentially weak and that she seemed not to have the temperament to perform the piano in public, she put wishful thinking to the side saying: 'If the thing you want beyond anything cannot be, it is much better to recognise it and go forward instead of dwelling on one's regrets and hopes.'

Dame Eva, who is a renowned influential singing teacher, approves of this direct, truthful approach as, although it is painful for both parties at the time to recognise lack of talent, it allows the student's life to flourish in another direction. When asked, during an interview for the BBC radio programme *Kaleidoscope*, if she ever told students that they had no chance of a future in music she replied, 'Oh yes, I've told one or two. I think it is only right. I don't think they should be left in a fool's paradise and waste their years.'

Dame Eva Turner, in January, 1976, travels with energy towards her own centenary, which is a mere sixteen years away. She looks like a little wise owl, with her hazel eyes looking intently from behind thick glasses, which she has recently started to wear, after a successful cataract operation. Her once-burnished-gold-waist-length hair is now short, thick and wavy, and is grey with the merest hint of blue colouring. She is positioned in front of her television, ready to bear witness to Concorde's first passenger flight and has interrupted a scheduled singing lesson to watch and wish the elegant bird, 'Bon voyage'.

The plane glides along the runway and her eyes never leave the screen as she clasps her hands in a prayer-like position. She could be Elisabeth in *Tannhäuser* as she sits, concentrating, with inner stillness, patience and a sense of bowing to the inevitable, whilst hoping for the best. Her back is straight in her grey, serge morning dress. A beautifully simple, pewter brooch decorates the neckline.

'No sparkling jewels before 6.30' is the golden house rule, never to be broken. She is also wearing three strings of pearls, as understatement is never her forte and they shine on her stunning skin, untouched by sun, as she waits for the plane to take off. She sits with her rather large hands clasped on the table and her upright figure surrounded by an aura of sacred respect as she honours a wonderful new happening; the breaking of the barrier of the speed of sound by a passenger airliner.

No relaxed easy chair is used for watching television at any time and so Dame Eva, Anne Ridyard, her secretary-companion, and the student, sit on high backed dining chairs, which live round the table where all important happenings evolve. The chairs are angled towards the smallish television, tucked away in the far corner of this large basement room.

26 Palace Court, Bayswater, London

Apart from teaching, (which happens in the studio/sitting room directly above) and Dame Eva's bedroom, also on the ground level next to it, most of indoor life at 26 Palace Court takes place in this dining room. There is a small back yard but no interest is shown in that and there are certainly no pots of flowers there, as dutiful care and watering, which they would demand, would divert precious time from focusing on the more important aspects of the life of a singer. Sitting in the sun would not be of interest either as this is considered a strange activity. Tenants occupy the upper storeys of this large, grand house and kindly overlook her, sometimes Victorian, living rules, such as; friends should be met outside the home lest their constant visits wear out the stair carpet leading to the upper

2   Dame Eva Turner   A Life on the High Cs

reaches of this six storey house. This carpet also has special attention if a hard-up student needs free lessons, or some extra cash in exchange for vacuuming it.

The three watch the television from a fair distance away. Anne Ridyard's chair is angled rather less steeply towards it, as her main attention is still on her typewriter, on which she is performing the almost saintly task of dealing with the Dame's perpetually full mail-trolley. Every scrap of paper which enters Palace Court is honoured with a thoughtful reply, typed by Anne and signed by Dame Eva. Dame Eva requests, rather coldly and over-politely, that Anne stops the noisy task in hand and gives the television her full attention for the few minutes it would take to see Concorde safely off the ground, 'Anne dear, I think we should respect this wonderful achievement and give it our full attention. Don't you?'

This request is made as a rather grand, imperious aside, given on stage to a lesser fellow performer, while not wanting the audience to take part in the discussion. With a sigh and a resigned look, Anne does as requested and Eva thanks her graciously and more publicly as Concorde gets up speed and leaves the ground. The little audience gives a small cheer and claps. Dame Eva leads the applause and very soon the boom of the plane breaking the speed of sound is heard and she once again wishes the passengers, 'God speed', as these British and French sisters fly off to Bahrain and Rio de Janeiro. 'Blessings! Blessings!' she prays aloud as the plane disappears into the blue yonder.

Anne Ridyard

Eva Turner as Leonore in 'Fidelio'

'Didn't you sing in Rio, Eva?' asks Anne after the television has been switched off.

'Yes dear, I had a grrreat success there with *Fidelio*. You know dearrr' she says turning to the student, 'in those days we had to travel with our own costumes. I will show you my travelling trunks and my Leonore costume one day when we have more time. It was hard work but sooo wonderful. Now dear', she says, as if the interruption of the lesson had been the student's idea, 'we must get on. We have a lot to achieve. Your placement has to be brrrought reallly forward if you are going to sing Madama Butterfly with success. The tessitura is verrrrrrrry high and challenging so let's get going.'

1892 -1915 Lifestyle And Family 3

Studio / Lounge Palace Court

'Annie dear' she smiles, walking round the table to take hold of her friend's hand, 'we will be down again in about an hour. Could you get the coffee organised? Thank you dear.' Anne smiles back. Perhaps a little touch of guilt at her sharp words has entered the room and with it, a touching love and a moment of human togetherness has certainly appeared.

Dame Eva leads the way on the steep stairs at a pretty fast rate for an octogenarian. 'I don't know what I would do without Anne', she says between breaths as she opens the studio door, first choosing a key from the large bunch which she carries around with her, and goes in, 'she is truly a wonderful person. I am so grateful for all she does for me.'

Hurrying across the room, round her treasured Blüthner piano, positioned near the window seat, which houses some of her many old precious scores and which curves round the high oriel window, she sits down with her back to the outside world, ('my piano is positioned here to gain the most light') on the long piano stool, recently re-covered in a tapestry sewn by Anne. Dame Eva arranges the pencils and rubber and other bits and pieces on top of the piano in an orderly manner, as she has been doing for many years. Perhaps she feels that external order leads to inner calm, allowing a place inside one's self to be claimed for study and improvement on the chosen path: 'Self discipline has to be maintained in all walks of life.'

She knows her *Madama Butterfly* score intimately and immediately turns to Cio Cio San's entrance music. Dame Eva is a good pianist and her long, red-painted fingernails click on the keys, as her mind takes her far away to the islands of Japan where she, dressed in a formal Japanese wedding dress, walks into an oriental garden, carrying her parasol above her head. Following are her faithful Suzuki, her cousins, her aunts and uncles, also dressed formally to be part of her wedding celebrations. There to meet this little 15 year old girl, is her American Captain Pinkerton, who will, during this duet, call her 'Butterfly' and become her beloved husband. A shadow crosses the garden for Butterfly, as Eva senses the memory of 'the other woman', who until that night she had been; Kate Pinkerton, a part and her first Puccini role, for which she had been paid half a crown. Eva, in real life, had never been the 'other woman' but had played many parts on stage in her career which did not reflect her own life.

At this moment, in her mind's eye, she is Madama Butterfly, the star and so she must, and would, focus and use this wonderful, unexpected opportunity to sing well and impress and thrill the public present at a Carl Rosa Opera Company production in 1922 at the Opera House Manchester. The next day's Manchester Guardian reported on March 3rd:

> *'Miss Kate Campion was unable to sing Butterfly and Miss Eva Turner took her place. If it was a last minute effort of Miss Turner's, her work in this most difficult character was extraordinarily good.'*

Madama Butterfly, written by Puccini, became one of her favourite roles and it was when she was singing it on June 3rd, 1924 at the Scala Theatre, Charlotte Street, off Tottenham Court Road in London, that Ettore Panizza, composer and conductor from Buenos Aires, heard about her. At that time he was conducting at Covent Garden and asked her to come there and audition for him and after hearing her, offered her an audition for that most famous of opera companies, La Scala, Milan.

That memory fades and she is now eighty-three years old with all of that glory and excitement both behind her and still alive inside her. 'Now dear, you must prrroject. The Royal Festival Hall is a tiny bit dry and it will take some singing but you can do it. I'll be there with Anne and I was wondering if we could include dear Gladys Parr in our party. She was a verrry fine singer you know and an excellent Suzuki. Thank you dear. Now, you must not sing too softly, no matter who says so. You must get the voice going and accelerate as you sing these wooonderrrrful ascending phrases – Don't move!!!' she advises in projected tones putting her finger in the space behind her front teeth and grimacing. Presumably this is where one does not move from. 'You must keep going. I can't hear you dear. Oh for goodness sake – just do it'.

These last instructions are shouted over the top of the piano as she looks up, turns the page and gets back to her orchestral task. 'Look in the glass. Smile! Don't move!' she insists, as the music continues. Nothing very specific at this stage, just the words of encouragement to a runner (the singer) from the trainer (the teacher) riding alongside on

Eva Turner as Madama Butterfly

1892 -1915 Lifestyle And Family

a bicycle, since the real work of bringing the voice forward has been achieved earlier during the exercises. Even then, however, she growled and shouted about doing it quicker, faster, better and most often 'properly', as she flew around the piano banging out notes, not talking about how to do it. 'If the forward placement is maintained then there is no need for words of explanation. Of course you can sing the top C. Just keep accelerating towards it, don't move. Just do it. I couldn't wait to show off my top C. I would have paid them to let me sing. Now don't let doubt enter the room. Well done that was excellent', she says as she closes her score at the end of Act 1. 'Now, dear Anne will have our coffee ready. We deserve it. Let's go down and join her.'

Identity Certificate for entry into Ireland

The lesson is ended abruptly at Dame Eva's bidding, with no thought that there may be a question or two in the student's mind. They leave the room and Dame Eva locks the door behind them. 'You could write what has to be said about singing on the back of a postage stamp. The rrrrreal task is to do it. Not talk about it. Just do it! Lamperti the great vocal teacher said '"Se vuol cantare, bisogna studiare al dimeno sette anni" (If you want to sing you must study at least seven years!)', she says into the corridor. 'Scusi dear! Scusi', as she passes the student to travel first along the narrow hall passage. She is like a small tank in full budgerigar flight: broad backed, straight as a post, her size eight feet carrying her five foot stature (she has surely shrunk a little from the five foot five inches declared on her Police Certificate of Identity for entry to Ireland in 1918!). She moves with an energy which could have moved mountains and brings Boadicea to mind. There seems to be an invisible battle being fought with life itself, as she makes every step count and leads this private little caravan forward to the top of the stairs, as if it were crossing the Sahara Desert.

'You know dear, Elizabeth Vaughan, a Welsh girl, I sang sooo much in Wales, is a verry fine Butterfly. When I went to Japan in 1967, to judge the world-wide *Madama Butterfly* Competition, I did not agree with the choice of two Russian singers to share the first prize. They had very good voices but were not, for my taste, Butterflies. I had been left a powder compact, made by Cartier, by a very dear friend Sybil Seligman, you know, the mother of Vincent who wrote the famous book *Puccini Among Friends*. Sybil knew Puccini intimately. I gave Elizabeth this very beautiful compact which was gold inside and engraved with an inscription, in Puccini's own writing "Sybil". I did this to let her know that for me she was the winner.'

'Anne dear', we enter the dining room. 'Son qui', Dame Eva sings Cavaradossi's words to Tosca quietly to herself.

'Your coffee has been ready for ages. You have been a long time', smiles Anne gently, as they sit down.

'Well dear we can't help that. Important work had to be done and we have achieved a lot. Did you hear us? I do hope you haven't let the pot boil over. You know how I adooore our Italian coffee pot. I hope you laid the milk bottle on its side to get the last of the milk, Love. Where is the mail? Has it arrived yet? There was nothing behind the door as we came down. Any phone calls for me?'

'Will you stop fussing Eva and sit down please?' says the long suffering, not so meek, little round, white-haired Anne, as the small galleon approaches the seat at the top of the table.

Dame Eva stretches for her diary and lays it in front of her. 'Let us make time for another lesson before your concert', she says as she opens the page-a-day diary. She likes to look at it without interference and digest her schedule by reading it carefully, sometimes aloud if there is an impressive entry like, '6.00 St James Palace', not an uncommon event in her interesting life. Her very bold clear writing fills the page. 'Now, I will phone Glad before you leave, to remind her about your concert. She will be so pleased to be included. Thank you dear that is most kind of you. She will of course thank you herself.'

Dame Eva charges three guineas for a singing lesson, while the going rate among fashionable teachers could be as much as £25, so the visit to the Royal Festival Hall box office for an extra ticket (which will now be necessary, since the three previously purchased tickets are already spoken for), although inconvenient, will not cause financial hardship. This moderate teaching fee is one of the ways in which Dame Eva makes it known that she understands the frugal life of a student. Her thoughtfulness creates camaraderie in the centre of the clearly defined boundaries between the international star and the aspiring singer.

'Linda, will you please fetch the biscuits from the boiler room? We keep them there so that they will be crrisp and tassty. Anne dear you love the music of *Butterfly*.'

Sotto voce aside, which could be heard out in the street, to me, 'Bring the sssugar from the top of the sssideboard dear.'

'Yes I do. Thank you', says Anne as she brings the tray with a jug of piping hot milk, an Italian coffee pot and three bone china cups and saucers, white with rosebud design on them, from the small galley kitchen, five feet away from Dame Eva's chair.

'What else are you singing love?' Anne asks in her lovely soft Lancashire accent.

'*Leise, leise* from *Der Freischütz* and *Ritorna Vincitor* from *Aida*', I reply.

'WHAT????' shouts Dame Eva, 'You didn't tell me THAT! We must get that diary organised.'

'For goodness sake Eva stop shouting and let the girl drink her coffee in peace'.

A chastened, childlike, hurt Eva appears from the midst of her frustration, apologises to the room in general and concentrates on her coffee.

Coffee at Palace Court is, like tea in Japan, a lovely occasion of natural politeness to, and interest in, other people's lives and

Dame Eva does not want this ritual to be disturbed, even in the face of such a shock, so recovers her composure, after this small huff, to take part in the exchanging of news that is happening around her. Coffee was served later today because of Concorde but it usually happens around 11.00, when the 9.30 student is leaving and the 11.00 one is arriving. The diary is now opened and two lessons are added for next week in her very strong writing. The book is closed and Dame Eva sits staring into space.

'You know dear, my father died of a heart attack when he was nearly seventy, while he was sitting in the stalls at the Royal Opera House on September 26th 1935. It happened just as the lights went down, seconds before the curtain went up on a new production of Weber's *Der Freischütz*, in English, in which I was singing Agathe. Sir Thomas Beecham gave clear instructions to all backstage that I was not to be told, so after a short pause, the opera commenced without my knowing about father. Norman, my brother, who had not been at the performance, was called to the hospital and when he arrived was told that father had passed away. Norman came into my dressing room after the show to break the bad news to me. Sir Thomas was just behind him and told us that father had in fact died in the theatre despite efforts to resuscitate him. Norman and I grieved alone for a few minutes and with his agreement I decided, after looking into my heart that I was glad Sir Thomas had decided not to tell me, as father would have wanted me to sing the performance, since he had always shared my dream of being a great singer and this had been a very important performance for me. Sir Thomas was wonderrful, wonderrful. The management announced father's death after the performance saying that I had only just been told.'

(The Times tells us that Eva Turner's singing of Agathe's great aria *Leise, leise* on that occasion was: 'as good as anything heard at Covent Garden for a long while.')

Eva Turner had spoken as if in a trance and was now in a very different place from that where she had been exuberantly performing, before coffee was served. It was as if she had become Agathe, singing the prayer in Act 3. There was a hushed silence around her which no one would have dared disturb, as she sat centre stage. Anne gently stretched out a hand across the dark green, linen table cover, to touch Eva's, while covertly looking at her with concern. The presence of her father whom she had loved was with us in the room.

Members of the Turner family - Charles (left)

Charles Turner

Charles Turner was born in Standish, Lancashire on May 13th, 1866 and had four brothers and six sisters. His mother was Hannah and his father, Martin, worked as an engine tender in the cotton mills which were the main employers at that time in that part of the world. Charles's grandfather, Daniel, had been a cotton weaver, living at the poetically named address of Almond Brook, and so it seemed obvious that Charles too should be employed in the cotton mills of Lancashire.

Charles Turner and Elizabeth Park were married in the district of Rochdale on January 23rd, 1889 and by 1891 were living in Victoria Street in Chadderton, a small suburb of Oldham, directly opposite the Manor Mill, where Charles worked. They then moved to Oldham itself, 5 Goddard Street, where Eva was born in 1892. Broadway Mill was on Goddard Street so once again Charles lived in

The name Turner comes from the French - someone who works with a lathe, a platform which turns to enable a wooden, bronze or pottery object placed on it to be worked on. In Ancient Egypt the lathe would have been turned by someone pulling a rope while another person used a sharp instrument to make shapes on the object on top. The early spinning wheels and looms had many complicated wooden pieces in them, probably turned on a lathe of their own time, so we might imagine the Turner family being involved in the wool industry which preceded the cotton one.

the street where he worked, by this time having been promoted to mill engineer. In the 1901 census, Eva was nine years old and her brother Norman, born in 1895, was six, Charles's stated profession was a cotton mill engine driver and the four Turners lived in Stanley Road. The head of the house, Charles, was a determined, hard-working young man, with drive and ambition for his family, who took home a good wage and enjoyed the special privileges and status which went with his job. He worked hard to realise his dreams for their future but as sometimes happens, it seems that in marrying Elizabeth, there was an attraction of opposites.

Elizabeth Park

Elizabeth Park, born on August 31st, 1868, was one of three daughters; her sister Salina and a step sister, Adeline Lees, a daughter from her mother's second marriage after the death of Elizabeth's father Thomas Park. Elizabeth was beautiful but not

10   Dame Eva Turner A Life on the High Cs

drawn to the domestic tasks of running a house. She had been a reeler in the cotton mills but her great love was poetry, which she could memorise easily, and she was of a sophisticated, contemplative, reflective disposition, different to the striving, thrusting nature of her husband. Elizabeth lost her own father at an early age and perhaps this was the cause of the periods of depression and erratic behaviour she experienced. In an unguarded moment, Dame Eva described her mother as suffering from 'melancholia', adding that she thought this unrelenting condition had been, in the end, the cause of her mother's death. Gladys Parr said about Elizabeth, whom she knew, 'She lived, I think, almost in another world. She was always reading novels.'

Dame Eva rarely spoke of her mother in later life, as if protecting her memory, but did say, 'One of mother's favourite books was *Uncle Tom's Cabin*, which she could recite from memory, so I think the gift of memorising, which I have, came from her.' Had the shadow of her maternal grandfather's death haunted Eva's childhood? Had she empathised with her mother in the silent way which children can and did this collusion of silence create a bond with which Eva never broke faith?

Eva, Elizabeth and Norman Turner c.1896

Life for Eva started in Lancashire where Charles was a 'modern man', before they existed, preparing meals and cleaning the house. These tasks must have been hard after such a long day at the mill, as he would have been early to the factory to get the engine running before the whistle blew at 6.00 am to summon the other workers. This big engine would then burst into noisy, oily, energetic, steamy life with him at the helm and the mill workers would hurry along so as not to be late for work, their wooden clogs clattering on pavements, adding to the morning cacophony. The roar of the engine starting would wake little children still in bed, as far as five streets away, when their houses shook as the mill vibrated into life. These same children were often employed to sweep up the cotton bits inside the mill after school was finished, making it a long day for them too.

The machines on the five or six floors of the cotton mill were powered by the steam energy, created by coal, coming from the huge engine which sat in one corner of the ground floor. The cotton bales would arrive from Eastern Mediterranean countries and be put through the processes of: opening, cleaning, picking, carding, combing, drawing, roving, spinning and then wound, as yarn, on bobbins and worked on the looms to become cotton fabric. The smooth running of these processes depended on the skills and reliability of the mill engine driver.

1892 -1915 Lifestyle And Family

The Lancashire water mills had been the original source of power for the spinning factories which preceded these big mills and the wet climate now had other advantages: cotton is stronger when damp and the dust created when working with cotton was kept a little under control. Nevertheless, the mill town occupants often had breathing problems caused by the air being full of floating cotton fluff which they breathed in and which stuck to their clothes, making it look as if it was snowing and also the air was foul with dirty smoke belching from the many chimneys. If the workers made too close contact with the machinery, many limbs and lives were lost. Money was to be made but at a cost.

Internal conditions in the mills, with their north facing windows to help prevent fires caused by strong reflections from the sun, were dark and gloomy, unlike the old weavers' cottages with their big south-west facing windows, with sills housing the looms, allowing the crofters to gain the best value from the daylight hours.

At the turn of the nineteenth century, the damp Oldham town where Eva grew up would not have been a place where a breath of fresh air could be easily found, nor would it have been a place of beauty, but it did house people with faith. William Blake, a poet of whom Eva was particularly fond, asked the questions: 'Did the countenance divine shine forth upon our clouded hills, and was Jerusalem builded here, among these dark satanic mills?' I think for the Turner family it was.

Dame Eva described her early life as simple and humble. Domestic duties were important to the Lancastrians because, although this dirt and grime was everywhere outside, they took great care of their homes and their personal hygiene. Cleanliness was indeed next to Godliness, with Respectability on its other side. The local baths were visited at weekends as most homes would have only a tin bath which was placed in front of the fire once a week, when the family stepped into the hot water, boiled on the cooker, the cleanest first and when a face flannel was a great necessity in life. The toilet would probably be outside and there certainly would not be a bathroom inside the house.

The door step and pavement surrounding their little terraced houses, which clustered round the mills, were mopped and cleaned weekly and all domestic duties had a particular day: Monday, washing; Tuesday, ironing; Wednesday, baking; Thursday, windows. All done and dusted by Friday so that the pleasures of the weekend could be enjoyed without guilt. Frugality was a great virtue: 'waste not, want not' being the motto of the times. Food was prepared to be eaten and not wasted, and the mending and darning of garments and sheets was a common activity on a winter's evening. Credit was not an accepted way of life for the respectable person and everything had to be paid for up front, so people at this time were careful and made a note of every penny they spent and earned to ensure that both ends met.

These practices and habits were ingrained in Eva Turner and she lived by their rules throughout her life, keeping very exact details of her income and expenses. In later life she had a book beside the telephone, in Palace Court, into which details were written of who made the call, to whom and how long it lasted. She embraced modernity, but the underlying ideas of cleanliness, frugality, respectability, learned in Victorian times, remained part of her and even her innate desire not to throw things away, probably exacerbated by her poor beginnings, was kept at bay by her ordered thoughts as far as housekeeping was concerned.

Nobody, in the working classes when Eva was a child, had much money and people pulled together to survive and to make the most of life. Eva's family had a sense of belonging to a Christian community, to which they would contribute their talents, enhancing the lives of others if possible. This gave her a keen awareness of who she was and seemed to empower her as a youngster, enabling her to gain the confidence that she needed to sing in public. Her public spirited approach to life, learned at this early age, allowed her generous heart to grow, although this did seem to have been born with her and was natural to her. Her outstretched hand, to help and to give of herself, was her special human quality.

We find Charles Turner at the end of the 19th century working hard for his pay, a small cut above his neighbours, earning a little more money than the ordinary mill worker and going home at close of work to keep the house in order, as his neighbours would have expected. Above all else, the face of respectability had to be saved and standards maintained. He wanted his family to be respectable and respected and impressed on Norman and Eva the necessity of keeping these virtues foremost in their mind.

Despite the area of friction concerning practicalities, the Turners shared happy times together, particularly when music making

In later life Dame Eva absolved her conscience, having sleeplessly tussled with the idea of throwing something away, by phoning students at an ungodly early hour and asking them to pop in that morning. On arrival, she would graciously present a gift which could be a plastic bag stuffed full of neatly folded plastic bags. The most remembered was to Keith Jones, a tenor, to whom she gave twelve lady's hats. On realising her mistake she asked the outgoing student if she would swap her present of 100 wire coat hangers, collected over time from the dry cleaners. The students were to be seen a few minutes later, sitting on the pavement wiping away tears of helpless laughter.

Manor Mill, Oldham

happened. Charles played the harmonium and had a good singing voice, as did Elizabeth, who would join in as he played and they would sing duets, encouraging Eva to add her young treble sounds to the occasion. As with most Victorian families, singing round the piano was a normal, happy activity and when they visited Eva's paternal grandparents' home after church, the family gathered there included good amateur musicians, who would be making music and having fun.

Uncle Alfred, a professional musician, played the violin in the Hallé Orchestra and her Aunt Jinny sang in the Hallé Chorus. It soon became obvious however that Eva had musical talents beyond those of her family and they needed to be nurtured. Who better to do that than this ambitious, musical father whom she loved? He taught her to play the piano and took infinite care to help develop her singing voice and she was soon invited to perform at local events, her first public singing being with the Copster Hill

Werneth Council School (2009)

Wesleyan Choir in Oldham, when she was about eight.

Education had become free in 1891 and in 1892, the year Eva was born, a brand new school, Werneth Council School, Oldham was built, which in the course of time, Eva attended, walking to and from it twice a day, as she and all the children went home for their dinner at midday. This was the main meal of their day, and was cooked and eaten at home where a family could spend time together round the table, exchanging the morning's news and gossip.

The mills too had this dinner break, during which the donkey-engine would take over and keep everything ticking gently along until the big steam engine got into full swing again after the dinner hour was over. The mill workers on the looms would knock their handle into a position for this donkey-engine to take the strain when they went off home and so the term 'knocking off' came into our language. The low 'chooooch, chooooooch' sound of the main engine starting again at around one o'clock would be heralded by whistle blowing which could be heard in the neighbouring streets as the workers rushed in their noisy clogs to get back to work on time, or even skidded along on their metal soles, if it was snowing. Everyone knew everyone else and their business, and most people lived their whole lives within the confines of the streets in which they were born. Eva's classmate Maude Thomson was later to become her relative when she married one of Eva's first cousins.

The Turners were the first tenants of their little terraced Stanley Road home, of the type we all recognise from Coronation Street, built, with an outside toilet, in 1900. It was while living there, that Eva marched into a new century hand in hand with her mother, father and Norman, her young brother, whom she adored. A year later in 1901 Queen Victoria died and the population of Britain was moving, filled with hope, into the Edwardian age. Optimism,

Eva Turner's front door in Stanley Road (2009)

1892 -1915 Lifestyle And Family   15

Eva Turner c. 1900

however, was not in the air for all the Oldham mill workers, as around the time when Eva was born, there had been a request from employers that the workers should take a 5% pay cut and a strike followed. The simple fact was that since the opening up of Japan socially, artistically and politically, Japanese cotton was finding a world market with cheaper prices and the industry in Oldham was in slow decline. It is a small irony that this negative influence from the Orient on the mills of Oldham would have such hugely positive effect on Eva Turner's later life and even at that time it made way for Charles to be offered a new position as Head Engineer in the Great Western Cotton Company in Bristol. Charles was quietly relieved by this change in his life and in 1902 the Turners, along with a thousand mill workers from the north, went to live in Bristol.

The Manchester Evening News on June 19th, 1929 published an article by Eva Turner:

How My Voice Gained Fame.
Early Days in Oldham – A Girlish Dream Come True.

'Before I was eight years old I had firmly decided I wanted to be a great prima donna. Instead of laughing at my ambitious ideas my father and mother were most sympathetic with my longing for a musical career. Many were the 'castles in the air' that we built around my future in these early days, even though the question of money for my training seemed likely to prove a serious stumbling block. Then all at once it seemed that my hopes might materialize. My father was offered the position of manager of an important cotton mill in Bristol and I really believe that his delight in the new position was more on my account than his own. For now he would be able to give me the musical education of which we had dreamed. At that time I and everyone else imagined my voice to be a contralto. It was only when I went to London to study under Levi that we discovered I was a soprano.'

The Turners stayed in the Gaffer's House when they first arrived in Bristol and after a couple of years, in 1905, they moved into a new house in Arlington Road where they settled into their new life, with the old Lancastrian habits of book keeping and frugality continuing, and with relations coming to visit, bringing with them treats from the north, like tripe, special cheeses and treacle toffee. Eva went to St Anne's School Bristol and was a hard working, clever pupil. Her memories of this time were that her favourite and best subjects were French, cooking and swimming but does not specify that they were part of the school's curriculum, which they probably were not. Her father made sure that extra subjects were obtained with his private funds, as he wanted the best possible education for both of his children and thought that knowledge and education were power. It was, however, once again music which took priority in Eva's life and she used every opportunity to practise, playing the harmonium for the Independent Order of the Good Templars and the Band of Hope, as well as the piano for the Sunday school where she was a teacher.

When she was about fourteen her voice was that of a mature woman and a sentimental ballad of the time, *Take My Head On Your Shoulder, Daddy* was one of her best pieces, which seemed to go down a treat with her listeners, leading to many more invitations to sing at all the important local celebrations.

'Even as a child my voice had great volume. When I was twelve, people who heard me without seeing me used to think that it was the voice of a mature thirty year old. Even at thirteen it was my ideal to be a singer.'

Her first real operatic experience was in the audience at the Colston Hall in Bristol on May 4th 1907. As she listened to this Wagner concert, she realised that these voices were like her own and she instinctively knew that she was one of this strange race called 'opera singers'. Shortly after she was taken by her father to *Il Trovatore*, performed by the Royal Carl Rosa Opera Company in the Princes Theatre Bristol and the die was cast. The direction her life would take was at this point decided, as we can hear from her own words, taken from a little interview by the then thirteen year old school girl Catherine David.

Dame Eva takes care and time with this interview which she gave when she was ninety six. The conversation has the ring of truth about it, created in part, I think, by her desire to tell her story for posterity to a young person who would outlive her by a number of years and so carry on her name and information of an operatic era which no longer existed.

Eva Turner c. 1905

'I knew from that moment on that I wanted to sing in opera. I returned home as if under a spell and lived in a world of make belief in which I invented operas and sang them as I went for lonely walks, imitating all the voices and making weird noises for the orchestral intermezzi. My dolls became operatic puppets and Norman would join in and sing other parts that I invented for him. Our great game was a gala performance of the "Miserere Scene" from "Il Trovatore", when we would dress up for the parts and when, to get a proper trailing effect for my skirt, I used to tie a dress round my waist. I dreamed every night about singing in opera and Norman would have to pull my ear to waken me for breakfast, as I was enjoying myself too much, receiving flowers and applause from an adoring public, to waken up.'

Eva adored Norman, her brother. He used to join in the games quite willingly as he too was interested in singing and was the soloist in a Ladies Night Concert a few years later, when he sang *All that I ask is Love* and *Dreamland*.

In that same year, 1907, Enrico Caruso and Emmy Destinn, who were household names, were performing *Andrea Chenier* by Umberto Giordano in London for the first time in their careers. Many great singers came from humble beginnings but were carried into greatness because they could sing and sometimes, like Caruso, they remained true to their beginnings and tried to help fellow, less fortunate, countrymen wherever they found them. These philanthropic thoughts appealed to the young Eva.

Wanting to be an opera singer then was a bit like wanting to be a film star, an internet tycoon or a footballer now. For the lucky few who made it to the top, there was the reward of status and money, but one needed special talents as well as ambition to reach the top branch of the opera-tree. A burning desire for this climb had to be accompanied by commitment to years of practice, and a devotion to training a potentially good voice, transforming it into a perfect vocal instrument. Since the instrument is housed in the singer's body, a certain careful way of life had to be learned and if the singer was also a good musician, that was a helpful attribute. The sooner the young singer learned how to achieve these goals, the better.

The Manchester Guardian on October 24th, 1907, talking about the production of 'Il Trovatore' which Eva had seen (although not the same performance), given at the Theatre Royal Manchester, says: 'Last night's performance was perhaps one of the best that has been heard here of late... The chorus and orchestra did well enough'. When this production travelled to Covent Garden later in the year, the same paper says on December 27th: '"Il Trovatore" went with a good swing owing to the conducting of Walter van Noorden who got some very spirited work from the chorus and orchestra'. Leonora at Bristol was Ina Hill and Azucena, Phyllis Archibald. Dame Eva recalled in later years, 'I must confess I do not remember absolutely clearly who the Manrico and the Count di Luna were but I think they were Hebden Foster and Ben Davies.'

Unlike many people of his class and generation who thought that being a singer just happened, Charles realised it would take more than her mature voice and intense interest in singing for Eva to become a great singer, so arranged for her to have proper training and found her local teachers with whom she studied piano and singing outside of school hours. She was a keen piano student, showing the necessary commitment and getting up at the same time as her father, who was off to the factory for 6 am. She would then practise before going to school, again at lunch time and after tea. Practising the piano was so important to her that she even ate her meals from a chair near it and stuck to this routine with devotion and dedication.

Ina Hill

Around this time Eva became great friends with George Washington Ivens, who walked with her to the church. They were soul mates, fell in love and became engaged to be married when she was sixteen. Her father felt that this immature love could never take the place of her singing and told her that she could either forget her music and get married, or he would help her financially to pursue a singing career. This may seem now to be a pretty stark choice but in those days it was a realistic one, as it was only since 1887 that a married woman, who had previously been a mere chattel of the man, could own property. As this was very recent history, Charles did not want even an echo of this kind of life for his beloved daughter.

Hebden Foster

A married woman was not able to enter a respected profession like nursing or teaching and certainly would not have been able to study the way Eva would have to, in order to climb to the very top of the singing world. Wifely duties were many and arduous with no machinery such as washing machines and dishwashers or even efficient cleaning materials which would, in years to come,

Ben Davies

1892-1915 Lifestyle And Family

Eva, Norman and Elizabeth c. 1908

make washing floors and keeping the house clean an easier task. The hard housework of that period would be time consuming, taking up most of a wife's week and would have taken precedence over Eva's heart's-desire to be a great singer, so she broke off her engagement to George and made the choice to dedicate her life to singing. Not long after this, George emigrated to Canada, became a sheriff, married and settled there for the rest of his life.

Another version of this breaking off of the engagement was given to me by a tenant and close friend of Dame Eva's who, on finding a letter from George Ivens among her personal possessions after her death, destroyed it, as he felt it was too personal to be shared. He told me however, that the letter suggested that George had gone to Canada hoping that Eva would follow but that conditions of abject poverty were so awful when he got there that he felt he could not ask her to share his life and so released her from her promise. Whatever the true version of the story, she did not marry George although they maintained a distant friendship and he appeared on a television link from Canada on Dame Eva's *This is Your Life* in 1959.

Charles Turner was clearly from a working class background but somehow had the idea that his children didn't need to stay in that class and could, with hard work and know-how, achieve social, upward mobility, so perhaps if George Ivens had been wealthy, things would have been viewed in a different light. We also have to remember that Charles probably felt that, apart from the birth of his two beloved children, his own marriage had not been totally ideal and so felt that marriage was not all it was cracked up to be.

It was not the idea of being unmarried which appealed to Eva but rather that the overwhelming need to be a singer was the centre of her being, linked with the firm idea that she could make a good living singing and rise in social standing in the world and please her parents. Charles knew that her talent was exceptional and he had the necessary inner courage to research the possible professional teachers with whom she could study in Bristol, as she outgrew her local tutors. Although professional musicians were outside his social circle in Bristol, he was himself quite a good musician and had enough personal confidence to enter their world where he could make contacts among those who knew the next rung on this ambitious ladder which he was seeking for Eva. He needed advice on how her dreams could be realised and, most importantly, he was prepared to put his money where his mouth was. He sought out Daniel Rootham.

Daniel Rootham had the necessary contacts which Charles was seeking for Eva and she flourished under his guidance as she respected and liked him, while he, for his part, was aware of her great potential. *Ocean Thy Mighty Monster* from Weber's *Oberon*, is a huge aria for any soprano, never mind a seventeen year old, but she studied it with him and he gave her a copy inscribed: 'To Miss Eva Turner with the hope that this will prove to be one of your greatest successes' and indeed it was. In later life she was to marvel at his foresight.

Her time spent studying with him and listening to his advice concerning the way forward on her chosen career, together with her considerable piano playing skill and developing musicianship, made it possible for her to be accepted for audition at the Royal Academy of Music. This idea had been encouraged when she sang for Miss Alice Bowdon of the Moody Manners Opera Company, who had agreed that the best route to becoming a professional singer would be to study in London.

For a woman, one of the few ways in those days to build an independent, liberated life, before the suffragettes won women's freedom, was through singing, since female roles were no longer sung by men, and women would be paid equally as their fame and prestige grew. Of course, to have a man looking after you was still helpful in the social scheme of things but not essential. Eva's relationship with her father was close and one has to wonder if any human qualities of personal possessiveness led him to give her a start in life that did not depend on another man. If this was an unconscious or even conscious thought, we must still give him credit for helping her make an independent life at a time when it was not the norm for women of her social class.

Daniel Rootham, born in 1837 and Eva Turner's first real singing teacher, was highly respected in the area around Bristol and had previously taught Dame Clara Butt, a British contralto of great renown at the time. Rootham's father had been a bass singer at Trinity College, Cambridge and he himself had been a chorister at Trinity and St John's since he was eight years old. After his father died, he moved to Bristol in 1852, became a lay clerk at the Cathedral and studied singing with Schira. In 1865 he became the conductor of the celebrated Bristol Madrigal Society and Bristol Festival Choir and was a respected personage in the world of music.

The Royal Academy of Music

So it was with her father's planning and money and her own talent that Eva, after her successful audition, entered the Royal Academy of Music on April 26th, 1912, aged twenty. She and her father travelled to London and he helped her settle into her lodgings south of the river.

George V was now on the throne and as they travelled to London the newspapers of the time would tell them that on March 1st, 1912, around the time of Eva's entrance exam, the Suffragette Movement, led by Emmeline Pankhurst, had attacked various West End sites, including Downing Street, by throwing bricks at windows and many women had been arrested. The Titanic sank on April 15th, 1912 (the newly formed London Symphony Orchestra had fortunately cancelled their booking at the last minute) and the Stockholm Olympic Games were on the horizon for that summer.

Carl Jung had written *The Psychology of the Unconscious* in 1912 and Scott and his companions who were adventuring to the Antarctic were found dead ten miles from safety on February 10th, 1913. The world at this time was full of journeys which were

1912 was an exciting time for the students at the Royal Academy of Music. The wonderful new building stood fifty feet back from the road, within easy access of various tubes and omnibus services. It has a frontage of 181 feet with five floors and a height of 100 feet, is built from Portland stone and red brick and has a green slate roof. All interior wood is teak, chosen because of its non-combustible properties and special attention was given to light, for health reasons, and to sound proofing, for the sake of its near neighbours. There was a telephone and a waiting room for lady students on the right and one for gentlemen students on the left. The Royal College of Music sent best wishes on the day of the opening of the Academy, which had cost £60,000 to build.

Entrance hall to the Royal academy of Music

22   Dame Eva Turner A Life on the High Cs

not for the faint hearted, but with joy and hope Eva set out to find her life as a singer in London.

Charles Turner paid the following: March 2nd – entrance examination fee of 1 guinea (£70 in today's money), March 29th – balance of entrance fee of 4 guineas on becoming a student and tuition fees for ordinary curriculum of 11 guineas per term from April 1912 to July 1915. Total of 115 guineas. Eva was given a little help as we can see from the following letter written on July 17th, 1913 to her address at 231 Kent Road, London S.E.

Royal Academy of Music
York Gate

Dear Miss Turner,

The arrangements for the allotment of the Students' Aid Fund for the ensuing academic year are now completed and I have great pleasure in telling you that we find it possible to make a grant of £3-3-0 per term towards the payment of your fees.

Yours sincerely,
FW Renant
(perhaps a little more.)

'You had to take the full curriculum. You know piano is demanded as a second study and so on and harmony and counterpoint, ear tests, sight reading and all this for which I was very grateful throughout my career... We had an opera class. I wasn't in the opera class.'

Eva studied piano with Cuthbert Whitemore and as a singer would also study diction and harmony and said in later life,

'You have to study. You have to furnish yourself. Equip yourself. I learned this at the RAM. Ear tests, music history and sight reading. All of these plus more.'

Three months after her entrance to the Academy, the new building in Marylebone Road, near York Gate of Regent's Park, erected on the sight of an orphanage building, was officially opened by His Royal Highness Prince Arthur of Connaught K.G., G.C.V.O. on June 22nd, 1912.

Sir Alexander Campbell Mackenzie, a renowned composer and conductor at this time, had become the principal in the old building in 1888. He had been a student of violin there in 1861 at the age of fifteen and had later been a member of the Sonderhausen Orchestra, his time spent there being said to have influenced his opera *Colomba* since it used: 'Teutonic operatic methods and ideas'. Sir Alexander was still the Principal when the new building

Eva's annual report from the RAM during July, 1913

First Study:
has a magnificent voice and good artistic temperament: she is a serious worker and should do well in the future.

Second Study:
most excellent progress, has worked splendidly.

Sight singing and reading:
could improve if she practised more at home.

Diction:
a good student, keen and interested much improved in accent and reading.

Harmony:
moderate progress.
(She studied harmony with Fredrick Corder of whom we will hear more in a moment. We shall now share a small secret; this 'moderate improvement' allowed her only just to pass her exam on June 25th, 1914 with 53 marks.)

Elements of Music:
She received 80 marks on March 30th, 1914.

Corder seems to have been a disappointed man with many unfulfilled imaginative dreams and said in 1911: 'My one passionate desire was, and is, to become a writer of music drama... Success danced before me and vanished with the death of our solitary impresario Carl Rosa.' Corder's history of the Academy is a most valuable, respected work and earns him a rightful place in the world of music of his time, as does his motet *Sing unto God* for 100 female voices written and performed at the opening ceremony. The Musical Times said of it: 'A very striking work and a remarkable example of the composer's skill. The climax near the end is gorgeous.'

was opened and his tone poem *The Inauguration of the House* or *Invocation* for an orchestra of 90 was performed at the opening ceremony.

Frederick Corder, a member of staff at this time teaching Eva harmony had, in 1887, had his opera *Nordisa* performed by the Carl Rosa Opera Company. Unlike *Colomba*, also performed by them around this time, Corder's opera was not a great popular success owing partly, it is said by Robin H Legge, to a strange happening during its first performance: 'The stage storm patented by Harris, went astray into the audience instead of over the stage and seriously damaged the evening clothes of the public.' Bearing in mind the cost of the elaborate evening dress worn at this time, this was indeed a minor tragedy.

The Royal Academy of Music, and the air its students breathed, was full of music of its time and the philosophy that comes with success and failure in the performing world. Eva had entered this very different world and was now breathing its refined, sophisticated air, instead of that of the cotton mills. She rejoiced in her new surroundings, while back home in Bristol on May 15th, 1912, a month before the great official opening of the new building. Someone, I surmise her father, still thinking of his daughter's life as a singer, had been at a Miscellaneous Concert in the Colston Hall for the Lord Mayor's 'Titanic' fund. He had saved the programme which Eva kept and stored with her own memorabilia. There are comments written alongside the performers' names in this concert, which included acts by comedians, dancers and actors as well as singers from the world of variety entertainment. Some of the comments are: 'not much class', this was about the Milton's Local Singers, of Miss Amy Richards, soprano: 'didn't think much of her' but of Mr Cyril Thompson's *Toreador Song*: 'very good' and of Miss Dora Bubbear, contralto, also: 'very good'.

Eva Turner said of the inauguration of the new Academy 'I was there for the opening and Prince Arthur of Connaught declared it open.' Her singing teacher was at that time Mary Wilson but very soon, after talking to her father about being trained as a contralto by her, Eva asked to change teachers and began to study as a soprano, which she undoubtedly was, with Edgardo Levi and his wife Gigia. Edgardo Levi was a famous teacher of singing and the editor of *Standard Songs and Arias* published by Ascheberg, Hopwood and Crew. These 'Arie Antiche' were given a new lease of life after he supplied them with cadenzas and phrasing marks and this new approach encouraged their everyday usage by singers of the time. Eva said that although her time of study with Edgardo had been too short, since he died suddenly of a heart attack, 'I owed my excellent Italian pronunciation to Edgardo's and Gigia's teaching.'

Having chosen to stay in New Kent Road, her journey to the new Academy would be by underground train or omnibus to Baker Street, both of which would be straightforward enough journeys once she got used to them and would make her cheaper accommodation, south of the river, possible.

'We had to fend for ourselves: I remember that I used to walk to St Martin's Church (Trafalgar Square) and then take the penny bus fare from there to the Elephant and Castle. I would walk from the Royal Academy to save the bus fare.'

She kept and cherished all her life a programme for a Special Benefit matinee concert on Monday December 8th 1913, in which Sir Alexander Mackenzie conducted his own ballet music from *Colomba* and in which Ben Davies, with whom she later sang in the Carl Rosa Company, performed along with other singers of repute; Evangeline Florence and Carmen Hill, with Hamilton Harty at the piano. Perhaps she spent the few pence saved on a bus fare on a ticket and a programme for this concert, and sat in the audience with hopes of one day joining them on stage.

In 1914, at the Royal Command Performance at Covent Garden, in the presence of King George V and Queen Mary, a suffragette attempted to address the monarch and when prevented from doing so, locked her arms to a metal rail. This was the year and political climate of her second year at the Academy. From June 6th to 12th, 1914, Eva along with her life-long friend Zoe Koerner, (later known as Corner) was one of the chorus of fairies in performances of Sir A.C. Mackenzie's opera *The Cricket on the Hearth*. The parts were given to members of the opera class while the chorus comprised of singers who did not take the class. Sir Alexander shared the conducting duties with Edgardo Levi, Eva's teacher and director of the opera class. The opera and its performances received excellent critical acclaim at the time and the Musical Times said:

'It will be to our everlasting shame as a musical nation if such a masterpiece is allowed to pass into oblivion.'

Eva Turner- March 1913

War was declared on August 4th, 1914 and life was changing for many women. They gave up domestic service work and drove trams, became lamp lighters, postal workers, nurses and served in the Police, Navy and Red Cross. During this time women began to cut their hair, hemlines rose dramatically to mid calf to accommodate this new way of life and the first bra was patented in America. This was an exciting time for women and Eva, the young woman, was part of all these fashion changes, since she was always interested in new ideas.

Eva Turner continued her studies and on February 26th, 1915, sang Aida's aria, *Ritorna Vincitor* from Verdi's opera *Aida* at a Student Concert in the Queen's Hall. In the orchestra playing his cello was the fifteen year old Giovanni Barbirolli, who later became the famous conductor Sir John Barbirolli and for whom Eva Turner often sang.

She said, in later life, of her time at the Academy,

'My time of learning was a most happy one. I was sympathetically encouraged but also had the good luck to win many prizes. When I should have left, I received a special grant of three guineas that allowed me to study longer than the allotted time span.'

Although there is no record of this, it is written in a publicity article of 1918 for the Royal Carl Rosa Opera Company that A.C. Mackenzie had given her money from the Students' Endowment Fund to enable her to continue her career after she left the Academy.

As no member of the Royal family was available to present the prizes at the Academy of Music on July 22nd, 1915, Madame Clara Butt, (called by Sir Edward Cooper who introduced her, 'A Queen of Song',) performed the royal duty and since she and Eva had both studied singing with Daniel Rootham in Bristol, life seemed to complete a small circle for Eva as she sat in that audience on the threshold of her professional singing life.

'When I was finishing my studies I told my father, who had sent me to the Royal Academy, I didn't wish anymore to have my allowance or so on. I wanted to see if I could fend for myself and what I would make of it.'

Gladys Parr

Around 1.00 pm on January 21st, 1976, Gladys lifts her telephone and answers the caller in her wonderfully deep, resonant voice. It is as low as any man's and is slightly booming but has a lovely lyrical quality which brings with it a certain gentleness. Her long upper lip lifts into a smile as she recognises the voice.

'Hello Eva dear! – Yes'

The loud projected high tones of Eva's voice travel down the line from Bayswater and Glad smiles to herself at the familiar sound which makes her feel part of a world to which she and Eva belong. They had given each other support inside and outside the profession over many years of friendship, a relationship which had survived all the ups and downs which life had presented. Eva is her oldest friend and she loves her as old friends do. She knows her failings and is irritated by her bossiness but treasures her, despite or even because of it.

'How very kind… yes of course I remember dear. I have kept the date free. I am so looking forward to the concert and to seeing you and Anne. I will have to return straight home as I have promised to listen to *Book at Bed Time* on the wireless. A very dear friend is reading it.'

Eva protests that they should spend some time together afterwards and must at the very least, visit the dressing room of the performers.

'Now Eva dear, a promise is a promise, as you well know, so I have to keep my word. I will leave you to pass on my congratulations, while I take the bus back home north of the river. Why don't we meet a little earlier and have a drink together? – Thank you dear I knew you would understand. Let's meet at the long bar at 6.30.'

Gladys Parr, who was a nine years old only-child with forty year old parents, at the time of the 1901 census, had known Eva Turner since they were students together at the Royal Academy of Music. They were drawn to each other, not only because they originated from the same part of England but because both their fathers had good positions in the cotton mills. They understood and shared a life style, so forgave each other's habits and Glad knew, through

Gladys Parr (left), Eva Turner (right) at Glyndebourne c.1976

years of practice, how to avert small disagreements without ruffling feathers: 'Eva dear thank you again very much for the cheque you sent me for my birthday. I bought wonderful black leather gloves, to go with my new coat with the astrakhan fur collar. You have not once forgotten my birthday, not even during your exciting first year in Italy where you were so busy building your career. There is a letter in the post for you and Anne. I am sorry to be so late in writing but time seems to have flown since the beginning of this New Year.'

No protestation from Eva that there was no need to write. Polite 'Thank Yous' are a way of life for these two rather grand old ladies as they are both Lancastrians and never take a present for granted, knowing that it took time, caring and above all money to give this gift.

'Who would have thought, Eva, we would still be here in 1976. I can't believe we are 84.'

Eva protests slightly nervously or is it gleefully, that she is still 83 and Glad smiles at this oft repeated joke that for two calendar months and one week, she is a year older than Eva.

'Bye, bye Eva dear. Thank you again for my ticket and I am looking forward to being at the Royal Festival Hall on Friday week. Where are you off to tonight dear?' she asks, knowing that 'evenings in' are foreign to Eva.

'Have a good time. I hope it is a good performance and they do their best' she replies, being told that Eva is going to a student concert at the Academy with a view to hearing the potential of any student who might deserve a grant for further study. Eva has fingers in so many pies and likes to be well informed as to who are the singers of the future.

'Blessings Glad, Blessings', says Dame Eva.

Gladys places the phone thoughtfully in its cradle and sits back in her big easy chair. Her mind returns to her own time at the Royal Academy, travelling from Streatham to get there and befriending Eva in 1913. Eva used to entertain their friends at lunch time in a room at the Academy by parting her hair in the middle and singing *Oh John* (see appendix) to make them laugh: but really they all knew that a desire to be a consummate artist burned brightly inside the young Eva Turner.

In a letter written to Angela Arratoon, who, along with her mother-in-law, was instrumental in making Dame Eva's 90th birthday at the Coliseum such a success, Gladys writes, 'That amazing vitality is something I have never met in anyone else. It is unique. I also was with the Dame at Swindon in 1915 when unbeknownst to each other we both auditioned for the Carl Rosa Company. We fell straight out of the Royal Academy of Music into that Opera Company.'

'How tremendously proud we were to have been chosen as members of the Carl Rosa Company. We lived together on tour and devoted all our time to the Opera and what that entailed, in fact we were dedicated. We were very true friends and have remained so all our lives and although our paths have often been very far apart owing to our various commitments, we have never lost touch. Our lives seem to have been extraordinarily linked together both in our families and those who have been closest to us in our studies and whenever some serious crisis has arisen we have usually managed to be together.' Those were words written by Gladys for the celebrations for the Dame's 90th celebrations at the Royal Opera House.

'Eva has such energy and good will towards this young generation', Gladys Parr thinks, remembering, as if it were yesterday, Eva's present to her on her 29th birthday, when they were touring with the Carl Rosa Opera Company. It had been a copy of the Musical Times of January 1st, 1921 which Eva had acquired at great trouble and expense in time for Glad's birthday on the 3rd. Under the heading of Opera in London, there was a review of the Carl Rosa Season at Covent Garden, the season in which they had both made their debut there:

> 'Much promise had been shown by the younger members of the company and Miss Eva Turner, like Miss Gladys Parr, has demonstrated how good is the material in our midst.'

A dramatic soprano and a lyric mezzo can become friends and remain so, without a great sense of rivalry, as their future lives are already set on different paths. Different voice types predict, to a certain degree, personality, realistic ambition, the amount of free time and interaction with the outside world. Neither of them at the time of that review was hugely famous and both were buoyed up by institutions and togetherness. Each, however, had to find her own inner strengths to allow her to fulfil her best hopes and step forward in this crowded operatic world to become an individual in her own right and to survive. They were both good singers but from an onlooker's point of view, weren't equally successful, as one was to become internationally well known and a Dame of the British Empire. The balance of power had shifted as life went on, so finding that Gladys and Eva in 1976 are still intimate friends after a lifetime in this hugely competitive world, competitive even after retirement, says a great deal for both of these ladies. What excitement and hope, not to mention digs of varying degrees of cleanliness and comfort, they had shared in their years of touring with the Royal Carl Rosa Opera Company.

> 'Many times when we arrived in the various towns on a Sunday night we walked for quite a long time trying to find rooms because it was different in those days, you had rooms; a bedroom and sitting room but I shared with a contralto who was Gladys Parr. We've been friends all those years and we shared. I remember when we had a double bed we used to put the bolster down the middle to make it single beds... I had wonderful rooms I remember in Hull and various places with wonderful landladies, where we went year after year because I was with the Carl Rosa until 1924.'

CHAPTER 2

1915 -1924 The Royal Carl Rosa Opera Company

Carl August Nicholas Rose

Carl August Nicholas Rose was the son of Ludwig Rose and Sophie Becker. He later changed his name to Rosa, because in English, the final 'e' was not pronounced, as it would have been in German, so he replaced the 'e' with an 'a' which brought it closer, in his ears, to his original name. It also brought with it recognition of his red hair. He had been a child violin prodigy, studying at the Leipzig Conservatorium where he met and became life-long friends with Arthur Sullivan. His English début was at the Crystal Palace on March 10th, 1866, twelve days before his 24th birthday, although he had made a private visit to London seven years earlier. However his stay in London was brief, as he was in New York by autumn the same year.

Carl Rosa

Euphrosyne Parepa (Carl Rosa's first wife)

Euphrosyne Parepa, a soprano born in Edinburgh on May 7th 1836, was a member of the concert troupe with which Carl travelled to America. She was the young widow of a British officer, of the East Indian Service, whom she had met in London and to whom she had been married only a short while.

Euphrosyne Parepa was a very successful singer, the daughter of a Rumanian nobleman who had died when she was a baby, leaving her 21 year old mother in poverty. Her mother, a singer of no repute, trained Euphrosyne (born Parepa de Bayescu) for the singing profession, in the hope that she would make a living for them. She made great progress in her musical studies and was also a considerable linguist, speaking five languages fluently. This linguistic ability, coupled with her father being Rumanian, allowed her to think of travelling through Europe in the days when it was slow and difficult to do so and foreign travel was done mostly by the wealthy upper classes. She had to make a living for herself and her mother and so at the age of eighteen, searching for success, she had travelled as far as Malta, where she was known as Eufrasina Parepa.

Malta's little Teatre Manoel was a renowned operatic venue, often starting singers on great careers and it was there that she made her professional debut in *La Sonnambula* during the 1854/5 season and in the 55/56 season she was Malta's first Violetta, to critical acclaim. Most singers were not highly paid in those days so benefit performances were necessary for singers to survive and occasions of this kind were managed by the opera houses, with the best times given to the most popular singers. Ageing singers were squeezed into matinees or into the hottest, most uncomfortable time of the year, but Parepa was given a prime spot for her 'Benefit Performance' and the Malta Times of Tuesday January 30th, 1855 reported:

Euphrosyne Parepa

'The Signorina Parepa's benefit came off on Thursday last week and the house was as crowded in all parts as it was possible to be. The front stalls in the pit were covered with damask for the occasion and were occupied by ladies, the whole presenting a gay and animated appearance the like of which we have not seen in this Theatre for very many years past... She sang two cavatine and a duet.

Nothing could indeed be better than her rendering of the well known "Una Voce Poco Fa". The applause which she received after it was as enthusiastic and hearty as she could have wished. We have also to speak in high terms of approbation of her other cavatina from "Ernani" and her Duet with tenor, from "Attila", which introduced Miss Parepa to us in the most dramatic and fervid style of Verdi. Great flexibility and great extensions of voice, combined with much chasteness of expression, are her marked characteristics. With those she must ever command a high position as a singer and the audience, who cheered, applauded and showered no end of sonnets, flowers, bouquets and garlands on her on Thursday night, could not have more clearly manifested the hearty and just appreciation of her merits.

The collection in Miss Parepa's plate was most satisfactory, bringing abundance of substantial proofs of the good will and high *regard felt for her and we doubt whether she will not in after years look back on her first benefit night in Malta as to the most pleasing of her triumphs and as the one of all the others in which there was not the slightest shadow of doubt as to the genuine warmth and true heartiness of the applause bestowed on her.'*

Euphrosyne Parepa and Carl Rosa set off together, as members of the same troupe of performers, when it left London to tour America. On February 26th, 1867, the talented couple were married in New York and this successful singing star became known as Madame Parepa-Rosa. Two years later, in 1869, they formed the Parepa-Rosa English Opera Company in New York and toured in America for three seasons with Parepa singing and Rosa conducting Italian opera sung in English. This was not pioneering operatic work, as Daniel Snowman in his book *The Gilded Stage* shows us but it was still very adventurous.

A document, thought to be the first contract 'made and entered into' by the new company on June 23rd, 1869 between: 'Carl Rosa of Belvedere House, New York, Professor of Music and Mademoiselle Rose Hersee of 22 Mortimer Street, Cavendish Square, London, Vocalist' says, among other things, that Miss Hersee was to sing five times a week in concerts and four times in opera in the U.S.A. and Canada. She was to attend the necessary rehearsals for the weekly salary of $300 (£60) and would receive $50 per performance for any addition to this. Her repertoire would include *Sonnambula* (her debut), *Bohemian Girl*, *Faust*, and The Countess in *The Marriage of Figaro* and she was asked to provide her own costumes for these roles. Rose Hersee was to become the most famous and best loved Susanna and Zerlina of her time, often singing alongside the equally famous Figaro and Don Giovanni of Sir Charles Santley. When she sang with the Carl Rosa Company in England a few years after her American debut, the Guardian tells us that Rose Hersee's Zerlina was:

Manoel Theatre, Malta

Malta's little Manoel Theatre was built, with an interior of fabulous wood, in ten months, and was opened in 1732. It was designed along the lines of the Palermo Opera House in Sicily and was (and is still) quite beautiful with a marvellous acoustic, said by the locals to be due to the deep underground water channels on top of which it was built, water being a marvellous carrier of sound. Euphrosyne Parepa, like many other singers of her day, went, after her success at the Manoel Theatre, to sing in Naples, Genoa, Rome, Florence, Madrid and Lisbon, so she was already a very successful singer, when in 1857 she appeared in London, where she sustained her career for nine years.

1915-1924 The Royal Carl Rosa Opera Company

'as artless as the village girl should be and as this young lady's style would lead us to expect it to be.'

Perhaps Carl Rosa had chosen well to whom he gave his very first contract.

In 1873, in England, the company called Carl Rosa's English Opera was formed, opening at the Theatre Royal, Manchester on September 1st. It then toured Britain and Ireland, without the singing of Madame Parepa-Rosa as she was now, at the age of thirty-seven, pregnant with their first child. Later that year, W.S. Gilbert approached Carl Rosa about writing the music for a comic opera *Trial by Jury,* in which Parepa would play the soprano lead, as part of a planned season at Drury Lane Theatre. Unfortunately the baby and Parepa died shortly after she gave birth, so this project was not to be and Eufrasina Parepa was not to have those later years when she could look back with pleasure on her triumphant first benefit in Malta. (A competing manager Richard D'Oyly Carte produced *Trial by Jury* in 1875, with music by Arthur Sullivan.)

In 1874, while trying to recover from his loss, Carl Rosa staged a second season at the London Lyceum Theatre, important as a London venue for opera, bringing with it a sense of operatic history and kudos. It had been opened in 1816 as the English Opera House, had burned down in 1830 and in 1834 had reopened as the Theatre Royal Lyceum and English Opera House. When Henry Irving took over the theatre in 1871, it had a new lease of vibrant life and because Irving's company was often on tour in America, the Royal Carl Rosa Opera Company was able to stage an annual season at the Lyceum.

During this prosperous time, in 1881, Carl married again and in December, 1885 the Lyceum Theatre staged the first night of *The Damnation of Faust* by Berlioz and the application for reserved seats would have filled twelve theatres, with thousands coming from Germany alone.

Carl Rosa died suddenly in 1889 leaving behind a worthy, living memorial to his great love of music and opera in particular. Fortunately, the company had become a limited liability in 1887 and so was able to continue after Rosa's untimely death. The custom of performing in English had been established, so that too continued, with many important and not so important first performances taking place with the support of this company.

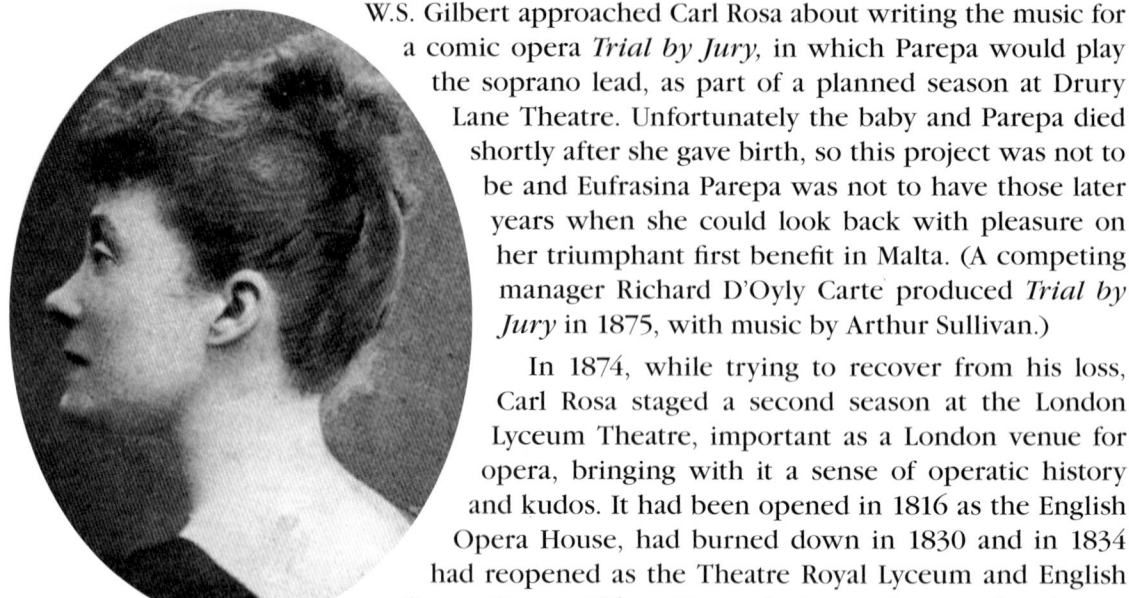

The second Mrs Carl Rosa

Sir George Grove wrote in 1880: 'The careful way in which the pieces are put on the stage, the number of rehearsals, the eminence and excellence of the performers have begun to bear their legitimate fruit, and the Carl Rosa Opera Company bids fair to become a permanent national institution.'

The Carl Rosa Company also tried to promote the birth of an English Opera School of Composition, encouraging composers of the day such as Stanford, Goring Thomas, McCunn, Mackenzie, Corder and Macfarren. Premières in Britain of other works, always performed in English, included: *Cavalleria Rusticana* in 1882, Berlioz's *The Damnation of Faust* in 1885, Hamish McCunn's *Jeannie Deans*, produced in Edinburgh in 1894 and Humperdinck's *Hansel and Gretel* at Daly's Theatre, Leicester Square, London at Christmas time in 1894.

La Bohème had premiered in Turin in 1896 and the following year was performed in English by the Royal Carl Rosa Company, in Manchester, with Puccini, its composer, sitting in the stalls. By this time the Company had been granted a Royal Warrant by Queen Victoria, for whom it gave command performances at Balmoral Castle.

The Royal Carl Rosa Company was at the cutting edge of musical performances in Britain when the new century was born and Eva Turner had seen a performance given by them in Bristol, in 1907, of Verdi's *Il Trovatore*, which had changed her life, so it seemed natural that her first port of call, on leaving the Academy, would be to audition for that company. Sir Alexander C Mackenzie would certainly have known someone to whom she could apply for an audition, since he had conducted for them and had his own compositions performed by them.

Eva Turner on Tour with the Royal Carl Rosa Company

Walter van Noorden and his brother Alfred, with the helpful presence of the second Mrs Rosa, had taken over the Company by this time, 1915, and were steering it in an altogether safer direction than it had been taking in recent years. Walter, who now devoted his entire life to this company, was the chief conductor, managing and directing it on tour and Alfred, whose business interests were in the City but who was also fascinated by opera, was his chief advisor.

It was for Walter van Noorden that Eva Turner auditioned:

'Walter van Noorden said of me when I auditioned that I had no stage experience and therefore he couldn't give me a principal's contract and I was to sing in the chorus for a year! Actually I was a little bit disillusioned and thought that maybe I should have done that before going to the Royal Academy of Music, but I have been grateful ever since because it gave me a certain freedom of movement. I made up my mind, even though I was in the chorus, I was going to

The second Mrs Rosa and Eva Turner

Walter van Noorden

Alfred van Noorden

be seen AND heard! (Laughter) My first solos were The Page in "Tannhäuser", the choir in "Cavalleria Rusticana", and Kate Pinkerton in "Madama Butterfly" and for that I got half a crown which I banked because in those days when we had time out, we were not paid as we are today... Glad and I used to go to the Post Office together and bank our earnings... I began my career with the Carl Rosa Opera Company, and I have very happy memories of those hardworking days, even of early Sunday train calls on draughty platforms, when ourselves and the milk churns often seemed to be the only travellers, and of Monday morning rehearsals in dreary dust-sheeted theatres. Touring was no bed of roses for a singer, but it was a grand life and I loved every moment of it.'

Eva Turner's first Carl Rosa contract, sent to her on May 18th, 1915 during the First World War, was for the period starting September 6th that year. The contract was for 'Soprano Chorister' at a salary of £2 a week and was signed by Alfred van Noorden. She waited, eagerly, for an opportunity to arise which would allow her to step out of the chorus and this happened very early on when she was asked to learn Papagena at twenty-four hours notice to save the show. She was also given the small part of The Page in *Tannhäuser*, a part known in the company as 'one and six tights' since 1/- extra was paid to sing it and the young Eva had to wear tights with 6 pennies stitched in the top to keep them up. The scene in the chorus dressing room must have been a moment filled with laughter, as she got ready for this small role, being ribbed by her colleagues perhaps about her rather big, 'sit-me-down' or somewhat solid, short little legs. As she stepped on to the stage, however, she did her job with commitment and delight, as this was her first Wagner role and she was surrounded by experienced performers of this repertoire whom she could 'listen and learn' from. She was twenty three years old, a single woman with a burning desire to be a great singer and she used every opportunity this job gave her to lay the foundations for her life and career.

£1 then would be worth about £68 today and a typical working class family budget per week for essentials would be about £1-5-0 that is 25/-, worth about £85 in today's money. One could buy a loaf of bread or a pound of apples for 3d (85p) and a couple of pounds of potatoes for 1d (28p). A pound of tea would cost 1/6 (£5-10), a pound of butter 1/2 (£4), a dozen eggs 1/- (£3-40) and a bar of soap 4d (£1-13). Her rent would be about 5/- (£17) a week so Eva, earning £2 (£136) and of a frugal nature, would be able to make ends meet as a single person and, as we have heard, save as much as possible.

It may be difficult for those who know how the Second World War affected the everyday life of the entire population, not least because of air raids, to understand that life during the first war could include visiting a touring opera company when it came to town. 'Keeping the home fires burning' meant that normal life should be maintained as much as possible until the war was over so that those risking life and limb would have a home to come back to. There were, however, notable exceptions to homeland safety, with Zeppelin night raids and also on June 13th, 1917, a daylight air raid by a German plane, which caused the death of 160 people in the East End of London.

The carnage experienced by those at the front line was felt in the hearts and minds of the British population, whose thoughts were constantly with those fighting and dying in the trenches and wishing them home safely. Eva's striving for excellence in her career reflected her inner feeling that singing was what she did best and to do it 'properly' was the way she would proudly, with honour, serve her nation. While these young men were being sacrificed in war, she was aware that she was lucky to be doing what she wanted, singing on a stage, and gave of herself in a dedicated, all consuming way to her audiences, with no holds barred. To enhance the human spirit and ease the troubled hearts of those she met along the road of life was her mission. She thought that success, through talent, courage and hard work, was an honourable way forward.

Eva was part of that young generation of whom Ivor Gurney, war poet and great song writer, born in 1890 in Gloucestershire, wrote in his sonnet, *To the Poet before Battle*: 'Now, Youth, the hour of thy dread passion comes; thy lovely things must all be laid away' and the generation of whom Siegfried Sassoon wrote: 'the unreturning army that was youth.'

There was a sense surrounding Dame Eva Turner that she had absorbed this sentiment as a young person and a potent mixture

Sums of money were written differently: e.g. 2/6 would mean 2 shillings 6 pence. 6d was six old pence. A shilling (1/-) was 12 pennies (12d) and there were 20 shillings (20/-) in a pound (£1). There were 2 halfpennies in a penny and four farthings in a penny.

of pride and guilt lived inside her, fermenting for the rest of her life. This mixture, together with her Victorian values of forward thinking and interest in the future, set alight a slow candle of sustained energy which burned brightly within her, leading her to actions and behaviour which, later in her life of service, sent her striving for a better future for young people wherever she found them in her world of singing and music.

Her second Carl Rosa contract, sent on September 11th, 1916, was that of Principal Soprano with a clause that she would sing in the chorus for the first 6 weeks of the tour. She would earn £2-10-0 for the first two terms of the contract with an increase to £3-0-0 for the last. The Company would provide: 'dresses for the roles but artists should provide shoes, tights, feathers, ornaments and all 'basso vestario' (underwear).The artist undertakes without salary to be present and assist at all rehearsals a fortnight prior to performances and not to accept other engagements during this time, the fine for doing so would be £25. The company will pay travelling expenses whenever it may require her services at a distance of more than 5 miles from London.'

Among the other rules were: artists were not allowed to write to newspapers, travel arrangements had to be followed or they lost the cost of the fare, artists had to perform any role required within the terms of the agreement or the fine would be one week's salary. The singer was not allowed to introduce or omit any songs and for the men all facial hair to be shaven if required. No one was allowed front of house during the performance or to bring anyone behind the curtain and there was no smoking, swearing, nor drinking of alcoholic beverages. The fine for the above would be one week's salary or dismissal and if ill for more than two weeks, the artist could lose his or her contract. The artist would not be given holiday pay for Passion or for Christmas and the preceding week.

It was with the knowledge of all these rules that Eva Turner became a principal member of the Carl Rosa Opera Company in 1916. The Manchester Guardian reported of *The Magic Flute* on October 24th, 1916:

> 'The Three Genii – Miss Florence Barron, Miss Eva Turner and Miss Gladys Parr - sang most effectively together, and the numbers in which they took part were amongst the most delightful of the opera',

and of *Maritana*, the evening before:

> 'Miss Gladys Parr a young contralto who is a native of Bury and the winner of a scholarship at The Royal Academy of Music sang

the ballad "Alas those Chimes" in the prison scene with richness and pathos.'

In her first year as a soloist Eva Turner also sang Arline in *Bohemian Girl* at Carlisle and Genevieve in *The Attack on the Mill* at Leeds. Just before Christmas 1916 she was in Nottingham singing Micaela in *Carmen* where the local paper reported:

'A feature of uncommon interest was the appearance in the role of Micaela of Miss Eva Turner, a young Nottingham artist (the address on her Police Pass to enter Ireland was Nottingham) whose future as an operatic artist should be assured. Miss Turner's voice is a dramatic soprano full of colour and attractive quality and her singing in the duet and her aria in the smuggler's cave was excellent.' (Gladys Parr was an excellent Mercedes.)

'I sang Micaela at the Lyceum Theatre in Sheffield and I really thought I had arrived when that happened but of course that was only the beginning of going on to the major roles'

Eva Turner studied the operatic soprano repertoire quite fearlessly and never missed an opportunity to hear and watch other performers, good and bad, from the wings. She conscientiously banked part of her salary in her post office account and saved for her future study needs or for a rainy day. She also needed money for tickets to other artists' performances, as she always followed closely what was happening in the outside world, visiting, for example, the Aeolian Hall on March 17th, 1916 at 3pm to hear a concert organised by Madame Edgardo Levi for the benefit of disabled Italian soldiers. This visit served many purposes: she would be in touch with her former teacher, would hear some music making and would be herself quite a celebrity at such an occasion. Tickets, available from Madame Levi at 5 Acol Road NW, were 10/6, 5/- and 2/6 (not cheap). Perhaps she would have sung if it had not been for the restrictions of her present contract.

Her third *Desert Island Discs* programme, in 1982, tells us a little more about her early performances:

Roy Plomley, 'What was the first small part you played, do you remember?'

Eva Turner, *'We opened in Swindon in 1915 and I sang The First Lady in "The Magic Flute" for which I got the sum of five shillings. That was extra to my chorus money. The chorus money was thirty-five shillings out of which we paid our rooms and board and so on.'*

When she celebrated her 90th Birthday at the Coliseum she told the audience:

'My first role was The First Lady in "The Magic Flute" in Swindon, Wiltshire and I should tell you that the conductor with whom I sang that role was Eugene Goosens the father of the distinguished musical family: Leone, Eugene, Mare and Sidonie Goosens. He was a marvellous musician. A strict disciplinarian and I profited enormously from him and I've ever been very, very grateful... I believe that Joan Sutherland's debut at Covent Garden was also in that role.'

During the 1917 season her salary was £4 a week for four performances rising to £5. Her friend from the Royal Academy of Music, Zoe Corner, billed as a New Zealand contralto, gave a recital at Weston-super-Mare in August, 1917 and Eva once again used her funds to be at the concert giving support to an old friend and fellow fairy in the chorus of *The Cricket on the Hearth* at the R.A.M.

The Royal Carl Rosa Opera Company toured Britain extensively and performed a variety of operas, some of which are unknown now. *The Attack on the Mill*, one of these, is an opera by Bruneau, libretto by Luis Gallet from a short story by Zola. It was popular at that time, however, and the Carl Rosa Company gave many performances around the country. Eva sang Genievive in a cast which included Hughes Macklin, E.C. Hedmont, Ida Carton and Beatrice Miranda.

Beatrice Miranda (left) and Hughes Macklin (right)

'The cast distinguished themselves by their talented singing and expressive acting and the orchestra left nothing to be desired':

was reported in next day's newspaper after a performance in Bournemouth. Another opera from their repertoire, seldom performed now, was Balfe's *The Bohemian Girl* and it was reported in the Hull local paper:

'We were fortunate in having as youthful and brilliant singer as Miss Eva Turner to deliver the music of Arline. This gifted lady's joyous voice and easy natural style captivated the audience. "I dreamt that I dwelt in marble halls" evoked a tempest of applause.'

Eva Turner had by 1917 graduated from The Page in *Tannhäuser* to the role of Venus alongside Beatrice Miranda (Elisabeth), William Boland (Tannhäuser) and Hebden Foster (Wolfram), the core star material of the company: rather a large step.

Beatrice Miranda, very much the prima donna of the Carl Rosa Company at that time, was the daughter of David Miranda, a Spanish singer, and had a Scottish mother born in Dundee, a soprano, who was said to be a favourite of Queen Victoria, known to be a great opera lover. Beatrice and her sister Lalla were born in Australia and Lalla, the older girl by about 10 years, came to Europe to continue her singing career which had begun in Australia, and became an internationally renowned singer, being probably best known at the Paris Opera. Beatrice came to Britain, first to London and eventually to Edinburgh, where she had many relations nearby. She was married to Hebden Foster, a handsome baritone with fine stage presence, and they were rather an influential, powerful couple in the Scottish world of opera in later years, claiming the name Scottish National Opera for the company they set up in the 50s, which was organized, directed and conducted by Miranda. The patenting of that name was the reason the professional company, which came into being in the 60s, had

William Boland (left) and Ida Carton (right)

to be plain Scottish Opera. She is said to have been rather waspish about Eva Turner's success in 1928 at Covent Garden saying that the Daily Mail had exaggerated her success. It is only fair to say that she was very kind and generous to her own students, of whom she had many in later years and to whom she passed on the tricks of the trade, which she also passed to her daughter (also Lalla), a very good singer, but who acquiesced to her American husband's desires and did not become a professional singer.

Beatrice Miranda is said to have been irritated by this rather too ambitious, eager young singer, Eva Turner, because she always stood in the wings watching and listening to Beatrice's performance and even sometimes, much to her annoyance, 'copied' her portrayal of the role. Eva followed in her footsteps singing the major dramatic soprano roles in the Carl Rosa Company's repertoire at that time and so we have a certain sympathy for this lady who was ten years older and in the full flow of her career. Eva Turner said of that time:

'I was terribly anxious to get on and was consumed with this idea to sing.'

When asked on radio during the programme *Frankly Speaking* in 1962 by Alec Robertson: 'Were your colleagues ever jealous of you in your early days?' she replied,

'No-oh they were all wonderful. I remember them helping me to get dressed when I had solos to sing.'

'So you didn't encounter enemies anywhere at all?'

'No. Of course, it is not always easy when you assume somebody else's part. You feel yourself a little - er, well embarrassed perhaps, but you feel if you fitted yourself that you are glad to have the chance.'

Eva Turner was using these lesser known roles and golden opportunities, amidst the singers of repute at the time, to gain experience and popularity with the provincial public and press, who said of her in Plymouth:

'As Maritana, Eva Turner employed a voice of marked and considerable range and won much appreciation especially with "Scenes that are brightest", which had to be repeated last night.'

In Birmingham she also gained praise:

'Miss Eva Turner the new soprano with the company has a great future before her and she is certainly an acquisition to the company being a young artist gifted with an excellent voice which is likely to develop in power and as Giulietta a courtesan in the Venetian scene, she certainly scored a success.'

Dublin

In December, 1918 women in the UK voted for the first time but out of 1600 candidates only 17 were women. Countess Markieviez won a Dublin seat as a Sinn Fein candidate but said it was against her principles to take the oath of allegiance to the King, so she could not attend parliament and so the making of laws was not, as yet, influenced, directly in Parliament, by women.

Armistice Day, November 1918, was celebrated by Eva Turner in Ireland where the company went on a regular basis and, among other venues, performed at the Gaiety Theatre, Dublin. On Friday 8th, she sang Venus in *Tannhäuser*; Saturday 9th, Giulietta in *Tales of Hoffmann*; Monday 11th, Armistice Day, Musetta in *La Bohème* and on Tuesday 12th, Santuzza in *Cavalleria Rusticana*.

The Freeman's Journal tells a little of her story at that time:

'Venus requires a voice of exceptional purity and strength and no little dramatic intelligence and in these respects Miss Eva Turner met the situation most admirably.'

Dame Eva adds a little memory,

'I remember being in Dublin with the Carl Rosa Opera Company and I was going to sing Venus and I went to the Art Gallery and I saw Venus attired in flimsy robes and all this and I thought this is how she has to be dressed but of course I got something like a flannelette nightdress so I had to give the illusion and so on. (Laughter) Well one did all that kind of thing went to art galleries, the history. Oh you do a lot of research because you like to portray the role from every aspect.'

The Freeman's Journal again:

'Miss Eva Turner, as Giulietta, lent particular charm to this remarkable creation...

Miss Eva Turner was a captivating Musetta - if indeed the character can be described as captivating. Her best vocal effort was the song in the café scene of the Latin Quarter. She was also remarkably good in the great third act scene with Rodolfo, Mimi and Marcello...

The Santuzza of Miss Eva Turner was especially deserving of note. Dramatically and vocally it was one of the best of many fine performances given by this gifted artiste.'

Eva Turner as Musetta in 'La Bohème'

In a box of bits and bobs which Eva Turner cherished, there were three small cuttings, referring to the Armistice Day performances in Dublin:

'Miss Eva Turner's Santuzza, in Mascagni's only work that counts, is what is being talked of today by all who were there. She is an actress if she had not a musical note in her composition. Her "Rejoice that the Lord has arisen" in the "Easter Hymn" was wonderful soprano singing, with the full, pure voice piercing through orchestra and chorus. The duet music with her and Mr. Ben Williams, the Turridu, was excellent'....

'Miss Eva Turner's Santuzza, a highly dramatic creation, lacked a little the sympathy which most ideally might have been infused into it; of its musical strength it is not easy to speak too highly'....

'The opera was excellently cast by the Carl Rosa Co. at The Gaiety Theatre last night with that fine dramatic soprano Miss Eva Turner playing Santuzza.'

Dame Eva's thoughts about Santuzza were: 'Nowadays there is a tendency to give the role to a mezzo, but I cannot agree with this. To interpret the role properly one must be able to produce some ringing top notes which do not lie within the compass of the average mezzo. Santuzza belongs by right to the dramatic soprano with complete security at both ends of the scale.'

1915-1924 The Royal Carl Rosa Opera Company

Eva Turner as Musetta

It seems that the reception given to an English girl or even an English company in hostile Dublin, was not dimmed or tainted by the civil unrest in Ireland at that time. In April that year there had been a general strike in Ireland, protesting against the idea of conscription and a rally in Dublin condemned it as: 'Declaring war on the Irish nation', going on to say that it would be a direct violation of the rights of small nations to self determination:

'What the English say they are fighting for.' This was all part of the long battle for an independent Irish Nation. As we shall see, Eva Turner had a life-long capacity for remaining outside politics as she concentrated on her chosen career so it should be no surprise to us that she never mentioned a word about this political situation either then or later.

'The war to end all wars', although it did not do that, changed lives forever, in particular the lives of working class women. During the war they had taken on men's jobs. These earnings gave them a taste of independence and freedom and they realised that it was no longer necessary to be supported financially by a man and the camaraderie of this new life style empowered them. This new situation for women emphasises how far sighted Charles Turner had been in encouraging his daughter to have her own career many years earlier.

Walter van Noorden, for whom Eva had auditioned, had died suddenly in April 1916, so she lost a useful ally in building her career. Nevertheless, build it she did and the resounding comment under her photo in the Royal Carl Rosa's Jubilee Celebration Programme 1918, was: 'Fine stage presence'. It seems that her year in the chorus gaining stage experience had borne fruits as had her decision: 'To be seen AND heard'. She was now a valued, flourishing soloist.

After one of her great successes as Turandot at Covent Garden, Eva tells us, in the Wigan Observer, a little more about the war years while touring with the Carl Rosa Company:

'It was a severe life. England was under the shadow of the Great War. Travelling was arduous and food was scarce. And I always seemed to be losing my coupons. One night we were locked up from midnight till dawn in Carlisle station. Enemy airplanes were about and to add to our discomfort the station was in blackout. It wasn't a pleasant experience for a cold and hungry company. At York all the lights went out and we had to finish "Tales of Hoffmann" by the illumination of candles.'

By law children could not take part in performances on stage as we see from this little anecdote.

'I remember the law said that children could not appear with our touring company and so a dwarf played Trouble, Butterfly's little boy,'

Dame Eva said in sensitive tones in case it was hurtful for anyone,

1915 -1924 The Royal Carl Rosa Opera Company

'and I still remember, with distaste, the smell of cigar smoke as I lifted him on to my shoulder for the last act. Oh dear! There was also some difficulty keeping him sober throughout the performance.'

Ida Carton's last professional performance was as Suzuki when Eva was singing Butterfly and Mr. Arthur Carton, the son of Ida Carton tells us: 'There was an epidemic of Spanish influenza in 1919 and there was no baby sitter available to look after me so I went with my mother to this performance and I remember being illegally enlisted to play the little boy "Trouble" because the "Lilliputian adult" who usually played the part was rather sozzled. As it was the last night of my mother's professional career she volunteered my services and these were completely successful (laughter) 'tho in order to keep me on stage at the end, lying folded as I was with a large orchestra in front of me and an even louder suicidal soprano behind me, my mother hid behind a suitable rock or some such and hissed "stay where you are" repeatedly until the curtain came down.'

Around this time Eva Turner asked for some singing advice, on how she could develop vocally, from the company's principal tenor, Christan Emanuel Hedmondt, but he merely pointed over her shoulder and suggested that she should work with:

Mr E. C. Hedmont, originally Canadian, had married Marie Kacerovsky, who was born in Austria in 1861. She had been a soprano, whose career was cut short after a throat operation prevented her from singing. Marie had at one time worked with the German composer Berta Block but now taught singing without making a sound, using verbal imagery alone and among her successful students was Elena Gerhardt. When Eva was looking for a new vocal way forward, this couple's shared interest in singing technique was the reason for Eva's asking Mr Hedmondt's advice.

Albert Richards Broad

Albert Richards Broad, an Australian bass, of Cornish decent, affectionately known as Plum, had been quite a well known singer, performing as a bass with Hans Richter at Covent Garden, and was a friend of Dame Nellie Melba. He was an authority on voice and had devised a very particular vocal method which he wrote about, in 1912, in one of his books *How to Attain the Singing Voice*. Eva made the ideas in Plum's book her bible and used them both for her own singing and when she was teaching in later years.

It is not quite clear when Eva started to study voice with Plum since it was a secret arrangement to avoid gossip, not of a sexual nature but rather to do with the politics of singing which every opera company experiences. We know that in 1920 he was employed in the chorus as a bass, taking small walk-on parts and as the company's librarian. It is generally thought by those who knew him that his sexual orientation was homosexual but this was never spoken of openly, as not only was it illegal but also socially rather hampering in those days. Plum agreed to teach Eva only on the strict understanding that she would have a daily lesson with him and follow his exact advice, so in every town they visited with the company, he would hire a room with piano and they would go off to practise.

Broad was quite a formal person but Dame Eva always referred to him as Plum, a rather informal pet-name, because he adored eating plums. He was Eva's friend and had her best interests at heart and it seems that in the early 1920s, he, Gladys Parr and Eva Turner were a little band of fellow travellers. Out on the road, touring all the time, it must have been a good thing for them to have created a mini family support group, where they could rely on each other for company and friendship. Gladys was overheard one day during this period, saying to Eva that she had managed to get a nice pot of bones for Plum's dinner that night. This pot of bones being turned into fine, delicious soup was an ongoing joke between Eva and Glad and when Gladys was her guest on *This is Your Life* in 1959 it was mentioned again in respect of a difficult, silent, hard to engage, dinner guest who had eaten the soup silently without comment.

When she was interviewed in her first *Desert Island Discs* programme in 1942, Eva Turner's fifth choice was a Melba record. Perhaps this was a tribute to the recently deceased Plum:

'I shall never forget when I was just starting with the Carl Rosa Company I went one night to Covent Garden and heard her (Melba) in "Romeo and Juliet". It was such beautiful singing. It made a great impression on me. It fired my ambition to try to emulate that lovely voice. It really was an inspiration. As there is no available recording of that music I have chosen Melba singing "Au Clair de la Lune"'

She kept a programme for *La Bohème* on May 17th 1919 with Melba in the cast and this was the same season she would have heard her sing Juliet. She had programmes for the Russian Ballet on July 14th and for *Louise* July 19th, 1920 so we can see that even though she was busy with her own performances she was always interested in the international scene and how she could improve her portrayals by watching and listening.

The Royal Carl Rosa Opera Company had more than one group on the road at any one time, so was able to carry a huge repertoire to very many places in the British Isles which, from a singer's

In *How to Attain the Singing Voice,* Albert Richards Broad states that you should start with deep breathing, then apply this to an airy consonant, preferably 'sh' and allow the vowels ee, ay, ah to follow through behind it to the same position behind the front teeth. Central ideas in the book include: you must be accurate in the aim of breath, not move from this forward placement 'behind the fringe of the top teeth' and that the singer's own ears must not deceive him. Correct production sounds clear and ringing but smaller to the singer than the round woolly back tones he or she produces when enjoying the sound too much themselves. The cords must meet, to avoid a breathy sound but on no account be forced together so that vibrating would become difficult. Mental positivity is crucial: 'I can't' is not acceptable.

Dame Nellie Melba

point of view was good, as they were able to learn roles and try them out in smaller towns before performing those roles in the big cities. From a management point of view, however, casting would have to be handled very carefully.

Greenock
January 1920

Dear Sir,

Perhaps the management of The Carl Rosa Company will explain why the same artistes appear night after night. Is it because there are no principals to play the different operas or is it their intention not to allow us to hear some of them? I have noticed that some of the photos at the entrance to the theatre and the artistes represented there do not figure on the programme. I trust this will be satisfactorily explained to the public.

Yours etc.
Regular Opera Goer

The King's Theatre,
Greenock

Sir,

The correspondent demands an explanation as to why the same artists appear night after night. Surely his knowledge of the past week's performances do not give him the right to style himself 'Regular Opera Goer,' as it may be of interest to him to know that during last week we presented eight operas and a total of fifteen different artists appeared, and on Wednesday evening the services of no less than eight principals were utilised in "Pro Patria" and "Cavalleria Rusticana".

Finally may I say that all the principals will appear this week.

Yours etc.
ED. Taylor,
Carl Rosa Opera Company

Dame Eva always talked about the Royal Carl Rosa Company with affection. She did not deny its limitations as it was a touring company but felt that the experience she gained with them was: 'Enormous' giving an opportunity to: 'Walk the stage and find myself.' When talking about stage rehearsals in her day, with Daniel Snowman, he asked her if they used to rehearse productions as much then as now and she replied:

'We did not.'

He then surmises that perhaps the tradition was much more that you simply stood and sang and in her anxiety to please, she nearly said yes, but then added:

'Well you did what your own ideas were really and we were left to our own resources. Of course that happened much more with the Royal Carl Rosa Opera Company which was a touring company but in a way it taught us a lot. One used one's own imagination and so on and it was quite good. Of course it could have been improved I'm sure but it wasn't a bad experience – bad for experience.'

Daniel Snowman: 'Was acting and physical appearance important?'

'I don't think as much as today.'

As part of her career-building experiences she would have had to buy her own stage makeup and learn to apply it. The small, pale, salmon-pink, metal box, containing her rouge, eye shadow and foundation sticks, and bits and pieces, such as hair grips and compact mirror, (among the things that she left to the Royal Opera House), was probably the one she used as a young singer with the Royal Carl Rosa Opera Company. When the lid was opened the grease paints used by performers at that time and the scent which hit the back of one's throat and the dry powdery bits, evoked a singing and acting tradition of bygone days.

Eva Turner's voice developed, with Plum's help, and her repertoire expanded into more dramatic roles and by 1920 she was singing Elsa in *Lohengrin*:

'We went to the Wimbledon Theatre, I was singing three or four other roles that week but I learnt Elsa in one week putting my light on through the night to see if I remember and so on. (Laughter). I am lucky in so far as I can play the piano and I can learn the parts.'

Another addition to her repertoire at this time was Leonora in *Il Trovatore* which she loved singing:

'What a wonderful role Leonora is, as it does, every aspect of singing. The superb lyric legato of "Tacea la notte" is followed by the florid "Di tale amor" each making its contrasting demands, while the famous "Miserere" calls for full, strong, dramatic voice. In "D'amor sull'ali rose", all three qualities are required, and if I had to chose the record on which to be judged I think this would be my choice.'

Brünnhilde in the *Valkyrie*, Elisabeth, Aida, Butterfly, Amelia in the *Masked Ball* and Leonore in *Fidelio* soon followed:

'I remember with the Carl Rosa, before I went to Italy, I did four performances a week - many times, and heavy roles; "Meistersinger," "Tannhäuser," "Trovatore," "Aida," "Ballo in Maschera," "Cavalleria" and I was in excellent voice at the end of the week so I thought to myself "well I must be doing something right".'

The company travelled by train as far afield as Scotland, where they performed not only in the important cities of Glasgow, Edinburgh and Aberdeen, where she sang her first Elisabeth in *Tannhäuser*, but also in the smaller provincial towns.

Eva Turner as Elizabeth Tannhäuser

Glasgow and Edinburgh

Glasgow and Edinburgh were always favourite places to perform for Eva and Gladys, as they were pleased to settle into digs for the six week season rather than, as sometimes happened when in the north of England, where small towns were close enough to travel to and from there base camp, they:

'often had to spend the night in stations waiting for the first or last train out of a town and perhaps even sing the next day without proper rest.'

The Lyceum Theatre, tucked in behind the then newly built Usher Hall, lies near one end of Princes Street, so perhaps, after: *'getting up early before a rehearsal to study and to practise any phrases that I thought could be better'*, she read a newspaper sitting on Princes Street. Was she well wrapped up against the

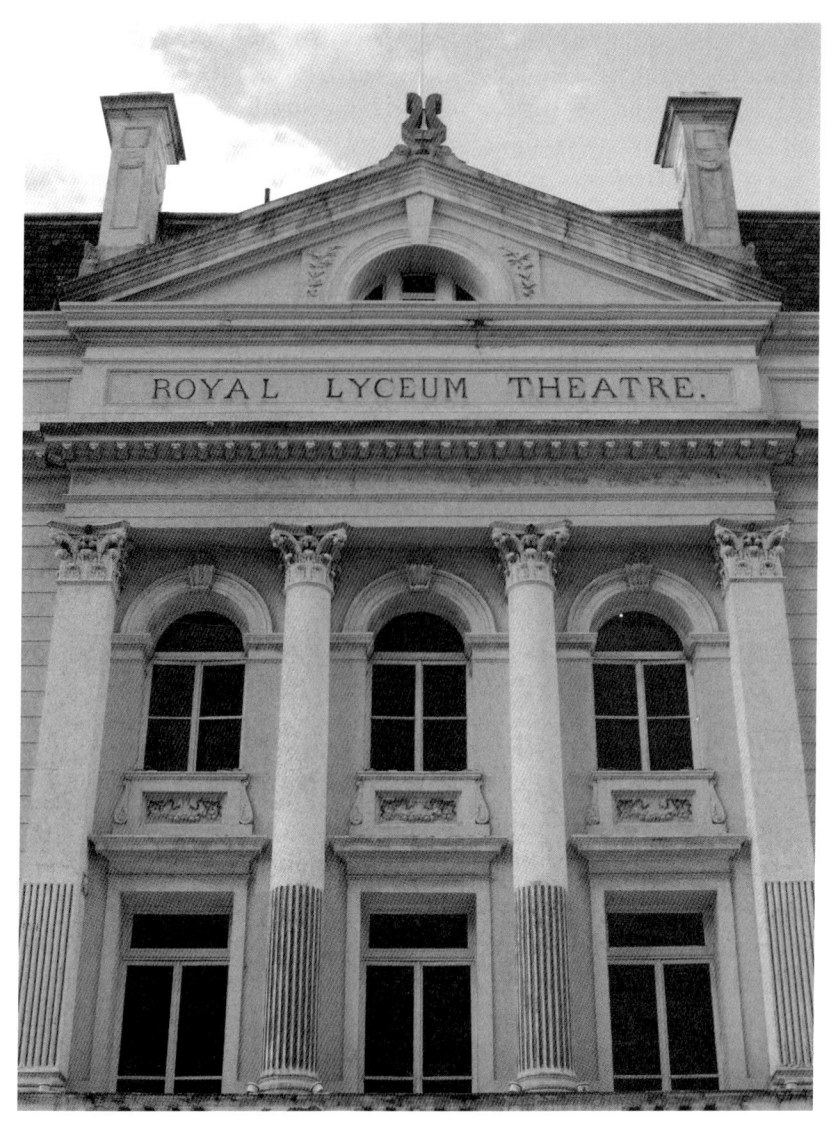

The archives, of the Royal Lyceum Theatre in Edinburgh, opened on September 10th, 1883, collected by Glasgow University, give us a clear view of Eva Turner's operatic roles between 1916 and 1924 and as a bonus we can have a look at the roles of Gladys Parr and see how their operatic lives were taking shape. Also included are the walk-on parts of Albert Richards Broad, (See appendix).

chill winds of Scotland's early spring, with the Scott Monument towering above her and the great castle with all its history looking down on her as she read:

> 'darkened streets and stormy nights were much in evidence during the engagement of the Royal Carl Rosa Company, but despite these and the many other claims on the public at this time the company received a gratifying measure of patronage from the lovers of high-class opera.'

The prices charged at the Lyceum were: Boxes 2/2 (£170), Orchestral Stalls and Dress Circle 5/- (£20), Amphitheatre Stalls 3/- (£12), Pit 2/- (£8), Amphitheatre 1/- (£4), Gallery 6d (£2).

'The Carl Rosa Opera Company announce that on the occasion of the opening of the Glasgow station of the BBC by the Lord Provost at Glasgow today, the musical part of the programme will be supplied by the artistes of the company who are now giving their season of "Grand Opera in Glasgow". This will be the first occasion on which grand opera has been broadcast in Scotland.' On March 6th, Station 5SC began broadcasting from an attic in Rex House, where the small space housed an orchestra, pipe band, choir, solo singer, actors and speech-makers as BBC Scotland took shape, sending news, current affairs, sport, religious addresses and entertainment into people's homes. I wonder if she was there.

Government Entertainment Tax extra. (See p.37)

Gladys said that when they were on tour and she and Eva shared digs, Eva never walked, but ran everywhere. They would run in the morning to the 10.30 am rehearsal at the theatre which ended around 1.30pm and then run home for a quick bite of dinner before they practised all afternoon, after which they would run back to the theatre for the performance in the evening. Neither of them wanted to miss anything of interest but although Gladys would have been happy to walk smartly, it was Eva's habit throughout life always to run so as not to waste valuable time.

They were clearly dedicated young artists and this was noticed as we read in the Scotsman of April 17th, 1920:

'"The Miracle" or "The Story of Antoine" by Reginald Sommerville. As Thérèse, Miss Eva Turner gave an excellent account of a part in which she had to contend with a good deal that is merely conventional... and Miss Gladys Parr as the mother of Antoine, Jeanne Marie was artistic in her study of a pathetic character... In view of the fact that the opera was new to Edinburgh there were too many empty seats in the theatre. Under such circumstances an impresario can hardly be expected to display much eagerness to produce new operas.'

Edinburgh Castle

and on April 26th, of a matinee of *Il Trovatore* a couple of days previously:

'Miss Eva Turner adorned the role of Leonora by the purity and high range of her voice, while Miss Gladys Parr, as Azucena, the gipsy woman, was fully equal to the demands, dramatic as well as vocal, which the part entailed.'

The Theatre Royal Glasgow was the venue for Eva Turner's first Brünnhilde.

'All they had to produce the ring of fire, through which only a hero could penetrate to claim me, was a smelly old boiler off stage, with a ring of perforated pipes around

Brünnhilde's rock. I remember lying there in the middle of that dreadful smell,'

she reminisced once when sharing a post lesson cocktail of Cinzano and lemon juice which:

'is good for you because Cinzano has herbs in it and lemon is a wonderful disinfectant for your body.'

She was also a great believer in rosehip syrup, castor oil and cod liver oil for their help in guarding against germs and contribution to inner cleanliness. These thoughts are a reminder that she grew up in the days when you had to be your own doctor and before the miracles of modern medicine, which she also enjoyed, having had her cataract removed when she was almost eighty-three. She went on to say that the effects of the boiler fumes in *Walküre* worried her, lest they caused her to be ill for her next show so:

'I went to bed with a raw onion wrapped in red flannel round my neck so that I would not get a sore throat for the next performance!'

The Theatre Royal, Glasgow was also the venue for an Earl Haig's *Warriors' Day* Fund Concert on Sunday, March 20th, 1921 and in later life she talked of this concert and others like it, in which she gave her services:

'with gratitude to those who had given me my freedom... It was my duty.'

When she talked about this particular concert she began to smile as she remembered how she and Gladys had been soloists along with Princess Iwa who was dressed in her Native Maori costume as she sang her ethnic songs. Dame Eva recalled that Princess Iwa's headdress was made of huge feathers and reached the floor.

Eva Turner purchased her Brünnhilde wig for the sum of £10 during April, 1921 from wig makers with 'Royal Approval' at 10 Long Acre, who proudly boasted of being wig makers to Covent Garden Opera. £10 was almost a week's salary for her at that time since on August 22nd, 1921 she had signed a contract which gave her £11 rising to £13 for 3 performances per week with the Carl Rosa Opera Company. Later in that year on November 25th she bought her Butterfly wig from the same firm for £3-3-0. Eva Turner was investing in her future.

Manchester

Manchester was the nearest city to Oldham, the town of her birth, so let us read a little of the local reaction in the Manchester Guardian.

February 2nd, 1921:

'Miss Eva Turner was a powerful Venus singing in a full and open-hearted way which left little of the possible enigma or romance in the attractions or lure of the character, though the vocal satisfaction of her singing was substantial enough and rather paled the unripened beauty of Miss Ethel Austen's singing as Elizabeth.'

August 25th, 1921:

'Miss Turner has a style too unreserved to give the suggestion of romance and mystery to the music of Elsa, and her quiet tones lose too much of vocal enthusiasm for them to be the charm of the whole.'

August 30th, 1921:

'Miss Eva Turner was more successful as Aida than in any previous part, for the admixture of melancholy in the music seemed to awake in her a greater sensibility and flexibility of style. But she revelled most in the moments which allowed of transcendent power, and whatever doubts we may have had about the wisdom of her efforts in this kind, these moments seem to prove that with a judicious training and control, hers might be, or might have been, the voice of a generation. As it was last night, one could not regard it as having any beauty of an ideal kind.'

September 21st, 1921:

'Miss Eva Turner was a more powerful Nedda than we have previously heard but scarcely a fanciful or captivating one'

March 1st, 1922:

'Miss Eva Turner has a voice that thrills often enough because it is naturally vibrant, but her movements on stage do not give the illusion that they are involuntary.'

Please keep this!

SALTAIRE PHILHARMONIC SOCIETY
THIRD SEASON - 1921-22

VICTORIA HALL, SALTAIRE
Third Concert of the Season

PROGRAMME
OF

GRAND CONCERT

On Wednesday, March 22nd, 1922
At 7-30 p.m.

PRINCIPALS

Miss EVA TURNER   Mr. WILSON THORNTON
Prima Donna, Royal Carl Rosa Opera Co.   *Late Principal Tenor, Royal Carl Rosa Opera Co.*
and Covent Garden Opera.

FULL CHORUS AND ORCHESTRA
Principal Violin - Mr. Whitby Norton

CONDUCTOR   -   -   -   Mr. J. DOUGLAS SMITH

WADDILOVE & CO. LTD., BRADFORD.

Hull

Hull was a venue which Eva, Gladys and Plum loved visiting on tour, as they had there digs and land-ladies who looked after them particularly well. (These ladies who later travelled to Covent Garden to hear Eva Turner sing in 1928 and whom she immediately recognised at the stage door, were given two of her bouquets.) The reviews from Hull are usually very much on the side of these young artists and remind one how to be accepted and appreciated helps the performer to relax and give a good show. It seems that the good people of Hull were opera lovers and great supporters of the Carl Rosa Opera Company, which spent Christmas 1921 and brought in the New Year of 1922 in that town.

Hull Daily Mail December 24th, 1921:

'Miss Turner as Elsa added another success to the many registered in Hull. Throughout the opera her brilliant soprano voice was used with consummate artistry. The moods of Elsa, the childish delight in the answer to her prayer, the suspicion engendered by Ortrud, and the final despair at having thrown away her chance of happiness, were all sincerely displayed. Vocally Miss Turner's Elsa was impressive and deserved the applause accorded to her.'

December 27th, 1921:

'Time was when "Trovatore" was the opera goers' pet – aversion. That was in the days when any sort of performance seemed to do:

Eva Turner

and that day happily is past. Give "Il Trovatore" a fair chance and the genius of Verdi will shine out - as it did last night. The attention paid to the musical details by the singers and orchestra raised the work to the level it ought to occupy.

One has to go a long way back to recall a more brilliantly effective quartet of principal singers than Miss Eva Turner, Mr William Boland, Miss Gladys Parr and Mr Kingsley Lark. Miss Eva Turner has 'arrived'. She is to be regarded as a prima-donna of rank. As such she sang last night, mastering all the varieties of song that Verdi has given to his heroine. She was equally effective, though in another way in the lyrical grace of "Breeze of the Night" as in the many impassioned scenes where the fullest dramatic force is required. Miss Gladys Parr's voice has grown greatly in volume without losing anything of its beautiful tone.'

January 2nd, 1922:

'It is nothing but the truth to say that "Aida" last night was the finest thing this young singer has accomplished. It is a far cry from "Maritana" to "Aida" on successive nights and the success of Miss Turner in each reveals her great versatility and value to the company.'

Of her Maritana it said:

'Miss Eva Turner renewed acquaintance with the part in which she made her debut in Hull three years ago. Needless to say the audience was delighted with the performance and encores were demanded.'

January 5th, 1922:

'Again the chief honours go to Miss Eva Turner, who simply amazed us by the ease with which she turned from the primitive savagery of Aida to the radiance and passion of the singer La Tosca. Miss Turner's wonderful voice simply played with Tosca's music and one reason for this must surely be found to be connected with her histrionic conception of the role, for it was undoubtedly a remarkable display of acting.'

Bristol

Bristol too kept an eye on Eva Turner, regarding her as a home grown product. Bristol Evening News October 4th, 1922:

'Miss Eva Turner, who though not born in Bristol, we can nevertheless claim as a Bristolian, has improved her idea of Eva Pogner. She sang with an intensity and clearness and made her an outstanding figure particularly in the quintet in Act Three.'

October 9th, 1922

'In Miss Eva Turner there is now one of the finest Santuzza in this country. She has immensely improved her rendering of the part, by her development of every detail of the passion and pain. To say the house was enthralled is but to state a plain fact'

Greenock (See appendix)

We can read a little in the Greenock Telegraph about the experience of visiting the Royal Carl Rosa Opera performances at the local Kings Theatre at that time: February 14th, 1923:

'After the solemnity and semi-barbarians of "Aida", it was something of a relief to listen to that gay and sparkling opera "Mignon". Thomas's work has been heard frequently in Greenock, but it is doubtful if it has ever had a better representation than that which it received last night from the Carl Rosa Company. The house was well filled and the opera from beginning to end was carried through with fine spirit. Principals and chorus alike were in excellent trim and the various familiar numbers seldom failed to rouse the audience to enthusiasm... In the title role Miss Gladys Parr achieved a vocal and dramatic success. The music suits her well, and both her singing and acting skills were satisfactorily tested in the merry dressing-room scene. The great song "Knowest thou that dear land" was given with fine emotional feeling....The "Masked Ball" which will be presented for the first time tonight in Greenock has a romantic career... Miss Eva Turner will play Adelia, (for reasons unknown they changed her name from Amelia) and that signifies an added interest to the opera.'

February 15th, 1923:

'Last evening will be remembered by the audience that attended the first performance in Greenock of the "Masked Ball". Seldom if ever has there been such a demand locally to see an opera. Every available seat was snapped up several days ago but it is doubtful if many anticipated such a rush for accommodation in the area and gallery... The "Full House" notices were posted shortly after the doors opened and a considerable number had to go away disappointed... Miss Eva Turner was in brilliant voice. The beautiful duet in the Gallows scene was delightfully rendered and she sang with great feeling in her impassioned appeal to Renato to let her see her child before he slays her.'

When Dame Eva re-visited Greenock in 1977, she was disappointed that the King's Theatre was no longer there but after eating fish and chips from a newspaper (her request), we walked along the esplanade to look for the house where she and Gladys had stayed in Greenock all those years before. She remembered clearly that the house had a monkey puzzle tree in the garden and that, 'the Scots had been most kind to them'. She walked smartly, taking deep breaths of bracing sea air, exclaiming at the beauty of her surroundings and saying how it didn't seem a moment since she had sung in this town. During this conversation, her back straightened even more and the performing mode was upon her. She was not boastful but was proud of her achievements and happy to share memories of her time on stage saying:

'I was so happy to sing in those days that I would have paid them to let me do it. It was never a chore and I looked forward to every performance.'

There had been nervousness in my parental home before her visit, as my mum and dad wanted Dame Eva to know by their actions, how grateful they were for all the ways in which she had helped me begin my career and in some strange way, they were anxious that they would 'let me down'. Dame Eva, however, was at her most gracious and inclusive during her visit, immediately sensing the situation and so, released from their inhibitions, they were able to give in the generous way they wanted. They were delighted with and cherished her 'Thank You' letter, which I found in a box containing family papers after they had both died.

Alexandra Theatre later known as The King's Theatre Greenock

When I sat in the Watt Monument Library, Greenock, my home town, researching for Dame Eva's biography, my complicated feelings, among them the sheer joy of finding a direct link to Dame Eva again after all these years, almost overwhelmed me. I was brought into her past, during which through thick and thin she had spun a thread of sounds which can still be imagined in the

Letter from Dame Eva to Mr & Mrs James Gray

> 01-229 7760   26, PALACE COURT,
> LONDON. W.2.
>
> 8.6.1981.
>
> Dear Mr & Mrs Gray,
> Words truly fail me to tell you what a great pleasure it was to be with you during this past week-end. I loved every moment of it, and it was quite wonderful to be in Greenock, Gourock, Glasgow, & Edinburgh again. Scotland has always been very special for me, and its people also. I was touched by your kindness in every regard, and all the transport, our sandwiches in Dungoon, and the HAGGIS. What a sweet kind thought! It was a pleasure also, to be in your home - I can now visualise you therein.
> My love and blessings
> Sincerely Eva Turner.

words of the reviews, linking us to the great universal, continuing, subconscious web of music, which has been created by dedicated musicians and singers down the years in whose number Eva Turner can be counted.

The dramatic soprano repertoire, which Eva Turner was by this time singing, requires very special abilities and qualities. These qualities are unusual and are valued commercially so it is not surprising then to find the sum of money in her contract with the Carl Rosa had now risen to £15 for three performances a week. Neither was it surprising to notice outside interest, as in this letter from the famous concert agency 'Ibbs and Tillett', addressed to her, care of Carl Rosa Opera:

9th November 1922.

> 'Dear Miss Turner,
>
> Would you care to make a test record for the Columbia Graphophone Company?
>
> If so we can arrange an early appointment for you. Please let me know by return.
>
> Yours faithfully,
> Ibbs and Tillett.'

There is no record of whether she accepted this arrangement or, if she did, what the outcome was. Had she written to them in the first place looking for concert work?

After a considerable lapse of time, there is another letter from them on:

17th August 1923

'Dear Miss Turner,
Chesterfield Amateur Musical Society March 12th
Barnsley St Cecelia Society March 13
Sheffield Amateur Musical soc April 1
With the object of obtaining concessions in terms, the above mentioned societies have co-operated and will perform Berlioz "Faust" on all three days under the directorship of Dr. Fredric Stanton. Will you kindly let us know, by return, what is the very lowest fee you would be disposed to entertain to sing the part of Marguerite on all three dates?
The management, Ibbs and Tillett.'

The British National Company had asked a couple of months before if she was free to repeat her performance of Santuzza on June 16th, 1923 at a matinee performance, after her recent success in the role with them. She accepted this engagement and also one to sing Venus for the Huddersfield Choral's performance (percentage to Ibbs and Tillett) of *Tannhäuser* on November 14th, 1923 at the fee of 15 guineas. A different agency wrote to her around this time asking her if she would entertain singing at the London Coliseum, which was a stage for variety performances. All this would suggest that if Carl Rosa Ltd. wished her to remain a member of the company, they would have to offer her a contract with more flexible terms.

The plans for the Carl Rosa Opera Company's 1923 autumn tour were completed by Mr. H.B. Phillips, the new proprietor, who said that the company would begin with old favourites such as *Faust, Samson and Delilah, Madam Butterfly, Tales of Hoffmann, Tannhäuser, Lohengrin* and *Trovatore* and would carry a larger orchestra than had been the case for many seasons with the total strength of the company exceeding a hundred: 'A feature of the performances will be the re-introduction of the ballets in certain operas and the season will open next Monday at the Borough Theatre, Stratford, whence the company will proceed to Richmond for a fortnight. Later they will visit Ireland and Scotland, in addition to many English towns.'

When visiting Ireland with the company in 1923, a publicity article for Eva Turner on October 1st in the Irish Independent shows how her reputation had grown:

> 'The Carl Rosa Opera Company, which will open a three-week's visit to Dublin on the 25th inst., will have Miss Eva Turner as prima donna. A Lancashire lass by birth, Miss Turner attracted attention as a vocalist in her 11th year. One of her most enthusiastic admirers is Madame Albani and she has a repertoire of more than 30 leading operas, her favourite roles being Aida, Butterfly and Brünnhilde.'

Dame Emma Albani (1847-1930) was a famous singer and renowned teacher who married Ernest Gye (the son of Covent Garden's director, Vincent) who later became the manager of the theatre; clearly an influential person to mention.

In Catherine David's interview, Eva recalled going to Dublin with the Carl Rosa Opera Company:

> '*I was singing Marguerite in "Faust". In the final scene - you know she is in prison and lying on straw - well I remember this straw! I don't know if they got it from a mews, or somewhere, but it was too horrrrrible for words. Horrible. I thought, I have to act as though this doesn't matter, so it helped my acting really... (Laughter)*'

It would have been a big job for the stage crews to dress the stage in the given time in the small theatres the Carl Rosa Company visited on tour. Some of them would not have had the high-tech of the day and although it would be exciting to sit in the audience for the opera, even in the gallery way up high, the conditions back stage could be pretty basic and facilities a little depressing.

It would certainly be crowded in these narrow corridors and perhaps smelly, backstage as well as on stage (!), where singers were trying to pass through to get on to perform, wearing elaborate, heavy costumes. On the other hand there is nothing like that smell back stage to get the adrenalin going if you are a stage creature, which Eva Turner was. Having said that, she was first and foremost a singer: 'consumed with desire to be perfect in my vocal emission' so it is a shame that her inflexible contracts with the company did not allow time for more concert work at that time.

London

In addition to the provincial tours, the Royal Carl Rosa Company performed in London, where the reviews would be taken very seriously by the management of the company and singers alike, as they were written by erudite critics who were used to hearing music, of all kinds, performed to a high standard. These reviews would capture the attention of the more discerning, bigger audiences which London could provide and bring recognition for the singers as well as a full house.

Roy Plomley asked Eva Turner: 'Did you have London seasons as well with the company?' She replied:

'I remember in 1917 I think it was, we came to the Garrick Theatre and I remember I sang in "Maritana" and Ben Davies was the tenor, (yes) then we went over to Shaftesbury Avenue to the Shaftesbury Theatre and again we were singing the "Maritana" and Adelina Patti was in the box there for the afternoon performance. She left early to return to Swansea. You know she lived in Craig-y-nos Castle outside Swansea so I didn't have the pleasure and the honour of meeting her'.

The Observer critic tells us about her Maritana on May 13th, 1917:

'Miss Eva Turner might gain in refinement of vocalisation, but her natural voice is a very good one'

Opera in the provinces had an enormous air of excitement surrounding it, with delight in first performances of new operas and the hunger and enthusiasm of the man in the street to see an opera, entertainment which was the forerunner in many ways to the habit, which later developed, of going to the cinema. Praise like that above, however, from the London press, would have been a big moment in Eva's development, putting icing on the cake of an already exciting life. This was a good beginning.

There was no resident Opera Company at Covent Garden during the war years (see appendix) and the only opera performances heard there between July, 1920 and the beginning of May, 1922, were twelve weeks given by the Royal Carl Rosa Opera Company; November 22nd/December 18th, 1920 and October 17th/December 10th, 1921. The Company's survival, providing jobs and opera in English, despite its own financial difficulties, made possible by years of tradition, experience and continuity which gave knowledge of how to balance the complicated schedule and expensive travelling arrangements, was nothing short of miraculous in the musical climate of that time.

In 1920 Mr Alfred van Noorden, of the Carl Rosa Opera Company, entered into an arrangement with Frank Rendle that the coming season at Covent Garden would be given by the Carl

Rosa Company, which would play for four weeks, beginning on November 22nd. *Lohengrin*, *Faust*, *Tales of Hoffmann*, *Cavalleria Rusticana*, (Eva Turner's debut at Covent Garden), *Pagliacci*, *Aida*, *La Bohème* and *Carmen* would be performed.

> *'The company will be greatly increased for the occasion... a chorus of 250 has been obtained especially for "Lohengrin". Over 60 musicians have been secured as a nucleus for the orchestra... The orchestra includes a tympani player named Kavanagh, who was a member of the orchestra at the opening performance of the company 51 years ago,'* said Mr. Alfred van Noorden.

In the following weeks further repertoire was added: *Madama Butterfly*, *Tannhäuser*, *Tosca*, *Samson and Delilah*, *Jewels of the Madonna*, *Il Trovatore*, *David Garrick*, *Susanna's Secret*, *Tristan and Isolde* and *Dante and Beatrice*. Prices including tax were: Reserved seats, 3/6 to 12/-, Unreserved, 1/3, Boxes, £3-13-0 and £2-8-0.

Gladys Parr was first to step foot on the stage at Covent Garden as she made her debut there on Tuesday, November 23rd, singing Siebel in *Faust* and the next night she sang Niclaus in *The Tales of Hoffmann*.

1920: Eva Turner's Debut at Covent Garden

Eva Turner made her debut at Covent Garden on Thursday, November 25th, 1920, singing Santuzza in *Cavalleria Rusticana* by Mascagni. Parry Jones was Turridu and Elsbeth Wakefield sang Lola. The Evening Standard said:

> *'Miss Eva Turner's Santuzza was brilliantly successful.'*

and the Morning Advertiser:

> *'Miss Eva Turner, Santuzza of the occasion has a voice of great brilliance, but lacking in sympathy.'*

On Saturday that week Eva Turner sang Musetta in *La Bohème*. The Globe reported:

> *'The biggest hit was made by Eva Turner who, acting as well as she sang made a most engaging Musetta',*

the Telegraph:

> *'Miss Turner, a very interesting Musetta, is so clever that she must guard against the overplaying which is one of the blots of our young artists in opera'*

and the Daily Mail:

'on Saturday the lively Musetta of Miss Eva Turner stood out.'

On November 30th she sang Elisabeth in *Tannhäuser* and in December: Leonora in *Trovatore*, Giulietta in *Hoffmann*, Venus in *Tannhäuser* and Madama Butterfly. Gladys and Eva sang together in *Butterfly* and *Hoffmann* during this Covent Garden season and Gladys also sang Mrs Smith in *David Garrick*, an opera about the life of the actor and playwright whose life spanned the eighteenth century and whose play *The Clandestine Marriage* served as a subject for Cimarosa's opera *Il Matrimonio Segreto*.

Carl Rosa production of 'Tannhäuser', 1920s

On December 3rd the Athenian tells us:

'The Carl Rosa performances at Covent Garden will be enjoyed by those who like opera for its own sake and are not distracted by appurtenances. The singers have to bear the full burden as they should: on them alone it depends whether the opera gets across. We think that the Carl Rosa Company do get it across. They approach the task not as an immortal work of so and so which has to be treated in the spirit of reverence but as something that has to be intelligible and interesting to the audience. The result is that "Tannhäuser" for instance has more go and more unity of purpose than many others that have been heard at Covent Garden at three times the price. Mr Boland showed signs of his training as an oratorio singer but he makes a convincing Tannhäuser. Miss Eva Turner sang well as Elisabeth while Miss Gladys Seager made a plausible Venus indeed.'

1915-1924 The Royal Carl Rosa Opera Company

Eva Turner as Santuzza

On December 17th the Times reported:

'It is announced that the short season of the Carl Rosa Opera Company at Covent Garden has been so successful that Mr. Frank Rendle has already arranged with the directors of the company for an extended season there, which will begin in the middle of next October and will run until nearly Christmas. In spite of the fact that many thousands of people have been turned away, it is not intended to alter the price of admission, the policy of the directors of the Carl Rosa Company being to present their work to the widest possible circle.'

The Royal Carl Rosa's 1921 season at Covent Garden included some of the same repertoire as the year before with *Valkyrie* and *Mastersingers* added. Eva Turner sang: Madama Butterfly, Santuzza, Musetta, Brünnhilde (*Valkyrie* and *Siegfried*), Giulietta, Elisabeth, Fricka, Elsa, Leonora in *Trovatore*, Jeanette in *Le Chant Fatale* and Aida in that season.

On October 19th the Times reports:

'Madama Butterfly can be given effectively enough by British singers, in spite of its wholly Italian style, if they do not try to sound like Italian artists. Last night the young soprano and tenor, Miss Eva Turner and Mr. John Perry, both seemed to be avoiding this tradition and they had Mr Eugene Goossens to help them as regards the vital matter of rhythm. The music was carefully sung; it went with a good swing, clearness and steadiness. More sentiment of expression was needed, but this is a matter for sensitive vocal colouring rather than for those fervid tricks of rubato, of which our people as a rule have not the secret. Miss Turner's voice is inclined to be a little unsympathetic in its cool accuracy; she must try to impart a little more naivety and charm into the tone. Her acting was much better in the more serious second act than in the first, where she was very nearly arch in her endeavour to portray simplicity.'

October 19th the Daily Telegraph:

'Compliments may go in no measured terms to Miss Eva Turner, (Butterfly) not only for her general conception of the role of the protagonist but for the skill and success with which she carried it out. This young singer has made very considerable strides in her art since we remember first to have seen her and there is about her work an ease and assurance that gives a note of real conviction to all she does. Her voice which she managed very cleverly answered all requirements without any suggestion of effort and if there were moments when one felt that delicate shades of vocal colour were not quite at her command, it was something to hear

the music throughout with a clear steady tone and unforced expression – though not with impeccably clear diction. Perhaps the next time Miss Turner will be able to contrive a somewhat more convincing make-up. But her petite figure suited the part admirably, and her simple unaffected acting and graceful movements were always in the picture.'

October 30th, the Sunday Times:

'Miss Eva Turner sang the music of Antonia finely. She is a young artist who is steadily making her mark. Her voice is a good one, and she has intelligence: but she would be well advised to give more thought to the question of diction. At present it is not easy to follow her words.'

Eva Turner as Antonia

November 10th Ernest Newman writes in the Guardian:

'I hesitate to write about the Carl Rosa Company's performance of the "Rhinegold" for fear of seeming unsympathetic... In vocal resource only Miss Eva Turner (Fricka) and Mr Boland (Loki) came anywhere being the equal of the music.'

Eva Turner's roles at Covent Garden in the 1922 Carl Rosa Season were: Madama Butterfly, Aida, Eva, Elizabeth, Tosca, Musetta, Elsa, Thais in *Thais and Thalmae* by C McCampbell and Santuzza. In a little interview given during that season in the Star newspaper, she said:

'I have played about thirty parts altogether. My favourite roles are Aida, Butterfly, and Brünnhilde. I am very fond of Wagner parts and hope someday to play Isolda.'

The Times on October 10th reports:

'"Madam Butterfly" First Night of Carl Rosa Season. The feature of last night's performance was an extremely clever study of the title part by Miss Eva Turner. Her acting was unforced, sincere, and at times touched with feeling. Her singing was clean and strong, a little cold maybe, but so sure and steady that she always held her hearers. In gesture and deportment she carried off the disadvantage of an un-ideal height for the part with genuine skill. We liked the Suzuki of Miss Gladys Parr and the Sharpless of Mr Booth Hitchen: both sang smoothly and both were very much in earnest.'

All continues well during that season when the Scotsman writes:

'The outstanding feature of the performance of Verdi's opera "Aida" at Covent Garden Theatre to-night by the Carl Rosa Opera Company was the singing of Miss Eva Turner, who appeared in the title part. Her phrasing was clean and clear and the cool purity of her piano tones was a delight to hear. In the beautiful Nile scene she was particularly fine in the duet with her father Amonasro.'

In her 1982 recording for her third Desert Island Discs she remembers singing Tosca at Covent Garden in 1922. The first theatre they went to after this was the Alexandra Theatre, Hull which was of course much smaller:

'Always after the second act I went out to see what the drop was, you know when Tosca throws herself over the castle walls? (yes) And at the Alexandra Theatre someone came to speak to me and I didn't look at the drop. Well the drop at the Royal Opera House was much deeper and this was very

shallow and I threw myself with much force and came up again.' (laughter)

Roy Plomley: 'O that's lovely – the bouncing prima donna.'

'Yes! Yes! (Laugh) Oh dear! (Laughter).'

Eva Turner, In March 12th, 1924, gave a little detailed interview about her life at that time in the Glasgow Weekly Herald's Stage and Screen Page:

> 'Eva Turner... When I saw Miss Eva Turner before her appearance in "Faust" on Saturday night, I found to my relief that she has a warm place in her heart for interviewers. Indeed our talk was more in the nature of a heart to heart chat than I had dared to hope and it needed little prompting on my part to learn her ideas and all the things that concern theatre goers in general. Miss Turner's labours on behalf of Grand Opera are obviously labours of love for she is an enthusiast. And she gave me an interesting account of how she came to be attached to the Carl Rosa and that she was now an Associate of the Royal Academy of Music. "Have I any particular favourites," she said when I asked the question. "Oh yes. I am awfully fond of Fidelio. I love Fidelio and I like Aida and Madama Butterfly and "Siegfried" very much". Thereupon I was told something of Miss Turner's personal ambition, chief of which is that in every part she plays she strives to improve on her previous performance. She aims at perfection. "I always try to excel myself," she exclaimed, "to do it better and better every time and try too to enunciate the arias clearly. It's not always easy – because of the orchestration for instance – but I try my best believing that it makes a great difference to the people".'

The interviewer goes on to ask her about hobbies and Eva says she has no time as she is so busy building her repertoire:

> 'It did transpire however that she likes piano playing and I observed she keeps an instrument in her dressing room. Miss Turner is also very fond of horse riding... she has fond memories of her time in Brighton last year when she did a lot of it. "Friends told me," she went on "that horseback would make me dreadfully stiff but it didn't really. Not a bit. I just loved to gallop over the rolling downs – miles and miles of open country you know. There are no trees and I could see the boats that called at Dieppe." Miss Turner, however, did not go in for hurdling and would not voice an opinion on the Prince's recent mishap but thinks that horse riding benefits the liver... Her hopes for respite after the present season ends are centred on Germany; whither she would like to study continental Opera. She already has 'done' France and Italy and holds the belief that a tour

of Europe is helpful to anyone associated with opera. They are then more receptive than one not so associated. Miss Turner then gave her impressions of Glasgow theatre goers which I will not repeat but briefly she loves the northern audiences for their discerning taste and applause. She agrees that attendance is disappointing and suggests the Depression and also some lesser known pieces may be to blame and suggests a more detailed programme would be helpful and agrees that the long interval is not ideal but says that she understands that although there are a lot of ready and willing stage hands they need the guidance of a good stage manager. She likes the acoustic of the Royal but best of all she likes singing in Covent Garden.'

When the Royal Carl Rosa came to London in 1924 they did not perform at Covent Garden Theatre but at the Scala Theatre in Charlotte Street and the Musical Times on July 1st tells us:

'"Fidelio", which has not been sung in London since the Beecham season of 1910, opened the series of operatic performances at the Scala Theatre by the Carl Rosa Opera Company. The Scala Theatre, which is certainly the most beautiful theatre in London, a theatre fit to be the setting of distinguished artistic enterprises, proved to be difficult of discovery by London opera goers during the Carl Rosa season and the valiant singers often had to face discouraging rows of empty seats.

We mention with respect the conviction with which it was sung in spite of an English text that seemed calculated to take the wind out of any sail. The principals were Miss Eva Turner and Mr. William Boland. These are singers of gifts that would, in a community less reckless of artistic values than ours, be held precious and worthy of the right fostering. We fear that both, who might be eminent, must be described as coarse in their performances. Both made the impression of singers too well accustomed to insensitive audiences – audiences for whom nothing counts but the gros moyens. No musical listener is above taking pleasure in the grand culminating tones in the right place but some of us like it artfully prepared for, and we know how much more effective it is then. Wherein lay the success of the singing in "The Rose Cavalier", which made it a nine-days' wonder last May, among all who cared for music in London?

Not in the prodigious gift of a single one of the singers, but in a cultivation of the finer shades. Miss Eva Turner is a most remarkably gifted young woman.

It is as much the blame of musical England generally as her own, that she is not a better artist.'

Interestingly, in the same edition of The Musical Times, a different critic writes about Ettore Panizza, who is about to discover Eva Turner and invite her to audition for Toscanini at La Scala Milan. The unflattering review tells us of his conducting at Covent Garden during the Italian season:

'M. Ettore Panizza made his way through the score as if nobody else was concerned in it. Such conducting night after night, neutralising much of the finer parts of the singing, was a great reproach to the season.'

In her own words in 1982 *Desert Island Discs* to celebrate her 90th Birthday, Eva Turner tells us of how she came to be invited to audition for Toscanini:

'I was doing three performances of "Butterfly" one week and three performances of "Fidelio" the next week at the New Scala Theatre, Charlotte Street and Maestro Panizza heard of this and he sent me a letter me asking me if I would go and audition at Covent Garden, which I did. Percy Pitt and Charles Moor the stage director were also at this audition and the stage was set for "Butterfly" as it happened. After the audition Panizza asked if I could leave at once to audition for Toscanini.'

A big decision had to be made at this point, as many factors had to be considered:

1. Eva Turner had already signed her contract for the 1924/25 season with the Royal Carl Rosa Company for £21 for three performances a week. Written at the side it says: 'It is further agreed that the artist shall be cast for leading dramatic roles only and that consecutive performances will be avoided. That the artist may accept concert engagements provided she gives the company 6 weeks' notice in writing of such engagements.'

2. Eva's father asked Plum to accompany Eva to Italy and, if the audition was successful, to travel with her and look after her affairs in her new career but Plum too had signed a contract for the following year. The contract requiring his signature was accompanied by a rather curt letter, addressed to Mr Peter Broad at 14 Wrotham, Road: (He was sometimes called Peter)

'Dear Mr Broad,
I enclose the above for your signature which please return to us. The salary specified represents our very best terms. In the circumstances we cannot consider a request for an increase.
Yours truly CROC Ltd.
Henry B, Phillips.'

His contract was for Librarian, 2nd bass in the chorus and to play walk-on parts when required. He would earn £5 for this.

3. If this audition for Toscanini was successful, Eva Turner would be in an awkward position as both she and Plum would have to be released from their signed contracts with the Carl Rosa Company.

4. This was a huge opportunity but not an easy one, as musical relationships within Europe were not always smooth. That year, the Vienna Opera Company, which included: 'the unknown Frida Leider' and Lotte Lehmann, was banned from performing in London.

5. Would this unknown English woman, Eva Turner, who had not sung in an International Season at Covent Garden, be accepted in Italy? If she was, she would be going where no British singer had ventured before; she would be the first English singer to sing at La Scala Milan.

Eva Turner, however, did not hesitate in giving her answer in the affirmative and she and Plum set off for Milan the very next day.

The following announcements in the Times seem to bring the Carl Rosa days in this book to an appropriate ending. October 21st, 1924:

'The death is announced of Mr. J.W. Kavanagh, who had seen 56 years service with the Carl Rosa Opera Company. Mr. Kavanagh joined the company in 1868 when a boy of 16 and was the last remaining link with Carl Rosa himself, the founder of the company.'

Mr. Kavanagh was the timpanist given special mention in the advert for the coming season at Covent Garden in 1920 when Eva Turner made her debut.

The Times, November 29th, 1924

'The announcement of the death, at Wimbledon Park on Wednesday of Mme Rose Hersee, at an advanced age, is a reminder of that period in the 'seventies when Carl Rosa first made the cause of opera in English his personal concern. Rose Hersee, born 1845, was then at the height of her powers as a soprano singer, and became one of the principals in the strong combination with which Carl Rosa attracted the London public. She was then known on both sides of the Atlantic, for she had sung in New York in 1869 in an opera company taken there by Mme Parepa-Rosa, herself a well known singer and wife of Carl Rosa. It was in 1875 that Carl Rosa gave the first of his famous seasons of opera in English at the Princess Theatre, and a certain performance of "Figaro",

the outstanding work in the repertory, in which Rose Hersee sang Susanna to Santley's Figaro, is still recalled by some old opera goers, as the best ever heard in the British language.'

It was Mademoiselle Rose Hersee whose contract for his American Company was the first signed by Carl Rosa when he started his journey to bring opera to the people.

As Eva Turner steps forward into another world, those announcements of the death of two people who had been closely associated with the Carl Rosa Company in its early days remind us of the honourable beginnings and standards of the company of which, all her life, she was proud to have been part. She carried the Royal Carl Rosa Company's high aspirations with her into her new life as an international singer and never forgot the company's influence on her as a young performer.

Her time spent with that company let her build her repertoire through early lyric beginnings into later dramatic repertoire on which she founded her international career. There must also have been a certain limited mileage in being able to sing and act roles to which she was not ideally suited but in which she managed a convincing enough performance. Her knowledge of operatic repertoire would also be very useful when she was a teacher much later in life.

Most importantly I think it can be said that an intuitive singer knows within about 50 bars of music of the new role they are studying if it is: workable, quite good, very good, or will in fact be a valuable, outstanding, award winning war horse in their life. There are probably only about half a dozen of those in every singer's life and I think Eva Turner met hers when she was with the Carl Rosa Opera Company: Leonora, Leonore, Madama Butterfly, Aida, Amelia and Santuzza. That she was given a seventh later on was a great piece of good fortune.

Eva Turner had star qualities so I have not at this point included any of the Wagner repertoire, as I think she was such an outstanding singer that the minute she opened her voice, the rest of the cast in a German opera would be in danger of being vocally outshone. The opera would be vocally unbalanced and since Wagnerian operas are essentially chamber music on a big scale this is not desirable. The German opera world is often inhabited by singers, whose first interest is not the voice, but is the text and although she loved words, they were for Eva a vehicle on which to place the voice. In the Wagnerian world, it is the other way round with the voice being used to illuminate the inner meaning of the text. In Italian opera the voice is everything and vocal stars are born in that repertoire. She herself regretted that there were not more recordings of her singing the German repertoire but I would suggest that this is one of the reasons for this gap in her life. The exception to this observation is *Fidelio* but this is an opera with a classical Italianate singing line and asks for a star in the shape of Leonore. Eva Turner could and did fill that bill.

CHAPTER 3
1924-1927 Italian Beginnings

When Eva Turner left London to travel to her audition for Toscanini at La Scala, Milan, in June, 1924, the world was a very different place from the one of the late 19th century into which she had been born. Queen Victoria had died when Eva was a child of nine and the Edwardian age had given way to that of George V by the time Eva began her studies at the Royal Academy of Music. The previous year, in 1911, King George had been crowned: 'King of the United Kingdom of Great Britain and Ireland and of the British Dominions beyond the seas, Defender of the Faith, Emperor of India'.

A World War had been waged and during it the face of Europe, not to say the world, had changed. Italy, Britain's ally in the First World War, had suffered huge defeats from the Austrians, making it vulnerable and ready for change. The Russian Revolution too had brought different alliances into being. A world-wide influenza epidemic had killed hundreds of thousands of people, the school leaving age in Britain had been raised to 14, British Summer Time had been introduced to save on coal, 'upstairs' were told to cut back on 'downstairs' expenses, Rodin, Degas and Debussy had died and ten million people were prematurely dead as a result of the War.

After the end of the First World War, women voted for the first time in a UK election and in 1919, Britain voted in its first woman member of parliament, the American heiress Nancy Astor. In the first three years of 'The Twenties Decade' Britain, America and the Empire had many 'firsts':

1920   The League of Nations was launched in London at St James's Palace.
        Nellie Melba made her first advertised wireless broadcast.
        Fox's Glacier Mints were invented and named after the New Zealand Glacier.
1921   The Helicopter lifted off in its first proper flight.
        America saw *The Kid*, Charlie Chaplin's first full-length film.
        Unemployment in Britain topped 1,000,000 for the first time
        The King opened the first Ulster Parliament.

1922   The first regular news broadcast was made from a room in Marconi House on the Strand.
The isolation of insulin discovery in Canada gave hope to diabetics.
The Reader's Digest was born.

1923 brought great changes in the balance of power between the sexes: there was concern in Britain among the male population about the new found strength of women in society, hemlines of skirts rose and with them, fear of a decline in moral standards. This concern was shared even by some middle and upper class women who were happy to be attachments to their husbands. The first birth control clinic opening in London did nothing to alleviate the worries about the rising power and independence of women. Princess Alice launched a new programme on the BBC called *Woman's Hour* and her inaugural talk, about adoption issues, was discussed. *Woman's Hour*, not the programme which we know today but a forerunner, gave women a voice, where concerns such as a bill allowing women to petition for a husband's adultery and, in a lighter vein, the idea, of using cardboard tubes to style ladies' hair, was talked about.

Britain still had a huge gap between the rich and poor with abject poverty being quite common, despite philanthropic work by men like George Cadbury, a Quaker, who built Bourneville Village. The houses there could be bought by his workers at cost price, thus allowing them to rise in social and economic status and to take pride in themselves and their families. Cadbury died on 25th October, 1922 at the age of 83, leaving behind a valuable, lasting legacy for the working class population in his part of the world. In America, alas, we can see an example of the very opposite of this spirit of fairness, with the forming of United Artists to protect the huge salaries of the stars. In the end however, death has no favourite and does not take sex, talent or riches into account: the great Caruso died on August 3rd 1921 age 48 of peritonitis and the Tokyo earthquake left 300,000 dead in September 1923.

News on the art front in 1923 included: Edith Sitwell and William Walton collaborating to write *Facade*, W.B.Yeats winning the Nobel Prize and in February 1924 the first performance of *Rhapsody in Blue* with Gershwin the composer at the piano. The piece and Gershwin's brilliant piano playing transfixed the audience which included Rachmaninoff, Stokowski and Heifetz.

In 1924 Elgar was made Master of the King's Musick in Britain and the King and Queen made their first visit to the Promenade

Concerts in London's Queen's Hall. The concert was conducted, as always since 1895, by Sir Henry Wood.

The Olympic Games opened in Paris, with forty four countries, but not Germany, taking part, where the runners Harold Abrahams and Eric Liddell, of *Chariots of Fire* fame, won gold for Britain. Britain's first national airline, Imperial Airways, was launched and the U.K. became a more accessible place to live, as world distances shrank. Even without travelling, communicating across the world became easier with wireless conversations taking place between Britain and many distant Continents including faraway Australia.

Eva Turner's mind, body and soul had been, through all these happenings, concentrated on her singing and she had, it seems, lived in a little capsule headed 'my singing career'. This is not to say that she did not enjoy life but her enjoyments and thoughts were filtered through the prism of vocal achievement within one operatic company. She breathed, ate and slept singing, living out of a suitcase while on tour most of the time. Being part of a company, which would also be her extended family, would have created an illusion of safety and protection from everyday life, since the pecking order in that family would have been judged by one's artistic abilities and allowances made for eccentricity, if those talents were greater than the norm. In short I think she had become institutionalised as she lived more and more within the confines of the Carl Rosa Opera Company. Nine years is a sizeable portion of one's life to be lived under one set of rules.

This makes her decision to audition in Italy even braver perhaps, or we could say that she lacked the experience of the outside world to see how difficult it might be. Alongside singing, one of her lifelong loves was that of travel and we can now ask the question, was this nature or nurture? Had she been dreaming of foreign travel as she sang the length and breadth of Britain? Was she so used to it that she thought it was easy? Remember all her travel arrangements up to this point had been made and paid for by the company. Her father, however, knew that as a woman she would need a travelling companion and since his wife Elizabeth, Eva's mother, had many bouts of serious illness and had to be cared for, Charles asked Plum to go with Eva. He would otherwise, I imagine, have travelled with her himself.

Elizabeth Turner – Eav's Mother

1924-1927 Italian Beginnings

The world was a melting pot for change in 1924 when Eva was still touring Britain, then governed by its first labour controlled parliament. The performances of *Fidelio* and *Butterfly*, which led her to audition for Panizza at Covent Garden, were in June that year and she left England immediately after them to travel to Italy where Mussolini's fascists had recently won a sweeping victory in their general elections. The young Eva, unsurprisingly, did not notice this. Neither did she consider nor realise the possible consequences of a fascist reign of power. Her ideal was to be a great singer and she set off for a country with song and music in the very heart of its soul – just like her. Albert Richards Broad travelled with her and he became not only her teacher but also her manager, an association which continued for the rest of his life. His travelling expenses were written into Eva Turner's contracts and they became an inseparable duo for sixteen years, until his death.

I say glibly that Eva and Plum travelled to audition for Toscanini at La Scala, Milan, Italy but to get a flavour of that statement, we have to consider a few things: exactly who was Toscanini and what was the status of La Scala in 1924 where the audition itself took place. Neither Eva nor the Australian Plum spoke Italian, so how did they manage when they arrived in a foreign land with the fascists in power?

'Now I don't know whether it is possible for a generation who did not know Toscanini to realise what it meant to be summoned before him. He was the greatest man in the Italian opera world. A name before which even the most distinguished artistes bowed. To be considered worthy of his attention was an accolade in itself and so to be given the opportunity to sing for him was something which one dreamed of but really never expected to happen.'

These were Dame Eva's words when giving a little talk, interspersed with records, in which she expressed her pride in the invitation to audition. Toscanini did not ever conduct Eva Turner during a performance but it was he who, as musical director and therefore responsible for the general standard of all the performances, and who, after hearing her in 1924, gave her the job which changed her life.

Arturo Toscanini

Arturo Toscanini was born in Parma in 1867 and later went to the Parma Academy of Music. At the age of eighteen he became principal cellist and assistant chorus master of an Italian opera company which was to tour South America and in 1886 was called upon, while at Rio de Janeiro, to conduct a performance of *Aida*, doing so with great skill and from memory. When he returned to Italy as cellist in La Scala orchestra, he took part in the world premiere of Verdi's *Otello*, with the composer conducting and soon after began his own conducting career. In 1892 Toscanini conducted the world premiere of *Pagliacci* and in 1895 became the artistic director of the prestigious Teatro Regio in Turin, where he conducted the world premiere of Puccini's *La Bohème* and also the first Italian production of *Götterdämmerung*.

His reputation grew with each magnificent performance and, after marrying Carla de Martini in 1897, he became the musical director of La Scala in 1898, the year their first child, Walter, was born. Wally, their first daughter, was born in 1900, quickly followed by another son in 1901, Giorgio, who sadly died of diphtheria when he was five years old. Their daughter Wanda was born in 1907 to complete his family. He then left La Scala to become principal conductor at the Metropolitan Opera Company, sharing the position with Mahler for the first two seasons and stayed there until 1915 when he returned to Italy, where he remained for the duration of the First World War, conducting only benefit performances.

After the war, despite having run unsuccessfully, in 1919, as a fascist candidate for Milan, he quickly became disillusioned and disenchanted with fascism, repeatedly defying Mussolini after his ascent to power in 1922. In the early twenties he set about rebuilding La Scala Opera Company which had not existed, as such, since 1917, and in 1920/21 took the Scala orchestra on a massive tour of Italy and North America. In December, 1921 he inaugurated the first season of the reformed La Scala, by conducting *Falstaff* and by 1926 his world-wide fame was so great that he was the first conductor to feature on the front cover of *Time Magazine*. He remained the artistic director of La Scala until 1929.

In 1901, during Toscanini's first period as artistic director, La Scala installed the most modern stage lighting system in Europe, and an orchestral pit was constructed in 1907. Toscanini fought hard for these reforms and insisted on darkening the lights in the auditorium during the performance, as he believed that for a performance to be artistically successful, the audience's attention had to be drawn to all the ingredients of an opera: singers, orchestra, chorus, staging, sets and costumes. Theatre since

The Teatro alla Scala was built on the site of the church of Santa Maria della Scala from which the theatre takes its name. The name means Holy Mary of the Staircase and honours an icon placed on the staircase of the house of a mother of a deformed child who prayed before the statue for the healing of her child who was then restored to full health. Building expenses were covered by the sale of boxes, which were lavishly decorated by their owners and the theatre became the most important meeting place for the noble, wealthy Milanese. (See appendix)

Shakespeare's time had focused on the audience as much as the performers, so this was a huge change, especially for the Italian operatic public, who treated the opera house as a superb venue for doing business and for meeting the right people. In order to achieve his visions for opera and the high musical standards he set himself and others, Toscanini fought many battles, using his terrifying temper, which was renowned in the musical world, to good effect.

By the time of Eva Turner's audition La Scala had 2800 individual seats as well as those in the boxes, above which there was a gallery, from which the less wealthy could watch the show and to this day the loggione (gallery) is crowded by the most critical part of the audience, who can by their reaction make or break a performer. We now imagine this English singer of thirty-two, standing in the middle of La Scala's huge 145 feet deep and 98 feet wide empty stage, where great Italian singers, like Amelita Galli-Curci, Beniamino Gigli and Enrico Caruso, and others, who had grown up in the Italian tradition of the past one hundred and fifty years, had performed.

Eva Turner, with only a small upright piano, taking the place of the orchestra, for company, looked out into the auditorium, shaped like a horse-shoe-piazza, up past five tiers of 194 boxes to the gallery, felt the silent, judgmental Italians, with their huge tradition of singing and music in their bones and sensed the great Toscanini sitting 'out there' in darkness. Alongside him were the associate conductors: Maestri Scandiani, Panizza and Gui. Four powerful men, who usually conducted from the orchestra pit which housed 100 players, were now her audience. They waited for her to sing. It was her moment and she grasped it with both hands.

'If you want to be a singer you have to go along with blinkers on to achieve your goal,'

was one of Dame Eva's mantras by which she lived. Aligned with this thought, her mind was always on her next performance and how to improve it. Her desire for perfection of vocal technique was so strong that perhaps, to the person in the street unfamiliar with a singer's way of life, this pursuit of excellence might seem almost to the point of obsession. This concentrated commitment would perhaps have saved her from the normal human fear in the difficult situation of this audition. All her energy would have been concentrated on the excellence of her performance and no time or energy would have been left for negative thoughts. She knew she was good and was about to prove it. She sang *Ritorna Vincitor* from the first act of *Aida* in Italian and Eva Turner tells us:

'Then Maestro Toscanini asked me to sing the "Nile Scene" aria and I did, in English because I didn't know it in Italian'.

Had she prepared a different aria in Italian, while he wanted to hear this one as he tried to compare her with the great Aidas he had conducted?

She was no novice and had performed Aida many times in English. Dramatically and musically Aida offers the artist almost everything. The emotional conflict between the characters is of a timeless, universal nature which could easily exist today. If you played *Aida* in modern dress representing invaded and invading nations, the situation would still ring true and except for the loss in spectacle, it would remain a great piece of theatre. Musically it is a singer's joy.

'Perhaps even Verdi never achieved a greater master-stroke than the moving pianissimo of Aida's lovely prayer "Numi Pieta" following upon the passionate outburst of "Ritorna Vincitor".'

Eva Turner's own words. She loved singing Aida, understood the character and felt drawn to her emotionally.

Eva Turner as Aida

'Don't ever sing an aria for an audition if you don't understand the character or feel instinctively close to the piece.'

She had not sung the great aria from the third act in Italian because all R.C.R.O. performances were sung in English but international performances were not always in the original language either and singers in the same opera often sang in different languages. Perhaps Maestro Toscanini would not be unduly disturbed by an English rendering, although Eva Turner:

'hoped most anxiously, singing the "Qui Radames Verra" in English would not make an unfavourable impression on the Italian maestri'.

When Aida threatens to throw herself into the River Nile if Radames rejects her, perhaps she, as Eva Turner, felt drawn to the water, thinking of how, its magnificent flow had been strangled at Sadd el Ali and rerouted, this cruel act having been executed to increase the production of Delta cotton and help the output of the far off Lancastrian mills, on the doorstep of which she had grown up. Her hard-working father, with his earnings from those mills, had provided the finances for her to survive as a child and blossom as a young adult. Did she consider her imaginative death by drowning in the great waters of the Nile to be a just sacrifice for one of its own small deaths? It is certain that whatever her imagination presented, she would also be ready to show off the

1924-1927 Italian Beginnings

magnificent top of her voice during the arduous ascending passage to the top Cs, as she reached the climax of the second verse.

Toscanini had known Verdi and had seen him conduct. He also had his own ideas of how these arias should be performed, formulated from many years of conducting great Aidas and so he knew what he wanted to hear. Had the clever Plum realised that this high tessitura was Eva Turner's passport to the world of great singing and advised her well that her Aida was comparable with many of the great singers? Her own good singing instincts would certainly have told her that she was an ideal Aida.

Whatever the reasons of chemistry, or of thoughts, her performance was good enough for her to be given a contract for the coming season at La Scala there and then: Freia and Sieglinde in *L'Anello del Nibelungo*, the *Ring* cycle which would of course be performed in Italian. If she was disappointed by the roles, probably the only ones as yet uncast for that year, she never mentioned it. The joy of being immediately accepted for the coming season was, for Eva Turner, a moment in her life which never could be repeated but would be cherished. This moment was often recounted down through the years and although she had many other great moments, she regarded this as her most defining and never tired of reliving it.

When Eva first arrived in Italy she had only a few words of Italian but this did not really seem to bother her:

'I got on pretty well. I was a little talker you know and that might have helped. Yes, I got on quite well.'

She loved the sounds of a foreign language and was never frightened or embarrassed to try out her skills. As she said:

'I also quite liked the sound of my own voice and had plenty to say for myself being from Lancashire.'

She projected her speaking voice as if she was already singing and so foreign words had a familiar ease and she was able to pronounce them as she was thinking. This, together with her listening abilities, meant that she had a natural gift for language. She was also prepared to work hard to build her vocabulary and had a good memory from years of learning and memorising her operatic roles, sometimes at very short notice. All this and an eagerness to be part of Italian life very quickly brought with it an early fluency, on which she built vocabulary over the years. She did not allow a language barrier to get between her and a successful career in Italy and after Eva had lived there only a few months Tetrazzini asked: 'How is it a young English girl like you can speak such beautiful Italian?'

Madame Tetrazzini

Eva Turner c. 1924

When Teleri Bevin interviewed the eighty six year old Dame Eva for Welsh Radio, she said of her in the introduction to the programme that she was lively, warm and energetic and on asking her about the difficulties of the Italian language, Dame Eva replied:

'When I went to the Scala, I didn't speak Italian, only a few words then, in 1924. I remember I sang "Ritorna Vincitor" of Aida in Italian and then they asked me to sing the "Nile Scene" aria in Italian but I knew it only in English so they asked me to sing it in English and then Toscanini said "Bella voce, bella pronuncia e poi una bella figura", Good voice, good pronunciation and good figure, so I thought as to the last, well I never thought that, maybe distance lends enchant-

ment or something like that. (laughter). So I was accepted. I had a contract.'

She adds:

'Thank God'

to this when she was interviewed for *Kaleidoscope* by a thoughtful, incisive Elizabeth Hutchings and says of Toscanini:

'He was verrry demanding and you know he had very bad eyesight. He conducted everything from memory but that was per forza...' 'his wife claimed she could tell when he had been reading through new music by the smudges of printer's ink on the tip of his nose.'

Elizabeth Hutchings: 'Was he very extrovert?'

'Oooo noo, au contraire, absolutely. He used to go through like this you know.

(Demonstrating, Dame Eva put the back of her hand to her brow to hide her eyes.)

Nobody dare approach him and verry demanding. I believe that once Toti dal Monte walked out, he was so horrible and said she would never go back...' 'When I saw the prova generale, and the ante prova generale, he really attended much more to the orchestra. The singers were already ready for the performances. Generally he was very nice at rehearsals, although he was a man of few words;'

she told Teleri Bevin.

'In order to make Italian my own, I won special permission to attend rehearsals as well as public performances. With Toscanini conducting that was a rare privilege. I clearly recall, how after each rehearsal, the maestro would make a bee-line for his dressing room, there to remain throughout the night, studying scores for the next day's work'... 'A very powerful personality and very enooormously committed. He was a man that really went along with blinkers on for the objective .No doubt of that. Very demanding. Verry demanding. A disciplinarian of the OOO;'

she said in an LBC Interview.

Rasponi writes in his book *The Last Prima Donnas* that Eva Turner said:

'I had never sung for a great conductor before and to my surprise I was not half as scared as I had anticipated,'

and yet in a wonderfully sensitive interview by Sue MacGregor for Dame Eva's 95th Birthday for Radio Four, when asked the same question she replies:

'O yes I was very nervous. I was always very nervous but I learned to gain control over that.'

Sue MacGregor: 'How did you do that?'

'Well, by well, experience and also time allowed me to overcome it.'

The fascists were in power at that time but had she been on the moon, with the Daleks in power, would singing still have been her major activity and consumed all her waking thoughts? We hear proof of this suspicion in an interview for London Broadcasting Company Radio, when the interviewer asks her: 'What were your impressions when you first went there? Were you conscious of the fascist situation when you first arrived in Milan?' At first she is a little confused and reminds him that it was after the First World War that she went to sing in Italy. He agrees and reminds her that they are talking about 1924, which seems to bring her mind to the right time. This confusion was quite unlike her usual precise answers and clarity of thought when she was interviewed about her career. She was always alert, 'on the ball' and happy to go exploring in a conversation. Her vocal inflections, as she tells her story with well chosen words, are a delight. The vocal subtexts express her inner thoughts and her voice never switches off from this area of the subconscious. Her voice, when asked the question about fascism, suggest that she had not thought of that aspect of her arrival in Milan until that very moment and if she had, her long ago thoughts were lost in the wings of La Scala Theatre but she tries to answer, saying:

Eva Turner

'Not a great deal. I saw Mussolini appear on balconies and make speeches and things like that.'

The interviewer persists with: 'What impression did he have on you, then, perhaps an impressionable young girl?'

'Well I don't know. I don't think I gave it all that importance.'

'You didn't realize how important it was going to become?'

'No! No!'

1924-1927 Italian Beginnings

She lingered thoughtfully on the second 'No!' as if she herself began to wonder why she hadn't noticed what was going on around her. She had lived in a world apart which was governed by music, with its politics ruling and bringing satisfaction to the lives of those involved; artists and audience.

Eva Turner said of Toscanini on another occasion:

'His beliefs transcended all adverse ideas of race and politics. At the height of Hitler's persecution of the Jews he made it a point not to accept an invitation to conduct at Bayreuth – an open slap at the German dictator. And his opposition to Italy's own fascists is well known.'

She aligned herself with these thoughts, as although always a pragmatist as far as using every opportunity presented to improve her own career and those of her students, there were certain honourable, unspoken rules which Eva Turner would not breach, among them: no prejudice about private lives, class, race or creed so long as those beliefs did not affect the lives of others.

The LBC man, not being quite satisfied that he had squeezed the last word from her on politics asks: 'Did you find you were treated with any suspicion as an English singer?' Dame Eva finds her feet at this point and says with great decisiveness, cutting any further political thoughts off at the pass:

'No, no, not at all. No, not at all'

and diverts him back to singing by telling him how the only thing that she had objected to was being asked to change her name to an Italian one. She tells him how she had refused as she felt that if she could not make it with her own name then she wasn't much good in the first place.

Among her papers, which were kept at Villa Junesca until she sold it, were a few diaries from these early Italian years which I was thrilled to receive from Dame Gwyneth Jones who helped her clear out the villa before selling it. I was distressed however, to find that not only had I the greatest difficulty reading edge to edge pencil writing but that when I did manage to decipher the words, they were such as:

'I slept late then I had breakfast with Mr Broad. Got all ready. I wrote P.C. to Beal and after to Dada. Had our meal. On to see Mr Wall, talked a lot, on to the Scala. I had a letter from Bessie Taylor – taxi to the Samuels, nice time there and tea etc. Met various folk. Talked a lot. Got ready for my evening meal. Enjoyed it. Mr Watson had our tea all ready – nice. On to bed.'

All the entries contained this endless flow of conscious thought, even on the days of performances. Apart from the fact that I would have probably gone blind, I would have, and did up to a point, persevere with the intermittent transcribing of her diaries but in the end came to see that she was not going to share one internal thought or point of interest with us. It would have been so lovely to have her own thoughts, written at the time, of this part of her life.

Eva Turner thought of herself as a rather practical person as we see during her first *Desert Island Discs* programme in 1942:

'I am a very practical person really. I should try to make myself a comfortable home. Then I should swim a lot – if there were no sharks – and experiment with new dishes. I love cooking but a thing I should miss terribly is motoring.'

Roy Plumley: 'With your sense of the practical, I expect you would get around to harnessing a turtle as a means of transport?'

'At any rate he would provide soup when he got too old for running about.'

Her friends were very nervous about her driving, one of them refusing to drive to Italy with her, later on in life, until she had passed her driving test. (In those days one didn't need to pass a test to drive). Much to everyone's surprise she did pass the test after sitting it three times and she and her friend drove to Italy the very next day. The travelling companion said in jest that she had suffered a minor nervous breakdown as a result of the journey being fraught with so many dangers caused by impatient driving. Gladys Parr said on this subject: 'Eva was so impatient to get to the destination that she regarded red traffic lights as optional.' Dame Eva did have the grace to smile about her driving in later years when this activity was a thing of the past, but hesitation and lethargy in everyday life, always gave her cause for impatience, and the slowness and indecisiveness of others drove her insane. There was also the small issue that she memorised her words and music while driving!

It was not that she was being disingenuous when she answered Roy Plumley, about being practical, rather that her self-image on these points was a little out of focus. She was very decisive and clear when she was making arrangements in advance, but the actual method of how these would become reality was expected by her to magic itself into place after the planning was done: she had managerial skills rather than practical ones. Plum was, however, at hand, so their initial journey to Italy would be well organised. Eva was not a great fuss-pot about practicalities either however, and after arrangements were in place, she helped make them work. She never mentioned the long journey in a crammed, hot train with bugs that bite coming out of the woodwork, for which trains at that time, even the Orient Express, were famous. Nor the simple hotel which they would find at the end of their journey, because, to her, these would be unimportant details, which had to be lived through calmly, to allow her goal to be kicked, spot on, into the net.

After the successful audition, the elated Eva Turner and proud Plum returned to England where the business worry of a couple of signed contracts would have to be dealt with. Fortunately an amicable arrangement was reached whereby they would both be released from the year's contract with the Carl Rosa. Eva did agree, however, to sing with the company in 'Grand Opera at Hammersmith' in August that year. The three weeks at the King's Theatre Hammersmith were sponsored in conjunction with the Wimbledon Theatre and she sang Leonora in *Trovatore*, Leonore in *Fidelio*, Eva, Butterfly, Marguerite and Aida. The cheapest seats were 1/3 and the dearest 7/-. Fish Suppers and 'Dainty Teas' could be enjoyed at the Royal Cafe on Hammersmith Bridge Road, '2 minutes from the Broadway.'

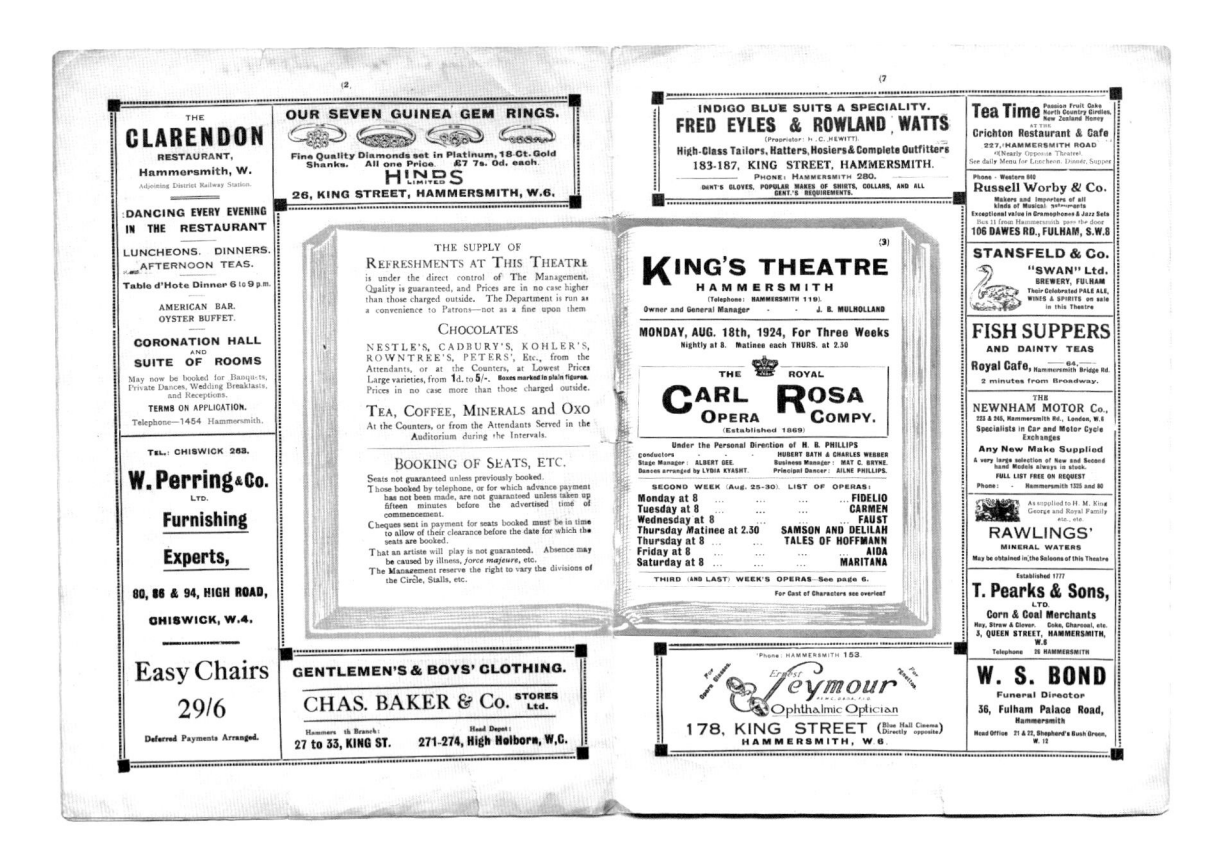

On her return to Britain she began a four month study period of the Italian language. Her roles at La Scala would be sung in Italian to an Italian audience so work would be hard and serious. Freia, a small but important part in *Das Rheingold* conducted by Gui, would be followed by Sieglinde in *Die Walküre*, conducted by Panizza, both sung in Italian. The Wotan would be Nazzareno De Angelis of whom she said:

'I really did not know what a true basso was meant to sound like until I met him.'

Eva Turner's debut at La Scala Milan
16th November 1924

Freia is not a starring role even with the best voice in the world and passed without much comment. She did, however, make the most of an opportunity during the rehearsal period:

'My own first role was Freia in "Das Rheingold". It called for a difficult run and I became so disturbed at my own ineptitude of the moment that I broke off and exclaimed aloud, "Hang it this simply won't do!" Toscanini was standing on

1924-1927 Italian Beginnings   89

stage at that moment, hands behind his back in the familiar pose, watching the rehearsal. His amusement at my outburst was obvious and I was flooded with embarrassment. Yet later I came to see that I could not have helped myself more, for this incident served to impress the maestro with my determination to do the best within my power.'

Freia was soon followed by Sieglinde which is a major part and would show her voice in a better light. Lilly Hafgren was her Brünnhilde and the Corriere della Sera tells us on December 2nd:

'The exhaustive part (Sieglinde) was taken by Signora Eva Turner, who in status is very much valued for the expressive clarity of her singing, for the intelligent interpretation and for the effectiveness of her outstanding personality.'

'I still recall vividly how awed I was at first entering La Scala, those portals wherein Toscanini held utter command and sway. To me it was an operatic paradise; a place of dreams-come-true, for it featured not only superb singers, but spectacular physical facilities as well, including a striking open-sky panorama which attracted the attention of visitors from all over the world.'

Eva Turner

She went from the local hotel, where she and Plum were staying at this early point in her Italian life, to rehearse at La Scala on December 3rd and as she passed through the foyer to go to the rehearsal, was greeted with people saying 'presto, presto.' She quickly joined them at the window to see Puccini's funeral with its mile long cortege pass by in the street below, on its way to the Cimitero Monumantale. Dame Eva remembered this occasion with great sadness until her own dying day, as her grief for Puccini was heightened by the recent death of her mother, on October 22nd, while Eva was in Italy. Her father and family had said that since there was nothing she could do, she was not to return home but was to stay and get on with her important contract. A double loss was felt by her that day in Italy.

The body of Giacomo Antonio Domenico Michele Secondo Maria Puccini, who had died in Brussels (see appendix), arrived in Milan on December 2nd and the next day a State Funeral took place in the cathedral, followed by a procession to the cemetery. Eva Turner watched the cortege from the windows of La Scala Theatre where his operas *Le Villi* (third version in two acts), *Edgar*, *Madama Butterfly* and *La Fanciulla del West* (second version) had all been premiered. Of *Turandot*, his final opera, he is reported to have said to his son shortly before dying: 'I am sorry that *Turandot* remains unfinished. I have not done the final duet of the third act. I am afraid I shall not be able to finish it. Well, they will produce the opera incomplete and somebody will come out and say to the audience, 'The Maestro died at this point'.'

The opera was premiered at La Scala on April 25th, 1926: Rosa Raisa sang the title role, Fleta was Calaf, Zamboni was Liu and Toscanini conducted, while Eva Turner sat in the audience. Mussolini, however, was not in that audience because Toscanini had resolutely refused to play the Fascist anthem, *Giovinezza*, as requested by him. Dame Eva tells her story about this first performance in an article by Eric McLean in the Montreal Times. She was in that city celebrating her 81st birthday, whilst judging their International Voice competition having flown straight from Nagasaki, where she had been on the panel of judges along with Maria Callas and Giuseppe di Stefano for the International Madama Butterfly competition the previous week:

'At the point where Puccini had stopped composing, Toscanini turned to a stunned audience and said "A questo punto moriva il Maestro." (At this point the Maestro died). We all rose quietly to our feet and along with a veiled Turandot, Calaf and La Scala chorus, observed two minutes silence. Then Toscanini picked up his baton and resumed the performance with Alfano's ending to the opera which was scored using Puccini's ideas.'

The usually accepted version of this performance suggests that at the point where Puccini stopped composing, mid-way through Act 3 after Liu's death and cortege, Toscanini turned to the audience and murmured: 'Here ends the Maestro's work.' The curtain then came down slowly and the promising young composer

1924-1927 Italian Beginnings

Franco Alfano's ending was not performed. Toscanini was not happy with the ending, later cutting some of Alfano's writing and adding some bars of his own, so Panizza took up the baton for the rest of these early performances. It seems harsh that the distinguished young composer Franco Alfano, a friend and colleague of both Puccini and Toscanini, should have been treated thus. He had been employed to complete the opera and had spent the previous sixteen months doing so, scrupulously using the notes Puccini had left, creating an appropriate ending. Was Alfano's ending disregarded in a cavalier and insulting way or was the silent ending, on the occasion of the first performance, a tribute to Puccini?

When Eva Turner performed the opera in the early years after Puccini's death, the two minutes' silence that she described was always observed before the opera continued with Alfano's ending and so it is possible that she was remembering those occasions when she was interviewed in Montreal. She knew Franco Alfano, who was head of the Turin Conservatory and who said of her that she was the perfect Turandot. (See appendix for the story told in Eva Turner's own words). Despite admiring Alfano's ending, Dame Eva thought:

'if Puccini had finished the final duet, it would have surpassed all the earlier great ones of "Manon Lescaut", "La Bohème", "Tosca" and "Madama Butterfly".'

While singing in the *Ring* cycle, Eva Turner was at La Scala until March 1st, 1925, during which time:

Claudia Muzio

'Amongst the first performances I attended at La Scala, as a member of the public, was one of "Il Trovatore" conducted by Toscanini with Claudia Muzio singing Leonora. I shall never forget how thrilled I was to hear this singer and to see her. She was absolutely gorgeous. When I was with the Carl Rosa singing this opera, we made a cut in the Bridal Scene. This cut, Toscanini restored and the duet was sung with an organ behind the scene – it was beautifully done. Many times before going to Italy, I had heard people scoff when they heard the "Miserere" and I could not help but greatly wish those who had thought Verdi's music bordering on the banal, could have been privileged to have heard the performance I heard, conducted by Toscanini and sung by Muzio.'

She also heard many mezzos and had the thought that maybe:

'The Italian tendency in mezzos was to bring the chest too high.'

Eva Turner was then invited to visit Germany as part of a Milanese Touring Company, organised, rehearsed and funded by La Scala Milan Theatre. The standard of Der Mailänder Opern Stagione, as it was known in Germany, had been variable in the past and so the possibility of its returning to Germany was not greeted with enthusiasm by the German theatre managers, who provided not only the venue but also the chorus, orchestra and small part soloists. These managers felt that this company's work was not of a high enough standard of Italian singing to merit this tour.

The German manager of the tour, Mr Norbert Salter, had prolonged correspondence with the artistic director of the Stuttgart State Opera House and other directors of opera houses to be visited, as he tried to make the tour possible. In the letters, Eva Turner was described as being a member of the Scala ensemble; a native English woman who had had huge successes in London's operatic society. They also state that there was no single native German in the ensemble, even if some names did not sound Italian at all. Letters indicate that Stuttgart would not have the same cast as Berlin; apparently Riccardo Stracciari was too expensive, and Eva Turner would not be part of the ensemble in Berlin.

This Milanese Opera Company, with Egisto Tango conducting throughout the tour, gave their first performance in Karlsruhe on March 10th, Eva's 34th birthday. Eva Turner's roles on this tour were: Aida, Tosca, Santuzza and Leonora, (*Trovatore*) and the towns visited were Nürnberg, Mannheim, Braunschweig, Wiesbaden, Frankfurt, Kassel, Bremer, Breslau, Dresden and Hamburg. Reviews for that tour were placed by Eva Turner in small envelopes, with the names of the towns and cities written on the outside in her own handwriting and sealed for safety. She had given care and attention to preserving the life she loved and when opening the letters which she had carefully closed all those years before, I was moved and felt close to a cherished friend. Here are some of those reviews,

Der Mailänder Opern Stagione. When the opera director of Stuttgart State Opera, Albert Kehm wrote of concerns of the director's office regarding the quality of the touring company, the publisher Ricordi of Milan assured him that the Milan Touring Opera was recommendable and some of the cast was: 'even outstanding', but still a special offer from the tour management to the opera houses was rejected. There were objections from the police and authorities regarding the legitimacy of the company and it soon became clear that N. Salter did not have a license to manage the tour through Germany. However, a contract between Stuttgart and Milan Touring Opera was eventually signed on June 10th.

MAILÄNDER OPERN STAGIONE

KARLSRUHE
LANDESTHEATER

DIENSTAG, DEN 10. MÄRZ 1925 7½ UHR
TROVATORE

DONNERSTAG, DEN 12. MÄRZ 1925 7½ UHR
CAVALLERIA RUSTICANA UND BAJAZZO

BILLETTVERKAUF AN DEN BEKANNTEN VERKAUFSSTELLEN

Eva Turner (far right)

which give us a flavour of her performances at that time in the different roles.

On March 19th, the Fränkischer Kurier reports on a performance in Nürnberg:

> 'This was the second evening of their visit and this time they put on Aida. The first night was a complete disaster. (Doesn't tell us which opera.) This time the Italians were much more traditional and the group worked well together, although it was not as good as the usual South German staging but the conductor Egisto Tango has fantastic musicality. Eva Turner, if you ask me, is a German and did far the best that evening. Her voice is delightful and when she goes up to the top, it gains in volume, and so shows her technical ability. She coped well with the very high tessitura and her high Cs in the last duet with Radames, showed that she had the same crystal clear, full resonance and fresh voice at the end as she had had at the start of the performance. She has stamina! On the downside however she couldn't put together the lower register with the higher one but if she could overcome this she would be perfect. The tenor, Lindi, was very Italianate with the real Italian melting creaminess and with a fantastic bright and high top voice.'

Marone was Amonasro and Lotte Dörmald was Amneris.

March 21st, the Mannheimer Volkstimme reports on *Cavalleria Rusticana* at the National Theatre:

'We shouldn't talk about the "Milanese Opera Stagione" but about the "Turner Company". Eva Turner sang Santuzza in the dramatic tradition, ruling and dominating with her high register and following the art of singing with a very passionate melodic voice production. Her joy was infectious to her colleagues.'

Turridu was sung by Battaglia.

April 2nd, the Braunschweigische Tageszeitung:

'The Landes Theatre: It is quite unusual for Braunschweig (near Hanover) to have Italian Operas on stage and we are pleased that this company is visiting us. Eva Turner's Tosca was full blooded and her singing generous, while the other singers were a bit shrill sometimes. Her singing is of a very high standard and when she sings with the orchestra she rises above them when necessary, so that we can still hear her very clearly. She handles this very well. The tenor Francisco Giorgini has a very light, bright tenor voice but he seemed not free in his attacks and could not always cope with the orchestra. All the performers, however, received great applause at the end.'

April 24th, the Frankfurter General Anzeiger reports about *Tosca*:

'It is typical for an Italian opera theatre to have very young talented singers who have finished their studies recently. They are usually outstanding in these most important roles and afterwards come to fame most of the time. As always Eva Turner the high dramatic singer was outstanding, especially in Act 2.'

Miss Eva Turner writes to us, in a local English paper, from Frankfurt:

'Singing here now with great success. The public is one of the most critical in Germany. I love the German opera houses; they are full of such great accomplishments in the past. What memories they possess!'

May 4th, the Kasseler Tageblatt:

'People were not enticed to come to the theatre to see "Il Trovatore", so sadly there was not a full house. I don't understand this as it was an outstanding performance. It was a very Italian-like troupe although I am not sure it was genuinely full-blooded 'echt' Italian but the production was very good. Battaglia, as Manrico, sang the serenade beautifully; in fact I have never heard it sung quite so beautifully. Beside him there was Eva Turner singing Leonora who shone forth with her phenomenal high voice. Maria dal Monte as Azucena gave the best all round performance and was the star of the night. The small roles, however, were without disciple and the conductor the same and because he was so undisciplined; the singers did their own thing, so you could hear that it was not always together, especially in the last act where there were many little vocal accidents. Tango did not look after the singers at all well.'

May 25th. In the Breslauer Neueste Nachrichten, the critic in Breslau (now in Poland but in Germany at that time) tells us about *Aida*:

'It is unusual to hear such voices, so full of power and rich in colour that it takes one's breath away. At this moment bel canto singing is out of fashion but I enjoyed the performance although I had not expected to. When one comes across the beautiful great and cultivated voice of the human being then we have to accept it as if it were a perfect figure made of stone or bronze and look up to it. Eva Turner has a soprano voice, whose shining embers glow. She conquers the situation with victorious power. This voice reminds us of Rempsche but Eva Turner's voice is sweeter and purer in her pianissimo. Her ability to act is better than anyone else in the ensemble. Tango didn't do well with the singers but strangely we did like how he dealt with the instruments in the orchestra. Tempi were quicker than we are used to but the difference in tempi and dynamics was such that the drama worked better. When Tango is building up his finale the nerves are heightened and we are excited.'

June 2nd, the Neue Mannheimer Zeitung:

'Eva Turner is well remembered here from her appearances as Santuzza and Tosca over Easter but Leonora is not really her role. At the beginning of the opera her voice was a bit flat so that "Tacea la Notte" was not really melodic but after a little while this charming attractive voice warmed up and it became enriched by the way she expressed her emotions which are not diminished by her technical timbre and security. She was not anxious about the orchestra and showed them her tempos by leading. The whole thing in this way is outstanding and to be taken as an example of how she can sustain the tone, so we forgive her for the beginning. However, the resonances in her chest voice are not giving her the dramatic touch she needs as an open chest voice can never go into the head voice. When she has learned to do this joining of the registers, she will be an even greater artist.'

Eva Turner then sang at the Vienna Volksoper (see appendix for cast and dates), again with Egisto Tango conducting. He was an important conductor of his day, born in Rome in 1873, and had conducted at La Scala and the Metropolitan. He had also been chief conductor with the Budapest National Opera 1913-19 where he conducted the premiere of *Bluebeard's Castle* in 1918.

August 14th, *Ballo in Maschera*:

'Eva Turner, singing Amelia, is a highly dramatic, Italian soprano. She did not make a fuss of the bel canto technique but she made a dramatic explosion. The tone quality, powerful in her high register, was fiery and very noble. The tenor Oreste de Bernardi reminded us of Gigli but the surprise of the night was Luigi Montesanto. You could see that he was shaking with nerves in the beginning, nearly unable to speak his recitative, but in the big aria in the third act he showed the high quality of his beautiful singing and won the hearts of the public. He triumphed like a baritone can in Vienna. He was also a gorgeous young man and because he is young and handsome with a beautiful voice, he will be a favourite in Vienna. Egisto Tango used well his unusual way of conducting and is a musician with freedom, taste and full of temperament. This premiere was fantastic.'

August 17th, *Aida*:

'Eva Turner was the star of the whole ensemble. Her registers were beautifully blended and she showed that she was highly dramatic, as her voice was happily combined with, and complimented by, her interesting and urgent acting. She well deserved the applause of the people. At her side was the Radames of Taccani with his free voice, so she was well matched and he was worthy of her. The third one in this group was Fregosi who sang Amonasro but not that well, as he was lacking the powerful, demonic touch but he had a lyrical softness and a noble posture.

August 18th, *Aida*:

'Praise for Verdi and especially to Egisto Tango. Even on this quite small stage, the mass scenes were very well done and believable. The evening was ruled by Eva Turner with her fantastic, easy rising voice; better than this has seldom been heard. Her big arias were fantastic but also very touching and the finale at the end of the second act was magnificent. For a long time we have not seen such a good artist. Beside Fräulein Turner was Giuseppe Taccani as Radames who coped quite well even if it seemed at times that he was forcing his tender instruments. Gulio Fregosi was Amonasro and Amneris Eugene Besalla. Applause was given by the public in between the scenes, showing that they enjoyed the performance.'

1924-1927 Italian Beginnings   97

I would draw your attention to the continued comments about the technical ease at the top of Eva Turner's voice. It seems too that she is developing skills such as her use of *pianissimo*, and that her acting ability is developing apace. It is interesting also to note that, while she comments disapprovingly on the Italian mezzo-soprano taking the chest voice too high, she too may have temporarily fallen into the same trap. The mixing of the chest voice is a subject on which a whole book could be written and often is (!). Suffice to say that when I was learning from her experience, she was adamant that the chest voice should be mixed and never taken higher that an F. Even this is a little too high in the opinion of many singers.

Although all of these performances were giving her working experience, one has to ask why La Scala let her go on a sight-seeing tour of Germany rather than using her in the big house itself. I would suggest a couple of reasons: Italians love their own singers, no matter how good foreigners are, and the roles which she was singing on tour require expertise which the normal young house singer employed by La Scala would not necessarily have. In other words she could have sung smaller roles in La Scala or could be employed more usefully, for them, by gaining a better reputation for their associated touring company, performing big dramatic roles. She was, too, perhaps earning more money singing the big roles and we have to remember that she was now supporting two people, herself and Plum, as well as sending money home to her father. Whatever her thoughts about those issues as she struggled to become accepted in Italy, with Plum's help she kept raising the standard of her game.

Still not back in La Scala but clearly gaining recognition in Italy, Eva Turner, following on from the tours of Germany and Austria and having obtained the services of an Italian agency, sang 30 operatic performances in the northern Italian opera houses, between October 15th, 1925 and February 16th, 1926, for a fee of L1500 per show, so despite Italy's preference for its own singers, she was making headway.

In the Bristol Evening News on February 26th, 1926, there is a rather inaccurate, retrospective article suggesting that Madame Albani was financially responsible for Eva Turner's training at the Royal Academy of Music. This was not true as her father had paid for her training, even refusing financial help from a kind relative who thought sending Eva to study at Manchester would be a good idea. Charles was adamant that the Royal Academy of Music in London was of the very highest standard and, wanting her to have the best, he had paid for the privilege. We can't quite trust the writer of the Bristol News piece because of this inaccuracy, but he does tell us that 'his old friend Arthur Winkworth', the one time famous Mephistopheles before becoming the director of Carl Rosa Company, had shared with him the thought that Eva Turner would go far. He also tells us that, when he had met Eva Turner humming to herself just before going on to sing one of her early parts, he had stopped to congratulate her on her success in Bristol. She had replied, much to his surprise: 'It is nice to know someone likes me'. The writer muses that, therefore, at that time she was a young artist struggling to find her feet. He then recalled being in the foyer of the Prince's Theatre one night and hearing her sing the *Easter Hymn*: 'with her silver voice rising above the chorus and orchestra as it soared out through the doors of the theatre.'

Charles, Eva's father, replied to this article, not contradicting the part Mme Albani had played in helping his daughter (at least if he did, it was not printed) but wanting it to be known that: 'she is quite as good a daughter as she is an artist.' Eva, throughout her life, was an avid post card and letter writer, collecting addresses, of friends old and new, in very fat little books, and looked forward to receiving replies to them. Her 'Dada' was top of her list of family and friends with whom she kept closely in touch by letter, despite a gruelling touring schedule, in her early years on the continent. Her letters were mostly of an inconsequential, chatty nature but were her way of sustaining friendships in her peripatetic life. She always replied to fan mail, of which there was a lot, even in her early days, and letter-writing became a habit which she enjoyed, as it gave her contact but allowed space between the lines. Although one does have to wonder how her kind heart would have dealt with begging letters, some from quite intimate people in her past, even an old piano accompanist from Bristol who asked her for a loan of £500, which, she claimed, would be the difference between life and death. Giving her heart and soul and even time was Eva's belief but not, as far as I know, money. In any case she was never hugely rich and was always concerned with her future survival and her financial commitments to Plum and her family.

During March and April, 1926, Eva Turner went to Portugal, again on tour from La Scala, and sang Aida, and Minnie in *La Fanciulla del West*. *Aida* opened the opera season at Lisbon's Sao Luis Theatre on February 27th, under the baton of Maestro Emil Cooper. The tour, after performances of both operas in Lisbon, went on to Oporto with the same repertoire and her fee was L2000 for each performance, so finances are taking a turn for the better.

On March 1st, the newspaper Diario del Lisboa reported:

'The honours of the night's performance ought really to go to Emil Cooper for his assured direction but also we ought to mention the chorus direction of Achille Clivio. Bianca Sereno as Amneris was adequate in her part and Lindi pleased us as he is an intelligent artist. But it was Eva Turner as Aida whom we preferred to hear. With regards to this artist the following occurs to us: this is hardly a school of singing that our public is accustomed to hear, Eva Turner has rare qualities in a singer and she attacks well and has a fine high register especially in the romance of Act 3 which was tight but right.'

Another paper tells us:

'The outstanding performer Trantoul fully confirmed his reputation as a singer with a potent and wide ranging voice. He has well accentuated dramatic diction and gave a virile performance of Radames. The part of Aida was taken by Eva Turner who was applauded with ample reason given the clarity of interpretation she brought to her part. Her performance was quite sombre with a certain brilliance, especially in the "Nile Scene" to which she brought an emotional element. The mezzo-soprano Albertina dal Monte was quite pleasant as Amneris, and Daniani as Amonasro gave a good dramatic interpretation'

Eva Turner gave very few performances of Minnie, so let us read about those in Portugal:

April 9th, the Oporto Commercio reports on *La Fanciulla del West*:

'The performances were quite brilliant especially that of the notable soprano Eva Turner who sang with rare polish and dramatic vigour. The tenor Voltolini was suffering from lack of voice but managed to overcome it like a true artist and Tenta the baritone was highly appreciated.'

April 10th:

'Eva Turner's representation of the part of Minnie was admirable. This part is not without great difficulties and has unpleasant modulations for the voice, demanding accuracy of pitch and musical knowledge which not all singers have. Minnie is a complex part and Turner's genius is such that she put this across and won over the public who responded with spontaneous applause especially in the finales of Act 2 and 3.

It is difficult to highlight anything in particular in her singing because Turner was perfect in the whole work but in the second act we might mention the drama she brought to the scenes. At the first appearance of Rance, the eminent artist Eva Turner's facial expressions and vocal inflections brought to life the different and successive feelings which dominate the psychology of the character: anger, anguish, pain, passion and piety, in all, the whole emotive range which is capable of moving the human soul. We should also point out that this is the first time Eva Turner played the part which shows the merit of her work. Voltolini is a fine artist with perfect style and great purity of diction...'

'We would like to give the place of honour to Eva Turner who has already appeared here as Aida. The part of Minnie involves a lot of work as a singer and as an actress and demands superior artistic faculties and perfect command of vocal technique to triumph over the difficulties of the part of Minnie. She conquered the public with a perfect interpretation and was enthusiastically applauded especially at the end of Act 2.'

Eva Turner was performing in Portugal until May 2nd and shortly afterwards returned to Milan to record: *Gloria all'Egitto* from *Aida* and the ensemble of Act 3 of *La Gioconda* with the Scala orchestra and chorus conducted by Molajoli. Eva Turner tells us of this occasion:

'they put me right at the back, behind the orchestra and chorus so that they could get the balance correct. I am happy to say I think you will have no difficulty hearing me... After these recordings there was a big banquet, big supper and I ate oysters and I had typhoid fever. I was terribly ill. They even sent for my father because I had nurses night and day but I got over it. You must never eat oysters in Italy. Never. Never!'

In 1926 Charles Turner tells us in the Glasgow Evening News:

'Miss Turner is confined in a Milan nursing home with typhoid fever from where I have just returned. Mr Lindi with whom she sang recently on tour wished her better soon and said she was the finest operatic soprano of the day and he was proud to be associated with her... I think she has been run down with over work to do honour to herself and her British Homeland'.

Mr Turner goes on to say:

'She had crammed four new operas including "Don Carlos" and "Ernani" since her arrival in Italy and was preparing a fifth, "La Gioconda" for a visit to Trieste when she was taken ill. Unfortunately

her breakdown has cost her cancellations at Turin and at Madrid Royal Opera House.'

She made the recordings of *Aida* and *Gioconda*, after which she was ill, at Milan on May 10th and 12th and so would have been at La Scala during the rehearsal period of *Turandot*. When one is in the house during the rehearsal period of an opera, the music is in the air and one catches snippets of it in the atmosphere and even without knowing it, begins to absorb a sense of the work. The minute she heard it, she had a feeling that it was for her. This feeling was confirmed by a house repetiteur who gave her his score so that she could start learning the music and become the character of which she said:

'I feel that critics and singers alike tend to place too much emphasis upon Turandot's cruelty. To me her overriding emotion is fear: a fear from which all her other qualities stem. In the great scene after Calaf has solved the riddles, when she attempts to persuade her father, the Emperor to release her from her promise, her voice mounts and mounts in the ecstasy of fear "Non guardarmi cosi" she cries to Calaf "Don't look at me thus." This is not a cry of anger but of fear. She knows that she has met her match, a man for whom she has a real affinity – and he for her – pre-ordained and inescapable. And as she feels the self imposed barriers crumbling, she is terrified. Calaf shares this instinctive certainty that they are for each other and this is why he offers her a way out of her dilemma by challenging her to discover his name. In the last act, which Puccini never lived to finish, she finally surrenders, not only to Calaf and to love but, to a destiny which all her efforts have been powerless to avoid. This last act was, of course, completed by Puccini's friend and disciple, Alfano, who often visited me in my dressing-room when I sang in Turin where he was head of the conservatoire. I valued his friendship and enjoyed his conversation. It was he who told me how he had learned from Giuseppe Adami, one of the librettists of "Turandot", that during his last illness Puccini kept writing to them, imploring them to hurry with the text of the last act.'

It must have been very frustrating for Eva to be so terribly ill at this crucial point in her career. The incubation period for typhoid is around two weeks and she was in a nursing home for six weeks. Her next performance, as far as I could trace, was her first Gioconda on October 30th, at Il Piccolo Teatro in Trieste. Eva said of *La Gioconda*:

'I sang it first at Trieste in 1926 but it was not one of my favourite roles and I never sang it in England. However, no dramatic soprano worthy of her name can resist the challenge of the great "Suicido".'

In November she sang Aida in Treviso on the 4th, and again on the 12th, 16th, and December 2nd, in Genoa at the Politeama in a cast that included Albertina Dal Monte and Ettore Bergamaschi under the baton of Mario Parenti. During that time she travelled to and from Turin for more performances of *Gioconda* between November 20th, and December, 5th.

Later in December, Eva was presented with a wonderful new opportunity when she was invited to sing her first Turandot. It was at Brescia's Teatro Grande on the 18th and she made headlines throughout Italy following her brilliant performance. A dispatch to England from Milan noted:

'At the moment of going to press, we learn that Eva Turner, having completed her engagement at Brescia went to Trieste to sing Turandot and was again an outstanding success.'

She had been studying the score since first hearing it eight months earlier at its first performance.

Eva Turner was, at this time, earning about L1700 for each performance - this varied a little according to the opera house's status - and a piece written on Sunday March 1st, 1927 in Turin and printed in the Daily Mail on Tuesday gives as an idea of her performances around this time:

'Casually visiting the Turin Opera, I found an English girl established as the leading soprano and enjoying an unquestionable success. I heard Miss Eva Turner last night sing Leonore in Beethoven's "Fidelio". The great theatre was crowded and Miss Turner was warmly applauded. She deserved it for she sang with a flood of tone and in her performance made an impression of buoyant vitality. After her great song in the second scene the performance was held up with a storm of applause. Her success was the more remarkable as Fidelio includes much dialogue. Miss Turner was quite confident yet when she left England two and a half years ago she knew no Italian... In the last two years she has vastly improved and has sung at the Scala Milan and is in great demand by all Northern Italian opera houses. She has sung in Verona, Trieste and Brescia and has toured Germany as the Prima Donna of an Italian Opera Company

Eva Turner's diary for the first few months of 1927 included:

14th Jan – Trieste, 'Turandot'.
22nd Jan – Turin, 'Fidelio', 7 performance.
13th - 21st Feb – Padova, 'Aida'.
24th Feb – Turin, 'Aida' with Pertile as Radames and Marinuzzi conducting.
12th March – Verona, 'Turandot'.
23rd March to 10th April – Genoa, 'Turandot'
9th April – La Spezia, 'Turandot'.
14th - 24th April – Florence, 'Turandot'

104   Dame Eva Turner A Life on the High Cs

and also Portugal. The Scala has invited her to sing Brünnhilde and she has offers from South American opera houses.'

Before setting off in May to tour South America, Eva Turner received a letter from Charles Moor, whose father was a former Lord Provost of Edinburgh. He had worked as a director at Covent Garden since 1922 and was present at Eva Turner's famous audition for Panizza, the conductor who sent her to sing for Toscanini. In 1925 Charles Moor had been given leave of absence to go to the Chicago Civic Opera where he gained a lot of operatic and administrative experience and became very influential in the opera world around this time not least because of having the all important links with America. Later, in 1929, he became the artistic director at Covent Garden.

Eva Turner as Turandot (opposite)

*Bella Vista
Brusino Arsizio
Switzerland
April 3rd 1927*

Dear Miss Turner,

I have been thinking over the question of German parts for your career & I would advise you leave the Brünnhildes for a time, taking up Elsa, Elisabeth & and Senta to begin with. I am sure that these three parts which you know already, musically, will suit you very well. They will also not collide with your Italian repertoire in the way that the Brünnhildes would. Then we shall get someone to make arrangements for guest performances in Germany & and after having sung those with success you will tackle the Brünnhildes. I am emphasising this, as I think it is the best road, vocally and histrionically.

Don't forget what I told you about Eurythmics (sic). Get hold of a good dancer, or Ballet master, & have a course of two lessons a week for about four weeks & and you will find you have mastered all that is necessary & it will do you a world of good.

Dress very well! Add the expenses of your dresses to your fees and you will find that the impresarios will pay for them. But otherwise, you will also find, after every success, that the best firms will make special prices, if you go about it the right way. Don't neglect this, look at the way Muzio dresses when you see her in Buenos Ayres, (sic) it brings in bigger fees!

And when you get your own costumes made, which you must eventually do, then go to Caramba at the Scala, tell him you are a friend of mine, give him my love and he will advise you on this

1924-1927 Italian Beginnings

point. Tell him how much you can spend and he will find a way out of any difficulty.

If they offer you America for next season, Chicago or New York, don't accept! Sing another year in Italy at the Scala and Rome, make a great name for yourself there, then you can command better prices in America, you must go as one of the very first, with your own dresses & and everything. They must pay for it.

Remember me very kindly to Mr Broad.
Goodbye and God bless you.
Yours always sincerely
Charles Moor.

A movement seems to be apace to enter the big arena. Eva and Plum know she has the goods and they are now asking for help in wrapping them and presenting them to the big world out there. Three years away from the limits of the Carl Rosa Touring Opera and time spent with the more sophisticated continental audiences are having their affect on the performing business of this partnership. It is interesting that she had inquired from Charles Moor about German roles. In later life she often expressed regret that she had not been adequately praised or employed for the German roles which she loved singing. Perhaps this question takes us back to a fork in the roads where she lingered before fate took charge in the shape of Turandot.

Eva writes at the top of Charles Moor's letter: 3 points Hands, Money, Scala and how to study German. Unusually we have a little draft of a reply written on the empty page of this letter:

'I was so glad to receive your most kind letter and thank you sincerely for all your wonderful advice and support with the hope that I shall ever merit its continuance. I shall certainly do all possible to prove myself to you and show how I appreciate your interest. I shall keep your letter with me to buoy me up and onward. It has already given me much hope and also satisfaction to learn that my constant attention to ideals has met with the approval of one so much higher up in the art world. If you will let me know the date and time of your visits to Chicago and London I will let you know direct of my doings. I return to Milan on the 11th. C/O Tho. Cook & Com will always find me and they always forward. After May 1st I am with the Colon Opera-Buenos Ayres for some time and after I believe up to Rio Janiero – I am not sure. Doubtless you will know more than I. Did you know that the Scala wanted me to learn "Fidelio" for them? I received the score after you had left but found every word was different to the edition I had at Turin. I realised

that it would be impossible to relearn the opera at such a time as would allow of my giving sufficient number of performances to compensate me for all the trouble it would cost me so I respectfully declined the opportunity. Besides I have to learn "Don Carlos" for the Colón opening and also to rearrange all my wardrobe for the voyage which will occupy a lot of time and between the two stools one section of the responsibility will have to suffer and my nerves through the harassing they would be called upon to experience. So I chose, as I have said and trust I have acted in the best interest of all concerned.'

An extract from the diary of an eighteen year old tells us on April 21st:

'We went to "Turandot" at the Politeama Fiorentina. (Florence) The part of Turandot was sung by an English girl Eva Turner. She had a very fine voice and a beautiful figure'.

But as we see from her letter above she is not entirely convinced as yet that fate has earmarked this role to decide her future.

As planned, she set off on tour to South America and the Evening Times of Friday June 3rd, tells us:

'Miss Eva Turner is now in Buenos Aires for a season with an Italian company that includes such celebrities as Fleta, Volpi, and Schipa. They will present 20 operas some of them such as "Don Carlos" and "Ernani" new to Eva Turner. An opera star's life must surely be a strenuous one. Miss Turner was rehearsing daily aboard ship during the voyage from Italy. Before she sailed, a gala performance was given in Genoa.'

Claudia Muzio, (see appendix) mentioned in Charles Moor's letter was also on this tour. Muzio had established a special relationship with audiences at the Teatro Colón in Buenos Aires, where she first appeared in June, 1919 in Catalani's *Loreley*. She continued to appear there until 1934 by which time she had sung in 23 different operas, becoming known as *La Divina Claudia*. Dame Eva said:

'You know Claudia Muzio was the Prima Donna Assoluta and it was her company really. I remember she asked Toti dal Monte, (with whom a friendship, formed early in Eva's international life, lasted the tests of time) and me to have tea with her in her suite during the voyage. Muzio was a lovely, lovely singer.'

Eva admired Muzio perhaps more than any other singer and described her as:

1924-1927 Italian Beginnings

'the singer who had made upon me the most unforgettable impression of all. As a recitalist every word was pregnant with meaning and she encompassed the phrases so beautifully with her flowing tone. She held us all entranced and any chance to hear her was an opportunity not to be missed'.

'"La Traviata" is an opera which I greatly love but one in which I have never sung. Muzio was the finest Traviata I have ever heard. Indeed she was Traviata. I never cease to be enormously moved when I hear the way Muzio speaks the words: "E tardi, e tardi." The first time I heard this opera with Muzio was at the Teatro Colón of Buenos Aires in 1927. Actually it was made possible to me by the kindness of Tito Schipa, the tenor in that performance. By chance I met him during the morning of the day of the performance and he asked me if I was going to the opera in the evening. I said: "No - since I understood it was sold out". He insisted that I should go to hear Muzio, and said I must use his box. Tito spoke in glowing terms about Claudia. I was everlastingly grateful to him for this experience, because her performance was truly supreme.'

Dame Eva often talked of 'Dear Claudia' when she was teaching in later years. She took recordings of Muzio on all three of her *Desert Island Discs* programmes and on one of them was so upset at hearing Claudia's voice that the remainder of the recording had to be postponed until the next day.

Eva Turner made her debut at the Colón, Buenos Aires on June 17th, 1927 in *Fidelio*, given to a huge audience. She, Antonio Melandri (tenor), Benvenuto Franci (baritone), and Marinuzzi, the Maestro, were all generously received at the four 'full houses'. On July 15th, Eva Turner, Antonio Melandri and Ezio Pinza, the famous bass appeared in the local premiere of Rimsky Korsakov's *Tsar Sultan* and again there was praise and warm receptions for all involved. The company then visited the Teatro Municipal at Rio de Janeiro, where both operas were presented. At São Paolo only *Tsar Sultan* was presented, this time with Tancredi Pasero in the title role of which the local paper tells us:

> 'The acting was excellent. There was a good orchestra and the artists were very dignified, which gave the piece a splendid homogeneity. Fortunately no "great voice" stood out too much but Mrs Turner deserves particular praise as she sang her part with particular vocal flexibility. The opera is a delightful work.'

During this South American four month tour, a Milan newspaper of 21st, July tells us of *Fidelio* on 26th, June in Buenos Aires:

'We eagerly awaited the revival of "Fidelio" by Beethoven, a unique species of grand opera, and it had a true and noisy success in this magnificent presentation, directed by Marinuzzi. In this opera we came to know a new artist to Colón. She was Eva Turner who has a beautiful, big voice and who has had great successes in the major Italian opera houses. Full praise must be given to Maestro Marinuzzi who has commemorated Beethoven with this classic production and with his perfect interpretation.'

The cast included Antonio Malandri, Marengo Franci and Ezio Pinza.

'I had to return for fulfilment of contracts in Italy and I travelled on the Italian ship "Principessa Mafalda". This voyage was indeed filled with apprehension as often while mid-ocean her engines ceased to function and all the passengers were quite agitated as to whether she would "make it"; in fact that proved to be her penultimate journey as on her next journey she blew up off the coast of Brazil.'

(The *Malfada* took water after her propeller broke and she capsized, near the coast of Brazil with the loss of 303 souls on October 25th, 1927. 956 lives were saved.)

In early October, 1927 Eva Turner returned safely from the tour of South America during which she had heard, admired and befriended the great Claudia Muzio whose singing she adored throughout her life and of whom she said:

'No one has ever surpassed Claudia's Traviata'.

Part of this admiration was about her mystical persona, a feature which Eva never acquired and despite valiant intermittent efforts with her dress sense, encouraged by friends and powerful men in the opera business, sadly, Eva fell short of that great diva's high bench mark on that one too. Charles Moor again:

September 12th 1927

Dear Miss Turner,

You must forgive my not writing before. In London I never have a moment to spare and when I did get back. I had to leave again after a week to travel right through Germany up to the north, by aeroplane, then right round the principal towns and back to Zürich, then down to Milan etc. I got your letter safely and all your press, which I followed with great interest.

That day in Spezia I knew you were having a great success, without reading any press, but it was interesting to see it documented

1924-1927 Italian Beginnings

by the press. Now will you let me hear how you got on in S. America if you have time? It is difficult to follow things in that part of the world

Now there are two matters which I must remind you about.

1. The careful adjustment of all your motion and emotions on the stage to the rythm (sic) of the music. I suggested that you might go to some modern ballet-mistress or master for a short time for this purpose, not for dancing lessons please, but for rythmic (sic) gesture and movement. Once you get to understand this, you will be able to make your parts a harmonic whole, not a piece of good singing, then a piece of good acting stuck together as even many famous people do, no, you require one whole thing in which singing, acting, movement are melted together to one big personal form of expression.

2. That delicate matter, to which you referred yourself, the matter of dress & personal appearance. If you want to earn the biggest prices, you must become a little extravagant in this matter. You must be dressed & shoed & gloved in an absolutely personal way. You will find that agents & directors will pay you for this. It is quite superficial, but it has got to be done. The same thing refers to your costumes, which you must get, one after the other.

All good wishes for the coming winter.

Remember me very kindly to Mr. Broad.

With kindest regards,
Yours very sincerely,
Charles Moor.

I sail on the 17th for America.
Address: Aditorium Theatre, Chicago (Ill.) U.S.A.

In November Eva Turner sang Turandot at Ferrara and in the final days of that year, again at the San Carlo in Naples. On December 28th. Il Mattino:

'Eva Turner, not known to our public has revealed herself as a wonderful singer. Her voice is indeed beautiful, strong, vibrating and of a wonderful range and with a particular facility of utterance both in her high and low notes. In the second act her high notes rang out over both chorus and orchestra vibrating and dominating with an artistic effect. She deserves the applause she received, as she combines all the best qualities of the singer with the intelligence of the actress...'

Brescia 'Turandot'

Il Giornale Roma:

'The new edition of Puccini's last opera has had yesterday an exceptional Turandot in Miss Turner. Her voice was truly a wonderful one for range, volume and resilience. Not for many years have we had the opportunity to listen to a singer gifted with such extraordinary melodic talents. She uses these liberally and prodigally and gets her effects without apparent effort. The public found in her yesterday the exceptional Turandot which Puccini would have certainly chosen for his opera. The spontaneous applause and approbation of the public was well deserved by Miss Turner...'

Il Mezzogiorno:

'The new protagonist had to submit yesterday to a dangerous comparison. Miss Eva Turner was heard for the first time on the stage of our Maximum. But as soon as her voice with its limpid sounds thrilled out in the tale of the ancestral misfortune, the theatre was invaded with an agreeable expectation which became admiration when Turandot is enumerating the enigma. In the dramatic refrains she sustained and overcame their difficulties without any diminution of the rich warm tones of her voice. Her success was immediate. After the final duet Miss Turner besides the beauty of her tone *revealed herself a very intelligent singer in her musical intuition and expressive accentuation of the very dramatic interpretation of the scene. She is a valuable acquisition to the San Carlo.'*

The San Carlo at that time paid her L3000 for her performances, which was more than double her fee for Turandot when she first sang it a few months earlier in Brescia. *Turandot* with its very high tessitura is hard to cast but Eva Turner could sing it and so was able to command this higher fee, helping her to rise in status as well as reap some financial reward.

The Musical Standard reported to the public back in Britain:

'Miss Eva Turner, the operatic soprano, after her triumphs in South America is now singing at the famous San Carlo Naples. She is singing the role of Turandot there until the end of the month. She writes that she is now more than ever convinced that were it not for her adherence to the principles laid down by Mr A Richards Broad in his book "How to Attain the Singing Voice" it would be an impossible attainment for an English singer.

CHAPTER 4

1928-1933 Eva Turner Triumphs

Dame Eva tells us why she was not Britain's first Turandot on June 7th,1927 when Scacciati sang Turandot with Schöne as Liu, Merli was Calaf and Bellezza conducted:

'Well as a matter of fact, I was rehearsing "Fidelio" at the Teatro Regio in Turin and the previous autumn I had sung the Aida in Genova and the impressa, the impresario, was going to Buenos Aires to book for the next year and they came to that performance of "Aida" and when they returned to Italy after their business there, they came to Turin specially to hear me and were hidden in the shadows when we did the rehearsal with the orchestra, the first rehearsal, and I remember Maestro Marinuzzi asked me would I sing the "Abscheulicher", the aria, at full voice which I did, and then in the interval Rosina Torri, who was the Marzellina, said "You know why you were asked to do that, it was because the impressa are here from the Teatro Colón of Buenos Aires" and the next morning when I entered the theatre Maestro Marinuzzi said, "I would like a word with you Signorina" and he said "would you give me your word that you won't accept anything else until you've spoken further with me?" I gave my word and then later he asked me if I would go to the Teatro Colón of Buenos Aires but I was not aware that Colonel Blois who then was the head of the Royal Opera House Covent Garden had come especially to Milan to engage me for the first performance of "Turandot". I did not come that year and Bianca Scacciati sang the first performance and in the audience was Florence Easton who was on holiday going to Monte Carlo. She shared the role with Maria Jeritza at the Metropolitan and they asked her to do the next performance and then it was put away and the next year I came and I was engaged for six performances and we did ten - sold out I am happy to say.'

Opera fans had queued for up to fifteen hours for unreserved wooden seats in the gallery to hear and see the first performance in London of Puccini's *Turandot*. Among those avid fans, who inhabited the gallery every night of the then short season, was Ida Cook, the writer of many novels and an autobiography: *We Followed Our Stars* published by Mills and Boon. In her autobiography

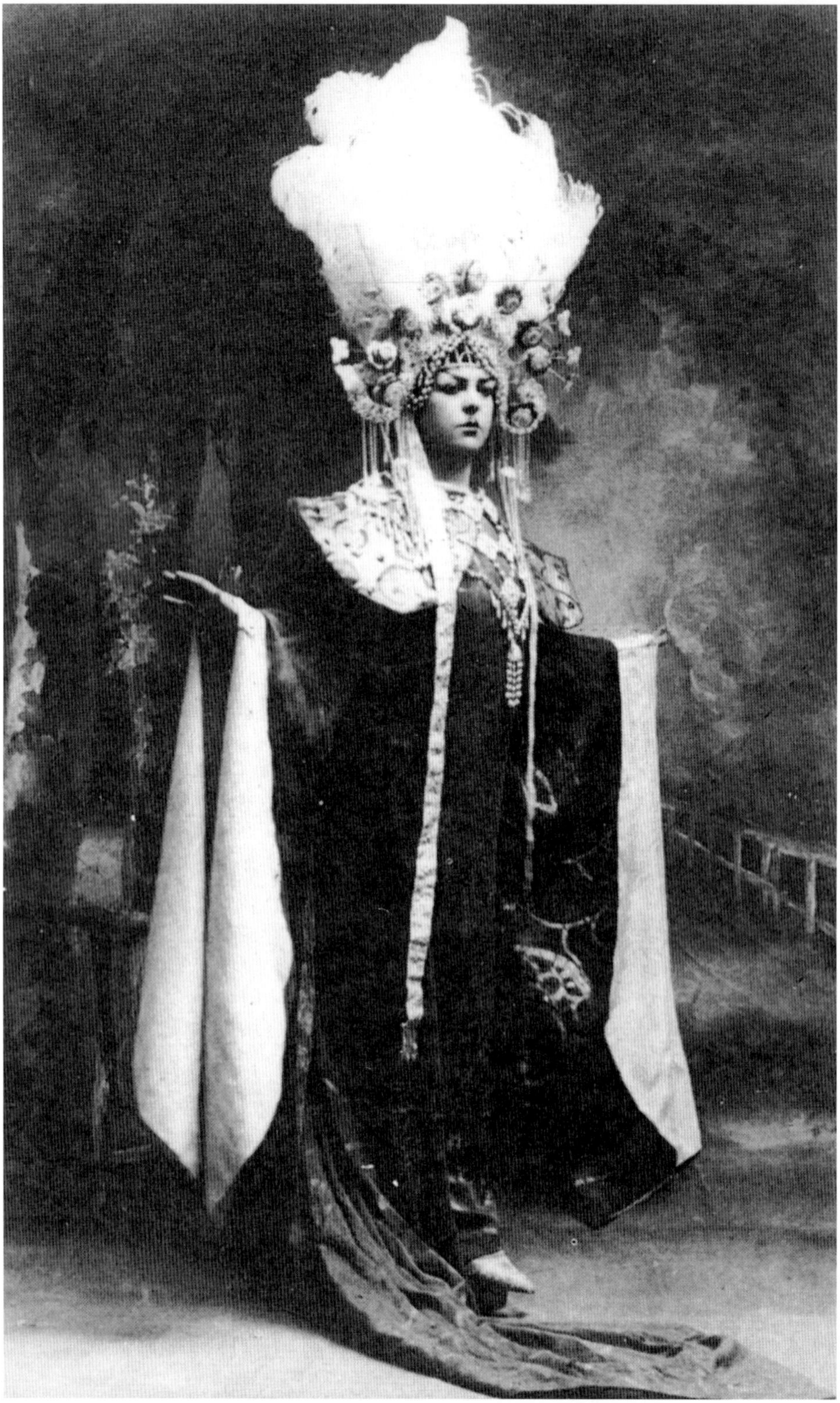

she describes how she and her sister Louise followed the famous singers at that time and she tells us, in her tribute to Dame Eva at her 90th Birthday Celebration, given by the Friends of English National Opera, about when she was a 'Gallery Girl' at the first performance of *Turandot* in London:

'We all knew each other. It was like a great club... We had one or two performances of "Turandot" and hadn't been madly impressed. I remember very well that the critics, you know, were very off-brushing about "Turandot" at first.'

Ida Cook had paid 3/6 for her unreserved seat and 3d for her programme. The cost of booked seats in the rest of the house was: for the most expensive, £9-9-0 for four people in the Grand Tier Box and in the Balcony Stalls, the cheapest, 18/6.

Having unwittingly made it impossible to be free to sing the first *Turandot* at Covent Garden in 1927, Eva Turner eagerly accepted a contract to sing there in the International Season in 1928. Her contract was to sing six performances of *Turandot*: June 5, 8, 27, July 5, 9 and 13, one of *Cavalleria Rusticana*: June 13 and three of *Aida*: June 20, 25 and July 14. (£75 per performance).

'I was thrilled to be going home to sing Turandot along with Aida and Santuzza all of which I adored singing.'

In another newspaper interview, however, she confessed to feeling far more nervous than ever before:

'just the idea of facing an English audience again - si si they are so curious so difficult to please, the English but they have always been wonderful to me in England.'

Eva Turner sang Elena in *Mefistofele* at the San Carlo in January with Laurenti, Luigi Marini and Nazzareno De Angelis with moderate success. She was received warmly by large audiences and had good reviews but perhaps the role was not ideal for her, especially compared with the new found Turandot and she did not sing Elena again.

Eva had received her contract to sing her first British Turandot from Covent Garden at the end of 1927 and was preparing for her big moment in London, so she accepted a contract for the period March 5th - April 1st, to sing Turandot at the Teatro Verdi in Pisa and sang eleven more performances in the following three weeks,

Eva Turner as Turandot (opposite)

The Daily Chronicle of February 25th, 1928: 'The preliminary list of artists for the coming Royal Opera Season was issued last night. A particularly interesting engagement is that of Walter Widdop who was an employee of the Bradford Dyers Association until October when he had a trial engagement with the British National Company at Leeds. At Covent Garden on January 24th he had a great reception as Siegfried with even the stalls rising to greet him. Another interesting engagement is that of Eva Turner who has achieved wonderful success on the Continent, particularly in the Opera Houses of Northern Italy.'

after a successful first night. This would have been a perfect preparation for her London international debut.

The Daily Mail of March 1st:

'Singers for Covent Garden. Old Favourites and New Comers.

The new Covent Garden Syndicate has issued an impressive list of singers for their season which opens on April 30th... The singers in this year's list hail from at least a dozen different countries; Denmark sends us a tenor Lauritz Melchior and Belgium, a soprano Mme Fanny Heldy and a tenor Mr. Fernand Ansseau. Mme Lotte Lehman comes from Vienna and Mme Leider who excels in Isolde, from Berlin. Among the tenors, Mr. Pertile comes from the Milan Scala and Mr. Georges Thill a newcomer this year from the Paris Opera Comique. The list of basses is headed by a Norwegian Mr. Ivar Andresen, who if he sings as well here as he did last year at the Bayreuth Festival will be allowed to have one of the finest voices in the world. He is attached to the Dresden Opera. Mr. Walter Widdop the Yorkshire Tenor is down on the list and also Miss Eva Turner who has not been heard in England for three years.

Miss Turner who was born in Bristol (sic) and brought up in Lancashire sang for some years with the Carl Rosa Opera Company. Her fine bold voice won her much admiration and there is no ground for the suggestion that she was unrecognized here. Her performances were followed with great interest and again and again it was said that with a more mature and less brusque style she would be a great singer. Her experiences in Italy have taught her much as performances of hers one witnessed there last year amply proved. It is to be hoped that we shall hear Miss Turner's Aida and her Turandot.'

Las Palmas

Aida, also included in Eva Turner's Covent Garden contract, is a very taxing role requiring great stamina and she took the opportunity to prepare for this by accepting an invitation to sing the role at the opening of the new Opera House, Perez Galdos Theatre in Las Palmas, the building of which was made possible by the Fernandez de la Torre brothers. On May 20th, 1928 at Las Palmas in the Canaries, just before her first international season at Covent Garden, she sang Aida with Maestro Capuano conducting. The Amneris was Antonietta Toini and the Amonasro, Noto. The performance was said to be: 'A Triumphant night' and El Pais the next day referred to Eva Turner as having:

> 'an assured well defined voice, agile with her top notes, extensive in quantity, firm and gracious in modulation.'

In later years her interpretation on that night was said to have placed her Aida in that theatre's history and the people of Las Palmas did not forget Eva Turner. Of *Il Trovatore*, also in her Las Palmas contract, she tells us:

> *'They promised me in Milano that I would be able to get back to present myself for rehearsals at the Royal Opera House but when I got to Las Palmas I found there were no means of my getting back. You know in those days, 1928, there were no aeroplanes and I remember I made enquiries everywhere. To cut a long story short, I went to the Elder Dempster Line on the quay and I asked to see the very head man and he was from Liverpool and that already was my passport (laughter) and I told him my predicament and asked him if he knew of any ships coming or such. He did know of a ship that was cruising and was putting into Las Palmas for a dance and a banquet at the Yacht Club and anyhow he made arrangements that I should join that ship. Well the performance took so long I had to leave in my costume and I went out by tender and I climbed the rope ladder, hanging up the side of the ship in my "Trovatore" dress. It was quite hilarious. But I got to Covent Garden and I didn't pay the fine for not presenting myself. (Laughter)'.*

Trovatore did not begin till 9.00pm and had included many encores with standing ovations at the end, so was very late in finishing. Some of the audience were cruising on the *Arcadian*, the ship which took pity on her but they had left in time to board the ship in the quayside and were looking out for her arrival by tender. Once Eva Turner had climbed up the side of the ship and was safely on board, they helped her celebrate her success into the 'wee small hours'.

El Defensor de Canarias Las Palmas, on May 21st, reports on the first opera given in their new opera house:

> *'"Aida" was the work chosen to open the Perez Galdos Theatre in Las Palmas on the 20th. The performance went on till 2.35 in the morning. It was a very fine company with the hero of the night being Maestro Capuano, with his total command of the text and the work. Thirty eight years ago the former theatre was premiered with Libia Drog singing. Now there is another soprano with much*

greater and more outstanding qualities called Eva Turner and also the excellent contralto Antonietta Toini. Voltolini was not master of his voice but the baritone Giuseppe Noto was very good and it was unfair that he was not be applauded in the duet 3rd Act with Aida. The conductor tapping his feet on the floor was distracting.'

El Tribuno May 22nd:

'Before the opera there was a reading of extracts of the works of the well known Spanish author Perez Galdos. "Aida" was the work chosen for the opening and was performed by a magnificent company under the expert direction of Maestro Capuano who carried out the work with great skill, avoiding all the pitfalls and was very well backed up by the orchestra. The part of Aida was taken by Eva Turner and she made evident what a splendid singer she is, singing with great lucidity and good taste. She handled her wide ranging and timbrous voice with marvellous ease and clarity of expression and won over the audience from her first notes. They expressed their satisfaction in the applause.'

El Defenso on May 23rd:

'The second performance of "Aida" was better than the first. It is a pity that the season ticket holders chose not to go to this performance because they had seen it before. Last night's Aida was infinitely better than the first night, although even the latter was good in general. The Maestro seemed to settle down and all was better. Eva Turner and Antonietta Toini were simply tremendous. Eva Turner is a soprano eminently endowed with a plurality of valuable faculties which she knows how to use with a really masterful skill. She also has good timing. This Signora will always be a big draw for opera companies and an idol for the public. What a pity that her appearances were so fleeting! Last night she was so admirable that there was nothing to criticise about her fine work.'

Of the performance after which Eva had to scramble on board, we can read, on May 24th:

'"Il Trovatore" is not a favourite here. The performance of Eva Turner was the outstanding event of the night and she performed wonders with her prodigious marvellous voice. The public gave her repeated ovations with spontaneous effusiveness. Eva Turner possesses an enchanting magical ability to produce the notes in her throat with marvellous flexibility converting them into gold. How well Miss Turner sang last night in "Trovatore": even better in the 2nd part than the first and especially in the 4th Act, which was embroidered with the enchanting voice and beautiful gestures of a great artist. The whole of the Theatre gave Turner several *ovations for leaving behind her the unforgettable memory of hours of emotion. The andante which precedes the "Miserere" for which she was given a long ovation was repeated at the end of the work.'*

The tenor was Voltolini.

Covent Garden International Season

While Eva Turner was busy fulfilling engagements which would leave her in the best possible form to begin her contract at Covent Garden, speculation about her appearances there continued: Weekly Dispatch April 22nd, 1928, at the end of a long gossip column Gordon Beckles tells us:

'I have said a thousand times and I suppose I will have to say it a thousand times again. Everything that is wrong with drama and music of this country must be blamed on the managers. With one or two exceptions there is not a showman in the length of the kingdom: there is genius and talent everywhere but the men in power simply don't know how to find it, how to encourage it, how to present it. Four years ago there was a young singer - not good enough for the British National Opera Company - who toured all the year round with one of the Carl Rosa groups. Her name is Eva Turner and she is probably one of the most popular sopranos in Italy at the moment. If she hadn't had the luck to get to Milan, she would still be singing Marguerite at Huddersfield next Wednesday night and getting 5 shillings for the job. As it is, she has kindly consented to come and sing for us at Covent Garden as a "star". It is all rot about people not "liking" opera. They would like it alright if there was one breath of freshness, of vitality, one topical touch in the whole business as it exists today.'

On the very morning of her first appearance at Covent Garden in the International Season, as we imagine her preparing for Turandot, perhaps fearful and certainly nervous but above all wanting to sing, she may have read the following article which possibly gave her that final resolution to do a good job and 'serve up the goods'. The Daily News on June 5th:

'One of the most interesting events of the opera season will be the appearance tonight of Madame Eva Turner in "Turandot". She has a beautiful soprano voice but it is only since she made a series of phenomenal successes in Italy and Dresden that the British public has 'discovered' her. And yet she has sung dozens of times in dozens of operas with the Carl Rosa Company. Madame Turner is Lancashire born "jannock" to the core and always loyal to the friends of her early days. She has recently returned from South

El Pais: *'Miss Turner, a good artist, managed to overcome the ingratitude of the role, of Leonora. For her the work constituted a new opportunity to show off her vocal and stylistic qualities and her peculiar, old fashioned style of singing. Her throat redeems all she sings and her sense of shading, timbre, modulation and the vibrant high notes are all qualities which defer on her a distinguished position. Her brief stay was fully enjoyed.'*

PRICE OF PROGRAMME 3d

May Fair Hotel

BERKELEY SQUARE W.1
Telephone: MAYFAIR 7777

GARDEN GRILL ROOM - RESTAURANT

Dancing Every Evening to

AMBROSE AND HIS **BAND**

Managing Director—FRANCIS TOWLE

THE SHAFTESBURY HOMES AND "ARETHUSA" TRAINING SHIP
164, Shaftesbury Ave., London, W.C.2 President: H.R.H. THE PRINCE OF WALES, K.G.
Earnestly appeal for help in Training, Clothing and Feeding their 1,100 Children
PLEASE SEND A GIFT

ROYAL OPERA
:: COVENT GARDEN ::
Lessees: Covent Garden Opera Syndicate, Ltd.

THIS EVENING'S PERFORMANCE

Thursday, July 5, 1928, at 8.30

PUCCINI'S OPERA

TURANDOT

In Italian

Turandot	EVA TURNER
Liù	MARGHERITA SHERIDAN
Calaf	AROLDO LINDI
Ping	ARISTIDE BARACCHI
Pang	NELLO PALAI
Pong	GIUSEPPE NESSI
Timur	SALVATORE BACCALONI
Mandarin	MICHELE SAMPIERI
The Emperor	OCTAVE DUA

Conductor VINCENZO BELLEZZA

Best wishes Eva Turner

SUPPER AT THE SAVOY
DANCING AND ENTERTAINMENTS

J. C. VICKERY
145-147, Regent Street
For Gifts of Distinction

BY APPOINTMENT TO HIS MAJESTY THE KING

Jewellery - Watches - Enamel - Shagreen
Ivory - Gold & Silver - Fine Leather
Goods - Bags - Dressing Cases

Call and see Vickery's Novelties

USED EXCLUSIVELY AT THE OPERA
Bösendorfer
"An Aristocrat among pianos"
Harold Bauer

HOLBORN Restaurant
5 MINUTES FROM THIS THEATRE
DINNER 7/6
SUPPER 6/6
SERVICE À LA CARTE
Dancing:- NIGHTLY

Elizabeth Arden
Muscle Firming Skin Toning Treatments
VENETIAN TOILET PREPARATIONS
25 Old Bond Street W.1
New York 673 Fifth Avenue
Paris 2 rue de la Paix

Estd. 150 years. A bit of Old London
RULES RESTAURANT
Maiden Lane, Covent Garden
Two minutes from this Theatre
DINNERS & SUPPERS till MIDNIGHT
Excellent Cuisine Fully Licensed

BECHSTEIN PIANOS
Speciality Decorated Cases in Period Styles
Only Address
65, SOUTH MOLTON ST.
Corner of Brook St.
W·1

GOWNS FURS CLOAKS HATS LINGERIE
Debenham & Freebody
Wigmore Street, London, W.1

Exclusive COLUMBIA RECORDS—
PAMPANINI
EVA TURNER
BORGIOLI
TOM BURKE
GEORGES THILL
AROLDO LINDI
STABILE
ROY HENDERSON
BRUNO WALTER
(Conductor)

Columbia
New process RECORDS
ELECTRIC RECORDING
For all gramophones. Lists from Columbia, 102 Clerkenwell Rd. E.C.1

SCHWEPPES TABLE WATERS
Ask for "Whisky & Schweppe"

Beautiful Shoes for all Occasions
Raynes SHOES
58, NEW BOND ST., W.1

The Tricity RESTAURANT
Top of Savoy Hill in the Strand
TEA DANCE—Daily, 4-6 p.m.
OPERA DINNER, 5/6 (or a la carte)
DINNER or SUPPER} 9/6
with DANCING (or a la carte)
X. N. TRICITY BAND, with JAY WILBUR and other Artistes
Ger. 1392 G. STONE, Gen. Mgr.

FINDEN BROWN AND CO. LTD., CRAVEN STREET, W.C.2

America, a singer's Tom Tiddler's ground, where her operatic triumphs were remarkable, even for a country remarkable for its enthusiasms. She will also sing Aida later in the season'.

We know that the rehearsal period began on May 28th, a week before this first performance, not very long by modern standards, so with all this fuss, let us fervently hope she has had enough time to get to know the production and is in good voice! She had many, telegrams from old friends, wishing her well and cherished them all her life. Below, are a few which may be of interest:

'All best wishes for great success. Love Glad. (Gladys Parr)', sent from Belfast.

'Every good wish from us both for a new triumph tonight Reginald Somerville.'

'All best wishes tonight. Hughes Macklin'

'Wish you heartily great success tonight Gigia Levi.'

'Best wishes for great success Astra Desmond.'

'Delighted to read, in Ireland, of your terrific success. Lancashire again. Norman Allin.' (Sent after the event)

How did she pass the day of this rather nerve wracking return performance to London? It was to be a defining moment of her life and she would have a sense of this as she prepared for the evening performance:

'People sometimes ask me how I spend the day before a performance. Well, the old fashioned theory was that a prima donna more or less went into retreat and spent the day in silent seclusion never venturing to speak above a whisper but in practice it does not work out like that. Still one does not talk on the telephone more than one can help and personally I spend a lot of time thinking of the role I am going to sing and trying to get the feel of the character. Each character has to be studied, or else however perfectly you may sing the role, you will not give a complete performance.'

She would have time to read, enjoy and think about her telegrams and many other best wishes cards, sent from all round the world:

'I always make a point of being in my dressing room early enough to allow plenty of time before the performance – sometimes there are gremlins in the room you know, hair won't go right or make up looks all wrong and then there is

nothing for it but to start all over again. Then I myself like to have a look round the stage, after the scene has been set and before I go on to sing – we all have a pet whim as to what makes us feel happy before a performance and this just happens to be mine... Turandot is I think perhaps the most exhausting role physically and dramatically. The Chinese robes I wear are tremendously heavy and in the second act my headdress is interlaced with ostrich feathers, which look very imposing, but I have to confess that I always have a secret misgiving as to whether they are going to stay in their places or fall out at a critical moment'.

Her headdress stayed on and there were no gremlins in her dressing room on that evening, certainly not of the evil kind. She was well prepared, knew she could do a good job and above all else she was courageous.

We have a huge choice as to which papers to look in to read of her historic success on June 5th, 1928 but since it was the Daily Telegraph which Dame Eva Turner liked to have each day in later life, let us look there first to read about her debut at the International Season at Covent Garden. Daily Telegraph June 6th:

Covent Garden Opera
Eva Turner's Debut – 'Turandot' by Giacomo Puccini

Turandot - Eva Turner
Liu - Rosetta Pampanini
Calaf - Aroldo Lindi
Conductor - Vincenzo Bellezza

'There is always a certain curiosity on the part of any audience just before the revival of a great or much discussed work: speculations as to whether, if it be old, it is still outwearing the ravages of time or, if it be modern, whether it will sound a little less novel or striking than it did say a couple of years ago. Last night when the curtain rose on the posthumous "Turandot" of Puccini for the first time this season those thoughts were undoubtedly mixed with speculation as to how the English Prima Donna would come through the ordeal of the title role part she has just been playing in the opera houses of Italy but was now to play for the first time at Covent Garden.

For Turandot, not a very long part, is exacting and requires first class singing. How would this artist who had graduated from the Royal Carl Rosa Opera stand this promotion to international rank? There could be no doubt as to the answer. From the moment when she first takes her place at the foot of the throne in the second act, impassive, like the image of gold, it was clear that the new Turandot was mistress of the situation. There was no uncertainty in the initial phrase in which – like an uncanny inversion of Elizabeth's greeting – she seemed to apostrophize the ancestral hall.

Her tones were imperious, declamatory and dramatic. The composer did not spare the singer in this act and the Englishwoman seemed to be as happy declaiming on high Bs and Cs as elsewhere in the range of her rich voice. One does not of course ask for tenderness from the frigid Princess of the Celestial Empire and Miss Turner made no apparent attempt to read it into the part. The riddles were asked in a strictly impersonal way and it was only towards the end of the great act when Turandot becomes the perfect Puccinian heroine, dropping the pseudo-Orientalism of her begetter at the phrase "Non guardami cosi" that the sphinx became a human being.

Aroldo Lindi was an admirable Prince Calaf and sang especially well in his duet with Turandot in this scene though not quite her vocal stature. He might have made more of the passage in the first act where he thinks of Turandot's mysterious beauty "O divina bellezza! O meraviglia!" but he rose uncommonly well to the importance of his position in the climax of the second act.

At the fall of the curtain the scene was remarkable. All had done well. The orchestra playing under Vincenzo Bellezza's masterly hand had been in fine form. But the honours went to the Englishwoman. That ancient prejudice against the native artist was once more blown to the winds and again and again Miss Turner had to appear before the curtain alone. She had produced "the goods" and the big critical house was delighted.

Rosetta Pampanini who had made such a vivid impression in Butterfly last week gave an altogether charming and perfect impersonation of the slave, Liu. Her singing of the poignant and lovely song in the first act was most moving and above all else she did have the authentic touch of the born artist.

Musically speaking the big trio of Ping, Pong and Pang at the beginning of Act II is by many popularly considered the best piece of writing in the opera and its performance last night was a joy. Artistide Baracchi was new comer to the role of Ping and proved himself to be a rare acquisition to a capital company.'

The papers on the days following her Covent Garden debut as Turandot, without one dissenting voice, helped lift her into operatic history. Headlines:

Daily Express
'English Singer's Triumph. Opera Ovation for Eva Turner'

Daily Express
'England's New Prima Donna. Lancashire Girl's Triumph'

Daily Mirror
'English Singer. Success of Mme Eva Turner as Turandot at Covent Garden'

Daily Mail
'Miss Eva Turner. British Soprano's Triumph. Covent Garden Ovation.'

Daily Mail:
'Miss Eva Turner's Big Thrill. Her Country-men's Praise. Had to go abroad to make her name'

Evening Standard
'England Finds a Jeritza. Brilliant New Soprano's Covent Garden Triumph.'

Daily Sketch
'Eva Turner Triumphs as Princess Turandot at Covent Garden'

Manchester Guardian
'Puccini's Great Legacy. Revival of Turandot.'

Morning Post
'Turandot at Covent Garden. Miss Eva Turner's Fine Singing.'

Sheffield Telegraph
'Puccini's Turandot. English Singer's Success'

Daily News
'Great British Singer. Miss Eva Turner's Triumph.'

Daily Chronicle
'Charm of Puccini's Last Opera. Turandot at Covent Garden.'

Bristol Evening Times
'Bristol Lady's Great Success. Tumultuous Cheers at Covent Garden.'

Glasgow Evening Times
'Eva Turner in Turandot.'

Aberdeen Press and Journal
'British Singer's Triumph'

Oldham Eve Chronicle
'A British Prima Donna.'

Oldham Standard
'Miss Eva Turner. Oldham Singer's Big Triumph, Covent Garden Ovation.'

The Star
'British Singer's Triumph. Miss Eva Turner in Turandot.'

Liverpool Post and Mercury
'Miss Eva Turner. Covent Garden Triumph.'

Glasgow Daily Record
'British and Unashamed.'

Manchester Evening Chronicle
'New Prima Donna. Miss Eva Turner talks of herself and her hopes.'

Oldham Standard
'I am Proud of Bolton. Opera Star wants to sing there. Fight for Success.'

Evening Express
'Miss Eva Turner. Lancashire Lass's Opera Triumph.'

Oldham Weekly Standard
'Famous at a Bound.'

Birmingham Post
'English Singer's Triumph.'

The Observer
'Music of the Week.'

The ongoing rumblings about English singers not being recognized still persisted.

Evening Standard on June 8th 1928:

'Sir, Although I have no desire to defend Covent Garden, I question whether English singers are denied a hearing here merely because they are English. As to Miss Eva Turner can P. P. produce any evidence that English music critics hailed her as an English Jeritza during her English period? When last year there was difficulty finding a good Princess in "Turandot" I wrote to Covent Garden saying that I had heard Eva Turner sing that part in Florence and had been greatly impressed by her? Colonel Blois wrote back and said that he too had heard Miss Turner and had liked her but that as she was engaged for South America there was no possibility of getting her for Covent Garden. So it is wrong to presume that she was overlooked until this year.'

The telegram sent from a proud father who had set his daughter on the road to stardom: June 6th, 1928 sent from Ashton-in-Makerfield, to Hotel Metropole, London: 'Glorious reports. Loving congratulations you/Plum. Dad.'

Daily Sketch:

'Voice like an Iceberg. I have seldom felt such a wave of patriotic feeling as when I heard Eva Turner sing for the first time in "Turandot". It is wonderful the way this glorious artist has beaten the Italians at their own game. Her voice cut through full orchestra and chorus like a knife through butter. I know exactly what young Willie Walton meant when he said her voice was "like an iceberg" – absolutely transparently clear yet overpoweringly strong. Except for Melba and Chaliapin, I don't think I remember a young singer taking a solitary call at Covent Garden before Eva Turner's fellow artists made her take it.'

Basil Maine:

'Miss Eva Turner is an English singer. Her success therefore has reflected more than ordinary glamour. Howbeit in the workings of the Covent Garden machinery her nationality is no more than an incident. We should be in grave error if we imagined that her arrival points to some fundamental change in the official outlook. In the high places there is the same fundamental mistrust of our native performers and it can be safely assumed that any English singer who has come through the Covent Garden ordeal is an exceptional artist. Miss Turner is certainly that; her singing of Turandot will remain as one of the most impressive of my operatic memories. She encompassed this extremely difficult part with no sign of misgiving and her voice rang as clearly at the end as in any other time. I have heard complaints that she varies her quality too little; but the role of Turandot calls for a firm steady relentless stream of tone, so that the significance of the character may be conveyed. There is a point in the second act where the vocal line becomes almost lyrical for a moment. Miss Turner marked this change with great subtlety.'

Eva Turner's Turandot was a British success such as the public had not witnessed in years and so the press gave her a special celebration luncheon and plenty of newspaper space to express herself. The following couple of interviews contain her own words; the words of a young woman riding the crest of a wave, so let us read them and let her tell her own story at that time.

The Evening News of June 6th:

'Miss Eva Turner on her Success. A Lancashire Lass. Her singing was simply irreproachable. The volume was outstanding... for the strong soaring singing required in Turandot there is probably no one to surpass her... Miss Turner returned to Covent Garden last night after five year's absence and her brilliant success as The Princess in Puccini's "Turandot" has brought her showers of praise *and congratulations from the critics. The story of her triumph, she told me in one sentence today. She says simply: "I am just a Lancashire lass who has worked hard, believed in her star and always hoped to be a great prima donna"... The opera singer, who was born in Oldham, declared all her success was due to her maestro Mr. Albert Richards Broad who had taught her practically all she knew. "He has taught me for the last four years (sic) going with me wherever I went - He's still teaching me... I think that young English singers find success very hard to obtain largely because there are so few good masters available in England to teach them" she said... A Change of Plan? Miss Turner has been asked to sign a contract to sing in thirty-five performances in Italy next season but her great triumph at Covent Garden may cause her to change her plans.'*

The Evening News of June 15th:

'Her manner is that of an unaffected girl, happy because of her success, a bit overwhelmed by the tributes paid to her. She has a wide smile and a desire to pass on her happiness to her friends. She told me she fully understood why the solar plexus punch was so completely effective in boxing. "The solar plexus is the real seat of the nerves" she said. "When I am nervous that is where I get a sinking feeling." The waiter put some English strawberries and ice cream before her. I became aware of a white haired benevolent looking man, sitting at a far table next to Mr. Percy Pitt the Covent Garden Musical Director, who was looking hard at her.

A Sign

I did not have to direct Miss Turner's attention towards the concentrated gaze of the white haired gentleman. It must have been mental telepathy.

She looked at him nodded and smiled when he made a sign that must have meant No. "That is Mr. Broad," she said to me, "he gives me my singing lessons. I don't do anything without him. He has taught me all I know."

She ate the strawberries but not the ice cream.

Her Teacher

Mr. Richards Broad, to give him his full name, is a lecturer on the science of singing. Miss Turner was introduced to him when she was playing small parts in the Carl Rosa Company. She asked him to give her lessons. He said he would but only if she worked as if her life depended on it. He has devoted himself to making her a great singer. He talked to me afterwards about his methods.

"One of the dictums is that the singer should forget all about the throat. The vocal vibrations must go straight to the bottom edge of the top front row of the teeth. The tongue must be trained to lie as flat as possible. Keep your mind ever between the teeth and not on the throat,' he says."

Mr. Broad received the following invitation from Columbia Graphophone Company Ltd. for a 'Complimentary Luncheon to Miss Eva Turner on the occasion of her signal success at Royal Opera House Covent Garden'. It was to be held at the Savoy Hotel on Thursday June 14th 1928:

Dear Sir,

May we have the pleasure of your company at a Complimentary Luncheon being tendered to Miss Eva Turner, the young British soprano who has created such a sensational success at Covent Garden?

The Columbia Company's interest in this tribute to Miss Turner is that in furtherance of a wider interest in music, and particularly in British musical affairs, we believe the occasion to be one deserving some such special mark of honour.

We regret the very short notice possible but trust you will be able to be present.

Will you very kindly indicate your acceptance on the attached postcard?

Yours very truly
Louis Stirling
Managing Director.

Weekly Dispatch 17th June:

'Anyone can learn to sing by Eva Turner

People say to me: "Why is that you are blessed with such a wonderful voice. Why cannot we too learn to sing?" I say YOU CAN. It is not an endowment of God why I can produce beautiful sounds form my throat is because I know how to produce them to the best possible advantage. It is simply a question of how we are taught to sing. When I say taught I mean taught to sing properly and when I say properly I mean my way of 'properly'.

There are hundreds of ways of different methods but I consider "My" way is justified by results and the amount of appreciation accorded to it. If I wanted to sing badly with what I would call a sweet pretty voice, I could easily do it – by producing my voice in such a way that I could hear myself sing. It is like this when I sing properly I cannot hear myself sing. All I hear is a buzz. I can tell by the way I buzz that it is going to give the effect that made me a Prima Donna.

Not Too Simple

Sometimes I wish that we could hear ourselves as other hear us. The trouble is that my voice is too loud for a room. In the first place people think I have a special voice for speaking and another for singing. Really we have only one mechanism for speaking, singing, shouting, whispering – they are all done with the same mechanism.

This is how I do it.

First, to make sound the air comes from my lungs. I turn that to sound when it gets to my vocal cords in my Adam's apple. The purity of the production of sound depends on the position of those cords. Automatically they should be shut but not tight. You cannot see yourself down there but I could tell you at once if they are in the right position by the sound you make. Then the air made into sound comes up my throat and out and the volume and tone depend on the path taken out.

If the sound gets to the roof of my mouth then the sound is deadened because the gum is soft and non resilient. It must go straight towards my teeth. The sound waves shoots off them into the outside air. And there is your perfect note. How I get the sound straight to my teeth is more than I can tell you – on paper – unless I wrote a book full of diagrams and things. But this is roughly how I get the sound to go straight to my teeth. Most people learn to sing aaaaah but I sing sheeeee. This is why: with the beginning of the word the sh sound is made by the air rushing through the chords (sic) and through the teeth. The eeee sound which follows is naturally then on the right path and the vowel sound of the word shee is produced by vibrations that are centred on the teeth. Singing is not a monstrously difficult accomplishment and matter of a fluke when it is stripped of its obscure anatomical mysteries. It is quite plain and simple and once you can do it properly you need never vary it.

No Strain.

My voice is uniformly good because I know how. It does not depend on temperament or atmosphere. I am always equally good because I pursue the same law of causation and by so doing the effect is always the same.

Singing should be performed with the utmost ease and freedom without any strain or fatigue. But remember to reach all the nooks and crannies of the Covent Garden Opera house it is necessary first you should not be able to hear your own voice.'

Below is a letter referring to that article:

The Weekly Dispatch London
Northcliffe House, EC4.
June 15, 1928
Telephone Central 6000

Dear Mr. Broad,

Herewith an amended proof of the article.

I have altered what you wrote somewhat and I hope you don't mind. The substance is the same but the wording a little less technical. We have to treat all readers as potential idiots!

The editor is very pleased with it.

Yours sincerely,
WJ Rayne .

PS Can you let the boy have it back with correction?

Daventry Experimental (5GB) had broadcast the first act of the 'Turandot' performance on the 5th June but Turandot herself says nothing during that act, merely gesturing that the Prince of Persia should die. It then broadcast Act 2, Turandot's big act, on Thursday July 5th, 1928 and the third act of 'Aida' on June 25th, 1928, with Bellezza conducting.

Ida Cook - 'I shall never forget the first impact of that incredible voice of such brilliance and colour and projection coming over at us. It didn't matter that you were in the gallery or the front row of the stalls or anything, as with a great voice it must be, it sounded the same everywhere and we were so proud of "our Eva" we couldn't get over it.'

Eva Turner's second opera in the season was *Cavalleria Rusticana* on June 13th. The Daily Mail June 14th tells us:

'Pertile's singing in "Pagliacci" like Miss Eva Turner in "Cavalleria Rusticana" made one marvel afresh at the human voice. In both there was an element of the stridency which is more admired in Italy than elsewhere, but both singers are great technicians and know just how far they can safely go. Miss Turner and Mr. Pertile together would challenge a Military band and come out smiling. With both there are moments more astonishing than beautiful but both are marvellous singers. Mr. Pertile's outcries were nearly terrifying and Miss Turner's high flying phrases – so bold and brilliant and dead certain were of their sort, the most remarkable known in these latter days at Covent Garden.'

Eva Turner said:

'I never sing "Cavalleria Rusticana" without remembering a certain Saturday morning when we were unsuspectingly rehearsing that particular opera at Covent Garden, and the impresarios of the Chicago Civic Opera suddenly stepped out

from behind a screen, where they had been listening unobserved, and inquired if I would like to go and sing in Chicago.

I sang for them next day in the foyer, which greatly intrigued the theatre firemen, who let us in and who were not accustomed to such doings on a Sunday morning.'

Lionel Powell, who established his concert agency in 1876, (after his death in 1931 this agency was taken over by Harold Holt) was eager to have such an illustrious star on board and so he wrote to her on June 15th at Hotel Metropole, Northumberland Avenue, S.W. from his citadel in New Bond Street London W.1.

Dear Miss Turner,

I have just come back into town for an hour.

I was wondering, whether you could take lunch with me on Monday next (18th inst.) in which case I will call for you. I think it is important we have a little talk as early as possible.

In case you do not know, I am very interested in AUSTRALIA, and have a very big connection there and broke all records in that country with KREISLER a short time ago, so if anybody speaks to you about AUSTRALIA, do not say anything until you have had a talk with me.

Yours sincerely,
Lionel Powell

Shortly followed on 16th by:

Dear Miss Turner

In the absence of Mr Powell, I am writing you this letter.

This morning, we have had an enquiry for a 'Private at Home' on July 5th to sing before H.R.H. Princess Helena Victoria, and shall be glad to know whether you would accept this engagement and at what fee.

I do not know what your position is with reference to your contract at Covent Garden, but perhaps you will let Mr. Powell know this on Monday when you meet him.

Yours faithfully,
Hilda M. Day (Private Secretary)

Eva Turner would in fact be singing Turandot that night so had to graciously and sadly decline the invitation but she did keep her appointment with Lionel Powell on the 18th and received this letter on June 20th:

Dear Miss Turner,

Very many thanks for your charming letter of the 19th inst.

You need have no doubt as to the best advice I shall give you to make your art the success it deserves in the British Isles – Australia and America.

Before you leave we must have another little talk.

Yours sincerely,
Lionel Powell

So it was that Lionel Powell became her agent in Britain.

Letters poured through Eva's letter box, as word spread of her great success, but not all were happy:

33 Holland Park Avenue. W. 11.
15.6.28

My dear Eva,

I was so delighted to see you yesterday that I would not mar your charming visit with any troubles of my own, but I feel I must tell you how your public attitude towards me pains me. That you ignore me as your teacher and inspirer of your first years of study is a fact. You said yesterday that you could do no more than publish that you were my husband's pupil. Of that I am proud, but you know that I did as much and more than he did and it is silly and ungenerous of you not to acknowledge at least that you were also Madame Edgardo Levi's pupil. The help you have received by others since and the experiences you have gathered are the salt that makes artists but the solid ground on which you were founded cannot be shaken.

You must forgive my harping on the subject, but besides it paining me considerably you must understand your attitude is doing me a lot of harm and my own pupils who are so faithful seem to doubt my word when I tell them about you. We said something yesterday about always doing 'the right thing', so my dear Eva all I can ask you is to do me a good turn at the first opportunity you may have to set things right.

I shall look forward to hearing you and seeing you next Wednesday and we won't mention all this, as I shall wish to give myself up entirely to the happiness your great success gives me

Yours affectionately,
Gigia Levi.

Ouch! What a sour, sad letter. However Eva Turner included Gigia Levi's name alongside that of her husband for the rest of Eva's life despite never really rating her as a teacher. We learn from this: Eva was kind, perhaps a little too obedient and thought that some things are not worth making a fuss over or fighting about. She had a capacity for being grand but also enough humility to stand down from her pedestal if necessary.

Another letter of interest was a kind one from Ina Hill who had been the Leonora in *Il Trovatore* in 1907 in Bristol, that fateful night when Eva Turner heard the opera and decided she wanted to be a singer.

Next week
C/O O'Mara Opera Co.
Sligo, Ireland.
Sunday June 17th 1928.

Dearest Eva,

I cannot express to you the joy I have known to read about the wonderful success you have made at 'Covent Garden'. May you still continue.

How you have worked my dear and I am proud to think that our Englishwoman has at last come into her own.

Of course by this time your dear father will have told you of our meeting since I have been with this com. He was so kind in every way and gave me one of the loveliest bouquets I have had for many a day and the opera was 'Tannhaüser' (sic).

How proud he must be of his 'Eva' Whenever he used to speak to me of you his eyes just used to fill and all he could say. 'Yes My Eva has worked hard.'... In the meantime accept from one who has always had your interests at heart.

Every good wish and loving thoughts.
Affectionately yours,
Ina Hill.

I think the outside world sometimes forgets that to sing is, as well as being a pleasure, a full time occupation and so invitations to grace tables of important people of the day, flow in without much thought as to surrounding performances. Eva Turner never made much of such things and, if she could, she accepted all invitations as she loved to be part of the social whirl, so I guess this next reply from 11 Downing Street, on June 18th pleased her.

My dear:

Bring anybody you like. Each and all of you friends will be welcome. My husband looks forward to making your acquaintance. The Prime Minister is also coming. And Princess Helena Victoria has promised to come. I hope and believe we should have a jolly evening, and I shall not permit it to be formal.

Affectionately yours,
Ethel Snowden.

Pertile, by the time of the 1924 Covent Garden season, had already appeared at the Metropolitan in 'Tosca' with Jeritza in 1921, (his only year at the Met), when his other roles, were: des Grieux, Turridu, Radames, Pagliacci and Julien in Louise. He was the leading tenor at La Scala from 1927 until 1937 and a favourite of Toscanini and had, earlier in 1928, recorded *Celeste Aida* with the Scala orchestra, a recording which shows an ideal Radames with strength of voice, vocal light and shade and great understanding of the character.

Aureliano Pertile was to be Eva Turner's Radames on June 20th and 25th and, in later years, Dame Eva remembered singing Aida with him. He was eighteen days younger than Martinelli and both tenors were born in the same town of Montagnana, in 1885. In 1916 while Eva was singing with Carl Rosa on tour, he was already singing at La Scala where he appeared in *Francesca di Rimini* with Rosa Raisa who was the first Turandot. Dame Eva fondly recalled that he had, 'wonderful stage presence and a great voice'.

The Times on June 21st 1924 reported:

'The success of Miss Eva Turner has been one of the notable events of the present opera season at Covent Garden. Last night she won fresh laurels as Aida. The heroic part suits her enormous voice which will overtop a chorus and orchestra without ever ceasing to be musical in quality. Its only defect is a lack of veiled colour; the range is from brilliant to smooth but it goes no further towards the more subdued shades. This deficiency in an exceptionally brilliant and serviceable dramatic soprano voice made itself felt in "Cieli Azzurri" (sic) and in the last scene of all. Everything that phrasing can do – and that is more than half of all tonal expression – but the purified emotions of the final tragedy call for more hushed tones than Miss Eva Turner can quite command, just as the sentiment of the patriotism in Act 3 demands tender as well as ardent expression. But it is magnificent singing, not only from a technical, but from a dramatic point of view: the notes are sung true, and the character is strongly felt.

Daily Dispatch 22nd June: 'The Lancashire Prima Donna. I took the air in the intervals of last night's Covent Garden production of "Aida", with Ivor Novello. He is just back from Germany and while there heard and made the acquaintance of Miss Eva Turner the Lancashire prima donna. Like everyone else with any pretension to musical intelligence Novello was enthusiastic about Miss Turner's singing. 'She is wonderful' he kept on repeating. 'Don't you think so?' This question was sheer rhetoric of course because never have I been so moved as during her singing and Novello knew that too!'

Signor Pertile, as Radames, was inclined to over-sing and sometimes to be too nasal, but he did bring out the dignity and pathos of the end of the opera, which gives to the listener many of the conventional pleasures of Italian opera and produces the true catharsis of tragedy and so qualifies to be numbered among the great works of art.'

'A British Triumph. The Italian season at Covent Garden provided the only sensation and a British one at that - Miss Eva Turner. Her performances in "Turandot" have been remarkably fine. Her voice rings out through a great blast of chorus and orchestra as easily as a red hot needle pierces a butter pat: yet it remains true and retains its tone quality. To Signor Bellezza goes much of the credit for the interest of the last few weeks. He started away in a hurry and raced both Puccini and Verdi off their feet. But he soon sobered down - the expression is strictly musical - and all went well.'

Wonderful Covent Garden Triumphs

EVA TURNER

Records EXCLUSIVELY for

Columbia New process RECORDS

ELECTRIC RECORDING WITHOUT SCRATCH

12-inch Double-sided, 6s. 6d. each.

L1827	Good-Bye (*Paolo Tosti*). O Lovely Night (*Sir Landon Ronald*).
L1836	CAVALLERIA RUSTICANA—Voi lo sapete (*Mascagni*). TOSCA—Vissi d'arte (*Puccini*). In Italian.
L1976	AIDA—O Cieli azzurri (*Verdi*). In Italian. LA GIOCONDA—Suicidio (*Ponchielli*). In Italian.

10-inch Double-sided, 4s. 6d. each.

D1619	TURANDOT (*Puccini*)— O Principi che a lunghe carovane. In Italian. In questa reggia. In Italian.
D1578	AIDA (*Verdi*)— Ritorna Vincitor. In Two Parts. In Italian.
D1563	Because (*G. d'Hardelot*). Sometimes in My Dreams (*G. d'Hardelot*).

THE recent return of Eva Turner to Covent Garden, after four years on the Continent, provided one of the most wonderful evenings in the annals of that historic opera house. Her success in the difficult and most exacting role of the Princess in Puccini's "Turandot" was so triumphantly brilliant that the audience was swept away with unbounded enthusiasm. Never has a British artist received such a magnificent ovation. The marvellous effect of her great dramatic voice, which rang out above the chorus and orchestra with thrilling brilliance and power, will long be remembered as a wonderful piece of vocalism by this Columbia artist.

[See over

Miss Eva Turner having caught the public's attention is now in demand as a recording artist:

Columbia Graphophone Co. LTD
26th June 1928

Miss Turner
Metropole Hotel,
London, WC 2.

Dear Miss Turner,

Further to our conversation, we should like to know just what titles you would like to make, because we feel it is better that you should sing just those which you find most suitable.

I have attached a list of possible titles, but I would ask you not to let this affect your decision in any way; regarding the ballads, these are difficult to find, since really good ballads do not occur so often.

If it is possible, however, we would like to have one or two English ballads for the English market and perhaps Mr Broad will be able to look out some in time for the recording. Regarding the two Weber numbers, If you should consider these, they could be done either in English or Italian, just as you wish.

Would you please let me know as soon as possible the titles you select, say ten or twelve, in order to have five or six records. The Turandot we propose to make again with your permission. At the same time, if you could let me know the dates when you would be free to record, we could proceed at once to get the music and fix up the sessions for the orchestra or piano as the case may be.

1. Ave Maria	*2. Hear Ye Israel*
3. Oberon	*4. Hiawatha's Spring Had Come*
5. Tosti, Goodbye	*6. Gioconda, Suicido*
7. Norma, Casta Diva	*8. Cavalleria, Voi lo Sapete*
9. Tosca, Vissi d'arte	*10. La Wally, Ebben*

11. Aida Duet with Amonasro.

From John Bull to Miss Eva Turner.

Dear Madam,
That a little Lancashire lady should by the power of a golden voice overcome the prejudice of years proves that miracles can be worked even today. Recently at Covent Garden, you were the recipient of one of the greatest ovations ever accorded to a singer yet the programme furnished evidence that you were British to the core. May your triumph smooth the path for native talent.'

Eva's situation at this time is summed up very well on July 8th, by The Referee which reported:

'Physical beauty has played no part in Miss Turner's success but charm, wonderful vitality and a sweet childlike nature certainly have. Added to which is an implicit faith in her own power to succeed, to win the world with her God given voice. Her enthusiasm, her confidence, her vitality draw others to her as to a glowing radiant fire and the homely name of Eva

Turner will go down in the history of music among the great ones of the earth.'

On Wednesday July 4th at 8-30 pm Eva Turner was invited to:

'A National League Recognition of Recent Stirring Achievements by Women Pioneers of Empire, at the May Fair Hotel. A vivid call to the: National Spirit of Enterprise for Country and Empire. It is a moment vital to the History of our Empire when WOMEN are coming forward in PIONEER ACHIEVEMENT, and this National occasion will be representative in every aspect of work that makes this country great. It will give to individual effort a National value. MEN of noted achievement also will be there, coming forward to play their part in honouring women.'

Not only was she invited but:

'she would receive a Tribute for distinctive achievement in Recognition of her contribution to opera.'

Alongside her would be women from aviation, air travel, motoring and motor boats, chemical research, exploration, and polo.

The 'occasion' received this letter:

145, Piccadilly, W.1.

The Duchess of York and I desire to express to all those present at the gathering of the National League this evening our very sincere thanks for the kind message we have received. We have watched with sympathy and admiration the magnificent exploits of women who, regardless of danger and hardship, have given themselves to the interest of the British Empire, and indeed, to humanity at large.

An organisation such as the National League, which has been formed to give further encouragement to such efforts, is deserving of the fullest support, and we cordially wish it success.
(signed) ALBERT.

She was also very pleased to receive a special invitation to the annual dinner of the RAM Club at her old home the Royal Academy of Music on July 20th and while resting after her triumphs, Eva Turner wrote the following piece for the Daily Mail on July 30th:

'Our self-conscious singers. The Lancashire Prima Donna who after four years of continental triumphs won a sensation success at Covent Garden recently asks:

Why do so few British singers actually succeed as operatic stars? Is their nationality a serious handicap? Since my return to England

I have heard these questions hundreds of times. And perhaps this very fact is illustrative of our national talent – I had almost written genius – for self deprecation, furnishes a significant reply.

Actually given certain essentials most of which may be acquired by sheer hard work, on right methods, any singer of any nationality can win success if she believes in herself and allows nothing to dishearten or deter her. And what are these essentials? Before all else the voice must be rightly posed and to be rightly posed the voice must be rightly trained. Wrong methods of tuition are responsible for many a promising young singer's failure. Travelling all over Europe I have met numbers of disillusioned students who having spent thousands upon training with first one teacher and then another have at last faced the ruin of their hopes.

Often their stories have made my heart bleed. Yet no singer is made by voice production alone. Adaptability particularly in mastering foreign languages is essential to success on the operatic stage. A popular fallacy that the English are poor linguists exists because they will not take the trouble to learn. But in the singer's vocabulary the world has no place. When one may be called upon as I was to master Italian in four months sufficiently to memorise five roles in long operas it is important to cultivate one's linguistic abilities. Accuracy too is essential. Continental audiences often complain that British artists slur over details of pronunciation with a carelessness that would ruin the finest voice.

Largely on this account I consider foreign travel and experience essential. To any singer with ambition I would say "Go abroad, soak yourself in the life language and conditions in which the great operas were created." For how can a British singer hope to compete with those born and bred in the atmosphere of the art? Many critics argue that the British have not the artistic temperament of foreigners.

But I maintain that "temperament" – the power of entering into and expressing the inmost emotions of a character – can, to a great extent, be acquired. Not only must the artist learn the technique of the stage, she should also study human psychology. Books on psychology are always at my bedside. Reading intensively, I gain insight into the women I portray.

How can one express convincingly the mental anguish of Tosca the callous cruelty of Turandot if one has not first within oneself their reactions? Content to possess lovely voices many British singers are inclined to neglect the mental and emotional side of vocal education. Before we can hope to become great artists we must break down our inbred fear of expressing ourselves in speech and action – a handicap unknown to continental singers.

But the British artist's fiercest struggle is waged against our devastating native sense of artistic inferiority. Unfortunately foreigners are too ready to accept us at our own valuation. During my four years abroad I was constantly advised to adopt an Italian name if I hoped for recognition. But I always refused. If I have helped to destroy the prejudice against British artists I am proud and happy. For once shaken, prejudices are doomed before the realization that, given the opportunity and training, British singers can hold their own.'

The important monthly magazine the Musical Times in its July issue in 1928 says:

'"Turandot" was once again a handsome spectacle whatever you may have thought of it as an opera. Miss Eva Turner formerly of the Carl Rosa Opera Company and the British National Company returned to her native land after some years of enriching foreign experiences and triumphed in the difficult part of the Princess. Years ago we knew that Miss Turner had a huge voice but the effect she made with it was always rather prosaic. Turandot *proved that, as a technician, she has enriched herself impregnably. On the trying high phrases of the riddle scene, she let loose again and again a stream of brilliant tone as a trumpeter's, without a tremor or shade of uncertainty.*

It was marvellous singing; an achievement comparable with the fiddling of Heifetz. What else there is in the gallant little singer we shall have to wait and see. It may be that nothing will suit her quite as well as the misanthropic Princess's high and daring music but it is unlikely that in that part, any soprano in the world can match her... "Cavalleria" gave Miss Turner another and different chance. She expressed Santuzza's passion with simplicity but with effect and the strong stream of her vocal line suited the music.'

Eva Turner and Plum returned to Italy to prepare for her hoped for debut at the Chicago Civic Opera. They spent the summer months in Italy recovering from her hard work and enjoying a little the satisfaction of having achieved a huge success in London. This success was very important to both Eva and Plum for many reasons, not least of which was that an English soprano was finally recognised as being of the same standard and on the same level as a foreign one. The prestige she was awarded as an English singer had no precedent in the history of Covent Garden.

Albert Richards Broad (Plum) and Eva Turner

Chicago Civic Opera

While resting in Milan, Eva jotted down a few points regarding her expected appearances at Chicago. The notes are in her hand writing:

'A certainty of 20 guaranteed appearances. Do not wish to be paid for performances without making appearance. Seeing there are so many of the same voice thought there may be a lack of opportunity of appearances – and kept in background.

Ferone (her Italian agent) even assured me I should get extra shows.

Is there any intention of using me on tour next year?

Do you think it would be wise for me to tour seeing that I have a Continental clientele that I wish to hold on to?

If you booked me at all for the tour I suppose I would be expected to do the whole of it.

Seeing that I would like to raise my income to the status of many of the others, would you aid me in securing payable concerts and the facility for fulfilling the same?

In the event of my returning for next season would you favour me with the roles you want me to sing so that I might prepare them?

I desire to sing the Italian Roles in preference.'

In September Eva Turner, keeping a long standing engagement, sang in *La Forza del Destino*, by Verdi, at the New Mirandola Theatre, Italy and enjoyed good reviews:

> 'La Turner in the part of Leanora is very strong and powerful vocally and she plays the part in every respect. The grand scene in the church is splendid as her limpid voice, with its subtly blended registers, rings out above the orchestra.'

Another review tells us that she is the perfect Leanora in every way and her magnificent voce and enthusiastic acting were applauded by an appreciative audience in an appropriately long and loud way.

Plum and Eva set off from Milan to Genoa by train and on October 2nd 1928 travelled first class deluxe, in separate cabins, on the liner *Augustus* which sailed from Genoa down the coast of Italy to Naples, through the Straits of Gibraltar and out across the Atlantic Ocean to New York. In the brochure describing their bookings it tells us: the liner carried cars as well as; 420 second class, 450 intermediate and 766 third class passengers. Eva was a very poor sailor and was usually sick when travelling by boat and on one voyage she was up on deck feeling ill, when a young sailor said to her: 'I can see you're not used to the high seas ma'am.' She promptly replied rather wittily:

> 'On the contrary my man, I live by them.'

Despite feeling queasy, she worked with Plum at her singing, using her travelling piano of about three octaves, the forerunner to the neat little electronic keyboard, and after about a week's sailing they arrived in New York. She was not, however, bound for the Metropolitan Opera House but for the Chicago Civic Opera House, where she would make her North American debut. These houses were on an equal footing at that time.

Eva Turner recalled:

> 'I sang "Ritorna Vincitor" and the "Nile Scene" from "Aida" when I successfully auditioned for the Chicago Opera people on the Sunday morning after they had heard my rehearsal for "Cavalleria Rusticana" at Covent Garden'.

But it was for: 'Sieglinde in *Die Walküre*, La Contessa in *Le Nozze di Figaro* and to be prepared for the Italian roles if needed', for which she originally signed the contract.

In late September, however, Rosa Raisa, the first Turandot, cancelled her 1928/9 season in Chicago due to complications of a difficult birth while vacationing in Italy. Claudia Muzio, the other Italian star, cancelled her season saying that she too had family difficulties. Since the death of her father, a chatty little man, Claudia was accompanied by her mother, an altogether different creature, and Claudia was considered to be a shy difficult person, something of a recluse, refusing invitations to parties and public gatherings. It is thought that Claudia's mother did not like the winters in Chicago and because of that, Claudia agreed not to sing there that season, allowing space in the otherwise occupied Italian dramatic repertoire.

It was because of these cancellations that Eva Turner started her first season at Chicago in the Italian repertoire, making her debut as Aida on November 3rd, in a matinee performance with Lappas as her tenor. There had been some debate and confusion about repertoire, as the following telegram from Chicago shows:

'Letter third just received stop sorry but evidently misunderstanding regarding repertoire stop we shall not produce "Walküre" or "Fidelio" coming season stop "Giovanni" and "Figaro" will be given first performances about same time stop will arrange regarding costumes stop regards Johnson'

A letter of August 22nd, only increases confusion:

'We have special scenery for "Giovanni" and "Figaro" and costumes for these operas are furnished by the company. We can of course also furnish you with costumes for "Cavalleria" and the other works in which you will appear accept "Aida" which you stated you have. (Her Aida costume was bought by her in Italy and cost L1200 for Act 1 and L2000 for Act 2 costumes).Word from Mr Weber stated he has been working with you on "Walküre". I am sorry if the other works have been neglected for "Walküre", but the time has not been lost because we shall probably give "Walküre" next season. Mr Weber also stated that you are a very hard worker and this of course always pleases the management.'

(See appendix for the complete list of dates and casting in her Chicago seasons)

Eva Turner's roles in Chicago Opera's 1928/29 season were confirmed as: Aida, Amelia in *Ballo*, Santuzza, Leonora in *Il Trovatore*, Sieglinde and La Contessa in a new production of *Le Nozze di Figaro* and her fee for each performance was $450. From among the many reviews let us read a little about each role.

The Chicago Evening Post - Karleton Hackett:

'"Aida" last evening at the Auditorium. The triumphal scene was given with tremendous power and above the tonal mass Miss Turner's voice ever soared as the dominant note. In the Nile scene her singing was very fine; the tone vibrant, firm and in tune; honest

CHICAGO CIVIC OPERA COMPANY
1928—SEASON—1929

SATURDAY MATINEE, DECEMBER 8, at 2

Die Walküre
(The Valkyries)
(In German)

Music Drama in Three Acts
Music and Drama by Richard Wagner

Wotan, the God	Alexander Kipnis
Fricka, Wife of Wotan	Maria Olszewska
Hunding	Edouard Cotreuil
Sieglinde, His Wife	Eva Turner
Siegmund	Forrest Lamont
Brünnhilde	Frida Leider (début)
Helmwige	Ilma Bayle
Gerhilde	Irene Pavloska
Ortlinde	Alice d'Hermanoy
Waltraute (Valkyries)	Maria Claessens
Siegrune	Clara Platt
Rossweise	Coe Glade
Grimgerde	Ada Paggi
Schwertleite	Constance Eberhart
Conductor	Giorgio Polacco
Stage Director	Charles Moor

Baldwin Pianos Used Exclusively

SYNOPSIS ON PAGE 26   ENCORES NOT PERMITTED

singing. Great power for the big phrases with a high C to which she rose with gratifying certainty. The lighter passages had not quite the finesse, the diminuendi not fading into nothingness but ending abruptly but she is a straightforward singer with a fine voice and is a sincere artist.'

'"Aida" was the opera in which I debuted with the Chicago Civic Opera in 1928. The Radames was the Greek tenor, Ulysses Lappas, in very truth a Greek God! He was so handsome and looked superb as Radames. I clearly recall that when he did the rehearsal of "Aida" in Chicago, he sang and sang and sang – and I fear over sang, not sparing himself at all. At the performance next day, I realised, much to my dismay, as the opera progressed, that my fears of the previous day were not groundless. When we came to the end of the "Nile Scene", I had grave doubts that he would be able to finish the opera. Giorgio Polacco was the conductor and I clearly recall when, just as I had whispered to Lappas, "Zitto

1928-1933 Eva Turner Triumphs   143

The Chicago Daily Journal reported: 'From the point of view of absolute song, Eva Turner is the greatest singer who has been heard in Chicago. Miss Turner's genius in realising with her singing the elemental mystery of music's sway over human thoughts and emotions is apparently without flaw as it is without contemporary example.'

zitto canto io." Polacco put up his hand to me to sing and to Lappas to cease, thus saving the day.'

The Chicago Evening Post:

'Mme Turner again presented, this time as Amelia and showed that she is a singer with the voice and style of the heavy dramatic roles; an honest singer with a voice of vibrant timbre and firmly knit texture and a sure upper range'

Dame Eva recalled:

'Galli Curci came to my first "Ballo" in Chicago and said that she was singing herself tomorrow and "I came to hear you in just one act but you kept me to the end... May I compliment you on the extraordinary manner in which you were able to preserve a most beautiful singing tone throughout the performance".'

Eva Turner later received this letter:

My Dear Eva Turner,

Thanks ever so much for sending that sweet telegram of yours for – In bocca al lupo! I appreciate your kind thought very much. I am in fine voice and spirit and enjoy my work. I wish you a lot of good things and good luck for you deserve it and so does your beautiful voice.

God bless you.

Sincerely yours,
Amelia Galli-Curci.

Chicago Post, Karleton Hackett:

'M'me Turner gave an excellent performance as Santuzza - in fact it looked as though she were about to strike the spark. In the hymn her voice was full and rich and with the timbre that soared right out over the choral tone and they were giving her a backing of solid volume. But over it her tone came clear and true and without sense of effort. The "Voi lo sapete" was very fine dramatic singing; genuine feeling and the voice with great variety of shading to follow the meaning of the words.'

Eva Turner had not as yet sung the German repertoire in the original but that changed when she sang her first Sieglinde at Chicago in German on December 8th. Frida Leider made her debut at Chicago in that performance, singing Brünnhilde. After hearing her Sieglinde, the Chicago Opera Company took up the option for Eva Turner to sing Sieglinde and La Contessa on the tour to Boston and guaranteed passage back home on Contegrande on February 9th.

Her first performance of *Le Nozze di Figaro* was broadcast live on January 3rd, 1929 with Henry Weber conducting. The cast was: Eva Turner (La Contessa), Edith Mason (Susanna), Claire (Cherubino), Lazzari (Figaro), Bonelli (Count) and it was reported on January 4th:

> 'Miss Turner sang well if cautiously as the Countess but the performance as a whole lacked the lightness and charm which recasting might perhaps give it... Mme Turner had the air of a grand dame and sang the music with understanding, although with a certain angularity that needed rounding off. The "Dove Sono" was a bit of fine straightforward singing yet lacked something in grace of line and delicacy of shading. In the "letter duet" with Mme Mason she better expressed the feeling of the music. They did it charmingly.'

After visiting Boston on tour with the Chicago Company, Eva and Plum returned to Italy where they were making plans to make a permanent home for themselves:

Eva Turner as La Contessa

'The pay in Chicago had been very good and I was advised by Charles Moor where to buy land in Switzerland and had my villa built on that land. A friend had an astrology map drawn up and charted the villa and that was why I named her Junesca.'

It was Charles Moor, who, while working in Chicago at the time and known already to Eva, advised her where to build her home in Switzerland. The villa, built near the Moor's own, just over the border with Italy, on the Swiss side on the shores of Lake Lugano, near Brusino, was finished and ready to be lived in eighteen months later.

She returned to Italy from America in February and in March 1929 Eva Turner was invited by Maestro Tango to Copenhagen,

Charles Moor

146   Dame Eva Turner A Life on the High Cs

Eva Turner (opposite)

Villa Junesca

Villa Junesca (bottom left)

where he was then working, to sing Aida and Tosca in an audience which would include the King and Queen of Denmark. After this, she went to the San Carlo to sing *La Forza del Destino* by Verdi between March 23rd and April 14th, with Merli as her tenor, when she earned L3500 per performance.

Eva Turner went to La Scala on April 26th, to sing a single performance of *Turandot* and the Milan press reported:

'For this last performance of "Turandot" last night, there was a large concourse of enthusiastic spectators. The special attraction was the appearance of a new singer, Miss Eva Turner who showed herself to be quite capable of her difficult part, thanks specially to the extended range of her voice and its dramatic accents. These qualities were shown to their best advantage in the second act, but the singer was appreciated all the time and was applauded. Along with the tenor Melandri, the other interpreters and Maestro Panizza, Miss Turner was recalled to the stage several times.'

Eva Turner's appearances in La Scala itself had been so few that the reporter thought she was a new singer to the house.

In May, 1929, Eva Turner returned to Covent Garden to repeat her triumph of the previous year singing only Turandot this time, at an increased fee of £100, with equal success. Lionel Powell her agent in London, advised her about her Covent Garden contract:

5th June, 1929.

Dear 'little lady'

Be sure and fix up your contract with the Covent Garden authorities before you leave and in STRICT CONFIDENCE – be sure and put your pen through the clause with reference to 'BROADCASTING' – Only do not say I have said so. If there is any broadcasting to be done there is no reason why you should not have a big fat fee for it, as this is killing the concert business. Several other artists have deleted this clause and there has been no trouble about it, but as mentioned above, please treat this in strict confidence.

Yours sincerely,
Lionel Powell.

Lionel Powell has set his mind to re-launching Eva Turner in Britain and makes the suggestion that she should tour with the London Symphony Orchestra. He asks her to spare a month a year to tour in England and promises the fee of £1000 for 16 concerts, rising perhaps to £1600 the next year, telling her that there is no future for a star singer in the opera world and that she really should consider the possibility of touring with an orchestra.

There is perhaps some truth in this statement, as well known British oratorio and recital singers sang over 150 performances each year all over Britain. These fees were paid by the individual choral societies, however, and were not as big as those earned in the opera world, but nevertheless, the average British singer at that time had an annual income of about £2500, so if Eva Turner could have incorporated that very English way of life into her operatic life, she would have earned a substantial amount more; after all Lionel Powell is not suggesting piano accompaniments but concerts with orchestra and her life as a youngster had included both oratorios and recitals.

There is no record of her thoughts about this idea but she was careful that her operatic success in London was known in far away Chicago as we can see from this reply to one of her letters:

Chicago Civic Opera Co.
June 15th 1929

Dear Miss Turner,
Many thanks for your letter of the 28th and the press clippings which followed – also heartiest congratulations on your success

as Turandot in London. We have made good use of the clippings, incorporating them in the weekly music letter from Mr Johnson.

There doesn't seem to be much opportunity of my getting to Europe this summer. Mrs Clayton is still quite ill and I have a pair of youngsters to look after. They haven't been so lively the last day or two as both are in bed with measles. The nurse tells me that they are quite all right, however, and they will go to camp for the summer in another week.

We got your Copenhagen, Naples and Milan press notices and sent them out to the papers. I want to thank you for your co-operation as it enables us to keep your name before the public this summer – something of vital importance to yourself and to us.

Don't worry about my working too hard. I manage to get in a couple of rounds of golf each week which should be play enough for anybody.

With every good wish,
I am very sincerely yours
John Clayton,
Director of publicity.

Among the cuttings of which she was understandably proud was the Daily Telegraph Thursday May 30th, 1929:

'Eva Turner in "Turandot". A great Dramatic Soprano. Triumph at Covent Garden.

Great singers are appearing in fairly rapid succession at Covent Garden this season. Last night the central figure was Eva Turner who was making her rentrée in 'Turandot', Puccini's posthumous opera. Her success in the title role was one of the most striking events of the operatic season last summer; it was now repeated and emphasized, the English artist, being once more acclaimed by a full house as a prima donna of international rank. How that rank has been attained (and maintained) by one who had graduated from the Carl Rosa, the opera houses of Italy and America have excellent reason to know. Not to every dramatic soprano is the strange and repellent part of Turandot fitted, comparatively short, though it is. Miss Turner has emphatically made it her own. This sphinx like Princess of the Celestial Empire must be the embodiment of cruelty and arrogance from the moment she appears in the second act; she must be metallic in

Eva Turner as Turandot

The Daily Mail May 30th:
'A Wonderful Soprano
Again she astonished, astounded the listener. It was simply the most astonishing, simply astonishing singing I for one have ever heard. At the same time it could not but be remarked – our one criticism of Miss Turner's singing last night- that she has not the art to conceal altogether in her facial movements, the effort entailed.'

The Morning Post, May 30:
'Everything that need or can be written about Eva Turner's wonderful interpretation of the name part was written last year. Suffice to say that her splendid voice sails through the great difficulties of the music as surely, as brilliantly as easily as ever. There may be better Turandots, I have not heard them.'

propounding the fatal riddles, callous as to the penalty; and in the last act she must dissolve into womanliness before the heroic ardour and will of the Prince.

Glorious Singing

Miss Turner was more than equal to one of the severest tests in modern opera, even though the actual timbre of her voice is not of the dissolving kind. It may be that in the last scene of all she left too much to our imagination, for does not the Prince tell Turandot that her glory only begins with the charm of her first kiss and first tears? It was in the second act that she triumphed most gloriously even if she addressed the appealing "Figlio del cielo! Padre Augusto" to the audience, Italian fashion, rather than the Emperor on his throne. With Bellezza in command (and he had worked intimately with Puccini on this score) the performance had authority and verve. Merli, a little stiff as an actor, sang well always particularly towards the end. The living sympathetic part of the slave Liu was taken at short notice by Ina Suez, whose effortless acting and singing were good to the point of being distinguished.'

Mr Johnson the General Administrator of Chicago Civic Opera wrote to Eva during his visit to Milan:

June 19th 1929

Dear Miss Turner,
I received your note of 6th insts.

As Mr Ferone has informed you, we would like to have you prepare the role of Elisabeth in Tannhäuser in German. We have not yet completed our plans but expect to do so on the boat going home and if there are additional roles I will cable by July 5th. Just as soon as I return to Chicago I will talk over the tour situation with Mr Shaw and if possible will give you a decision regarding 1930/31 tour without delay. In any event we will of course give you definite word at the earliest possible moment. We are remaining in Milan until the afternoon of Monday 24th and will be pleased to see you if you care to come. Tel. 24196

With Best Wishes,
Yours sincerely,
Herbert M Johnson.

In July, 1929 she sang her first Isabeau in Mascagni's opera of that name at the Verona Arena, for which her fee was L4000 and where she was partnered by the legendary sensational top voiced, handsome tenor, Hipolito Lazaro. Of Isabeau at Verona she said:

'I sang a special Sunday night performance before the princesses of Italy who were in the royal box. I was greatly touched on returning to my hotel to find the lady-in-waiting waiting for me to convey lovely messages from Their Royal Highnesses. She remarked to me that they had spent much time in my country and knew and loved London very well.'

Verona July 23rd:

'The formation of the vocal performance was accomplished by the company with an exquisite artistic sense: from the protagonist to the last actor, the singers discharged themselves of their parts with distinction and perfection. What more ideal artist than Miss Turner could be imagined for the tremendous role of Isabeau? She has just the voice for an open air theatre: a voice of a clear, warm and penetrating tone, full of intensity, strong, resisting dominating and wonderfully trained. Her natural gifts can be put to the hardest of tests: they know no difficulty and enable her always to infuse a communicative and persuasive accent to the pure music. Mascagni could hardly obtain for these scenes a more precious collaborator. All that could be asked of the interpreter has been done by her with great intelligence and admirable spirit. The audience was not slow in perceiving the superior qualities of this singer. It was carried away by her most beautiful art and applauded her in the middle of the scenes, particularly in the first act and especially in the duet of the third act, and at the end of each act she was accorded the warmest ovations.

It was with infinite pleasure that the tenor Hipolito Lazaro the idol of Verona in the season of 21 at the famous reproduction of Piccolo Marat was listened to again. He fully lived up to his fine reputation and was a magnificent and efficacious Folco. The public after the applause of welcome that greeted his first appearance on the stage always followed the artist closely with the most affectionate interest and could not have been more satisfied. The "Falcon song" full of difficulties in intonation, the phrase prolonged for some time in the upper register as well as an abundance of high notes, was perfectly rendered and enthusiastically applauded. He intensified his success by the rendering of the duet in the third act so rich in passion and inspiration: this was sung with wonderful ability and sureness, together with Miss Turner and here, particularly, he seemed to have given full scope to his sublime artistic and vocal gifts, and to have shown us clearly the perfect maturity of his exceptional theatrical temperament.'

The Bass was Baccaloni, the conductor Armani.

Dame Eva recalled:

'I had to wear a body stocking to give the illusion of being nude, as the story of "Isabeau" is that of "Lady Godiva" who rode naked on horseback. I wore a long wig which covered all the important parts but on the occasion of the first night I thought I would make a good picture at the end and so stood with my arms up at the back of the stage for about 10 seconds as the curtain dropped. The fascists came and asked me if I could get off the stage more quickly as with the lighting, the public could see more than I supposed, so I did at the next performance. (Laughter)'

Mascagni did not witness any of this run of eight performances. He was however, so impressed by word of mouth stories about how marvellous her singing had been that he gave Eva a contract for the Reale of Rome, where she would appear, under his baton in the same opera, during the following season.

In the early weeks of September, 1929 Eva had to cancel performances of *Aida* in Vicenza because of a heavy cold but was well again in October when she sang *La Forza del Destino* in Genoa before once again setting sail across the Atlantic Ocean, this time on the liner *Roma*, to sing in a second season with Chicago Civic Opera from November, 1929 to February, 1930. She sang Sieglinde in *Die Walküre*, with Frida Leider as Brünnhilde and Kipnis as Wotan, and Elisabeth in *Tannhäuser* with Leider as Venus.

Chicago Daily Tribune on November 29th reported of *Die Walküre*:

'Given in Full and Finely Too. The Civic Opera house is making a great effort to popularize Wagner and Wagner at full length. If the quality of performance has anything to do with it the effort will be successful. These two acts came near to an all star performance. If one feels like awarding special honors to Mme Leider and Mr Kipnis there comes the immediate thought that Miss Turner was a Sieglinde such as has not been heard since the days of Emma Eames sang the part. And if Mr Strack's singing of the "Spring Song" was *not quite of ideally lovely tone, his dialogue with Miss Leider was so fine and dignified that it sticks in the memory.'*

The Chicago Herald and the Evening America report:

'Eva Turner gives colourful portrayal of Elisabeth. Eva Turner sang the music of the innocent Elisabeth with tone of crystalline purity and unfailing beauty. Mme Leider was a queenly Venus, a Goddess of song who gave no very decided point to her pagan court.'

New Year's Day 1930 was celebrated by Eva and Plum in America but as we see in the piece below, she had not forgotten her friends back home.

Hull Evening News, January 22nd:

'I have received a post card this morning from Miss Eva Turner, the world renowned opera singer and who is so popular with Hull audiences. She is at present time singing at the opera house Chicago and the post card depicts this building – staggering in its size as American buildings are, yet unique in conception. Miss Turner says it is wonderfully equipped and that the acoustics are perfect. The next engagement Miss Turner has is in Italy. She then proceeds to Germany and later comes on to England to sing at Covent Garden. Best Wishes for 1930 are heartily reciprocated.'

In the following letter, sent to her c/o Chicago Civic Opera, we see her generous desire to share with her relatives and let them have a little taste of the good life. Friends were always happy to put themselves out to help Eva. We also see her impatience that actions should be quicker than lightening since her telegram arrived sooner than the recipient.

Dear Miss Turner,

I got your telegram, although it arrived just before I got back, and I have arranged everything just as you wish. The box has been sent on to Mrs Bottoms at Wembley and everything seems to be in perfect order: I want to say that I did not have any trouble with it.

I am enclosing herewith your copy of the contract, and I sincerely hope that it is going to bring you plenty of good luck and returns.

Also I want to thank you very much again for the great kindness which you showed me in Milan, and I can assure you that it was very much appreciated.

Kindest regards,
Yours very sincerely,
Manager Continental department

The female stars of *Die Walküre* from the Chicago Opera arrive in Boston and lament:

'Polish, English and German Wagnerian singers wail of hardship as vanguard arrives in Boston. Madame Olszewska has got twenty pounds lighter pining away for her husband in Vienna. Attractive Eva Turner the English Prima Donna complained that she never had time to find a husband and Frida Leider star of the Berlin Stats Opera wailed that all her life consisted of was singing, eating and going to bed.

Even when I rest I can never enjoy myself explained Miss Turner. I have a very hard time because I am English. The world does not think that an English woman has enough temperament for an opera singer. I went to La Scala and Toscanini could not believe I was English. He was very wonderful to me and I worked so hard to prove my merit. Not until I had sung for some years in Italy did I sing at Covent Garden in London.'

'Envies American Women

The English audience, my own people greeted me with frozen silence. Not until I began singing did they applaud. They gave me fourteen curtain calls and Mr Pollak of the Chicago Civic Opera was in the audience and so they engaged me for America. I came a year ago and I have time for nothing but work and sleep. American women, she continued, have a beautiful life. Their husbands think they are perfect and they never do housework just enjoy themselves. I envy them and I think we singers sacrifice too much for our art. Perhaps art is not everything. Ours is a lonely existence when we are not singing.'

Eva Turner did not sing any of the Italian repertoire during her second season in Chicago as both Raisa and Muzio were back in their powerful places and on February 15th Eva and Plum travelled, first class as always, on *S.S. Minnewaska* from New York to Italy where she was to sing, during March, four performances of *Isabeau* in Rome, with Mascagni conducting.

This hand written letter sent from Charles Moor on March 18th 1930 would have reached Eva probably a little less than a week later. It has Royal Opera House Covent Garden headings and he uses the paper, despite having typed, in a small corner,

'Dear Colonel Blois I am having the divils job with this machine. The ribbon wont go round the right out'

My dear Eva & Plum,

Many thanks for diverse letter duly received. I am sorry I have put a spoke in your wheels as regards Germany, but Covent Garden is more important at the moment & Germany can wait. What are you doing in Frankfurt and when? Who is working for you in Germany?

As I expected Chicago did not renew my contract, which was, I think, a very good thing for me. Not a word of thanks for the years of slavery.

As regards "the house that Eva built" tell Bollen he must finish it in 3 months. If the flat in Milan is expensive, I should not keep it. You can quite well bring the furniture along to Bruzino where Moors will store it or get it stored at a very small cost until you require it. Then you can have your rest there, contemplating the house and overseeing Bollen. The kitchen sink is a small matter, but the water problem should be solved beforehand. I leave here at the end of this week going to Baden-Baden then to (? can't read) and getting back at the beginning of April. Let me know your movements.

Love to you both,
Yours aye,
Charles Moor

Letter sent to Covent Garden from the Hotel Continental in Rome

20th March 1930

Dear Colonel Blois,

After much correspondence to clear the way for the acceptance of your offer of "Sieglinde" on May 15th I think it is very probable that I shall be able to be with you.

However we shall leave it that way & if I hear anything to the contrary within a day or two, will wire you in accordance so that you will not be unduly put about. I should have got to know earlier than this but you understand the difficulties in hastening up correspondence.

Mascagni is nearly killing us with his rehearsals for 'Isabeau'. Already he has knocked out one Tenor. But so far he has not beaten me. His persistence in making me hang on to my top notes after approaching them with broad ritenutos is most inconsiderate. But what cares he so long as he can get his opera cheered by Mussolini. He visited the Pope the other day and had a great time. Was some pleased with himself.

Weather is lovely here but not many visitors so far.

Expect to be here till the 30th. Then go to Florence to do 'Fidelio' for a month & on May 1st sing Turandot *following the Aida etc.*

Trust all is going well with you & your projects & that your success will never be dimmed
Yours sincerely with fondest love to Mrs Blois.
Eva Turner

March 25th, 1930:

'"Isabeau" by Mascagni at the Teatro Reale Rome. Isabeau has found in Eva Turner a true, intelligent and passionate interpreter. Her strong voice, vigorous and vibrant, dealt victoriously with the high and difficult tessitura with complete dedication and assuredness... The tenor Carmelo Albiso, with his powerful unfading singing, has immense drive, ascending with an effortlessness and naturalness into his higher register and creates the ardent core of the primitive heroic Folco with great effectiveness... The soprano Eva Turner endeared herself to the hearts of her audience from the very first notes and during the opera she was accorded repeated ovations. Particularly enthusiastic was the applause granted to the duet of the last act for which an encore was demanded in vain.'

Eva said that Mascagni was a great party man and after these performances he would entertain the cast with wonderful food and conversation.

'One was expected to stay well into the small hours of the night chatting, eating and drinking and it would have been considered rude to leave early, although my thoughts were on being well rested and in good voice for my next performance.'

Between April 10th and 27th she sang five performances of *Fidelio* in Florence, conducted by Gui, where she opened the season and had another great success with this role. (L4000). After that run of performances, she went on to sing other favourite roles around the northern Italian Opera Houses having engaged an agent to find her good work and help her build her European career and just before coming to London for the 1930 season, she had yet another success with *Fidelio* in Frankfurt.

Eva made herself free to sing Sieglinde on May 15th 1930 in the second *Ring* cycle at Covent Garden, replacing Lotte Lehmann who had sung the role in the first cycle. The Times on May 16th reported:

'Mme Leider repeated her fine performance of Brünnhilde. Sieglinde and Fricka were taken by singers new to the parts. Miss Eva Turner has of course sung Sieglinde's music before but her reappearances at Covent Garden in the last year or two have been

At Covent Garden, singers for the first year of the new decade, 1930, included: Odette de Foras, Lotte Lehmann, Frida Leider, Rosa Ponselle, Elisabeth Schumann and Eva Turner and the conductors were: Bruno Walter and Robert Heger for the German repertoire and John Barbirolli and Vincenzo Bellezza for the Italian operas.

in Italian opera. She uses her magnificent voice with intelligence and has enough savoir faire of the stage to bring any role to life, but the quality of her voice is not really suited to the tender and unfortunate Sieglinde. Its brilliant quality of tone was magnificent in the scene with the Valkyrie maidens at the beginning of the third act and she had previously modified it into something much more feminine in the scene in Hunding's hut, but its essential quality is out of keeping with the character. The orchestra under Herr Heger has now settled down and played with accuracy, flexibility and responsiveness so that in sum the performances reached a high standard.'

The Telegraph on May 29th:

'A packed house witnessed the revival of "Aida" at Covent Garden last night. No opera of the Italian repertoire, certainly none of the earlier Verdi operas, grips a modern audience better than this spectacular work of the seventies – when it is reasonably well done... Verdi concentrated so much of the drama of this opera in the role of the Ethiopian slave, on her actual lips, that a mediocre performance of that part always endangers the whole... No such danger was run last night with Eva Turner to bring her superb voice, her intelligence and experience into play. From beginning to end she was mistress of every situation. No climax found her voice swamped by an exuberant orchestra and her singing of "Ritorna Vincitor" especially, was all but matchless.'

Her other role at Covent Garden in the 1930 season for the Grand Opera Syndicate managed by Colonel Blois, was Aida which she sang on the 28th of May and on June 2nd and 12th and finally on July 1st. The cast was: Eva Turner (Aida), Minghini Cattaneo (Amneris), Merli (Radames), John Brownlee (Amonasro) and Pinza (the King). Barbirolli conducted as Bellezza was indisposed. Her fee for each of these performances was held at £100 less commission to her agent of £6, plus travelling expenses for 2 people.

As with her Turandot, the press rose to her over the next couple of days and she was once again given press coverage to make her ideas known:

Glasgow News, July 14th:

'To become a prima donna you must go to Italy by Eva Turner. The world famous opera singer.

Now had I been asked this question a few years ago I would have said "Sing sing and sing on until you convince operatic audiences that your voice has the qualities essential to merit the trust and confidence of the great Maestros of Italy and Germany. Such is the simplicity of the tyro."

How many and how endless were the days of practise, days of trial, days of disappointment and apparent futile endeavour before I found myself feted as a star in Milan, Vienna, Paris, Chicago and London. Do not mistake me I am not boasting. But since this

The Monthly Musical Record: 'A fair number of British singers were heard, (during the Covent Garden Season) the best of them, Eva Turner, who sang Aida with startling brilliancy and also more sensibility than formerly: a brave astonishing little person.'

is meant to be a candid narrative – confession if you please – of a Lancashire lass who long ago set out to win a place among the leading singers of Europe and America and the Prima Donnas of Italy and Germany, I need not disguise pride. For the plain truth is that I am proud of my position as an operatic singer – proud that I have won the approval of my countrymen in Covent Garden and still more proud that in a unique manner I have won the sympathy and respect of Italian and German audiences to whom the idea of an English singer is still alien.

Insularity

It is that pride that makes me sad when I meet girls and boys beginning life inspired by ambitions similar to those that inspired me in my early Carl Rosa days, when I toured England from Land's End to John O'Groats. I meet them in Milan, the Mecca of operatic singers. Sometimes I could cry when they tell me their stories.

Understand, the operatic community is unlike other artistic communities – we are in every sense a community of artists. Yet there is insularity. It is this very insularity that makes it so tremendously difficult for inexperienced English aspirants. Often I meet countrywomen of mine, bitter, disillusioned, and slowly becoming estranged from their original ideas. They have arrived in Milan eagerly ambitious. Many of them have genuinely pleasing voices, clearly organs that have the promise of being cultivated.'

Dame Eva tells us many years later:

'I returned, after this season at Covent Garden to Italy to rest and then to embark on the voyage to Venezuela where I was the prima donna of a company specially engaged by General Gomez for a festival to commemorate the memory of Simon Bolivar the liberator of the South American States.'

In Caracas she sang in *Turandot*, *Aida* and *Lohengrin* from the end of November until the middle of December. The date nearest to the centenary of Bolivar's death, December 15th was commemorated by a special performance of *Lohengrin*. Eva Turner was very proud to have been part of this enormous celebration for such a great man, who had fought so long and hard for independence. It has to be said however that she was at heart a Royalist through and through.

Bolivar, who died on December 17th, 1830, together with José de San Martin, had played a key role in Latin America's successful struggle for independence from Spain and following the triumph over the Spanish Monarchy, Bolívar participated in the foundation of Gran Colombia, a nation formed from several former Spanish colonies. He was President of Gran Colombia from 1821 to 1830 and is credited with contributing decisively to the independence of the present-day countries of Venezuela, Colombia, Ecuador, Panama, Peru, and Bolivia and is revered as a national hero by the people of those countries.

Together with the excitement of travelling to such distant lands, one sometimes thinks of the loneliness of leaving friends behind. Communication, as we know it, did not exist and speaking on the telephone was prohibitively expensive. Eva, however, seemed quite content to leave each part of her professional life behind to embark on the next, where she met a new set of colleagues as she forged her career path. She did however, throughout her life, have an enormously thick address book and diligently kept in touch by letter. Plum travelled with her, giving support and company and she never mentioned being homesick but it is nevertheless delightful to see a name common to both the *Isabeau* in Rome and this tour in Caracas. Afro Poli (who later became a leading baritone at La Scala) sang the small parts of: Il Cavalier Faidit in *Isabeau* and the Herald in *Lohengrin*.

On January 7th, 1931 Eva and Plum left Colón for Le Havre on the *Guadeloupe*, a small ship carrying only 203 passengers, and Eva was once again seasick. From Le Havre they returned to Italy, where there were many opera houses of artistic repute in the central belt and the north, and where it was that Eva Turner's career was centred during the thirties, giving her easy access to her new home at Brusino on the Lake of Lugano.

Lionel Powell is still trying to get Eva to commit some time to working with an orchestra in Britain, however, and has halved the time he requested in his last letter from a month to a fortnight, in the hope that she will agree.

February 13th 1931

Dear 'little lady',

Many thanks for your letter, and I too have been thinking about you a great deal. Now, would it be possible for you to give me say a fortnight for England – either in February or March 1932?

Very sincerely yours,
Lionel Powell.

COMUNE DI PERUGIA
TEATRO MORLACCHI

Sabato 30 Maggio 1931 - IX - Ore 21

PENULTIMA RAPPRESENTAZIONE DELL'OPERA

TURANDOT

Dramma lirico in 3 atti e 5 quadri di G. ADAMI e R. SIMONI
Musica di GIACOMO PUCCINI — (Proprietà di G. Ricordi & C.)

SERATA IN ONORE
della celebre Artista **EVA TURNER**

che canterà la Romanza:

"O CIELI AZZURRI"
dell'Opera "AIDA" di G. Verdi

ESECUTORI

La principessa Turandot	Eva Turner	Pang, Gran Provveditore	Giuseppe Giusti
L'Imperatore Altoum	Millo Marucci	Pong, Gran Cuciniere	Giuseppe Marchesi
Timur, Re Tartaro	Duilio Baronti	Un Mandarino	Vincenzo Cassia
Il Principe Ignoto	Franco Battaglia	Il Principe di Persia	Ines De Vincenzi
Liù, Giovine schiava	Lina Brunazzi	Il Carnefice	N. N.
Ping, Gran Cancelliere	Emilio Ghirardini		

Le Guardie Imperiali — I Servi del Boia — I Ragazzi — Sacerdoti — I Mandarini — I Dignitari — Gli otto sapienti
Le ancelle di Turandot — I Soldati — I Portabandiera — I Musici — Le ombre dei morti — La Folla
A PECHINO NEL TEMPO DELLE FAVOLE

MAESTRO CONCERTATORE E DIRETTORE D'ORCHESTRA Cav. Uff. **ALDO ZEETTI**

GRANDIOSA MESSA IN SCENA
250 ESECUTORI

PREZZI (oltre la Tassa erariale del 10%)

Ingresso Platea e Palchi L. 8
Poltrone L. 15 - Poltroncine L. 10 - Distinti L. 8
Palchi di I e II ord. L. 60 - III ord. L. 30 - IV ord. L. 15
Loggione L. 4

But Eva persists on her operatic road and we find her back at the San Carlo in Naples at the end of March singing Aida and then travelling on to Frankfurt, a city where she often enjoyed success. This time, in April 1931, the Frankfurter Zeitung tells us:

> 'The soprano Eva Turner from the Metropolitan New York, renewed, with her Aida, the impressions of her last year's guest performance. She uses her metallic, cool and splendid voice, coming from the best belcanto school, with a sure government in all registers. Despite all her vocal art, her acting is a little impersonal and there is a separation of language as the artist sang in Italian. However, this beautiful soprano is full and flexible and made a wonderful effect in the role.'

On May 30th 1931 in Perugia, Eva Turner was given a special celebrity evening, where she would sing Turandot conducted by Aldo Zeetti. Her Principe Ignoto, (Calaf) was Franco Battaglia and her Liu, Lina Brunazzi and Eva would also sing the *Nile Scene* from *Aida*.

There was, at the end of 1931, a disagreement between Eva and her father, Charles, about his domestic arrangements and in particular about his perceived treatment of his housekeeper in Ashton-in-Makerfield. I imagine Eva, who was now devoted to her life just over the border from Italy, in her Swiss villa which she considered her permanent address, was worrying about her father as he was not in the best of health and was, it would appear, becoming a little cantankerous and demanding. Eva Turner, a well travelled woman of forty, was a family person at heart but since she had no husband or family of her own, perhaps her boundaries with her father, who had given her so much help in her early life, were not clear to either of them and so feelings of abandonment and guilt arose between them. Operatic archetypal feelings of this sort would, one might think, be the everyday fare of an opera singer but when it comes to the reality of one's own life, not so easy perhaps.

The housekeeper wrote to Eva and she, having only one side of the story, wrote to her father who then sent a private letter, parts of which I am going to include, despite some guilt pangs of my own, because Eva wrote at the top of the letter that Norman, her brother, should destroy it after reading. He never did and I include it despite her request, because it gives us a flavour of Eva's relationship with the father, who had been so fundamental in helping her achieving her dream of being a great singer. In reading it we can perhaps catch a small glimpse of Eva Turner's private life which she seldom shared.

'My Dear Daughter,

Yours to hand (from Junesca), this a.m. So it has taken 5 days to come here, I have waited for it as I thought you might be in Constantinople, and since your last saying this possibility, I have also heard you were in Germany. Anyway I am glad to have your letter (of course) from anywhere, for certainly I feel a lot lonely nowadays, despite the fact of a sister being here.

Now Eva I want you to take notice of the remarks re Annie I am mentioning, and I also want you to know it is not piffle and silliness on my part. I have not mentioned it before because I have deemed it unworthy the time to explain, but as you always (in all your references) seem to think I have acted unkindly, I am speaking the truth and facts for once and finally.'

He then states his case for having been wronged by Annie, who seems to have been sacked in an underhand manner, and includes his brother John who witnessed her neglect of him and goes on to say:

'Now you know it all and you can digest it as you like Eva, if you give others the more credit than me, it is your business.

I hope you are quite well Eva and that all goes well with you of course. Your true interest is all I want and has always been so from birth. Of course it applies to my son as well.

Your loving father,
Charles Turner.

Love to Plum of course.'

CHAPTER 5

1933-1939 Day to Day Life and Performances

In 1933 Albert Richards Broad, (Plum) then aged sixty seven, was still guiding Eva. He gave her a daily singing lesson and travelled with her everywhere, tending to her daily needs. He did all their shopping, even for her personal needs such as stockings and underwear, paid the bills, attended to banking business, arranged her diary and generally organised her life so that she was free to get on with her performances. He was only a couple of months younger than Eva's father and it seems that their relationship included something of the parental authority with which Eva had grown up.

Plum kept meticulous page-a-day diaries recording their lives and daily expenses, writing in small, scripted handwriting, which although beautiful on the page and very neat, was actually rather hard, though not impossible, to read. The happenings of the day are at the top of the page and underneath, relevant expenses with a number code at the side, according to the type of expenditure. Every penny was accounted for.

Four of these diaries survive and exact details from a few early days in the first diary of the year 1933 are included here. Selected entries from the remaining diaries are incorporated, not only for the information itself but because this record keeping gives us a flavour of Plum and Eva's life together. It was, I think, a shared project, so perhaps Eva dictated parts and checked it as, although Plum was the boss in many ways, Eva was the main earner and her money paid the bills. She would have wanted to see where her money was spent, as she had not for one moment forgotten the frugality with which she was brought up and relied on those old habits as a structure for her daily life. I am very thankful that it is Plum's writing and so I can now let the diaries tell the story of Eva's life at this point. Plum refers to himself as A. R. B. (* denotes a performance.)

1933

January

2nd London
Charles came. 11-30 a.m. went to see Holt. Arranged tickets for Norman (Eva's brother) for Glasgow and planned date for extra concert at Queen's Hall for 15th inst. Heard of Press Dinner to E.

Book	3/-
Buses 3p, 3p, 9p.	1/3
Lunch 2/2 Tip 3	2/5
Tea 2/5 Tip 3	2/8
2 Songs @1/9	3/6

*3rd London
Holt came to concert and was very pleased.
(Harold Holt the Concert Agent)
Glad and Heddy came for night meal

5th London

Light1/- Gas1/- Tel. 8p.	2/8
Butter 8p Fish 9p	1/5
Torch and Glasses	12/-
Paper acc. up to Sat 7th Jan.	2/6

6th London

Chicory 3p Lemon 6p Chops 9p	1/6
Biscuits 4½p 4½p 3½p Envelopes 5p	1/6
Bus 8p Soda 1½p Soap 3p	1/1½
Butter 11p Lettuce 4p Beet 1½p	
Grapes 4p Currants 2p	1/10½
Buses 6p1p 6p	1/1
E 1/- Tea 1/9 Tip 6	3/3
ARB Shirt 10/6 Tie 1/6	12/-
Eva Hose 8/- Gloves 16/9	£1-4/9
B. I. K. Velvet Costume Trim with white satin at Harvey Nicholls with Allortiano and Hat	£19-0-0
ARB paid by cheque this dress acc £19	

*15th London
E Sang at Queen's Hall with Philharmonic Orchestra. Landon Ronald conducting at 3pm Thrilling success

Received on acc from Mr Holt	£20
Gas 1/-	1/-
Bus 1/- Taxis 3/6 4/- 4/6 Porter 6p 1/-	14/6
Left Euston 12.35 midnight.	
Fares to Dundee: Two 1st class returns	£12-14- 6

	Two 1st class sleepers	£2
	Dad Allowance	£3-0-0
*16th	Arrive Glasgow Central Hotel.	
	Rooms 321 and 322	12/6
	E. for doing hair etc.	£1
	1st Concert on tour at St Andrew's Hall proved great success.	
17th	Left Glasgow 11 arr. Edinburgh 12.30	
	Caledonian Hotel	10/- each
	Glasgow Hotel acc.	
	Two rooms at 12/6,	
	5 afternoon teas 7/6, 2 suppers 6/-	
	Telephone 1/6 Ironing dress 3/6	
	Tea for morning 1/6.	£4-1-6
*18th	Usher Hall Concert.	
	Had special supper with the	
	Inchs' family at Caledonian Hotel.	
19th	Left Edinburgh 4.25 arr. Dundee. Royal British Hotel.	
*20th	Caird Hall nice.	
21st	Left Dundee 8.20 arr. Euston 7pm.	
*22nd	Concert at Queen's Hall at 3 with Philharmonic Orchestra. Geoffrey Toye conducting, Sang Liebestod and Ocean. Great Success	
	Tube 8p	
	Tip Hall 2/- Taxi from Sterlings 5/-	7/-
	Harold Holt drove us home from the rehearsals and called at 2.30 to take us to Concert. – After the Forses drove us to their home for tea and then drove us to the Sterlings for Dinner – Left there at 12.30 midnight.	
23rd	Left London 2.20 arr. Birmingham 4.25	
	Received from Harold Holt for 5 performances in Scotland.	£262-10-0
*24th	Birmingham Town Hall	
	'Poor affair' 'Artistic Success'	
	Queen's Hotel Room 321 and 323 at Station	11/6 each
25th	Left Birmingham for London	
	Sent Betty cheque for the £3 we borrowed	
	Eva for Dad	£4-0-0
27th	Left London 12.25 arr. Manchester 4.35	
	Hotel	12/-

	ARB got flu en route.	
	Train tickets	£2-00
*28th	Free Trade Hall Bad House	
29th	Left Manchester 10.15 arr. Sheffield 1.45	
	Royal Victoria Station Hotel	8/-
	Food-good salads but fish very dear	2/6
	Carl Rosa Opera travelled on the same train	
*30th	Concert tonight in New City Hall	
	Lovely place Poor House	
31st	Left Sheffield at 2 on train (dirty) that had to be specially run owing to break down of night train in Loughborough. Changed York arr. Newcastle 5.30.	

(Always notes tips, food, papers, porters and Eva's expenses.)

February

*1st	Newcastle City Hall	
	nice Hall	
*2nd	Left Newcastle 2.17 arr. Middlesboro 3.48.	
	Splendid Old Hall like a church.	
3rd	Left Middlesboro at 10.45 changed at Darlington arr. London 4.15.	
4th	Went to Huberman's	
	took Nance to Queen's Hall.	
5th	E, Dad, John and 2 Miers went to Philharmonic Concert to hear Beecham	
6th	Irish sweep z;J.57652 10/- as Evaplum. E sent China F50 (China is house keeper at Villa Junesca.)	
*14th	Left London 2.25 arr. Leicester 4.14	
	Concert at De Montfort great success	
16th	Left Leicester 10.14 arr. Birmingham 11.16	
	Left Birmingham at 5.50 arr. Liverpool 8.25	
	Left Liverpool at 10pm aboard the *SS Connaught* for Dublin arr. 6.30a.m.	
*18th	Concert at Theatre Royal Dublin	
19th	Special Bus Left Dublin10.10 arr. Belfast 2.30. 104miles.	
*20th	Belfast Concert at Ulster Hall.	
21st	Left Belfast on Splendid boat	
22nd	Arr. Liverpool 6.30 a.m. Southport 10.	
23rd	Southport 42 Walnut St. (Uncle John's)	
	Left at 3.45 arr. Liverpool 4.33.	
*24th	Liverpool Blizzard and Gale. Terrible	

25th	Liverpool 2.10 arr. Wigan 3.10. Then bus to Cousin Jane and Ted. Terrible day. Sleet Blizzards.
26th	Standish. Cousin Jane and Ted's. Terrible weather remained inside all day by fire and enjoyed it.
27th	Left Standish in Ted's car 9.30 called to see Jane's father – Very ill. Left there at 9.40 got to Wigan 9.50 – flew – got bags from cloak room and caught tram at 10.00 for Manchester.
*28th	Manchester and Oldham Grand Orchestral Concert at 7-30 Empire Theatre packed 2,800 Tremendous Success – Artistically, Appreciatively and Financially. Grand Reception Supper after.

March

1st	Left Manchester 12.20 arr. London 4.17
10th	Eva's Birthday. Had lunch at Nance's and Albert's and Bill
*12th	London Concert at 3 at Queen's Hall with Albert Coates conducting Sir Thomas took ill. Duets with Walter: *Götterdämmerung* and *Les Troyens*
15th	Left London 10 a.m. 3rd class.
16th	Lugano 12.33 noon. Left Lugano for Brusino (Villa Junesca.)18.10 E lost spectacles and comb
19th	Brusino. Dad enclosed in letter to him £1
22nd	Brusino. Received from Holt cheque £40 today for Queen's Hall appearance with Philharmonic Orchestra on Sunday March 12th 3pm Holt says this fee was arranged but such was not the case.
27th	Left for Milan by 12.10 train arr. 1.36.
29th	E went to Torino to see Borioli. Left at 6 am returned 6.10pm

April

6th	Lesson with Caluzio
7th	Lesson with Caluzio 100 francs.
10th	Attends to letters:

10/4/33
'Permanent Address'
Junesca,
Bruniso-Arsizio, Ticino,
Svizzera

Dear Mr Taylor,

I had hoped to write you 'ere now to thank you for your card but I have been so busy it was not possible. I returned here a few days ago from Italy and I take this opportunity during the respite of trying to cope with this mass of correspondence before I return to sing in Italy. Circumstances in Liverpool allowed of my complying with your request by singing Wagner's 'Dich Teure Halle - Tannhäuser'. I was truly sorry that I could not do 'Elsa's Dream' owing to having left the music behind.

Indeed it was only by chance I happened to have the 'Tannhäuser'.

By no means could I think your request impertinent, on the contrary, I am happy to try and comply with what people desire, and want to hear.

The weather here is very different to that I experienced in Liverpool / beautiful sunshine. Here we are on the lake of Lugano and it is very beautiful.

All best wishes,
Sincerely, Eva Turner

I return to England soon to sing Aida

13th   Left Milan 3.15 arr. Brusino 5.20.
China and ARB. E came by next train owing to seeing Ferone and with no satisfaction re Arena date bookings.

14th   E and ARB went to Lugano to meet Uncle Arthur and Addie.
Arrived late at 1pm. Uncle Arthur brought us:
Garden Chairs 3/6, Garden Table 3/6, 2 rugs 17/-
Marmite 4/6, Horlocks(sic) 3/6, Butter Beans.
Whilst with us he loaned us £2 on two occasions.
Then we ordered 3 tables and 3 chairs for London. For these we gave him a cheque for £6-10/- Plum added later that up to 1/3/35 the cheque had not been cashed.

17th   Sent Dad 10/-note

May

11th   Left for London with Frau Mooser at 7. Arr. Mendrisio 7.30.

> Permanent Address
> 10.4.33.
>
> Dear Mr Taylor,
> I had hoped to write you ere now to thank you for your card but I have been so busy it was not possible. I returned here a few days ago from Italy and I take this opportunity during this respite of trying to cope with this mess of correspondence before I return to sing in Italy. Circumstances in Liverpool allowed of my complying with your request by singing ...

Left at 8.41 arr. Lugano 9.40. Lucerne arr. 12.56. Basle arr. 14.35.
Left 15.15. Arr. Paris (est) 9.55. Had return tickets.
Took own food had good journey From St Gothards.
Then 12 left Paris St Lazare 10.36 Arr. Dieppe 13.9.
Left Dieppe 13.30 Arr. Newhaven 16.40
Left Newhaven 17.10 Arr. Victoria 18.43
Dada's Allowance £3-0-0

13th   Dada's Birthday.
Uncle John arrived. Norman and Florence (Norman's wife who had been a chorister with the Royal Carl Rosa

Opera and sang the coloratura repertoire) came to night Banquet.
Trousers for Dad's present £18.

Norman and Florence Turner

15th   Aida Covent Garden Syndicate Contract in Italian £50 per performance.
18th   Went to *Parsifal*.
       Wreath for Col Blois £15.

*22nd	1st Aida tonight E sang well but lacks magnetism in first act.
*25th	2nd Aida. Betty and Donald came down to hear it. All had supper at 396 City Road got home at 3.30 a.m.
26th	Gave Luncheon Party to Betty, Donald, Gladys and Heddy. Arrival of Uncle Arthur and Addie from Brusino. Great dinner party Arthur, Adelaide, Selina, Florence, Dada, Uncle John, Eva and me.
29th	Went to Columbia at Clerkenwell to see Mr Langley re making record. Then lunch at Overseas Club with Selina. 8-30p.m. went to *Tosca*. Raisa, Formichi Minghetti.
June	
2nd	Baroness gave an at Home to Giannini at which she sang to 200 people. *Othello* tonight. Good show with Melchior, Pampanini and Rimini.
5th	Went to Gladys to see the printing idea for Theatrical Costumes.
7th	Last Aida the best. Tips at Covent Garden to Milly wigs 10/-, Harold 5/-, Jackson 10/-, Donation Stage £1, Lift man 2/6.
9th	Made records of *Tannhäuser* and *Lohengrin* this a.m. Charles Webber 4 lessons £1. (He was the pianist who had played for the Earl Haig Concert 1921, in which Eva and Gladys sang and Princess Iwa wore her national dress. Presumably he worked with the Carl Rosa Opera as a repetiteur and Eva was now working with him privately. When a singer finds a coach with whom he or she is comfortable, it can be a lifelong relationship.)
*16th	Recording
*17th	Recording
21st	E went to *Ballo* at 4. E bought a ticket to see Gladys Cooper E had to go with Baroness so I went with Betty. Rotten!
23rd	Bought Russell Road W14.
26th	Left London 10 a.m. Arr. Newhaven 11.26. Left 11.45 Arr. Dieppe 14.55 Left 15.24. Arr. Paris 17.58 Gave Ada 1/-/- for bed and 10/- for food. (Ada, Plum's sister)

The Times tells us of her Aida: 'Miss Eva Turner was the only one of the singers who seemed to have grasped the more subtle qualities of Verdi's magical cantilena. All the rest relied on the big dramatic climaxes for effect and indeed it was only by the most strenuous exertions that they could make themselves heard above the orchestra in many of these too frequent climaxes. Miss Turner gave us some beautiful singing in the scene by the Nile... Mme Giani was inclined to scoop to the high notes and wobble down from them... Signor Battaglia is a robust tenor but rarely anything else... Sir Thomas Beecham makes his orchestra play but he does not necessarily make them accompany.'

27th   Left Paris 7.50. Arr. Basle 14.15. Left 14.43. Arr. Lugano 20.26 Arr. Mendrisio 20.43. China absent for three days.

30th   China came at 8 pm and received her dismissal.
E went to Milan 8.50 am and returned at 5.30pm.
Did not see Ferone or Fabroni

July

3rd   E went to Milan saw Fabroni

8th   Ida the new girl commenced today

9th   £2 sent to Dad for expenses he has incurred; fanlight etc.

18th   left Brusino 7.37

19th   Arr. Victoria 18.40

21st   Prize presentations by Eva

28th   Lesson Charles Webber 5/-

29th   left London 10.40 for Isle of Man. Arr. Douglas 7pm. Choppy Sea Packed boat

*30th Concert tonight at Palace ¾ full appreciative audience. E Off.

31st   Left Douglas 9 am Terribly rough all the way S.W. gale Ship rolling at deck level all the way. Arr. Liverpool 1.00
Left 2.15.
Arr. Euston 6.5

August

1st   E for Dad £3-0-0

6th   Left London 10 a.m.

11th   Holt sent wire as follows;

Sir Thomas suggests opening Concert at Queen's Hall with 'Des Adieux Jeanne D'Arc' Tchaikovsky. Please confirm as am starting advertising. Regards Holt.

Replied some days later
'Have tried aria fear tessitura is against my doing justice to aria or myself'

14th   E went to Verona

15th   E at Verona

16th   E returns from Verona at 1pm

20th   Jonathan, Selina, Wilfred, Dorothy and Florence Arr. at Lugano 14.38. Both met them.

September

18th   London

19th	Dad left by Charabanc for Woodley Lancashire.
20th	Letter from Dad saying that he has decided to stay away from London for all time
23rd	Lesson Charles at 10.30
24th	Dad sent letter definitely refusing to return to London.
27th	Lesson
28th	No Lesson Seeking Concert Dress Commencing

October.

*5t	Left London 12.15. Arr. Sheffield 4. City Hall opening concert of tour. Fine success in dress and voice. (17 Celebrity Concerts £30 each /£510. Beecham and the L.P.O.)
*6th	Dundee 2nd Concert
*7th	Edinburgh 3rd Concert
*8th	Aberdeen 4th Concert
*9th	Aberdeen. Rotten cold, wet, windy day. Remained in Hotel all day doctoring cold of Eva's. She got through splendidly at night. Concert great success and Hall packed.
*10th	Perth New City Hall 5th Concert
*11th	Glasgow Cold getting worse. St Andrew's Hall 6th Concert great success. Full Hall. Eva just got through creditably. Audience got no sign of cold condition.
12th	Arr. London by sleeper. Eva's cold much worse.
15th	E went to see Frank Duncan at Nose and Throat Hosp at 2
20th	Went to Parr's @ 5
23rd	Went to Ball
26th	From 8am to 4 pm. Great day shifting Dad's belongings from 67 to 51
*28th	Left London 11.50 arr. Manchester 3.20 E for hair and nails 10/- ARB Braces 2/6 Hotel a/c for dressing Room 2/6 Room 482 Left Manchester in Sleepers to London midnight for Bournemouth
*29th	Arr. London 6am. Remained in sleepers till 8.

Then went to Lyons Marble Arch and had breakfast till 10. Then took train to Bournemouth 10.25 Arr. Bourne 1.07 Left 7.05 Arr. London 0.38. Slept at 67 after meal at 51

*30th London-Leicester

*31st Leicester – Middlesboro.

November

*1st Middlesboro – Newcastle.

*2nd Newcastle – Liverpool.

3rd Liverpool 11 pm by boat for Dublin... £150 for 5 concerts

*4th Dublin.

*5th Dublin – Belfast.

6th Left Belfast

*7th Arr. Liverpool – Birmingham.

*8th Birmingham – Nottingham.

9th Nottingham – London

10th Dad for November £3-0-0

15th £150 for 5 concerts

18th Charles Webber 5 Lessons £1-5-0

*19th Concert at Queen's Hall with Philharmonic Orchestra and Sir Thomas. Hall packed 350 turned away. E sang Elizabeth's (sic) Greeting and Liebestod.

26th Left London

28th Brusino A bit miserable and stove brought in.

December

9th E and P went to Milano to see Flats. Disappointing results. Flat we liked owner objects to singing. Sought others but without avail.

11th E and P went to Milano re. flat to see if the one desired is sound proof for singing. After tried flat for singing and found the voice penetrates the next apartment above so abandoned the idea of taking it.
Found another in Via Angera which we think suitable,

13th E and P went to Milano to see about fixing on flat at No1 Via Angera 600L from 29 Dec to March 29.

18th Went to live in Milan.
Got through customs splendidly.
We came to train at 1.25 arr. 2.55 arr. about 4 at Via Angera 1. Soon unloaded and gave them meals.
Then had ours and got to rest 11pm.

19th   Milan freezing.
       Lesson Bruni.

20th   Lesson with Bruni.

21st   Lesson with Bruni.

22nd   Lesson with Bruni.

23rd   Lesson with Bruni.

24th   Lesson with Bruni.

25th   Lesson with Bruni

26th   Left Milan 12.30 arr. Torino 15.15.

27th   Torino.
       Miserable weather. Had difficulty with a young fool in the Police re right of singing in Italy. Had to write to Rome.

28th   Received advance payment for 1st show.

29th   Very heavy snow.
       Took Butterfly and Brünnhilde gowns to be cleaned

30th   Heavy Snow

31st   Snow melting. Terrible underfoot.
       Shops open all day on account of closing tomorrow.
       3 Vermouths to see New Year in – No fuss. Came out of the Hotel at 11.30 and went to Theatre and then to Cafe. Then went to Hotel and had Panattone and Orvieto wine, which I disliked, till one a.m.

       (41 performances in all that year)

1934

Plum's diary guides us in 1934 but this time in a condensed form: Eva's singing year began on January 6th, with the first in a group of performances of *La Wally* by Catalani at Teatro Regio Turin with Ghione conducting (Afro Poli once again in the cast). Plum comments: 'E had a great success and outshone herself'.

She sang *La Wally* again on the 10th and 13th. On the 14th they sent a wire to Marinuzzi about the death of his son in Genoa. Eva Turner sang her fourth performance of *La Wally* on 17th and on the 18th she got flu and went to bed but still had to sing the performance on the 20th. After the show she went back to bed immediately but her flu turned to bronchitis. Despite this, she sang again on the 23rd and Plum said: 'Got through splendidly despite bronchitis and cold'. Eva once again went back to bed immediately after her performance as her bronchitis was worse after singing on it but by 28th she was much better and went to a rehearsal for her pending *Walküre*/Brünnhilde. A couple of days

TEATRO REGIO
(Società Anonima TEATRO REGIO)

SABATO 6 Gennaio 1934-XII, ore 21 precise
PRIMA RAPPRESENTAZIONE DELL'OPERA

LA WALLY

di W. DE HILLERN - Riduzione drammatica in 4 atti di LUIGI ILLICA
Musica di ALFREDO CATALANI
(Proprietà G. Ricordi & C.)

PERSONAGGI:

Wally	EVA TURNER
Stromminger, suo padre	MICHELE CUPERI
Afra	JOLE JACCHIA
Walter, suonatore di cetra	RINA MASSARDI
Giuseppe Hagenbach di Sölden	ANTONIO BAGNARIOL
Vincenzo Gellner dell'Hochstoff	AFRO POLI
Il Pedone di Schnals	VITTORIO BALDO

Alpigiani - Paesani - Borghesi - Vecchie - Contadini - Cacciatori
Giovinotti - Fanciulle di Sölden e dell'Hochstoff - Suonatori ambulanti
DANZE DI FANCIULLE E CACCIATORI
Alto Tirolo - Epoca 1800 circa.

Maestro Concertatore e Direttore d'Orchestra

FRANCO GHIONE

Maestro del coro: ACHILLE CLIVIO
Maestri sostituti: VITTORIO CAMPANELLA - EMILIO SALZA - EMIDIO TIERI
Maestro suggeritore: AMLETO TORNARI
Coreografo: GIUSEPPE CECCHETTI - Direttore di scena: RAOUL SIMONI

ORCHESTRA MUNICIPALE

80 Coriste e Coristi - Bandisti - Ballerine della Scuola di Ballo del Teatro
Comparse
Scene del TEATRO REGIO dipinte dal pittore LEANDRO CAVALIERI

---

later she was paid in advance for her first performance and looked for silk to make underwear spending L200 on the material when she found what she wanted.

Eva Turner sang Brünnhilde on February 4th, 7th, 10th, 13th and 17th and had a tremendous success. On the 15th she sang the *Liebestod* at a Gala Concert and left Torino at 16.05 on the

18th for London, with packed trains all the way to Paris, arriving in London on February 20th. On the 27th she gave a concert at Bristol with Cortot as her pianist and Plum wrote: 'Fine success. Better than the previous one. Coal 2/7.'

Plum's diary continues:

> 'Left Bristol on 28th at 5.15 pm arr. London 7.17 pm. Went to see Nell's grave with Monty at 12.30 and had lunch at the Iven's. (The family of the young man to whom she had been engaged years before.) Then Joe drove us to see Lily and on to Herbert and then over Clifton and down the river under bridge and on to Station.

March

5th	100 Bristol Posts 8/4 100 Bristol World 8/4 100 Bristol Press 8/4
	Carriage 3/6
7th	Dispatched the 300 Bristol papers today.
	E 2 dress preservers from Derry and Thom's 4/-
10th	Eva's Birthday.
	Tea at Norman's. Dinner at Nance's. Great Time.
	Charles for Lessons £1-10-0.
11th	Left London at 10.5 am for Italy.
	Florence gave us luncheon basket.
	Had carriage to ourselves the whole journey. 3 Railways.
12th	Arr Torino at 11.45 am. Rehearsal at 4pm.'

This rehearsal was for Beethoven's *Missa Solemnis* in Turin on the 22nd, 24th, 25th and 26th March. The other soloists were Borgioli (Tenor), Anna Massetti Bassi (Mezzo) and Giulio Tomei (Bass) with Busch conducting and the Gazette del Popolo reported:

'Eva Turner is a soprano of ample and secure voice.'

Plum writes on March 28th: 'Rehearsals begin for Verdi's Requiem - They didn't'. They arrived back in London on the April 5th. Eva was utterly exhausted and tried desperately to rest before the rehearsal, on the 8th at the Columbia Studios, for her Verdi *Requiem* on the 9th.

Manzoni's Requiem (See appendix) – Verdi's *Requiem*, with the London Symphony Orchestra on April 9th, 1934, should have been conducted by Hamilton Harty but he went to Australia and left Adrian Boult to hold the baton. Other artists were Muriel Brunskill, Frank Titterton and Harold Williams. 'Great Success even though E very tired. Notices were fair for *Requiem* but the Times was exceptional so I ordered 100 – No others': wrote Plum.

Sir Adrian Boult

Eva caught a bad cold going down to the tube at Shepherd's Bush and on April 30th, rehearsed with a bad head. She was then in bed with flu from May 1st until she was better on the 9th. Not a moment too soon as she was to perform, on the 11th, at a 'Grand Concert' in the Albert Hall in aid of Royal Amateur Musicians Fund under the patronage of the King and Queen.

'Now perhaps up to date what was one of my biggest thrills was my first appearance at the Royal Albert Hall. This was on the occasion of the Gala Concert in the presence of Their Majesties, the King and Queen (King George V and Queen Mary). I was presented to Their Majesties who were more than charming to me...'

She sang *Elisabeth's Greeting* from *Tannhäuser* and *In Questa Reggia* from *Turandot*. Richard Tauber and Conchita Supervia were the other soloists.

Plum:

May

13th Dada's Birthday. Had Norman and Florence to tea and supper.
In the afternoon we all went to the Albert Hall to hear the French girl Lily Pons. Not bad but needs more finesse.

17th Went to Ricordi's to hear about an opera venture to Australia. Did not learn much, so an appointment was made to see Day.

18th Saw Day the agent for Fuller re. opera co. for Australia and found Austral had been offered the premiere position so left the matter.

(Florence Austral born, in Richmond, Victoria, Florence Mary Wilson, was by general agreement the best Wagnerian sopranos ever produced by Australia. Melba referred to her as one of the wonder voices of the world.)

24th Guest at Foyles' Literary Luncheon – Speech by Frances Toye on Rossini. There were 800 guests.

25th C/G for *Arabella* 1st Act not bad, others fair.

29th E. Went to Gigli's Concert with the Baroness. Tremendous success. E very enthusiastic. Bus 2p.

29th ARB shoes soled E shoes soled 5/- and 4/-

30th E for tea with Compton and to buy corsets £1-13-9 bus 6p

(*Turandot* was revived on the 31st of May with Marinuzzi conducting and Roselle sang Turandot but, according to the press, she was a pale image of Turner.)

June

1st   Advert to let 51 Russell Road 3/-

8th   Prova at BBC 11.30 Broadcast at 8.
E Did splendidly – orchestra applauded deliriously. (Eva sang the great aria *Abscheulicher* from *Fidelio* in the first half and two Strauss songs *Zueignung* and *Cacilie* in the second and said of the concert:

'The year 1934 seemed with more thrills than usual as I made my first broadcast on 8th June'

13th   E was asked to standby to sing Turandot the next night should Borgioli not be able to sing in *Cenerentola*, but he did sing as scheduled.

Eva Turner was always interested in her properties as a way of guarding against poverty in the future and in July she went to see Jones, a solicitor at Lincoln Inn Fields, regarding obtaining the freehold of 67 Russell Street but with no positive outcome. On the same day Plum and she vacuumed the whole house at 51 Russell Street with a cleaner, hired from Murfeetts for 2/6 per day, their share of the cost being 1/3. They then did some shopping and bought: Chops 4½p, Soap 3p, Sugar 2p, Beef 2p, Lettuce 2p, Lemons 2p, Bread 2½p and went on to Selfridge's for moth bags and 'knickers for E' 7/1(see p.37). The basement apartment was let to Mr and Mrs Smith at 18/- weekly with the proviso that Mrs Smith would do the steps outside plus the inside stairs and bathroom and work for them 2 hours daily, when they were in London.

On July 9th there was excitement in the air for Plum and Eva, as the Barone Paolo Mazzonis, the Managing Director of the Turin Opera House, arrived from Turin, unexpectedly, to visit them before their departure for Milan the next day. Shortly after arriving back in her villa, Eva went to Milan in a friend's car to collect a letter from Turin about which the stage-door man had phoned her and the Barone had hinted at the contents. She found it was an offer to sing Sieglinde in the Turin *Ring* cycle in February and March the next year.

Eva was in bed with a bilious attack, of which she had many throughout her life, on the first day of August but was cheered up at night by a great festival on the lake. Many illuminated boats were in the procession with a fireworks display provided at the expense of a visiting Baroness, who was renting the Moor's house. Later in the month, Eva went to Lugano, where there had been a great storm and on arrival, she received a wire from Giurana, offer-

Dino Borgioli

ing her the part of Kundry. She sent a wire by return, refusing, as the part was too low.

There is no date on the following correspondence, referring to the role of Kundry, which Eva clearly did not think a suitable tessitura for her high placed voice. In it there is a great discussion between Ibbs and Tillett on behalf of Sir Henry Wood about a Promenade Concert. She wants to sing the whole of the last act of *Siegfried* and also the first act of *Walküre* but Sir Henry says that those excerpts are too long and he wants her to sing Kundry's aria *Herzeleide* and Brünnhilde's *Immolation*. Eva writes back, asking if he remembers that Kundry lies low. She adds rather sharply:

'with cost of postage as it is, Sir Henry might like to save me the expense of replying to all these letters.'

Harold Holt then writes to her saying that he has received a reply and cannot do better than let her have a copy of it:

'Which speaks for itself and in the circumstances I propose to write and say that you will abide by the wishes of Sir Henry.'

From Sir Henry, who was not having an easy time in his private life at this point:

I do regret that I cannot entertain the Scenes this year as I found they bored the public, as they are so different on the concert platform as opposed to the opera stage. Do tell my dear friend, I would do anything possible to meet her wishes but again the 'Herzeleide' is sung abroad by the soprano, and only in this country has the mezzo 'bagged it'. I am sure Miss Turner will score a great success with it...

P.S. I do hope Miss Turner will try her hand at the 'Herzeleide' 'Parsifal'. She will sing it superbly, and I have purposely not let the mezzo soprano touch it.
Yours sincerely,
Henry J Wood.

(Despite Holt's insistence, she did not sing the Kundry aria.)

At the end of August, Plum strained his back and was: 'stricken down with violent fever, neuritis and with delirium. Phyllis waited on me. Perspiring terribly. Heart beating terrific. Could not move my left arm'. A week later, Eva returned to Brusino from Milan and Plum was slightly better but his arm was still bad. Dr Bauler came to visit, called the illness 'Neuritis' and said that it was not possible for ARB to go to London, as it would be three weeks at least till he was better. Despite this advice Eva and Plum left Brusino for London on September 9th. Once in London, they went to search for a new evening dress for Eva for the forthcoming Promenade Concert and Plum was quite ill after the outing. (I am not surprised as these symptoms would be generally recognised nowadays as a heart attack).

Eva sang at a Radio Concert in Bristol on September 18th, to inaugurate their new facilities and had a successful time but a couple of days later, she received a disappointing letter from Passadoro, cancelling the proposed recording of *Turandot* at La Scala, as Merli was not available for those dates and neither was the La Scala orchestra. It was hoped that the recording would happen in the New Year. This idea of recording a complete *Turandot* had been on the cards since Columbia Records asked her, on April 22nd, 1931, about the possibility of recording the whole of *Turandot* in Italy. That letter had said:

'Mr Passadoro is anxious that you shall sing the part.'

Her first BBC Promenade Concert that season at the Queen's Hall, with Sir Henry Wood conducting, was on September 21st, 1934. She sang there again on October 1st when in the first half she sang: *Elisabeth's Greeting* and her *Prayer* (which Sir Henry thought didn't suit her) from *Tannhäuser* and in the second: two songs: *Lament of Isis* by Bantock and *Spring Waters* by Rachmaninoff.

In Ashton-in-Makerfield, where her father was then living, having absolutely definitely decided that London was not the place for him, Eva sang in a celebrity concert on October 3rd and it was a 'great success'. The next day Eva, Norman and Dad went to visit relatives living close by and then to the cemetery to visit her mother's grave before going to the station for their train home.

On returning to London, Eva gave a concert for the Jewish Guardians at the Hippodrome, with John Brownlee. They were accompanied by piano and Plum tells us 'Great Success'. Eva then caught flu, but good news followed shortly as: 'Water conveniences were connected into the kitchen with a geyser to heat the water. Hurrah'

The Royal Wedding Day of the Duke of Kent and Princess Marina which was a 'Tremendous Occasion' took place on November 29th and Eva gave a donation to the Musicians' Fund, paid by cheque, of £2-2/- to mark the event.

As you may have noticed there was good singing work for Eva at this point but perhaps not enough, as she sang only 26 performances that year and Harold Holt gave Plum little encouragement on his visit to the agent's office on December 19th, as the long sought visit to Australia seemed to be eluding Eva Turner.

Plum bought Eva a clock at £1-13-4 and Dada cigars at 5/- for Christmas 1934 and on the last day of the year Eva Turner sang at the first of the Winter Promenade Concerts with Sir Henry Wood conducting, when Parry Jones was the tenor. The programme included: *Elisabeth's Greeting*, *Tristan Love Duet* and *In Questa Reggia* all in the original language. Plum said: 'E made a sensation with Turandot Aria'

At the beginning of 1935, Eva Turner sang Sieglinde in the new production of the *Ring* cycle at the Teatro Regio, Turin, marking

Eva Turner as Sieglinde

the centenary year of the theatre. *L'anello del Nibelungo* was conducted by Fritz Busch, Lotte Burck was the Brünnhilde and Isodoro Fagoada was Siegfried. The Gazette del Popolo of March 27th reported:

> 'The revival of the four operas of the 'Ring' cycle together, in this organic, united form, is a very important artistic moment for music making in Italy... The singers were also excellent. Miss Eva Turner, well known to the public, sang Sieglinde with enthusiasm and skill.'

The only time I ever saw Dame Eva really cry during a lesson was when we worked together on the role of Sieglinde which I was about to sing at the Royal Opera House. We reached the wonderful passage in act three of *Die Walküre* when Brünnhilde gives Sieglinde the broken sword, which she took from the battlefield where Siegmund was slain, and tells her to live for the sake of Siegmund's son, the boy child Siegfried, whom Sieglinde now carries in her womb and who will remake the sword.

As we approached Sieglinde's glorious reply, Dame Eva threw her hands above her head and then sang, (a couple of octaves lower), along with me as if she had once again become Sieglinde. After this we had to pause while we both recovered during which time she said, through our tears, how much the wonderfully joyous, hopeful *leitmotif* which Sieglinde sings and which is only repeated once at the very end of the cycle, had meant to her.

When I saw the photo which is included here, I immediately thought of that moment. But there is some dispute about whether the photograph is in fact one capturing Brünnhilde's awakening by Siegfried and as she sang many performances, including Brünnhilde, at Turin, it is not impossible that I have got this wrong. The photo, of which she had many copies made, was definitely taken in Turin, so coupled with my personal experience, it seems likely to me that it was taken to celebrate their new *Ring* cycle in which she sang Sieglinde.

Eva Turner tells us:

> 'In 1935 I sang Allegra Salvatore's new opera "Ave Maria", sponsored by the Queen of Italy, in her presence. On this occasion the house was filled with the aristocracy from all parts of Italy, and I understand was an enormous success.'

Allegra was born in Palermo in 1898 and died in Florence in 1993. His dark verismo drama *Ave Maria* was first performed in Milan in 1934, so she was tackling a role which was hot off the press. Ghione conducted.

A letter from the Royal Opera House Covent Garden arrived for Eva at her Villa Junesca on June 21st 1935:

Dear Miss Turner,

Sir Thomas Beecham and I are very anxious that you should cooperate with us in the autumn season at Covent Garden and also the subsequent tours in some of the leading provincial towns. I cannot yet give you a definite repertoire but I can tell you that the first period would be between September 23rd and November 18th or 23rd with some weeks rehearsals beforehand. The second period would be between February 1st and the middle of March.

I should like to know as early as possible how you are fixed for these periods.

Mr. Toye to Harold Holt.

That letter was written to her less than a year after *Turandot* was revived without her at Covent Garden, when Toye was the managing director of the Opera Syndicate and I think perhaps, knowing that, helps put her barely concealed anger in her reply, into perspective. If she had been given that group of performances, her anxiety for work, during 1934, would have been lessened:

Royal Opera House

Dear Mr Toye,

I thank you for your letter of June 21st to which I should have replied earlier had circumstances permitted. To deal with your suggestion is by no means an easy matter.

Undoubtedly you are aware that I have built up, solely by my own value, a unique position in the Continental Operatic World and that in the face of tremendous opposition and the subtle antagonism associated with the jealousies encountered in professional circles. The fight has been too intense and too uphill to allow of such a great achievement being undervalued and now lightly abandoned. So that what you now ask of me becomes momentous in the face of the circumstances and much as I should like to help my own country in its attempt to give to opera, a place in its Nation's Life you will appreciate somewhat, perhaps, what it must mean to my career to acquiesce to your proposition. It practically asks me to give up the whole of my Continental Season and the associated status. And for what?

Considering the magnitude of what one would have to abandon, wherein comes the due compensation? No scheme seems to be in the making to warrant any consecutive operatic seasons for this country so under such uncertainty it could not be called sound to discard a reality for a myth.

It seems to me that the only feasible way of meeting such a situation would be on a guarantee basis; say for a term of Five Years, ensuring 20 performances in the autumn and winter months and 10 performances in the Summer Grand Season, at a fee of 50 guineas per performance. It would also have to be understood that no restrictions would be placed upon my acceptance of any Concert or BBC engagements. Only by such precautions could one's career be protected.

One too cannot trifle with important managements such as I am associated with, by dropping and taking them up whenever one's whims might fancy. Doubtless in your own management you would exhibit forceful objections to such treatments and would therefore be in strong disagreement with this phase of professional conduct. Besides there are far too many opportunists waiting to fill any vacancy forthcoming through any delinquency of a refractory artist. So a step as you suggest has to be very wisely considered lest a life's work be ruined by some indiscreet move. Then again, an important factor is, that your treatment proves to me that I can look for little consideration or appreciation from your management.

Trusting my presentation of the facts will be in agreement with your wide knowledge of affairs.
Yours faithfully,
Eva Turner.'

Such is the diplomatic power of opera house managements throughout the world when dealing with miffed singers, in the next letter from Harold Holt the situation has been resolved sufficiently for dates to be discussed.

'My dear Eva,
I have had a long discussion with the Covent Garden people and unfortunately there is a suggestion now made to slightly alter the terms which we had tentatively fixed with Mr. Geoffrey Toye. Between ourselves, I must tell you that Mr. Toye is now no longer in charge of the organisation of the autumn tour.

The present proposition is as follows: that you should be paid £800 for 18 performances to take place on the dates listed.

Sir Thomas Beecham

(See appendix for Eva Turner's performance dates for the Imperial League of Opera 1935.)

Before this season of opera began, Eva Turner sang, in early September, at the opening of the Dome Concert Hall in Brighton, with Sir Thomas Beecham conducting the Philharmonic Orchestra.

Eva's father died on September 26th, while sitting in the stalls of Covent Garden, as he waited to hear his beloved daughter sing Agathe. Many people in the audience knew of his death before Eva did, as she learned of her father's death after the performance was over from Sir Thomas Beecham of whom she said:

'Sir Thomas was wonderful to me just wonderful. His kindness was extraordinary.'

She had many letters of sympathy including those from: Miriam Licette, Oda Slobodskaya, Dino Borgioli, Marie Goossens Lauritz, Lillian Baylis, Albert Coates, Peggie Sherridan, Hubert Bath and Arthur Fear. Gladys Parr wrote saying she wanted to help in any way she could and said she had tried to speak to Plum so as not to disturb Eva at this time.

Four nights later Eva Turner sang *Ballo* at Covent Garden and a wave of sympathetic applause greeted her appearance and a riotous burst of applause greeted her and Borgioli in the second act. The performance was stopped by this applause, much to Sir Thomas's irritation. (See appendix for cast)

Before his death, during his final years, despite their disagreements, Eva had continued to include her father as much as possible in her busy life. As we see from Plum's diaries Charles had hated living in London since he was at heart a northerner and needed to be with his own folk in his declining years. This made it harder for Eva to see him often but she gave him a small amount of money each month as an allowance, and birthdays etc. were celebrated together as much as possible. His once prominent position in Eva's life had ceased in the years before his death and a certain painful distance had grown up between them. As we all know, these complicated family feelings and misunderstandings, when love is involved, can cause pain, especially if left unresolved which is the northern way. These differences can be especially hurtful and lasting if the person in question is no longer available to share a healing conversation.

Eva, apart from Gladys in their young days, did not have a female confidante with whom to share such worries and she did not share this one with Plum either, as he was probably part of the disagreements. This lack of close female friends in her life is

Charles and Eva Turner

not uncommon among singers, as there is among women a kind of primitive competitiveness which is heightened in the life of a singer for obvious reasons. Neither had she had, for a long time, if ever, an intimate relationship with her mother, where feelings like this could be discussed. She had a brother whom she loved dearly, but that is different again and so she was out of practice at being able to talk about the emotional side of everyday life. With all this in mind, I imagine she put these big emotions behind her, considering them perhaps unnatural as she had never been able to share them by talking them through, and got on with her life, closing the book on them forever.

Of her Amelia on tour, the Birmingham Post reported on October 12th:

'The night was really Eva Turner's so far as the audience was concerned. It was glorious to hear this grand artist in an important Italian part – that of Amelia, of course. But, here, again (Eva underlined the next part in blue) there was not a sign that the Prima Donna felt she ought to be regarded as more important than the opera. Miss Turner for all her masterly singing, never once dropped out of the scheme. She took her opportunities when they came, and for the rest knew how to keep still or to fit her almost domineeringly powerful voice in with the others quite admirably. Her reward was that, whenever she was allowed to sail away over

the top of everything else with one of those broadly spanned tunes with which Verdi can stir one to the marrow, she was all the more thrilling... Miss Eva Turner again showed her command of emotions as well as her extraordinary power. Her study of the heroine was always well within the picture and even when she astonished and delighted her hearers she did so on lines of proper team work.'

This idea that she could be a team member clearly gave her a lot of pleasure as I think she was often accused of stealing the show which was not deliberately planned by her but was simply a result of her being the best singer. She was by nature a leader but she also liked to be in a team, a feeling of which she was proud and where possible she acknowledged generously the part of others in any performance. I think too she had sometimes sung too loudly not because she was showing off but the ability to sing pianissimo can be a lifelong quest for some singers and she was now achieving that ability with greater skill. (See appendix for historical piece included in a review about *Ballo in Maschera*)

Eva Turner

Of *Freischütz*, the Liverpool Echo on October 15th:

'On the stage Miss Eva Turner walked away with most of the opera. Since she first sang the opera in Liverpool, Miss Turner has improved out of knowledge and now the superb voice is controlled to the last fraction. It is indeed impossible to sing the first part of 'Softly Sighs' without such control and it is sufficient to add that it is difficult to think of any other singer today who could have done it more beautifully. Walter Widdop did what he could with a difficult and very operatic role. There was a very large audience and the greatest enthusiasm prevailed.'

(See appendix for more general review of the short Covent Garden Season)

The letter below is the first of a very long correspondence stretching over many years. The letters were donated to the Royal Opera House by Richard Baker, of BBC fame, to whom they were bequeathed. He became a friend of Sheila Wright's family when he was evacuated, with his school, to Northampton as a child during the war years.

Presumably Sheila Wright had seen Eva Turner perform in *Siegfried*/Brünnhilde at Birmingham; a pretty heavy 'first opera' to see but it did not put her off, as she followed Eva as a fan, and later a friend, for many years:

15th October 1935

Dear Sheila Wright (hand written),

I was pleased to have your letter and pleased that you enjoyed the first opera you have seen and heard. I am happy to be associated. I too hope you will be able to see other operas. Herewith I enclose a small photograph as you desired. I hope the future will permit of your wish to hear opera at Covent Garden being realised.

Thanking you for your kind wishes.

Sincerely yours,
Eva Turner.

Dame Eva recalled:

'I remember, when I was singing Brünnhilde, in English, in 1935 with Sir Thomas conducting, when Walter Widdop as Siegfried came along the top and saw me as Brünnhilde lying there and he sang: "That is no man" and someone from the gallery shouted: "You're telling us", referring I think to my ample bosom. (Laughter.)'

Now a business letter from Harold Holt on October 16th:

My Dear Eva,

The BBC have been in touch with me today asking me to suggest to you that you give a recital of songs by the French composer Bosquet, early in the New Year. I understand they cannot pay your usual fee, but feel that you may be prepared to accept a nominal fee for such a recital in an effort to help this composer, a recital of whose songs you once gave in Paris, I understand. Will you let me hear from you in this connection?

Hope you are well and with all good wishes.

Harold

Dear Harold,

Many thanks for yours of the 18th inst. respecting the suggested concert of Bosquet songs early in the new year at a nominal fee: let me say that considering the harm in one's future prestige as a concert draw and the consequent lack of dates with the accompanying loss of income which I have always understood is sure to come from appearances with the BBC. I feel the only means one has for protection against such contingency is not to make contracts for nominal fees even though by so doing one might be offered an increase in appearances which again should be accepted with extreme reserve owing to the staleness which the BBC would consider associated with the artists too frequent Broadcasting. So one can aptly conclude that there is much to lose and nothing to gain by consenting to accept 'Nominal Fees' with such an organisation to which, from your former attitude, I am sure you will concur. Under the circumstances, I can safely depend upon your protection against the introduction of such a ruinous policy.

Were a large number of Broadcasts offered over a definite period of years, 'Nominal Fees' might be entertained as then there would be some shield for one's compliance but without such I foresee regrettable finality which I have no wish to participate in. Until such safe ground is assured don't you think it wiser to act upon conservative lines?

With very best wishes,
Eva Turner.

Naturally these ideas are strictly between ourselves.

In a news paper article around this time she is quoted as saying:

'I wish that our government would take the necessary steps to make the people opera-minded for the refining influence of music must be reflected in the nation's standards. Also that our people would maintain and stand firm in the cause of peace and so work for the general betterment of the world.'

Eva Turner once again performed at the first night of the winter Proms on December 30th 1935 and sang: *Ocean Thou Mighty Monster* and *In Questa Reggia*, conducted by Sir Henry Wood. This concert was relayed from the Queen's Hall on the radio at 8.00pm. The second half of the programme was Beethoven's *Fifth Symphony*.

Death is still in the air for Eva, as at the beginning of 1936, her Uncle John died a few months after his brother Charles. John was four years older than Charles and died while cycling home from Standish where he had been visiting relatives:

'He died almost immediately after falling off his bicycle. Mr Turner, who lived with his sister Mrs C.H.Bottoms of Walnut Street, thought nothing of rising at 3 a.m. and cycling or running before breakfast. He was a keen musician and had a fine tenor voice.'

The Turners had a very strong sense of family and visits to them and from them were often in Eva's diaries. She sometimes stayed with them if singing in that part of the world and many relations and close friends attended her concerts to support her. A friend and tenant of later years remembered being a fan of Eva Turner's when he was living in Lancashire and when he walked ten miles to hear her in a concert. As a timid boy of about sixteen, he had gone to her dressing room to ask for her autograph and of course was given it along with a little chat. He had enough money to take the train home and while standing on the platform waiting for it, Eva, accompanied by four relatives, had arrived for the same train. Eva sent one of her male relations over to greet him and ask if he was the same young man who had asked for her autograph. On replying that he was, he was invited to join them on the journey home. Once installed in a carriage, apparently there was great conversation and laughter, not to mention a small sandwich to keep them going. When they arrived at Oldham it was pouring down and Eva asked Jack Blunden where he lived. He told her, and all seven of them piled into the car and he was driven safely home, amid good natured pushing, shoving and joking, on a sea of good will and happiness.

Eva Turner was always proud to have sung with John McCormack and Astra Desmond at a Memorial Concert for George V, on Tuesday February 4th, 1936 at the Royal Albert Hall, arranged under the direction of Harold Holt, the profits from which went to the Musicians' Benevolent Fund and she cherished the programme.

Eva Turner, later that month, went to Edinburgh and Glasgow to sing Isolde and the *Siegfried* Brünnhilde, both in English.

'My first performance of Isolde with Sir Thomas and the London Provincial Opera Company was sung in Edinburgh on February 25th, 1936'. (See appendix for cast)

The Scotsman tells us the next day:

'Last night's production was one in which great pride had been taken. No operatic and no orchestral performance can be greater than the capacity of the director, and the thrills of this occasion were the outcome of Sir Thomas Beecham's commanding genius. The power and beauty of his 'Tristan' has been known for long. Its ripe maturity was deeply moving last night. Stage and orchestra alike were sensitive instruments upon which he played with the aristocratic address of a true master and with a grand range of deeply human emotional quality. The Isolde of Eva Turner was indeed magnificent. She has established herself as one of the greatest singers in the world of music and last night she proved this to an enthusiastic Edinburgh audience. Her ability to override the most relentless orchestral fury provided a rousing experience. With Walter Widdop the great climaxes were completely within his power and this without abating one jot of real vocal beauty.'

Memorial Concert

in Commemoration of

His Late Most Gracious Majesty

King George V.

ROYAL ALBERT HALL

TUESDAY, FEB. 4th
1936

ROYAL ALBERT HALL　　　　**TUES. FEB. 4, 1936**

Memorial Concert

ORDER OF PROGRAMME

7.45 to 8 o'clock ORGAN SOLOS
HERBERT DAWSON

1. "Fanfare for a Ceremony" — *Walford Davies*
   KNELLER HALL TRUMPETERS
2. Funeral March — *Beethoven*
   BAND OF THE ROYAL MILITARY SCHOOL OF MUSIC
3. Recitative and Aria "Dido's Lament" from "Dido and Aeneas" — *Purcell*
   ASTRA DESMOND
4. Tone Poem "Venus; the bringer of Peace" ("The Planets") — *Holst*
   LONDON PHILHARMONIC ORCHESTRA
5. "The Lord is my Light" — *Allitsen*
   EVA TURNER
6. Prelude to "Gerontius" — *Elgar*
   LONDON PHILHARMONIC ORCHESTRA
7. Arias: "Caro Amor" ("Il Pastor Fido") — *Handel*
   "Vi sento si vi sento" (Lothario) — "
   JOHN McCORMACK
8. Overture "In Memoriam" — *Sullivan*
   LONDON PHILHARMONIC ORCHESTRA
9. Funeral March — *Chopin arr. by Elgar*
   LONDON PHILHARMONIC ORCHESTRA

INTERVAL

10. "Fanfare for Heroes" — *Bliss*
    KNELLER HALL TRUMPETERS
11. Aria "Angel's Farewell" from "Dream of Gerontius" — *Elgar*
    ASTRA DESMOND
12. Second Movement from Symphony No. 2 in E flat — *Elgar*
    LONDON PHILHARMONIC ORCHESTRA
13. Aria "Let the bright Seraphim" (Samson) — *Handel*
    EVA TURNER
14. Benedictus — *Mackenzie*
    LONDON PHILHARMONIC ORCHESTRA
15. (a) It is not the tear at this moment shed — *Old Irish*
    (b) Where e'er you walk (Semele) — *Handel*
    JOHN McCORMACK
16. Dead March from "Saul" — *Handel*
    BAND OF THE ROYAL MILITARY SCHOOL OF MUSIC
17. "Jerusalem" — *Parry*
    Sung by the Audience, Standing
18. Fanfare — *Bax*

"THE LAST POST"

"REVEILLE"

GOD SAVE THE KING

(Second performance March 2nd)

Of *Siegfried* in Edinburgh on February 27th and March 4th, 1936 we are told:

'The Covent Garden Opera Company staged a characteristic presentation of 'Siegfried' at the King's Theatre last night. There was a careful and shrewd note in the mounting and stage production that, taken in conjunction with first rate orchestral playing and direction, led to the most satisfying artistic results which the large audience received with deeply engrossed pleasure.

Impressive Singing. Mr Walter Widdop as Siegfried was well cast, presenting a youthful air alike in voice and demeanour throughout. Brünnhilde appearing only in the final scene was undertaken by Miss Eva Turner who again made a very deep impression with her singing. She filled the King's Theatre last night with her gloriously exultant clangour that easily vied with the full force of the orchestra. Mr Clarence Raybould (conductor) missed nothing either in the orchestra or on the stage. His direct interpretation was well suited in Wagner's nature painting in such scenes as the 'Woodland Murmurs'.

(The tour then went to Glasgow and continued into the middle of March.)

Eva Turner received a letter from Lillian Baylis at the Old Vic Theatre on April 15th asking her to do guest performances of *Aida* at a fee that would help English Opera but there is no record of her reply, and on May 25th, Eva went to see *Die Walküre* at Covent Garden with Kirsten Flagstad and Lauritz Melchior singing and Beecham conducting.

The next day, May 26th, her beloved Muzio died at the age of 47 after a short illness. Eva's thoughts about this great lady's singing did not ever waiver; for Eva, she was the best Traviata of all time and a great recitalist:

'investing the words and making them pregnant with meaning.'

During 1936, at a Promenade Concert on August 10th Eva sang Isolde's *Narration* and *Liebestod*:

'More faithful to the original text was a performance of the 'Prelude and Liebestod' from 'Tristan'. The solo was sung with noble restraint by Eva Turner who also gave us Isolde's narration from the first act' and: *'On Tuesday October 6th at the Queen's Hall, the London Symphony Orchestra with Albert Coates conducting performed the final scenes from 'Die Walküre' and 'Siegfried 'along with*

the Waltraute and Brünnhilde scene in 'Die Walküre'. The artists involved were Eva Turner, Walter Widdop, Harold Williams and Vera de Villiers. To these were added the 'Tannhäuser Overture', Siegfried's journey to the Rhine and the 'Siegfried Idyll' so making too long a programme. Miss Eva Turner hardly seems up to her usual form; her voice was less brilliant than usual and the articulation of her words was poor in comparison with that of Mr Harold Williams (Wotan).'

Walter Widdop was Siegfried.

Eva's neighbour in her home in Palace Court Bayswater was Ronald Crighton, the critic. He lived the other side of the wall from her studio and sometimes if things were going well she would open a window and ask a student to sing louder so that he could hear and be alerted to a new voice and perhaps give them a little newspaper space. The following review, again of October 6th, I think is by him:

'Wagner: Mr Coates and the LSO. The LSO was, last night, at the Queen's Hall, launched its 31st season with a concert of Wagner extracts conducted by Albert Coates. A section of the audience was so heartily philistine as to applaud Miss Turner's top Cs in the love duet before waiting to hear the end of the music. Miss Turner bore the brunt of the vocal pieces singing Brünnhilde to Mr William's Wotan and Miss Villier's Waltraute. She excelled in the brightest and most exuberant music viz., the 'Siegfried' extract. Her partner was in good form. R. C.'

A couple of weeks later she was singing Verdi's *Requiem* at the City Hall Sheffield, on October 22nd where her fellow artists were: Muriel Brunskill, Walter Widdop and Alexander Kipnis who:

'were all good and it was a magnificent performance by Henry Wood. The general pitch of the solo soprano's music is abnormally high but Miss Turner's true and ringing voice was admirably telling in the ensembles.'

Sir Henry wrote her a letter a few of days later thanking her for performance.

Harold Holt, her agent in London, had persuaded her that she needed to work more in Britain, probably with the political scene in mind and she had embarked once more on tour, this time as part of an International Celebrity Concert Tour. It was reported on Nov 23rd in Manchester:

'Celebrities in Quartet. There was a mystic atmosphere about the Celebrity Concert at the Free Trade Hall on Saturday. Fog which had

> 4, ELSWORTHY ROAD,
> LONDON, N.W.3.
>
> October 25th 1936
>
> My dear Miss Eva Turner
>
> Just a few hurried lines to thank you for your splendid work at the 1936 Sheffield Musical Festival. Your voice, your style & your interpretation gave me the very greatest pleasure
>
> Very sincerely yours
> Henry J. Wood
>
> mention luncheon

penetrated the hall presented people at the back of the place with a vision of wraithlike figures singing Verdi and Schumann. The unusual conditions in no way affected the standard of the singing. Interpretation of great dramatic power characterized the singing of Miss Eva Turner whose singing of the 'Greeting' to The Hall of Song and 'The Jewel Song' was superb... The other soloists were Sabine Kalter, Dino Borgioli and John Brownlee. The concert had an impressive finale, the quartet from 'Rigoletto.' Ivor Newton was as ever a faultless accompanist.'

Eva Turner tells us:

'The recent destruction by fire of the Colston Hall in Bristol brings to my mind quite clearly the concert I did there with Sir Thomas conducting on the occasion of the opening of the Hall on 12th December 1936'.

(The Colston Hall survived the German air raids of the Second World War only to be burnt to the ground in 1945, when a discarded cigarette caused a fire.)

On December 23rd, 1936, Eva Turner sang the *Abscheulicher* from *Fidelio* and Amelia's *Morro* from the last act of *Ballo in Maschera* at Broadcasting House and after the broadcast went immediately to Turin to rehearse and sing Donna Anna, in *Don Giovanni*, from December 26th, 1936 to January 12th, 1937.

Eva Turner in 1937 owned two properties in London as well as her Villa Junesca and, when she was not at Lake Lugano, stayed at 51 Russell Road, Kensington. 67 Russell Road where her father had once lived was now occupied by tenants. She had also made enquiries as to whether a loft conversion was possible in one or both of these properties so that she could have had a few more tenants but was advised against this possibility.

She was quite at home in London, although was always drawn more to Italy, at this time in her life.

'While I was in Turin in 1937, I received a very urgent cable from Sir Thomas on January the 13th, asking me to *sing "The Masked Ball" on the 16th of January in England. I had literally to fly to England and arrived at 4pm on the 15th. From the station I went straight to Covent Garden and rehearsed solidly, with the exception of a brief break for a cup of tea, until mid-night.'*

The News Chronicle:

'The famous British Prima Donna Eva Turner born in Lancashire and better recognised in Italy than in her own country came specially from Turin to sing Amelia and had tremendous success, her clear and telling soprano voice ringing true throughout. At the end of Act II she had an ovation worthy of a foreign star in the Grand Season.'

The Daily Telegraph reported:

'Eva Turner's command of the Italian style leaves no loophole for adverse criticism.'

She sang Amelia again on January 21st, when Francesco Salfi conducted, and paid tax on her £50 fee. This lesser fee was probably a sign of the times in Britain.

In 1937 Eva Turner set off once more on the International Celebrity Tour singing: the 'Rigoletto' quartet, 'Aida' duets, 'Pace, Pace' from 'The Force of Destiny', the 'Jewel Song' and 'Elisabeth's Greeting' of which the Aberdeen press reported on February 19th:

'Opera Stars in Aberdeen. Miss Eva Turner has been an Aberdeen favourite for some years now, both on concert platform and theatre stage: Borgioli is known to many here who have not seen him before through his broadcast performances and last night Sabine Kalter and Tomasini, by differing but equally successful personalities and artistry captivated and conquered their listeners.'

'My next great thrill was on May 12th 1937, the day of the Coronation of our present King and Queen. Immediately following the King's speech, I sang "God Save the King" from the stage of Covent Garden, before the commencement of the opera "Aida", to what was probably my greatest audience. Statistics have it that approximately 50 million people were "listening in"'

Regarding that occasion, there was huge disappointment among the British public that Eva Turner was not the Aida on that evening but she was never churlish about that and:

'Very much enjoyed singing God Save the King, with Sir Thomas conducting.'

Aida was sung by the great Italian soprano of French origins Gina Cigna. The cast included; Ebe Stignani - Amneris, Martinelli - Radames, Formichi - Amonasro and Salfi conducted. The Royal Box was not occupied but was filled with a huge crown of red roses, surrounded by blue and red hydrangeas and the auditorium was decked with pink roses.

Many years later Dame Eva was on the Board of Governors for the London Opera Centre and used her influence on occasion to

Eva Turner sang Aida on March 5th 1937 at Huddersfield Town Hall with Parry Jones as Radames, Constance Willis as Amneris and the Huddersfield Choral Society. Dr. Malcolm Sargent conducted. In a rather characteristic way, which continued into later years, the locals of Huddersfield placed their own choral society on a very high pedestal as we can see in this report:

'Brilliant singing by Miss Eva Turner and superb work by all the soloists in this Verdi Opera. The chorus, however, did not have enough to do in the concert version but nevertheless was truly wonderful.'

1933-1939 Day to Day Life and Performances

Eva Turner in front of the cast for 'Aida' performance at the Royal Opera House on the eve of GeorgeVI's Coronation, 1937

Gina Cigna

bring singers of distinction to work with the students. One such singer was Gina Cigna, who was a marvellous teacher and lived a long full life into her 100s, despite having had to give up singing after a heart attack in her forties. To hear these two great ladies talking together in Italian and English about singing was a very great privilege. They were both, in 1970, still full of the joy of singing and eager to pass on their knowledge from the Golden Age. There was not the slightest hint from either of them that there had been a historic dispute surrounding them and they enjoyed each other's company to the full.

Turandot, on April 30th 1937 was the first time Eva Turner sang with Giovanni Martinelli and he said to her: 'Signorina, you can only sing like that if you have a maestro and study daily.' Martinelli and Turner became firm friends and she valued this friendship throughout her life, saying that the days she gave master classes with him in London:

'were among the happiest days of my life.'

The Liu on that occasion was Faverò who also sang it on May 5th. On May 10th Licia Albanese sang Liu and in later life often spoke of Eva's generosity as a fellow artist. Barbirolli conducted and the director was Charles Moor.

198   Dame Eva Turner A Life on the High Cs

Turandot reports included:

The Telegraph:

'Eva Turner's singing of the whole scene was masterly and for the first time in my experience the 'Trial Scene' did convey to the spectator the emotions that the characters are supposed to feel – the pride and anger of the Princess: her coldness, the belief that her cruelty is justified: the anxiety and finally: the triumph of the lover. Mr Martinelli found Calaf better suited to his voice than Othello'.

The Evening News:

'Eva Turner mastered the situation. She sang brilliantly and well deserved the ovations she received at the end of the second and third acts. No Italian tenor of recent years has sung with such purity of note and such feeling for the music as Martinelli did on this occasion'.

The Times:

'Last Night the full effect was reached particularly in the performances of the two leading characters. Few sopranos can sing the high tension as Miss Eva Turner does without a screech or a whoop and Mr Martinelli has the true tenor quality of Italian Opera which can sustain each phrase, singing right in the middle of each note without apparent physical energy. The chief applause was naturally for them: for her repeated recalls after the great riddle scene (in which, by the way, she with her assistants managed her glittering train as easily as her voice) and for him the compliment of a spontaneous outburst at the climax of the love song which begins the final act.'

During August, Covent Garden was trying to fix dates on which she would sing on tour and despite her great success in the season, there seems to have been a bit of haggling over her fees for the tour. Management seems to land Covent Garden's

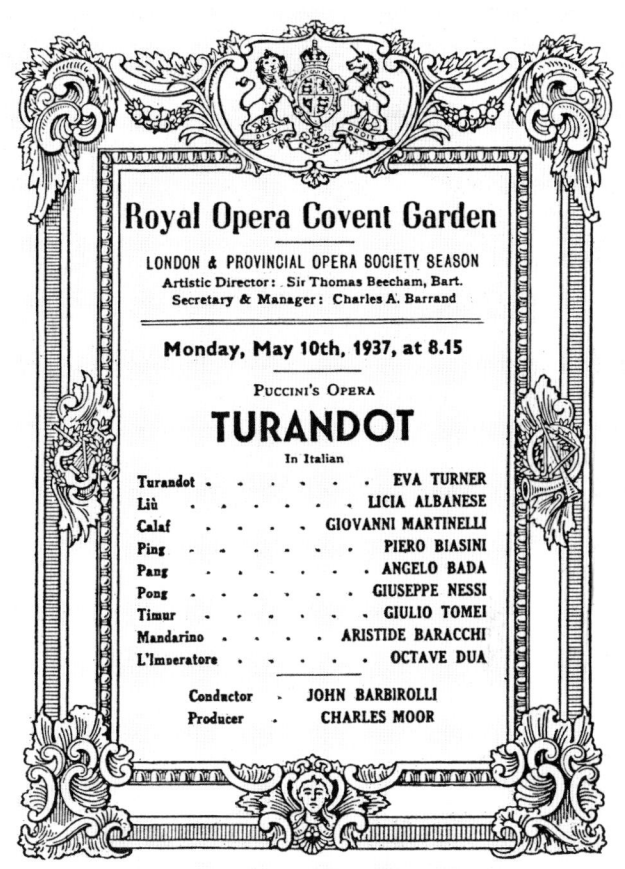

Playbill of a performance in honor of the coronation of George VI

In the Coronation Season of 1937 Eva Turner sang Turandot on April 30th, May 5th and 10th, and Aida on May 27th and June 29th. On June 29th, at the final performance of 'Aida': 'Eva Turner was at her thrilling best as Aida dominating the finale of the second act with her ringing tones; Rose Bampton was an Amneris whose clothes did credit to the dressmakers of ancient Memphis and Noble was an Amonasro of first rank'

inability to take *Turandot* on tour firmly on her doorstep, which I am sure would not be the whole picture:

> Dear Eva,
>
> Just off to Germany but must confirm the dates that you will do for us namely:
>
> Tristan *November 2 Liverpool*
> Turandot *November 5 and 9 Liverpool*
> Tristan *November 12 Liverpool*
> Tristan *November 16 Glasgow*
> Turandot *November 18 and 23*
> Tristan *November 25*
>
> Kindly let us know if these are alright.
>
> My love to you and Plum.
>
> Yours sincerely, Percy

6th Sept 1937

> Villa Junesca
>
> Dear Miss Turner,
>
> Many thanks for your PC which I received on return to the office this morning. I had a glorious holiday and wonderful weather all the time but I cannot claim that Ostend looked anything like as beautiful as Salzburg a picture of which you sent me.
>
> I have been speaking to Covent Garden people this morning and whilst they are anxious to have you for Tristan on the following dates, they have definitely ruled out any possibility of giving Turandot, because of the very heavy costs and because you cannot meet them over the question of fee.
>
> Tristan *Nov 2nd and 12th in Liverpool and 16th and 25th in Glasgow*
>
> First one with Beecham and the rest with Albert Coates.
>
> The fee for each will be £50.
>
> As the Turandot dates are out, we have accordingly booked you for Kilmarnock on Nov 5 at a fee of 75 guineas.
>
> I shall be glad if you would drop me a line confirming that all these dates are in order.
>
> With kind regards and wishing you and Mr Broad a very enjoyable holiday.
>
> PS Kilmarnock Nov 5th: There will be important people there expecting songs in English.
>
> From the office of Harold Holt.'

Eva Turner sang all the dates as requested and before them sang at a Promenade Concert in London on September 20th and was invited to Martinelli's daughter's wedding on October 2nd.

On December 1st she sang Isolde for the Imperial League of Opera at Covent Garden, where the tenor was Gotthelf Pistor who sang in German, while Eva Turner sang in English, although she occasionally sang in German to give him his cue. Albert Coates conducted. The press reported:

> 'Within the convention she had chosen, the human rather than the heroic, Miss Turner's performance was superb. Her voice we know has the exciting quality needed for dramatic expression and the power to surmount the Wagnerian climaxes and she did not fail to fulfil expectation in this respect. But she surpassed it in subtlety and warmth of her singing in the quieter passages and in the lower part of her voice. Her clean attack on the notes, her sense of style in phrasing and the distinctness of her words – we noticed incidentally some intelligent amendments of the usual translation that made for better sense both verbal and musical – were other elements in a splendid performance.'

Miss Edith Furmedge was the Brangaene, Booth Hitchin; Kurwenal, and Norman Walker; Mark.

Eva Turner took seventeen curtain calls, said to be only one less than the great Kirsten Flagstad in that role at Covent Garden. Reading between the lines we can see that her more subtle use of her voice and her improving technique was lending itself to performances that were noted not only for her power and vocal accuracy but for her thoughtful interpretation.

I think though it has to be observed that her apparently positive direct nature was challenged in the sometimes more complicated, turgidly emotional German repertoire:

> 'Turner is the mainstay of the company... yet the role demands a quality of predestined tragedy to which she, with that buoyant nature of hers, hardly responds'.

In life, I think few things are black and white, however, and I always got the sense from Dame Eva that her positive forward looking approach had been worked at and was not necessarily her first nature. It was one she had developed over many years of being taught, and so coming to think herself, that the sole most important thing that she had to give in life was her voice. We know that she had had sadness in her life: the death of her parents, which, because of her eager desires for her career always to forge forward, she had compartmentalised and locked away so that she could move on quickly.

We all approach these events in different ways and there are practicalities concerning them which when dealt with by a united family can lead to a sense of sharing. But what about sharing inner feelings about marriage, children, deep relationships which can cause sorrow, and sexuality, all the mainstay of ordinary lives, of which she never talked? Were they so difficult for her and hidden, even perhaps from herself, that she could not explore them without the fear of being caught up in them and slowed down by them? Being slowed down as one goes to the goal is not a thought which Dame Eva would have let enter her mind, at whatever personal cost. She was always quick. The containment of all of this, to my ear, leads to the very sound of her voice and perhaps even more so to the sound of her speaking voice from which all singing flows. Or we could look at it from a singer's point of view and say that since we have to contain the voice in order to control it, it is dangerous to release the singer's own default position, since singing is a game played between releasing the body and voice to allow colour and expression, and tightening it to gain supremacy over pitch and pianissimos.

At 3 p.m. on February 27th, 1938, Eva sang *Elisabeth's Greeting* and the *Liebestod* at a concert arranged by Holt at Covent Garden. The Philharmonic Orchestra was conducted by Sidney Beer and according to Plum: 'the concert was not outstanding'. The pending war and deflation was affecting everyone in Britain and Eva Turner's fees were also being squeezed even more, as she received only £35-6-3 for this performance.

During early March, which had the finest weather for 90 years, Plum bought Eva a ticket for America aboard *Isle de France* for £46-15-0; she would return on the *Aquitania* at the lesser cost of £43-15-0 and would take with her £105 in travellers' cheques. He also cabled the Metropolitan Opera House asking if she could visit it while in New York and on the 9th Eva left from Waterloo Station at 4.55pm to catch the tender which sailed from Southampton docks at 7.55pm and took an hour to reach the ship.

Plum sent her a wire, duly recorded in the diary as costing 10/-, to: 'Turner, cabin 205. Bon Voyage. Triumphant visit – Courage – Flo, Norman and Plum.' Eva arrived in New York on the morning of the 16th at 10 am and went straight to the Ambassador Hotel, Park Avenue on 51st and 52nd Streets. She had had an awful journey and the ship was twenty hours late because of the terrible weather, which meant that her audition for the Metropolitan Opera House was now only thirty hours away.

On March 17th, using the anonymous name of Rentur, at 4.30 New York time, Eva Turner sang the *Liebestod* and *Turandot* at an audition. Afterwards:

'*Bodamski was antagonistic but Johnson* (who had been the Canadian tenor Eduardo Di Giovanni before he was the General Manager of the Metropolitan and had been the General Manager of Chicago when Eva had sung there)*, was very, very impressed.*'

At the same time in London, Plum: 'sat in 'SILENCE' from 9 o'clock British time till 10.30 with mind on Eva. This despite a terrible disaster of flooding in Norman's flat during the day.'

I will now let Plum describe the awful tensions of this time through his diary:

March.

18th   Eva in New York.
ARB Very worried and agitated all day.
E Lunched with John B. Hears *Othello* to-night, with Martinelli.

19th   Eva in New York. No News. ARB Very worried and ill – through condition incapacitated
E Hears *Götterdämmerung* tonight

20th   Eva in New York. No News
ARB went out for first time since E went – up to park till noon
E Hears Barbiroli this afternoon
E Hears Martinelli Gala performance at the Met tonight after 25 years.

29th   Received cable 9 am from Eva re. engagement with Longone.
'Metropolitan interview delayed until the 14th – Johnson away. Longone offers 5 performances: *Aida*, *Ballo*, *Turandot*, *L'Africana* and Sieglinde from Nov 14th to Dec 5th in writing.'
ARB cabled the following night message: 'Beware Longone Think contract best through Simon. Consult Met – Don't upset. Fares. Good salary. Love.'

30th   Sent letter to Eva per *Queen Mary* sailing today. Should be delivered Monday am.

April

2nd 9a.m. Received cable from Eva: '*Longone* offers 5 performances at 300 dollars each Nov 26 to Dec 14. Have you received my letter?'
Replied: 'Terrible money – what about fares. What concerts probable? You receiving letter Mon. Then decide. Your last letter came by the Queen Mary. Love.'

12th Cabled Eva Night Cable: 'Who provides wardrobes? Get Langone's Italian Address. Tackle Johnson – Simon ask advise. Accept Holt's six performances of *Pagliacci*. Bon Voyage
Love Broad.'

14th E. 'Cable received 9.30. Interviewing Johnson 5.30 today American time.'

15th Langone leaves today for Italy.
E cabled: 'Happy Easter – Nothing Metropolitan – Accepting Pagliacci.'

19th E 'Booked to sing *Turandot, Aida, Ballo, Siegfried* and *L'Africana* with Chicago Opera Company next season.'

20th Eva leaving New York per *Aquitania*

26th April. Eva Arrived from NY.

We can only imagine the emotions which plagued Eva and Plum during the following month of May. What a waste of time and money and how depressing for this great singer to be treated thus. The answer to the first of the three riddles which Turandot sings must have been very close to her heart, although not once in her own life did she utter the words: 'Yes, Hope, which always disappoints'. Plum was travelling less with Eva, since breaking his knee cap in July the previous year, and career prospects seem to have been difficult for Eva at this time. Plum was assuredly feeling bad about that.

Eva, however, was made with true northern grit in her bones and before we know it she is off to America again. She did not accept an invitation to sing at Bogotá, Columbia, in Central America, from where, she was advised, she could go after singing at the Pasadena Bowl and then travel on via the Panama Canal to return to New York. She did, however, leave Southampton on the *Champlain* on June 2nd to travel directly to New York arriving on the 9th, a day late, after a foggy voyage. Plum, still in London, had two teeth extracted and was ill for the whole week while she was at sea.

Eva was joined in America by Nance, a relative and friend, to enjoy a little tour together. They set off for Pasadena where Eva sang Aida on June 24th:

'I once travelled 12,000 miles to sing at the Rose Bowl Pasadena. Ronald Colman and McCormack were very kind to me... I lunched with Ronald Colman and his wife at their lovely home and also went with Count John McCormack and his wife to see their renowned villa plus swimming pool.'

She was paid $1500, half in advance and the rest the day before the performance. After this they travelled from Pasadena via Los Angeles and Santa Fe to Chicago and arrived there on the 30th. Then went straight to New York to board the *Champlain*, which took them to Plymouth where they arrived on July 9th.

It was Plum's 72nd Birthday on July 19th and it looks as if he was really feeling his age when he wrote this little personal piece in his diary on August 22nd: 'At Burnham lost key of car. Hunted for hours for it. Sent for Dick to bring another. Meantime John found it in pocket of my over-coat I had hung up on arrival. I forgot I had put the key there, previous to hanging the coat up. I was greatly upset.' But life went on, as in September Eva rehearsed with Coates for Isolde and: 'ARB got another bottom set of teeth from Mr Ball – more satisfactory.' On Sept 19th Eva Turner sang, at the BBC Promenade Concerts at Queen's Hall, the closing scene of *Götterdämmerung* and in the 2nd half, *Spring Waters* by Rachmaninoff and Bantock's *Lament of Isis*.

Strangely, the famous performance of *Serenade to Music*, the music for which was written by Ralph Vaughan Williams especially for Sir Henry Wood's Jubilee Concert at the Royal Albert Hall on October the 5th, is not in Plum's diary. This performance with Sir Henry conducting the BBC Symphony Orchestra and the subsequent recording on the 15th, again not in the diary, at HMV Abbey Road Studios, became legendary and took the names of the British singers who took part into the lives of the public for many generations.

Dame Eva tells us:

'This was a most wonderful night in honour of Sir Henry who brought about the Proms. I saw Sir Henry on Paddington Station on my way to sing in Wales and he said, "O Eva I would like a word with you. You know I am going to have a Jubilee and I want certain singers who have been associated with me to perform but it would be impossible were they all to sing an aria, it would be far too long, so I propose letting them sing a few bars, do you mind?" I said Sir Henry I would

be thrilled even if it is only a cough and a spit. This was a most wonderful night you know, Rachmaninoff came over to play, paying his own fares, because Sir Henry had given many of his works the first performance. It was a most wonderful night - with Royalty, mounted police, Oh! wonderful.'

Sir Henry Joseph Wood, (see appendix) with whom Eva Turner had a long association, was born on March 3rd 1869 and founded the Proms in 1895. He had an enormous influence on musical life in Britain, improving access for the ordinary person to concert music and raising the standard of orchestral playing. On the great day of the Jubilee Concert, the Morning Post told its readers in a leading article:

'The vast circumference of the Albert Hall will be crowded with Sir Henry's admirers, and it is not too much to say that throughout the country, lovers of music, of all sorts and conditions, will join, one way or another, in the occasion. For he has become an institution; the crowd calls him "Sir Henry", sometimes "Sir 'Enry", hailing him as the inspirer of the most democratic concerts in the world.'

Sir Henry Wood

Sir Henry was anxious that it be known that the concert, given in his honour, was not for his own glorification but was a charity concert to raise money for beds in London hospitals for orchestral musicians and felt that not enough had been said of this in the publicity articles.

Many of the 8000 audience had arrived by special trains from as far away as Yorkshire and South Wales. Three orchestras, four choirs and the sixteen solo singers rose in their places to greet his arrival on the platform after which the concert started with his own orchestration of the National Anthem, followed by: Sullivan's *O Gladsome Light, Egmont Overture* by Beethoven and Rachmaninoff's *Piano Concerto No. 2* with the composer at the piano. Rachmaninoff received the reception of a lifetime, 'the greatest of anywhere in the world': he said.

The Serenade to Music by Vaughan Williams ended the first half. Felix Weingartner had begged to be present at this concert and Sir Henry treated this as a great complement from such a renowned musician and organised a box for him and his guests. Rachmaninoff joined them to listen to the Vaughan Williams work but was so overcome by emotion on hearing it that he had to retire to the back of the box, at which point Felix Weingartner, turning rigidly in his high stiff collar, inquired: 'He is not going to be sick?'

For this piece, Sir Henry chose singers he had worked with and liked and Vaughan Williams wrote the piece with their voices in mind, giving each singer only a few solo bars to sing, along with choral harmony which they sang together, marking their solo lines and their part in the harmony with their initials. Eva Turner's part is the most heavily orchestrated in this rather delicately scored work but as Ernest Newman remarked on another occasion: 'the scoring that could drown Miss Turner has not yet been put on paper'.

All the soloists, renowned in their profession, brought their own personality to Shakespeare's words, helped by Vaughan Williams' clever composition. They were not unknown to each other, far

Henry Wood surrounded by his chosen singers for 'Serenade to Music' by Ralph Vaughan Williams

from it, as, in different combinations, they had worked together and would go on working and teaching alongside each other as the years passed. They gave their services to the occasion.

Sopranos

    Isobel Baillie   1895-1983 (See appendix)
    Lillian Stiles Allen   1896-1982
    Elsie Suddaby   1893-1980
    Eva Turner   1892-1990

Mezzo-sopranos and Contraltos

    Muriel Brunskill   1889-1980
    Astra Desmond   1893- 1973
    Mary Jarred   1899-1993 (See appendix)
    Margaret Balfour   1892-1961

Tenors

    Heddle Nash   1894-1961
    Frank Titterton   1893-1956
    Walter Widdop   1892-1949
    Parry Jones   1891-1963

Baritones and Basses

    Harold Williams   1893-1976
    Roy Henderson   1899-2000 (See appendix)
    Robert Easton   1898-1987
    Norman Allin   1884-1973

A few days after the Jubilee Concert, on October 12th and 21st, Eva sang Isolde at Covent Garden with the English Opera Society. Albert Coates conducted with Walter Widdop, one of the sixteen, as Tristan and press reports included:

'Once again Eva Turner astounded her listeners with her astonishing stream of tone'

At an afternoon concert in November, three of Sibelius' works were performed by Sir Thomas Beecham, as part of his Sibelius Festival, a title which irritated Sir Henry Wood, a great rival, as he felt he had been conducting Sibelius works for years without the need to create a special festival. Plum said of Eva's part in it: 'Great Success. Most Difficult'. Eva Turner was, after the performance, presented to the daughter of Sibelius and received a congratulatory letter from Walter Legge about her performance, of *Luonnotar, Daughter of Nature* a Symphonic Poem written for soprano and orchestra. This composition has a mystical, cosmic feeling to it and is even ominous: after the birth of the world, a new beauty, but also new horrors become possible. These ideas were perhaps a little too relevant for 1938.

On November 10th Eva and Plum left for Chicago and the liner *Isle de France* immediately struck rough water which accompanied them all the way to New York. During this trip as often happened, Eva was sick daily.

While in Chicago, Plum's diary tells us:

November

19th Turandot. Staggering Success: Masini (Calaf), Garrotto (Liu).

26th *Aida* with Gigli and Maranzoni conducting.
Eva had been asked to sing *L'African* on this occasion as the management thought it would suit her but she replied that although she had studied the role she had not as yet sung it, so she would not wish it to be her debut opera.

Sunday Chicago Tribune November, 1938:

'Eva Turner noted English dramatic soprano made her re-entry in the spectacular title role after nine year's absence from Chicago. Although Turandot is one of her most famous roles, she had never sung it here. This proved overwhelmingly our loss for she delivered its superhuman high sustained music with almost unparalleled magnificence. Her large brilliant voice is as solid as a rock and contains the most glorious high C heard in a long time. If she does not greet a sold out house at next Saturday afternoon's Aida *and at a late repetition of* Turandot *the opera goers of Chicago will overlook one of the finest dramatic sops now singing.'*

28th Eva Turner (Sieglinde) with Manski (Brünnhilde), Rene Maison (Siegmund), Kipnis (Wotan) and Weber conducted.

December

8th *Turandot* with Tokatyan as Calaf. Conductor Leo Kopp.
17th Martinelli for Gigli.
Her fee for each performance at Chicago was $300.

At the end of the season, the Chicago Press thanked singers in three categories according to the size of their success. The following are all in the first category:

Kirsten Flagstad:

'Still the greatest figure in contemporary opera for the increased depth and maturity of her Isolde.'

Charles Hackett:

'Still the stylist among operatic tenors, if not indeed among all singers of older florid music for the immeasurable aristocracy of his Count Almaviva in "The Barber"'

Eva Turner:

'For her combination of spectacular vocal brilliance and superb musical security which made her singing of the title role of Puccini's "Turandot" the most striking new performance of the season and the finest version of the role ever heard in Chicago.'

Benjamino Gigli:

'Returning to America after years of absence, for representing on their highest meeting ground the smoothness of Italian vocal discipline and the warmth of Italian musical temperament.'

Eva and Plum stayed on in American during January 1939 and Plum's diary tell us:

January

2nd, 3rd Busy in New York re Met. Saw Simon Encouraging

4th – 13th   Busy re Met.

12th   *Fidelio* at Met with Flagstad - not outstanding.

13th   Teeth Broken in the making. Have to make new bottom part.
First Snow. *Simon Boccanegra* – liked it.
S.B was Lawrence Tibbett, Fiesco – Pinza, Soprano – Maria Caniglia. Conductor Panizza.

28th   Left New York @ Noon

February

4th   Arr. Plymouth @ Noon

6th   Eva Arrived in England from USA.

After her return trip Eva wrote to her friend and fan Sheila Wright:

I am happy to tell you that I have had a great success in Chicago and am invited to return next season when I hope other things will come along as a result.

I had quite a good journey back for this time of year but was very glad to leave the boat as always.

Yours,

Eva Turner.

Money matters concerning fees in Britain are serious, as we read in this letter:

Harold Holt
3 Clifford Street
New Bond Street
March 30 1939.

My dear Eva,

I had a long argument yesterday with Mr. Walter Legge concerning your fee for the Garden, and when I suggested that you were willing to take a reduction of 20% on what you received for the last Grand Season they all appeared to be quite shocked that you should want such a lot of money. You see, the contracts under which these Prima Donnas from Italy are engaged do not receive any such large sum of money, and I have now obtained a final offer for you of £50 per performance.

I would not hesitate, if I were you, to accept this as you must look upon it has having a thousand pounds worth of, in relation to your future at the Metropolitan and Chicago etc.

Will you telephone me in the morning and let me know that I can accept this offer on your behalf.

Kind regards,

Harold.

Despite this bad news, Eva went to Swansea to sing: *Great is Jehovah*, *Ritorna Vincitor*, *Elisabeth's Greeting* and *Vissi D'arte* and on April 30th bought a car, a new Hillman Minx, and took possession of it from the garage at a fixed rate of £18 yearly. It cost £108-19-2.

A couple of days later, in fighting mood, she wrote a brief letter to one of her tenants:

'Herewith I give you a week's notice dating from the 6th May to vacate my premises at 67 Elsham Road. I do not intend to tolerate further the constant expressions of dissatisfaction.'

(Elsham Road was at the corner of Russell Road, so this refers to the house previously mentioned.)

After writing the letter, she sang Turandot at Covent Garden and Plum tells us: 'Splendid Show'. The cast was: Luccioni – Calaf Faverò – Liu, Conductor - Constant Lambert.

Gracie Fields was at that performance and a newspaper of the day reported:

'Gracie is learning to sing in Opera. Gracie Fields queen of the English variety stage went to the opera at Covent Garden last night to hear a great English Prima Donna who is helping her to achieve the crowning ambition of her career. For Gracie from Rochdale, mill lass, plans one day to sing in opera and her idol Oldham born Eva Turner is coaching the famous plastic voice in the higher realms of music.

"Turandot" was the first grand opera Gracie Fields heard at Covent Garden: "Ever since I met Eva on board ship coming from America she has been nagging me to sing in operatic music" said Gracie as she sat in the Prima Donna's dressing room during the interval. "And she could do it" said Miss Turner matching Gracie's broad Lancashire accent: "She's got a wonderful natural voice..."

"Eva's been coming to my home to listen to me and go over arias from "La Bohème" and "Madama Butterfly" and has given me advice on breathing and producing the old voice... I've been messing about with it so long making my living as a comic, I thought it might be too late to get it to do the real stuff but Eva says NO. I've always loved real music best, and back of my mind all the time I have had that longing to sing an operatic role one day."'

The seat prices for the 1939 season at the Royal Opera House Covent Garden were:
Grand-Tier Boxes £10-10-0 and £8-8-0,
Balcony-Tier Box £5-0-0,
Orchestral Stalls £1-10-0,
Stalls Circle £1-6-0,
Balcony Stalls £1-1-0,
Amphitheatre Front Stalls 14/-,
Gallery 6/- and
Unreserved Gallery 3/6.
(see p.37)

Eva Turner had accepted the greatly reduced fee of £50 to sing Turandot on May 3rd and 11th and had also replaced Caniglia as Aida on June 8th for the same fee and Plum tells us: '*Aida* with Eva was a Grand Success.'

The Daily Telegraph reported:

"Aida' with Eva Turner. Wynn Reeves as conductor. There were two changes last night at Covent Garden when Eva Turner appeared as the heroine and Wynn Reeves one of the orchestral violins took Sir Thomas Beecham's place as conductor. Miss Turner has sung this part here before, but she won renewed admiration for the freshness, the appealing emotion and the absolute sincerity of her singing. She did not prance cavalierly through the score, as tho' it had been designed merely to afford her material for display. She treated it all as music – and as vitally dramatic music. The emotions of such a situation were reflected in her voice and the stage never became a platform. The whole of Act 3 was brilliantly sung and the end of the first scene of Act 2 showed the purest artistry.'

The reviewer goes on to say that it was a shame that such a good conductor should not be allowed to conduct after a rehearsal time although he took a while to warm up. The main dancer in the ballet scene was Margot Fonteyn.

'I recall so well the last "Aida" at Covent Garden, in 1939 prior to the war breakout. The cast was Gigli, Ebe, myself, Armando Borgioli, and I think Giulio Tomei and not Pinza, with whom I sang "Aida" so often and who was in every sense of the word a magnificent Ramphis, vocally and in stature. Mr Gigli was always such a dear. Do you know that when it came to our final duet in the 'Tomb Scene' he made a charming gesture to me to sit down on the stone bench before singing and said to me 'Prego Signora, s'accomodi' - "Please madam take a seat", and at the final curtain was so excited by the performance that he took me by the hands and swung me round and round. I have ever remembered this performance, since it seemed to be truly inspired. Little did we know then that was to be the last performance at the Royal Opera House for many years, since the war broke out soon afterwards. This performance was conducted by Sir John Barbirolli who I had known first when we were students together at the RAM and directed by my great friend Charles Moor. Ebe Stignani was a magnificent Amneris and we sang together often and when we sang the duet with Sir Thomas, also from Lancashire, he pushed us to the limit and took it at such a pace! I would fix him with my eye as if to say, "Well you may be from Lancashire too, but you're not going to beat us lad!" And when we pulled it off, he always gave us a wink.'

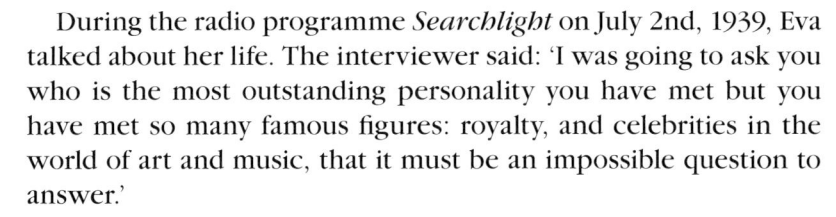

Ebe Stignani

During the radio programme *Searchlight* on July 2nd, 1939, Eva talked about her life. The interviewer said: 'I was going to ask you who is the most outstanding personality you have met but you have met so many famous figures: royalty, and celebrities in the world of art and music, that it must be an impossible question to answer.'

Eva Turner:

'No it is not so difficult. I can answer it but I think my answer will surprise you. I came back from America last year with Gracie Fields and we became very friendly. I think she is the greatest personality I have ever met. It is rather interesting that on the same day as she was given the freedom of Rochdale I was getting a civic reception at Oldham. I don't know whether Gracie will be able to hear this broadcast but I wish her a very speedy recovery from her illness.'

She also emphasised, during the programme, how important it was for a singer to keep fit. Mr Williams: 'Is this your first holiday here in Whitley Bay Miss Turner?'

Eva:

'Dear me no! I've spent many a holiday here. It's your tonic air I like. My favourite exercise is to walk right along the seafront from Tynemouth to St. Mary's Island - breathing deeply all the way.'

We look to Plum's diary once again for an exact sequence of events, and a flavour of his and Eva's life, as Europe travelled towards a war that changed the world:

August

5th   Mileage 43453. Left London at 6 am for Brusino in Buick with Norman, Florence, Eva and self.
Mileage at Brusino on 8th 839 miles from London.
Used Petrol 60 gallons average 14 miles per gallon.
Bought 65 and had 5 left. Distance 210 miles daily.

18th   Eva began to fast after night meal, broke it on 24th - 6 days. She felt much better despite contrary advice from Croaker.
Weight at beginning, 11-7. Weight at end, 10 stones.

27th   Frank and Maude Thompson (little girl in Eva's class at Werneth School who later married Eva's cousin) came today for lunch and tea. We went to their Hotel for supper.
In Buick to Lugano. Returned 11pm.
Eva paid for our two meals 11/- tip 1/-

29th   Norman and Florence left by Buick at 12.45 for London via Cento Valley under disturbing political conditions. They hope to reach French territory tonight.

31st   Norman reached London. Tonight the Germans broke through the borders of Poland

September

1st   Hitler commenced attack on Poland which is contrary to his prediction. I am very shocked at such a happening.

2nd   England declared war on Germany owing to time limit having expired of England's demand for Hitler to stop his attack on Poland.
France neutral at moment awaiting decision of Italy for some reason.

3rd   A state of War declared by England. France declares war. Italy still neutral

4th   Brusino: A state of war by England.
Bloody battle with Poles and Germans.
Wet a.m. France gone into battle.

Cut away ivy on right side. Roots to be found in time.
Benes suggested that Czechoslovaks and Slovenians should combine and fight for their past freedom.
Poles meeting German attacks. 24 hours rain.
Germans sank passenger ship off North Coast of Ireland by torpedo much indignation

5th Wet.
Hamburg bombarded by 25 British planes – 6 brought down.
422 foreigners ordered out of Switzerland.

6th Left Brusino by 8 pm boat for Geneva. Arr Lugano 8.50. Cooks Ticket for Geneva £60.

7th Left Lugano 7.23 am for Geneva arr. 5.38pm.

9th Supposed to have left for London but train cancelled. Much turmoil. Visiting consul re. same.

10th No meals. Consul says likely leaving date next Wednesday.
Much confusion

12th ARB Hair cut 1/- by Toscanini who has lived here 39 years.

13th Left Geneva 2.06 pm for London per special train and arrived at 11.45am in Paris then on to Dieppe.

14th Terrible confusion in getting through customs at 1am. Such a mess. Very badly managed just over filling in a paper concerning the taking monies out of France.

15th Left Dieppe 2.30 am in a black out with 598 passengers all British. I slept in a deck chair on deck till 4.30 am. E not good / below.
Arr. Newhaven 6 am terrible confusion getting through customs at Dieppe. At Newhaven we were early off and got through customs smartly – got good carriage – 4 in seat. The Indian acquaintance and girl inclusive. Had good cup of tea and left Newhaven at 7.30 am.
Arrived London at 9 and Taxi home.

The London Press reported on Monday the 11th:

'600 Britons on the Wooden Seat Express.'

The article tells that a collective visa was obtained for the Brits leaving Geneva. They were trying to cross the French frontiers but it was impossible to travel through militarized France.

'Eva Turner famous operatic star is among 600 British tourists who will leave Geneva on Wednesday on a special train in a dash

for England. The journey will tax the nerves and stamina to the outmost. The train will leave Geneva on Wednesday afternoon and should reach Paris via Lyon the next morning. The journey will mean 21 hours in wooden benched 3rd class carriages.'

At the end of the Promenade Concert on September 1st Sir Henry turned to the audience and in a subdued voice addressed them saying: 'Owing to the special arrangements for broadcasting which are now in force, the BBC very much regrets that the Symphony Orchestra will no longer be available for these concerts in London. I am therefore very sorry to say that from tonight the Promenade concerts close down until further notice. I must thank you, my friends, for your loyal support and I hope we shall soon meet again.'

This decision, taken by the management at Broadcasting House, to bring in emergency plans prepared long before was taken during the first half of the programme without his knowledge and came as great shock to Sir Henry. He had been refusing to take on board that this war was going to be very different from the previous one and that performances could not be kept going in the same way. His head had been a little in the sand and he was now quite traumatised for his own position and for all the musicians who would soon be unemployed because of lack of work. Eva's Prom with Walter Widdop on September 25th was among those cancelled.

Adding to their woes, on the 29th Plum and Eva went to the funeral of Mr Parr at St Nicholas, Kent at noon, a journey of 78 miles each way. This presumably was following the death of dear Gladys's father.

The Haven
Peachaven
4/10/39

My dear Eva
Thanks love for this, tell your friend to send the songs along, they may be the kind I'm looking for. It's a devil trying to find the right songs to please the folks. I'd much rather be in Italy doing nowt. Wouldn't you?
Anytime your this way come in love, will give yer a cup o tay affen we will and affen we want
Love to yer Gracie.

I think we all know the answer to the question of doing nowt:

London County Council
Public Health Department
Ambulance Service,
London
20th October 1939.

Dear Miss Turner

I wish to thank you for your application for enrolment in the London Auxiliary Ambulance Service but am obliged to inform you with regret that it is not at present possible to utilise your services. I would add, however, that you will be communicated with if in the future such a possibility occurs

Frederick Menzies,
Medical Officer for Health.

Maggie Teyte, a friend of both Gladys and Eva, four years older than them, had recently been accepted for a war job, driving trucks and, because she was so small, she had to stand up to apply the brakes. Hearing about this Eva had thought it a good idea that she too should do her bit for the war effort and could not quite understand the refusal. Perhaps the medical officer had heard of Eva's private confession to learning and memorising new roles while driving. However, now being freed from obligations and despite the awful journey homeward they had experienced, Eva and Plum decided to return to Italy, as it looked as if Mussolini had made up his mind to keep Italy out of the war.

Plum's diary:

October

26th   Left London Newhaven for Dieppe usual time.
       Boat took crisscross route across in day time.
       Arr Paris 11pm after long voyage.
       Arrived Milan on 28th

November

19th   11.30 this morning Swiss Consul of Milan Mr Mosiman phoned to say that Eva must be at his office at 9 am to receive the 2 visas. We have been held up in Milan for 3 weeks.

20th   Leave today on 11.15 am train for Brusino. Thank God after 3 weeks waiting

December

25th   Brusino Arsizio. Spent Christmas here: Eva, Plum and Angelina, who cooked us a lovely chicken for lunch. We brought a Cross and Blackwell's Christmas pudding and enjoyed the repast very much. Matty went home so we were very quiet. Still we had a sweet time.

27th   Left here noon this day for London via St Gothard, Lucerne, Olten, Lausanne and Geneva.

Gracie Fields wrote a series of letters in 1939 to the readers of the Sunday Graphic. This one tells its readers to look out for her special Christmas message to the troops next Sunday and goes on to say:

Villa Canzone... Song of the Sea. On my way down from France, singing for the troops at Bologna, there was my friend the Oldham lass Eva Turner who was having a big success as Turandot. Eva is a wonderful artist. Bless her.

The performance of *Turandot* in November, with Licia Albanese and Galliano Masini which Votto conducted, to which Gracie Fields referred, was the main reason for Eva Turner's return to Italy, and was her farewell performance in the country, which had embraced her as one of their own and was the land she loved almost as much as her homeland. But when war rears its ugly head, an individual's wishes and desires have to take second place and so it was that she left Italy with a heavy heart.

CHAPTER 6

1940-1948 War Years and Final Performances

Villa Junesca, on the shores of Lake Lugano in Switzerland, was off limits to Eva during the war years, which she spent in Britain, living in London when she was not touring and so she began trying to settle into this new way of life, without travel outside of Britain. No one had any idea of how long this situation would last and of course America was not yet involved but British thoughts went to perhaps a year, or even 18 months before normal life was re-established.

February, 1940

February, 1940 was a busy month for Eva.

Sir Hamilton Harty conducted on the 5th when she sang *Ocean Thy Mighty Monster* and the *Immolation* in London. A few days later, on the 8th, she was in Wales where she was a favourite of Ivor Owen, who was devoted to her and who conducted the Swansea Orpheus Male Voice Choir with Eva, as their soloist, singing all her big favourite solo arias and songs. The 11th found her broadcasting arias from *Masked Ball* and *Oberon*, conducted by Sir Adrian Boult, at nearby Bristol. She then set off for Scotland where she sang in Inverness and Glasgow and on the return journey from Scotland, sang in Liverpool. When she returned to London she took part in a concert for ENSA, Entertainment National Service Association, at Loughton in Essex.

It was very cold weather at the beginning of 1940 and Plum caught flu at the end of February. He was clearly quite ill and somewhat depressed as he witnessed his position in Eva's professional life changing. He was no longer able to look after her as a younger man could and they both knew this and were trying to think of solutions to a problem which if they were not careful, could end up with their roles reversing and Eva taking care of him. Neither of them wanted this, as Eva was anxious to keep her career alive until the war was over and had a sense that a pause now would not be good, so during Plum's illness she carried on travelling alone.

March

Eva went to the south of England where she sang with the Bournemouth Symphony Orchestra. On returning home to London, she received a letter from Plum's sister, Ada, with whom they had often stayed in France, en route to Lugano and to whom Eva had written before leaving for Bournemouth. Ada's situation on the continent, in wartime France was not ideal and so it seemed sensible that she should come to Britain and look after Plum. In her letter she offered this possibility and to share domestic cares. Eva wrote to her immediately by air mail on the 10th of March (Eva's birthday), gratefully accepting the offer and inviting her to spend her life with them, both in London and Brusino, helping in domestic responsibilities.

By the 13th, Plum was a little better and they heard a performance of *Traviata* with Joan Cross as Violetta but thought her: 'rather ordinary'... and Plum's diary the next day tell us: 'The Finns surrendered to the Russians and Norman presented a fine umbrella to ARB'. Eva gave a BBC Concert at Stratford Theatre on the 20th which was broadcast under the title: *Puccini, the Man and his Music* and Plum proudly recorded in his diary that he was there and: 'A high standard was maintained and all were delighted'. Eva then went to sing at the Blackpool Tower Ballroom Pavilion which was packed out and where: 'Reginald Dixon made a splendid effect on the organ'.

April

On the 14th she sang at the London Palladium with Dino Borgioli when they sang Puccini duets and arias. By this time Plum was clearly a little better and Ada had not as yet been able to arrange to obtain the official documents which she needed before she could leave France. Eva's diary had many Italian engagements in it for the next few months and with them gone, it looked a little bleak although she happily took on lesser engagements to sing for any charities in Britain.

June

Plum's Diary.

4th	British troops were evacuated from Dunkirk
10th	Italy declared war on Britain
14th	Swastikas flew from the Eiffel Tower and the Arc de Triomphe.

July

The country, not to say the world, was in a sorry state and it had all been too much for an ill man, so sadly we now have to say goodbye to Plum who died on July 26th, 1940, having reached the age of 74. (I have no idea what happened to Ada). Albert Richards Broad had a 'seizure' on July 25th and died the next day. It looks as if he did not ever fully recover from the flu, or even perhaps from his 'neuritis' attack of 1935.

The Daily Sketch of Monday July 29th 1940 tells us:

He found a British Opera star. Albert Daddy Broads 74 year old white haired maestro of opera, who gave up his life to the genius of Lancashire born Prima Donna, Eva Turner, has died at her Kensington home. His great protégé was at his side. Eva Turner tells us: "He was my master, guide and a second father. We were first brought together in the last war. I was with the Carl Rosa Opera Company. He was a famous bass and expert on voice production. He recognised the quality of my voice and he made my career his life's work giving up everything else. When I went to La Scala, my father asked him to go with me and look after me. After that he travelled everywhere with me".

On her triumphant tours Miss Turner travelled with this clause in her agreement that where she went Richards Broad went also and that his travelling expenses should be paid as part of her contract. The silver haired maestro saw to everything for his 'discovery'. For four hours a day he taught and advised her vocally. He made the travelling arrangements, labelled the luggage, studied her contracts, phoned her hair dressers and dressmakers for her and settled her bills. He was always in the audience at her performances, sensing opinion, signalling his own reaction.

Eva had many letters of condolence, among them Mr and Mrs Norman Walker, Ivor Newton, Elisabeth Welch and of course dear Gladys Parr.

August

Before he died Albert Richards Broad had negotiated what was probably his last contract for Eva Turner, which was for 8 Monday Promenade Concerts, the concerts having been resumed: August 12th, 19th and 26th, and September 2nd, 9th, 16th, 23rd and 30th at the Queen's Hall, for which her fee would be 30 guineas for each concert. The first of these, conducted by Sir Henry Wood as always, was the *Immolation* and *Ritorna Vincitor* and Norman Walker sang *O Star of Eve*.

September

During the run we read in a letter to Sheila Wright on the 11th:

'Last Monday was quite a happening. At about 4.35pm I get a phone message from Ibbs and Tillett the agents, saying the concert is likely to be cancelled but they would phone me definitely in a short while. At about 5pm they say they have decided to go ahead and will I make my way to Queen's Hall. I hurry and dress and my brother very kindly drives me to the hall. I arrive there to learn that after all it is cancelled so we turn tail and go home... Just after the receipt of your letter a 'Time bomb' was dropped outside here down the road and we had to go to the back of the house for 2 days.
Best Wishes,
Eva
PS. Time bomb was found to be piece of masonry shaped like a bomb so we were spared that! Thank God.

As often happens in the aftermath of death, grief takes a little while to descend, as we try to get on with our own lives, and it seems that this was the case with Eva. As we have seen with the death of her mother and father, intimate deaths and grieving did not have an obviously normal format in her life and so it was with that of her dear Plum. She just got on with things and enlisted the help of Norman when she needed it as we have seen in the letter above. Now looking after her own interests, we read of a little diversion in the tactics of keeping herself in the public eye. I wonder what Plum would have thought? The News of the World:

'Next Friday at 11.30 the blouses which are the subject of today's Fashion Company will be displayed in the Palm Court at Selfridges. The display will be sponsored by Miss Eva Turner the famous prima donna.'

Eva Turner was a member of the Proms Circle and at a meeting with nine members present, as well as Sir Henry Wood, the Circle broadcast their sentiments about the Proms in general and about their being cancelled.

'At the end of that meeting Olive Groves, accompanied by her husband George Baker, made an impromptu recording of *O tell me Nightingale* prefacing her song with the modest words: 'If I'd known you were going to do this on me I should have arranged to have an urgent professional engagement elsewhere' and then singing it as sweetly as Philomela herself.' Perhaps this was a little too 'impromptu' and unconsidered, as there was always 'a little something' between these two ladies.

1941

With her father Charles and her friend and mentor Plum both now dead and the War in full flight, it was a difficult, lonely time for Eva. But she soldiered on, spending her evenings writing letters of an empty nature, spending most of the letter saying how sorry she was not to have written sooner and how her commitments had prevented this. Gladys Parr spent a lot of time with her and was concerned for her usually ebullient friend, who was now a bit low.

Harold Holt was still her agent and she now dealt directly with him. There were more discussions between them on the telephone about a possible Australian tour and she visited his office for the express purpose of pushing this idea but it came to nothing. During February she sang: in Norwich, an Elijah in

Glasgow, a concert in the Queen's Hall with the LPO and a lunch time concert at the National Gallery.

In March, she remembered Sir Henry's birthday in her diary on the 3rd but there is no mention of her own on the 10th. The *Radio Times* tells us:

> 'On March 5th the first of a new series of studio operas was broadcast' and the feedback suggested that the public loved the broadcast which had been 'Cavalleria Rusticana'.'

In a small tail piece it said:

> 'Miss Eva Turner who has just returned from Chicago sings tonight at the Queen's Hall.'

There were terrible air raids in London during April 1941 but despite that, concerts happened and Eva went to see a performance of 'Messiah' on April 11th at the Queens Hall. A month later on the afternoon of May 10th, Malcolm Sargent conducted a performance of Elgar's 'Dream of Gerontius' there and that night, about 11 o'clock, this much loved and cherished Hall was hit by an incendiary bomb. (See appendix)

Eva sold her car in May and on June 1st went to Euston Station with Gladys to wave her off on tour with *The Beggar's Opera*, sending a good luck Telegram, at the cost of 1/5, the next day. Plum's war loan investments and his money were safely deposited at the bank for Ada. Eva went home to write a letter to Harold Holt about going back to America which as yet was not involved in the war and later in the month she sang at a celebrity concert for the BBC at Bristol on June 22nd.

Her old friend Glad, on returning from touring, and her brother Norman saw a lot of Eva during July and Eva spent the day with Norman on his birthday on July 13th but it was not so jolly as in times past.

With the Queen's Hall now gone, the Promenade Concerts took place at the Royal Albert Hall and on July 15th, Eva sang *Leise Leise* from *Der Freischütz* and *Elisabeth's Greeting* from *Tannhäuser* there. She visited Oldham at the end of the month and recorded in her diary on the 26th 'One year ago Plum left us'.

A letter to Sheila Wright on August the 9th gives us a little glimpse of her performances at that time:

> 'I am certain the bonny heather brought me luck and happiness because the concert on Monday went extremely well I am happy to say. So much so that I was in Lady Wood's box last night and Sir Henry in the interval came to tell me again how fine I was on Monday night and said he wanted to write me a personal note to tell me still again of the splendid performance.'

She had sung on August 4th, with Walter Widdop in *Götterdämmerung* and again on the 9th when she sang *Vissi D'arte* and *In Questa Reggia*. Eva went to hear Gracie Fields in a concert later in the month and recorded her mother's birthday on August 31st in her diary. It was almost 17 years since she had died.

In November, Eva Turner gave an afternoon concert in De Montfort Hall in Leicester and later that month, when she was rehearsing at Bedford for a forthcoming BBC broadcast of *Aida*, in St Paul's Mission Hall, which was freezing, she took a bad cold. Despite this she was in 'wonderful voice' when she rehearsed at the Corn Exchange on the 17th and 18th:

'Florence Austral had supper with us on the 18th and I woke the next day with very bad bronchitis. Could not sing Aida. What a grief. Stanford Robinson and Daphne Limmer were perfectly wonderful to me and the BBC gave me half fee as a consolation.'

The *Radio Times* reported:

'Singer's cold leaves BBC 3 hours blank. 'Aida' could not be performed because no substitute Aida, to replace Eva Turner, could be found, who could sing the new translation.'

She then left Bedford and went home to bed for a few days but was well enough, on the 23rd, to sing the *Immolation* and *In Questa Reggia* at the Royal Albert Hall with Sir Malcolm Sargent conducting and on the 30th Norman and his wife Florence went with her to Derby where:

'I wore my Madonna blue dress. Programme: "Ritorna", "Isis Lament", "June" and "Spring Waters". Encores: "One Fine Day", "Love Went a Riding" and the "Star Wake up Pipes of Pan". Drove home with Norman and Florence, after tea with Hooleys.'

Jessie Goldsack, now known as Lady Jessie Wood, had herself been a singer and knew and liked Eva from way back. Because of her non-marital situation with Sir Henry, the Woods were sometimes shunned socially but Eva had no problem with that and enjoyed their company on many occasions.

Her diary tells us: 'Dec 4th, Dined with Sir H and Lady Wood' and 'Dec 10th, Did lots of Xmas cards.' Eva became an insatiable letter writer and used her diary to record this often saying: 'Spent the evening writing correspondence' but the names themselves were not recorded and none of the letters remains.

1942

The new year dawns and life of sorts continues without many performances but on April 9th Eva took part in her first *Desert*

Island Discs programme for the BBC, where she would be allowed to take 8 records and: 'an inexhaustible supply of needles'. I include here her choices and a little flavour of her at that time:

1. The Prelude to Wagner's *Tristan and Isolde* because: *'It feeds my soul with imagination.'*

2. Rachmaninoff's *Rhapsody on a Theme by Paganini* because: *'I have a memory of hearing Rachmaninoff himself play the solo part (it was in fact his 2nd Piano Concerto he played) at Sir Henry Wood's Jubilee Concert, at the Royal Albert Hall, in 1938.'*

3. Elgar's *Nimrod* because: *'It is one of the most British pieces of music ever written and by a great British composer and to me conveys a deep religious sense which would come under the heading of sacred music. I am one of those people to whom worship means simplicity and I know nothing more moving than:*

4. Bach's *Jesu Joy of Man's Desiring.'*

5. Melba singing *Clair de Lune*, because there were no recordings of Melba singing *Romeo and Juliet*, which she had seen and heard at Covent Garden when she was just starting with the Carl Rosa Company and: *'it really was an inspiration'.*

6. *España* or *Spanish Rhapsody* by Chabrier because: *'It is exciting and there is a very fine recording by Sir Thomas Beecham and the London Philharmonic Orchestra.'*

7. *'I would want the finale to the "B Flat Minor Piano Concerto" by Tchaikovsky.'*

    Roy Plumley: 'Known to Tin Pan Alley as *Concerto for two*.

    Eva Turner: *'If you don't mind I'll have it just as the composer wrote it – and to my mind, Tchaikovsky expressed himself quite clearly in this wonderful work without the aid of crooners and vocal choruses... I would like Toscanini's interpretation with Horowitz at the piano.'*

    Roy Plomley: 'I can't understand the strange lack of opera'

    Eva Turner: *'The reason for that is very simple: on that desert island I should have my voice and should still have my imagination. I would sing, probably more than I do now, and I should hear in my head the orchestra and the other singers and the chorus, probably sometimes, even the applause. I should have, with my voice and my memories, a little imaginary opera house of my own. That's the only way I can express it. But my last choice is an operatic one, it's orchestral and it's from one I have sung all over the world. It is tremendous music and it should always remind me of all the great artists that I have had the privilege of singing with.*

8. The *Triumphal March* from Verdi's *Aida*.

Roy Plomley ends by saying that he hopes: 'It is not long before you'll be able to resume your travels and that nice English sounding name of yours will again be billed outside the great opera houses of the world.'

Eva Turner: *'Thank you Mr Plomley. That was a very nice little speech. I hope so too.'*

I am not able to tell you her choice of either book or luxury on that occasion as, in the early days of that programme, one did not take them with you but one was merely cast away with 8 records.

It seems that performing was less and less on the agenda, mainly because there were very few opportunities of doing so at that time, but Eva sang at the Proms as usual: July 6th Isolde's *Narration* and *Liebestod*, July 25th *Ritorna Vincitor* and *In Questa Reggia* and on August 21st *Beethoven's Ninth Symphony*. She also sang at one or two more concerts in favourite towns like Glasgow, Liverpool and Swansea during 1942.

1943

This was another lean year for Eva's singing but as always the Promenade Concerts featured in her diary:

June 28th *Prelude and Liebestod* from *Tristan and Isolde*. Roy Henderson sang *Amfortas's Prayer* from *Parsifal* in the first part of the programme, which also included: the Overture to the *Flying Dutchman*, *Venusburg Music* from *Tannhäuser* and the *Entry of the Gods into Valhalla* from *Das Rheingold*. The Wagner was conducted by Sir Henry and Basil Cameron conducted Tchaikovsky's *Sixth Symphony* in the second half as Sir Henry's health was failing and the help of close colleagues was enlisted.

July

Palermo, the capital of Sicily was taken by the Americans without a struggle and a couple of days later Mussolini, Italy's dictator for twenty one years, fell from power when King Victor Emmanuel assumed command of the Italian forces. In September, Italy surrendered unconditionally to the Allies and Mussolini was shot a couple of years later by Italian partisans.

On July 6th Eva Turner sang *Ma dall'arido stelo* from *Un Ballo in Maschera* at a Promenade Concert which was conducted by

> **Tuesday   6 July at 7   15**
>
> *Part 1 conducted by Basil Cameron*
>
> | | | |
> |---|---|---|
> | OVERTURE | Semiramide | *Rossini* |
> | PRELUDE AND ARIA | Ma dall' arido stelo (Un Ballo di Maschera) | *Verdi* |
> | RHAPSODY ON A THEME OF PAGANINI | | *Rachmaninoff* |
> | SYMPHONY NO. 1 | (First performance in England) | *Eugène Goossens* |
>
> *Part II conducted by Sir Henry Wood*
>
> | | | |
> |---|---|---|
> | CLOSING SCENE (Salomé) | | *Strauss* |
> | OVERTURE Benvenuto Cellini | | *Berlioz* |
>
> EVA TURNER
> *Solo Pianoforte* CYRIL SMITH

Other performers in the Proms in 1943 included names from the 'Serenade to Music' concert: Heddle Nash, Mary Jarred, Lillian Stiles-Allen, Elsie Suddaby, Frank Titterton, Roy Henderson, Parry Jones, Isobel Baillie, Muriel Brunskill, Astra Desmond and Norman Walker.

Basil Cameron. The second part, the closing scene from Strauss's *Salome* and the *Overture to Benvenuto Cellini* by Berlioz, was conducted by Sir Henry who had only conducted the second half because his health was failing.

On August 16th Sir Henry Wood conducted Eva Turner and Parry Jones in the *Love Duet* from *Tristan and Isolde* and Eva in the closing scene from *Twilight of the Gods*. Adrian Boult conducted *Symphony No. 4* by Schumann in the second half.

The photographer for the *Picture Post* on November 13th spotted Eva Turner at an art exhibition in London. The caption is:

'Whether you like it or not, it certainly holds the stage.'

And goes on to say:

'Eva Turner, left, goes round the exhibition. She is the English woman, an opera singer with the greatest international reputation, but takes an interest in painting as well as music.'

The next month, Gladys Parr and Eva Turner sang together again for the first time in many years, when they and Frank Titterton went to Swansea to give an *Opera Concert* at the Brangwyn Hall on December 4th.

1944

Eva had never lived alone before the death of Plum and so although Norman and Florence were very much in her life, living in the upper maisonette of her house, she was not only rather isolated and lonely, since they were a married (although unfortunately not happily) couple, but she was, more importantly perhaps, without someone who would organise her professional life.

When I asked in later years, how Anne Ridyard and Eva Turner had found each other, Anne took up the storytelling, saying that she had been out for afternoon tea in Lancashire with a group of ladies from the amateur operatic society to which she belonged, and they were chatting away about opera in general when the conversation turned to Eva Turner's Turandot. Anne Ridyard said in passing that she thought it would be tremendous fun to be part of a life like that and wondered if 'the diva needed looking after', a comment which brought general laughter to the group.

Anne Ridyard, who at that time had a good job in the Civil Service, was rather bored with her life and was keeping an eye open for a change but thought no more of the tea party. One of the opera lovers was a friend of a friend of Eva's and small towns being as they are, the bush telegraph was set in motion. Very soon Eva got to know of this story and on thinking about it went up north to be introduced to Anne Ridyard.

They liked each other immediately but there was one small blot on the landscape: Anne Ridyard was a heavy smoker. Eva liked her, and in those days anti-smoking was not so much on the agenda, so decided to turn a blind eye to this and asked her if she would come to London and be her secretary companion. Anne, aged forty with no immediate family ties, feeling that she had nothing to lose, accepted the offer and came to London on March 1st 1944.

Anne Ridyard

Things in Britain were beginning to look a little brighter with the lifting of clothing restrictions, allowing for demob suits to be more stylish, although ration coupons were still required to purchase them. Interest in women's fashions was also reawakening. In this slightly more optimistic climate, the two ladies got on like a house on fire from the very start, not only because Anne was a great help to Eva, answering her letters, attending to her diary and organising her home life but because she was able to stand up to Eva on the occasions when she became too bossy and demanding. Eva admired this quality in Anne and quickly learned never to overstep the employer/employee mark.

Eva Turner and Anne Ridyard

It is my personal belief that the two ladies fell in love at this early point in their relationship. They were two lonely people looking for friendship and love, and found it in each other. There is nothing in Eva Turner's papers to substantiate that statement and I have only my own observations, having known them for many years, linked with an instinctive gut feeling that there was something more than a professional arrangement involved in their relationship. Seeing them together, they were never less than the sum of the parts and were in many senses – one. They just felt like an old married couple by the time I knew them with all the history that that might suggest.

Eva took great pleasure in sharing the world of music with Anne and during Easter 1944, there was a performance of *Messiah* at the Royal Albert Hall, which Anne expressed a wish to attend. In her usual manner Eva set about obtaining a ticket for Anne to go to the concert, alone as it happened, as she herself was performing elsewhere. Kathleen Ferrier was the contralto, not long embarked on her dazzling career, and after the concert, Anne could hardly wait to tell Eva how glorious her voice was.

A few weeks later Eva was singing in Wales and an indisposed Mary Jarred was replaced by Kathleen Ferrier so Eva Turner now heard the great voice for herself and could not praise it highly enough. She also loved her personality, as did all who came in to contact with Kathleen, and felt the Lancashire bond embraced them both. Kathleen Ferrier died less than ten years later while Eva was in Oklahoma, from where Eva gave a very moving tribute to her on American Radio.

The great Rachmaninoff had died, on March 28th, 1943 and his friend and admirer Sir Henry Wood was but a mere seventeen months behind him, dying on August 19th, 1944. Eva Turner's Promenade concerts that year were on June 16th, July 10th and 14th, and August 8th. Sir 'Enry presented his last concert on July

28th and died just over a week after the 50th anniversary concert of the Proms, which he had been too ill even to listen to on the radio...

Eva Turner's hand writing was bold and big but never very clear, so the second paragraph of this letter makes one smile a little:

> 87a Westbourne Ter.
> 22nd August 1944
>
> Dear Sheila,
>
> The above address may set you thinking. I have to tell you that on the 3rd of July a flying bomb destroyed my house and most of the contents. My sister in law, who was in the upper maisonette was very severely cut and was removed to the West London Hospital. I am happy to tell you that she is now improving and has been evacuated to the north. I and my secretary companion and little dog were out at the time. The house along with six others in the row is to be demolished. I have to tell you that my piano was so badly damaged that it is going to take 6 months to repair it at a cost of £130.

(I have the bill for that exact amount which the repair to her beloved Blüthner piano cost her, as she left the piano to me in her will).

> I consider myself very blessed that my carpets and settee and chairs were away being redone for the Queens Gate flat.
>
> Sheila I have to tell you that your writing is really the limit as I have already told you before. I hope you will excuse me but someone will have to tell you eventually so better be me. It would lead me to think you were studying to be a doctor. It is illegible and for a person like myself with little time at their disposal, I begin to think I shall have to ask you not to communicate and just be content with seeing you when you present yourself and that is that. I know you will take it in the spirit it is meant.
>
> I cannot recall if you know that I have Miss Ridyard with me as my secretary. She has been a tower of strength through all these ordeals. She is also a 'lass from Lancashire' and a very enthusiastic amateur dramatic actress and singer so you should have much in common to talk about when you meet. Would it not be nice if she could come and do some of your parts with you in your company?
>
> Best Wishes,
> Eva.

Roger Quilter wrote to her the day after the bombing, saying how sorry he was about her house being bombed and offered her and Anne a roof over their heads in his house at Hampstead. Eva was very touched by this kind offer but did not accept it, as she and Anne found a flat in Westbourne Terrace in which to live temporarily.

On November 4th with all those changes happening round about her, Eva sang Aida with an all British cast: Muriel Brunskill (Amneris), Parry Jones (Radames), Roderick Lloyd (Ramfis), Dennis Noble (Amonasro) and Dr Malcolm Sargent conducted.

1945

Eva Turner was still singing in the provinces but not so much in London although, in April, she took the place of Oda Slobodskaya at short notice, when she sang at the London Palladium. It looks as if she sang Oda's planned programme, a group of Strauss songs: Morgen, Ständchen and Cacilie, along with her own repertoire, the *Immolation* with the London Philharmonic, which was conducted by Rankl.

By a strange quirk of fate, Eva Turner on May 8th, V.E. Day, was back in Dublin at the Gaiety Theatre. As you may recall she had been singing there when the 1918 Armistice was declared. Eire had not been without its own problems during the war, as travel between there and Britain had been banned in early 1944, for national security reasons but with relationships between the countries restored, we find Eva Turner once again in Ireland, singing Aida when victory in Europe was declared. The Irish press reported:

> 'In the name part one of the best known sopranos of the day appeared, Eva Turner, who, when she last sang here in opera, was a member of the Carl Rosa Company. She gave a very moving interpretation of the part of the royal slave, singing with great ease and power and richness of tone... Miss Eva Turner's Aida has been renowned for many years for its power and precision. The singer has a clear pure voice with tones that ring out in the ear and remarkably strong head notes: in all a truly great performance.'

In the audience that night were Count John McCormack and his wife Lily and also Margarita Sheridan (Peggy Sheridan).

On June 14th, she was the guest of Mr Frank Duncan when they dined at the Savoy and sat next to Sir Thomas and Lady Beecham, with Walter Legge opposite. After which she set off for the provinces once again singing in Wales, Scotland and the North of England, to celebrate the ending of the war. Work in London however did not seem to be coming her way although she did sing Promenade Concerts: on July 24th, the *Love Duet* from Tristan and on August 17th, the great aria *Abscheulicher* from Beethoven's *Fidelio*.

Flora Minns, a fan and acquaintance for whom Eva had often managed to procure complimentary tickets and who knew Eva only slightly, died around this time and as she had no family of her own, left Eva her house in Fulham, because of: 'Eva's great kindnesses to me'. This was a nice unsought windfall as she and Britain tried to recover from the financial devastations of the Second World War.

1946

On February 23rd Eva Turner sang a Verdi *Requiem* in London with the Philharmonic Orchestra and Choir and her birthday on the 10th of March was celebrated in style at the Savoy Hotel Grill where she had eleven guests including: her brother Norman and his wife Florence, Lady Jessie Wood who was now a widow and Anne Ridyard. That same month Eva Turner went up north to the Huddersfield Choral Society to sing Aida with them on March 22nd and while in that part of the world she went to Oldham on the 24th to give a miscellaneous concert of songs all sung in English.

Her Promenade Concert on September 5th, 1946 was: scenes from *Siegfried* with Arthur Carron singing Siegfried, Parry Jones as Mime and Sir Adrian Boult conducting. This was not broadcast and her fee was £50. Her Promenade on the 19th was: excerpts from the *Twilight of the Gods* conducted by Constant Lambert and Arthur Carron was once again her Siegfried. This was for the same fee but if broadcast, she would receive £65.

After singing *Cavalleria Rusticana* with the Stockport Choral Society, on October 5th, and despite the world still being in turmoil with many countries caught up in violence, Eva travelled across a still unsafe Atlantic Ocean to Chicago to hear Milanov sing Aida, one presumes to be seen, as well as to listen, with the hope of obtaining contracts from this old friend, the Chicago Opera Company. There were none.

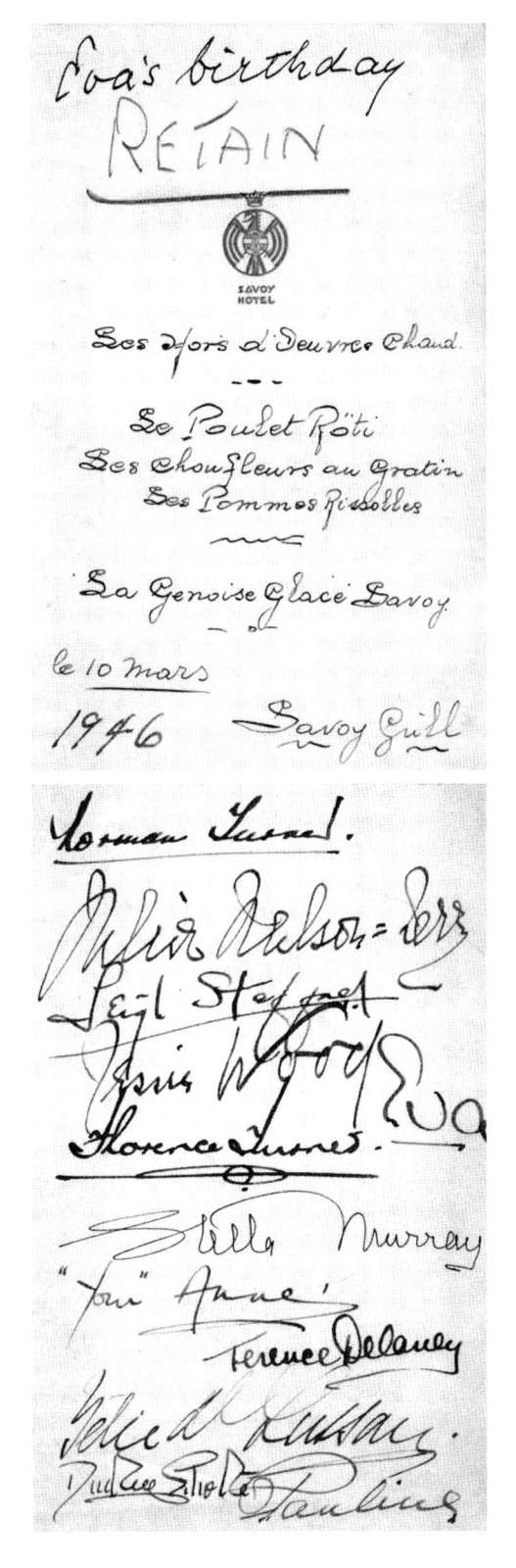

1940-1948 War Years and Final Performances 233

Thursday 5 September at 7

WAGNER—STRAUSS CONCERT

Conductor: Sir Adrian Boult

A Faust Overture	Wagner
Excerpts from Siegfried	Wagner
(a) Act I, Scene 3	
(b) Forest Murmurs	
(c) Love Duet, Act III, Scene 3	
Burlesque, for Pianoforte and Orchestra	Strauss
Dance of the Seven Veils (Salome)	Strauss

Brunnhilde EVA TURNER

Siegfried ARTHUR CARRON   *Mime* PARRY JONES

Solo Pianoforte DONALD HARGREAVES

Thursday 19 September at 7

WAGNER—SIBELIUS CONCERT

Conductor: Sir Adrian Boult

Prelude, Lohengrin	Wagner
Excerpts from Twilight of the Gods	Wagner
(a) Day-Dawn and Sunrise; Duet, beloved Hero; Siegfried's Journey to the Rhine	
(b) Prelude and Scene 1, Act III	
(c) Funeral March	
(d) Closing Scene	

Conductor: Constant Lambert

Symphony No. 6, in D minor	Sibelius
The Return of Lemminkainen	Sibelius

Brunnhilde EVA TURNER   *Siegfried* ARTHUR CARRON

Rhinedaughters:

Woglinde LAELIA FINNEBERG   *Wellgunde* EMELIE HOOKE

Flosshilde EDITH FURMEDGE

1947

In December, 1946, with the same hope of resuming her international operatic career, she had gone to Italy but returned to Britain on February 27th 1947 a disappointed singer, because the opera houses in Italy were still closed due to fuel shortage and Italy was struggling to survive. British opera on the other hand, was having a new lease of life with the repeat of Benjamin Britten's successful opera *Peter Grimes* at Covent Garden at the end of the year, after its first performance in 1945 at Sadler's Wells conducted by Reginald Goodall. Eva Turner, however, was never to be part of this new blossoming of opera in England, led by English artists, although Gladys Parr was.

After returning from Italy, Eva Turner sang, on April 5th, Verdi's *Requiem* and Malotte's *Lord's Prayer*, at Swansea, when she wore: a black velvet dress with Vogue sleeves. Edith Coates, Henry Wendon and Tom Williams were the other soloists and the conductor was Ivor Owen. Eva's fee for performances in the provinces was now 35 guineas and there was a little cluster of performances of such a type at: Nottingham, Wakefield, People's Palace and East Ham, of a miscellaneous nature, including some of her favourite operatic arias and songs.

At the end of May, 1947 Eva Turner returned to Covent Garden to sing Turandot in a new production with costumes and scenery designed by Leslie Hurry, directed by Michael Benthall and conducted by Constance Lambert. Covent Garden was now trying, at last one might say, to build a cohesive company which would include a nucleus of British singers. Eva Turner sang Turandot on: May 29th. June 3rd, 5th, 10th, 13th, 17th, 28th and July 1st.

Dame Eva tells a later audience at Covent Garden:

'Alfano was a composer in his own right. He made the Tolstoy's "Resurrection" into an opera and actually when I was at the Teatro Cólòn of Buenos Aires in 1927, this opera was given with Cobelli. I knew Mr Alfano enormously well. When I was singing "Fidelio" in Turin, he was then the head of the conservatoire and often used to come to the rehearsals and performances. Actually the last time I saw Alfano was here in this opera house in 1947. It was during one of my last performances of "Turandot" here. He had come to London to attend a conference of the Copyright Association and he told me afterwards in my dressing room that he had intended to return to Italy on the Thursday but as I was to sing Turandot on the following Saturday, he decided to stay over. He watched the performance from the Royal Box there. I must say I felt very honoured indeed.'

Some chorus members are renowned for their rather unkind humour about soloists, perhaps a way of coping with their own boredom when not on stage, and so Eva Turner at this time gained the nick-name among the Covent Garden chorus of 'the steam whistle', which rather contradicts Lord Harewood's opinion stated in his book, when he says that he could think of no other soprano: 'with that blend of opulence and blade.'

During that run of *Turandot* she fitted in a visit to the Regent's Theatre Chelmsford on the 1st of June, where she was the soloist for the Ford Symphony Orchestra whose conductor was James W. Sanderman. It seems that she sang anywhere she was invited and did not consider anything too lowly, even when she was also performing at the very top venue of the Royal Opera House, Covent

Garden. This performance was in aid of the National Farmers Union's, Flood Distress Fund.

Eva bought her house at 26 Palace Court in July and she and Anne Ridyard moved in, making it their permanent home. Eva was no longer dominated by an older man but shared her life with a caring partner and perhaps because of this, or perhaps her lifelong concern about money, who knows, the choice of concerts which she accepted was not always to her advantage but among them were these of note: the Winter Gardens in Weston Super Mare, the Royal National Eisteddfod in Colwyn Bay to an audience of 10,000, a celebrity concert at the Villa Marina, Douglas on the Isle of Mann and her Prom that year was on August 18th. All those, before going on tour with *Turandot* to: Glasgow on August 19th and 22nd and 30th, Liverpool on September 5th, 9th and 13th, Manchester on September 17th, 22nd and 27th and Birmingham on October 2nd, 4th and 11th.

Monday 18 August at 7.30
THE BBC SYMPHONY ORCHESTRA

WAGNER-SIBELIUS CONCERT

Conductor: SIR ADRIAN BOULT

EXCERPTS FROM THE TWILIGHT OF THE GODS — Wagner
(a) Day–Dawn and Sunrise—Duet, Beloved Hero—Siegfried's Journey to the Rhine
(b) Prelude and Scene 1, Act III (Siegfried and the Rhinedaughters)
(c) Siegfried's Funeral March
(d) Closing Scene

SYMPHONY No. 1, in E minor — Sibelius

Brunnhilda EVA TURNER
Siegfried ARTHUR CARRON

Rhinedaughters
OLIVE GROVES   EMELIE HOOKE   EDITH FURMEDGE

In October Eva Turner sang in Glasgow with the orchestra there and gave four performances of *Aida* at Leicester.

Grand Hotel Leicester
13th Oct 1947

Dear Sheila,

I could not agree with you more that there is such thing as doing too much but at the same time I should hate not to be busy. I think that to be really busy is to be happy – it gives one no time to ponder on political situations and such sordid things.

I am pleased to tell you that the tour has been an enormous success in each city. After this week in Leicester I sing two further performances of Turandot *at the Davis Theatre Croydon on the 20th and 25th of October. Then there is a further season at Covent Garden and I sing* Turandot *there on the 4th 8th 10th and 29th November...*

Best Wishes,
Eva

On November 14th she sang Senta in the *Flying Dutchman* at the Bradford Festival with Sir Malcolm Sargent conducting at a special fee of £35, half her *Turandot* fee, and after singing the performances of *Turandot* mentioned in the letter to Sheila Wright, Eva Turner received a contract with an accompanying letter which said:

'*I understand Mr Webster approached you regarding a further performance of* Turandot *at the Royal Opera House on January 8th 1948.*

I have much pleasure in enclosing herewith a contract for this date.'

There were also two more proposed performances of *Turandot*, on February 28th and March 20th.'

This last date was cancelled and so her final performance at Covent Garden was on February 28th 1948, at a fee of £70.

1948

Eva went to the Royal Albert Hall to hear the London Philharmonic Orchestra, conducted by Rankl, accompanying Kirsten Flagstad on January 29th and sang there herself on February 8th in a Holt Concert with Sir Malcolm Sargent conducting the London Symphony Orchestra, where she introduced a couple of new arias into her repertoire: *Divinités du Styx* from *Alceste* by Gluck and Elizabeth's great aria from *Don Carlos* by Verdi. She had, the previous week sung Aida at Stockport, to help celebrate their centenary at a fee of £50.

The Olympic Games were celebrated in London during August, at the Empire Stadium Wembley. The tickets for this event, costing 10/6 each, were sold on the strict understanding that the holder of the ticket would not take cinematograph pictures of any kind. Eva and Anne were at the hairdressers in the morning of August the 4th and on returning home were greeted by the kind bearer of two tickets for the afternoon session on that very day. Without a moment to spare, they jumped into a taxi which took them, just in time, to see the athletic events of that day and they were thrilled to have been part of this momentous occasion.

At the end of 1948 Eva sang a flurry of concerts outside London which included, on October 23rd at Birmingham, the soloist with massed bands where Stanford Robinson conducted. She was elected President of the RAM Club for 1949, an honour she considered to be one of the highest and dearly cherished in her career: 'My beloved Royal Academy.' The next President, in 1950, was Sir John Barbirolli, her old play-mate.

Of her final performances of *Turandot* in the 1947/48 season, The Stage reported:

'On Friday I met Constant Lambert who had conducted, and congratulated him. "Yes" he said "It's good to hear Grand Opera laid on with a trowel again isn't it?" It certainly is. It is good to see Puccini's grandest opera – not perhaps his most lovable and characteristic but certainly his most powerful and monumental – staged with a splendour that matches the brazen magnificence of the score. It is good to watch Leslie Hurry's grotesque designs whose magnificent and pernicious beauty suggests all the culture and cruelty of legendary China.

Above all, it is good to hear Eva Turner once more: to recognise the keen brilliance of her tone, the undeniable majesty of her presence; sometimes her intonation wavers a little – on the first night this was no doubt due to her train – a preposterous affair (there was evidently no clothes rationing in China) – less like a train than a gigantic carpet with a woman attached to one corner of it. On her entrance in Act 2 she was all but tripped up by it – an accident calculated to appal the stoutest operatic heart. I trust this encumbrance has been at least halved by this time.

Walter Midgley's Calaf is a lyrical tenor trying to be a heroic one and succeeding to a surprising extent. In the famous "Yes I will – no you won't" altercation in Act 2 between Prince and Princess where they bawl and brawl like a Billingsgate couple, each trying to go one better, his voice was not equal to Miss Turner's but when he sang alone it was true and resilient, and his high B natural was a refreshingly pure honest one.'

Another review from an unknown paper tells us:

'At Covent Garden, Eva Turner gives a Titanic performance as Turandot. No ordinary mortal could sustain such a role as this and at the same time manoeuvre a train such as she wears in the first Act – a blue and gold train that would nearly carpet Piccadilly Circus, borne along in her wake by a beauty chorus of six.

To walk upstairs with this formidable appendage is a feat in itself; and to turn and walk downstairs with it again demands much skilful tacking to and fro if she and the beauty chorus are not to be overwhelmed in its folds and disappear from view. Miss Turner not only survived this physical ordeal without getting pulled off her feet but has vocal power enough to sing the rest of the cast almost inaudible.'

She said of this train:

"We had three young ballet girls each side – one of them was Millicent Martin who must have been about thirteen years of age – they were quite wonderful. I gave hardly a sign and they responded immediately."

All reviewers were kind but some pointed out the flaws of age:

'For some twenty years Eva Turner has been the best Turandot in the world, and there are still some moments, notably in the last act, which recall the old magnificence; elsewhere (at any rate on the first night) the sense of strain was too pronounced and too continuous for comfort.'

Philip Hope-Wallace:

'What did move us was the return of Eva Turner to a role in which she had no rival in the world at one time (and for all I know even now has not). That sensational performance some twenty years ago has often been repeated

Eva Turner and Utu

1940-1948 War Years and Final Performances

and extolled. The sheer noise, intensity and punch of the high B and C in the big second act piece defy description. It was like someone hoisting steel girders and throwing them across the auditorium. One gaped at the upward speed of the phrasing, with the throat opening like a great crater. In many ways it was the most thrilling operatic performance of our day. Well, Miss Turner would be the last person to wish me to pretend that it is now the same thing. But you can hear enough to hear what it was. The voice is still wonderfully loud, piercing and majestic, and the famous train is carried in the grand manner.'

Harold Rosenthal, that most knowledgeable of opera critics who Dame Eva regarded very highly wrote, in September 1950, a piece in *Musical America*, which to my mind brings this English Prima Donna's international career into perspective:

'In an earlier article on the growth of the British operatic tradition, I sought to show why it has been all but impossible for continuous and steady growth of British opera to take place; how from time to time promising groups of composers and artists have been forced to give up the struggle, since the state was quite indifferent to the idea of a British National Opera; how at the same time, the British public was nurtured on international opera and "star" singers; and how against this background it was impossible to build up a British school of singing, with the result that the vocal student had little prospect of making a career on the opera stage. In continental countries, native singers are able to sing their native opera in their native tongue, and consequently have developed a national style of singing. In the days of great singing, if an opera director wanted a first rate Carmen, he went to Paris to find her: if he wanted an Isolde there were countless German opera houses to choose from: if he wanted an Aida he went to Italy. How did British operatic singers fit into this picture, and how do they fit into the operatic scene today?

Eva Turner

Since there has been no British national opera, British singers have developed no national style. The Carl Rosa Company, the British National Opera Company, the Sadler's Wells Company and the present Covent Garden Company are forced to adapt themselves, as best they can, to a diversity of styles, a practise that results in what Ernest Newman once termed, "a bastard style that is neither English, Italian, German or French". Moreover, the problem of finances has always impeded British opera singers. The average student of voice has always regarded opera as an incidental rather than a chief source of livelihood. British singers' careers have characteristically been on the concert stage, singing in countless London and provincial performances of "Messiah", "Elijah" and "Hiawatha's Wedding Feast". In the main they have had no real operatic stage training and they often come to the opera house entirely because they have gained reputations in the field of oratorio. Until quite recently, even if they wanted to, singers could devote only a fraction of their time to opera in Britain, for there was simply no demand for their services when the only permanent companies were the Sadler's Wells in London and the touring Carl Rosa.

Today the situation is somewhat better, for we have what is virtually a permanent national opera house at Covent Garden. But matters are still far from happy, for no substantial improvement is possible until the British provincial cities have their own opera houses, so that there will be chances of promotion from, say, Leeds to Birmingham, Birmingham to Manchester and Manchester to London, just as in Germany the promising singer arrives at Berlin or Munich by way of Darmstadt, Cologne and Wiesbaden. Only then will the young student be justified in devoting his full training period to opera, instead of regarding the opera stage as a precarious sideline.

Despite the many obstacles, however, there arose in England in the years between the two world wars a group of operatic artists who, if the necessary tradition and opportunities had existed, could have won international renown in Europe and America.'

Harold Rosenthal goes on to say that this piece is not exhaustive because of space but that he will deal with his chosen singers one by one in alphabetical order, so as not to incur disfavour. He then tells us about Joan Cross, Noel Eadie, Lisa Perli (also known as Dora Labette) and Maggie Teyte before commenting:

'Eva Turner became one of the greatest sopranos of the century, and a Turandot without equal.'

He then gives a brief resume of her career saying:

'Her success as Turandot brought her back to Covent Garden for the International Season of 1928. Prejudice against British singers in leading parts in these Grand Seasons was strong and this soprano had not even changed her name to an Italian sounding one. Nevertheless, her Turandot created a sensation, and she subsequently became world-famous as the heroine of Puccini's last opera.'

'If only,' she said to Ronald Hilborne

'If only Puccini had lived to complete that duet.'

Ronald Hilborne looked at the huge bowl of flowers on the table during the silence that followed her statement and went on to write:

'Although I was having tea with a prima donna, oddly enough there were many thoughtful silences. "Application" is for Eva Turner as important a word as "temperament". Not for her the ceaseless flow of chatter and the extravagant gestures one is conditioned into expecting from a traditional prima donna; she takes music too seriously for that. Instead, you merely see a hand occasionally and gently outstretched to emphasise a point and you hear an eager, self deprecating "Do you agree?" For the rest of the time she speaks with deliberate and deep sincerity... She put the score of Turandot on my lap. "See," she said, "see how the notes for the Princess go up, ever up, preparing with urgent excitement for that final revelation."'

Bernard Levin tells us in the Times of January 31st 1974:

'I heard Eva Turner right at the end of her career sing Turandot which she had made her own. Dame Eva, happily, is still with us – indeed she is clearly immortal – and every time I see her, which I do quite often, I go home and listen to her singing 'In Questa Reggia', which I truly believe to be the most amazing series of sounds ever put on a gramophone record; the final repetition of Turandot's terrible warning: "Gli enigmi sono tre la morte una" climbs so high and yet is sung with such exquisite purity of tone and such stupendous lung power that it becomes impossible to believe that it is coming out of a mere human being.'

'Such harmony is in immortal souls'
WILLIAM SHAKESPEARE

CHAPTER 7
1949-1959 Oklahoma

During the period when Eva Turner was singing, live performances were still a major source of relaxation. People made their own entertainment at home round the piano but the desire to see and hear excellence in the arts meant visiting a theatre or concert hall, as there was no television which could bring first class performances to people in their own homes. There were radio broadcasts from well known venues by great artists, which were welcomed into people's lives and when those same artists appeared in towns all over the country, the locals were even more anxious to see and hear them in person.

The days of reality television, or wall to wall sounds on many media, had not yet arrived and the singers and actors of that age were thought to have a very special gift. The working man, whose life was perhaps a bit humdrum and repetitive, not to mention a struggle, could be on the sidelines of those special lives, if he enjoyed singing in a choir or taking part in amateur dramatics, or if he spent some of his hard earned money to buy into that exotic world. His role would have been that of the admiring audience.

A great prima donna was, in the eyes of her public who loved her, merely an extension of her voice and was of iconic dimensions. Her public strove to hear every available performance and although they wanted in some way to be close to this icon, if they were too close, her magic faded, as she became one of them in her normality. This distant relationship had the give and take of friendship or even of simple love as the audience gave its money for a ticket and the singer gave their sounds in return, the audience gave due applause and the singer was polite when introduced to them in person at the stage door, or in the dressing room. These actions had in-built boundaries and were easily sustained, so long as the singer lived only in performance and in the admirers' imagination. There were some rumours about private lives and even the odd newspaper article but there were no magazines writing in a titillating exaggerated way, with salacious photographs, or chat shows, or personal blogs, where singers revealed their so called realness.

To be a great diva in those days, with all the time at one's disposal dedicated to one's voice and therefore one's self, as well as the slowness of travel and lack of easy communications, when one was abroad and removed from would-be loved ones, necessarily meant that private lives were limited and sometimes unfulfilled. In some cases, this obsessive desire and huge commitment to being the best in their profession, meant, as in Eva Turner's case, women singers did not marry or have children, as this situation would necessitate being part of someone else's normal needs and desires.

There were exceptions to this. As well as very committed, dedicated marriages, which produced much loved children, casual or convenient alliances also happened but singers' relationships usually had to take second place to 'La Voce' and so both members of the team became, in a strange way, the keeper of the voice. If not, the relationship broke down. I think we have observed, in both of Eva Turner's alliances with the men who looked after her as a person that they also cared, at the very least, equally for 'La Voce'. It would also be fair to say that Eva Turner cared most for 'the voice' part of herself, as from an early age she had been encouraged in the thought that her contribution to the world was through her voice and without that, she would be a lesser person. In 1929 during her successes at Covent Garden, an astute report for the Referee says:

> 'Miss Eva Turner is an artist full of temperament as far as singing is concerned, but a happy, almost child-like, woman in private life... In fact her singing is so much the greater part of her life that one gets the impression that she is a voice much more than a human being.'

Eva Turner

We find Eva Turner, at the age of fifty seven, for the first time in her life, faced with a diminishing number of performances and the possibility that with the main part of her singing career behind her, she would not perform again. How was she going to cope without the prominent frontage of her voice and the task of perfecting it, which until now had been her persona? If she had been married or shared her life with a woman partner in her early years, or with a child, life would have been viewed from a very different window, where she, as a person, would have played an important part in the lives of others who loved her and so their needs would have been part of her needs and the angle of her window would have been sharply changed, from the view through which she looked, as a single-minded, single person. Perhaps, with the inclusion of Anne Ridyard in her life, things were changing slowly. But as their relationship was at an early stage in its development, and still included duties of a professional nature performed by Anne, allowing Eva to get on with her own life, we still don't have the interaction which completely equal relationships allow. Normal interdependency can bring with it an understanding of how relationships work. Intimate relationships, you may say, are a mystery to most of us and I agree but they are even more unfathomable, if you don't allow space in your life to practise them.

The relationship between the singer and singing teacher can be of the most intimate, flexible and equal nature, but Eva's experience with Plum had been one of master and student in the studio and of mistress and servant outside the studio, both with very clear, inflexible boundaries. Nowadays, people go on courses to learn about teaching because we realise how important the way we teach, as well as what we are teaching is but in thossse times, singers became teachers of voice and taught how and what they themselves had been taught, sometimes in a non-healthy, bullying style.

The love of the adulation of an audience is slow to die in singers and the studio becomes another place for this admiration to happen and so demonstrations of one's own skill can, if one is not careful, take up a large part of the student's time. Demonstration is a good idea but only for specific purposes among which should not be seeking the student's praise for victories past. How is this great singer, Eva Turner, who, although in one way is very ordinary, in another, very extraordinary and on a pedestal in most people's eyes, going to deal with her new situation, leave performing behind and become a great teacher? With hindsight we now know that Eva Turner's personality would not only continue to shine long after her performances stopped but that it would grow in a way that she did not necessarily expect. She made a very big point of saying that she had never retired and my feeling is that because her personal life had never had time or space to develop, she was frightened of how she would survive in the unknown zone of retirement and this fear led her through the teaching door where she hoped to find another life and a different kind of stardom without which she could not imagine life.

The idea that she was a good teacher had been fermenting in her mind since she worked with Gladys Parr in the early '40s. Plum had also been one of Gladys's mentors and with him gone, she and Eva had a few sessions together, about which Gladys was complimentary. Early in 1949, the young singer Amy Shuard came into Eva's life, when she coached her in Aida, before Amy set off for South Africa. On the 3rd of May that year, Amy Shuard wrote to Miss Turner from Johannesburg thanking her: 'for your gracious help.' She wrote again in June thanking her for her interest and telling her how well *Aida* had gone.

These small forays into the world of teaching, as well as the fact that she was often asked by fellow singers for a bit of vocal help, gave her the inner confidence that she could teach, when the moment came. That very moment presented itself, when a fellow singer from her days in Italy, Joseph Benton, formerly the tenor Giuseppe Bentonelli, got in touch with Eva to see how she had survived the war in Britain. Their paths had first crossed at La Scala, where he went to study after training in Nice with Jean de Reszke, also Maggie Teyte's teacher, and later, when she and Giovanni

Joseph Benton was born in Kansas to humble farmers in 1898. Joseph studied medicine at Oklahoma University and, after switching courses, gained his bachelor's degree in music in 1921. He then went to Europe to study singing and after a singing career in Europe, was invited to sing with the Chicago Civic Opera in 1934 and in 1936 made his debut with the Metropolitan Opera. When he retired in 1941 he went home to Oklahoma where he completed a master's degree in modern languages before becoming, in 1944, Professor of Voice at Oklahoma University, founded three years after the first settlers in 1889.

were performing, in different operas, at the Arena in Verona. He had also sung with other prima donnas including Muzio and Gina Cigna, most famously in *Faust*.

In the January issue of Opera News, Joseph read an article written by Riccardo Martin, a tenor singing at the Metropolitan in the early part of that century. He was writing about the state of opera in Britain and Europe after the war. He said of Eva Turner after hearing her at Covent Garden:

> 'In Turandot, Eva Turner disclosed a phenomenally powerful voice to great advantage and looked every inch, the mighty Princess, acting in a convincing manner with great dignity.'

Joseph Benton wrote immediately to Eva, care of Covent Garden, ending with:

'Your life is busy but if you have time please write me and tell me all about yourself – years have passed so please be detailed in your telling.'

This letter renewed their friendship and a year later a post in the vocal faculty at Oklahoma University, where he was teaching, became vacant and he suggested to the President of the University that Eva Turner would be the ideal person to fill that job. Despite President Cross's misgivings, Eva Turner was invited to join the staff, beginning in the autumn term 1949. By way of encouragement, Joseph Benton described his teaching situation to Eva:

'I have a handsome studio, Steinway grand piano and a whole plethora of fine voices among my twenty (maximum number permitted) students.'

Among Dame Eva's papers was this letter answering her questions as to what to expect life to be like in Oklahoma, if she did accept a teaching post at the University.

Los Angeles, Calif.
July 26th 1949

Dear Miss Turner,

My very good friends John and Elsie Simmons have inquired about life and general conditions in Norman, Oklahoma. As I understand it, you are considering going there for a year and wondering if Oklahoma life will be tolerable.

It happens that I was born in Kansas City, Missouri, and that during my early manhood, I made many trips as a travelling salesman, through Oklahoma. I recall Norman only vaguely as a small 'county seat' which means that the public square or common in the center of the business district would be buildings containing the offices of the various officials serving the country around. The school itself, a State owned institution, has always had an excellent record and has grown steadily and rapidly both in size and tangible results.

Both the climate and the people resemble Australia. During the summer months – especially July and August – it is very hot and very dry. Quite often there are intolerable warm winds which blow steadily for days. During the winter it is cold – that is colder than England, because it snows. The spring and fall are beautiful, although in the spring tornadoes sometimes occur in this part of the world.

The people are definitely of the type you have seen in Hollywood 'Westerns'. They are friendly, open and speak with a drawly accent unpleasant to the English ears. Their ancestry is mixed, but probably mostly Scotch-Irish. They are distinctly the American type – exceedingly democratic. There are quite a few full blooded American Indians, numerous Negroes and some Mexicans. The Indians are normally wealthy, as they were the original owners of much oil bearing property. The Negroes and Mexicans constitute the servant class and after you become used to them, turn out to be very fine people.

The topography is generally flat and treeless. The rivers are dry throughout the summer.

This is a very rich country. There is tremendous income from oil wells and natural gas wells and from large scale farming operations. Everything is very new – Norman itself must be less than fifty years old. All of the conveniences of life to which you are accustomed are available, and many more typically American luxuries.

The automobile roads are excellent, and if one has a car, it is possible to reach the far famed Rocky Mountains (Colorado Springs) in one day. The Gulf of Mexico in two days, and Mexico itself, in a day and a half.

Norman is not far from the geographical center of the United States. Either New York or Los Angeles can be reached by overnight plane.

If you can tolerate a colonial atmosphere and put up with a fast moving civilization, almost without traditions, you can be very happy in Norman. If you value highly the small courtesies, the spirit of tolerance and compromise, the respect for the established position and the intimate personal considerations all of which constitute life in England, you will find yourself somewhat like a fish out of water. Great wealth is worshipped, but otherwise, men are 'free and equal'.

The general standard of living is much higher than in England and the cost of living about the same or perhaps a little less. Salaries and wages are higher in the United States. At the present time, there is some unemployment. The price of basic commodities is moving slowly downward as we have entered a buyer's market. Nothing is in short supply, excepting possibly cheap automobiles.

A year spent in Norman would certainly lead to many fresh experiences and you might find it intriguing and enjoyable. I recommend it as a way to understand the United States, if such knowledge will be useful to you.

If you do decide to come over, please make a note of our address. Perhaps on a holiday trip, you might visit California. We would be most happy to have you visit our home and see our Camellia Gardens (700).

The last page of the letter is missing but I get the feeling that this gentleman, whose name we do not know and who has offices in New York City, Mexico and Los Angeles, is no longer a travelling salesman.

Eva Turner thought the situation over, and the expected salary of $4000 for nine months (in September 1949 the £1 was devalued by 30% and so suddenly Eva had an extra windfall as the exchange rate became £1 for every $2.80. It had been £1 = $4 until that point), might have given her a little encouraging nudge and she said:

'You know I have always loved being in America since my time with the Chicago Civic Opera and I have finished my contract at Covent Garden so, after consideration, I will come for nine months.'

She published a brief notice in the Telegraph about her new position, made the necessary travel arrangements which all had to be paid for before leaving Britain and organised the £20 which everyone was allowed to carry abroad with them for incidental purchases. These monetary measures imposed by the government, were in addition to the usual rationing of every day foods and clothing, which had helped Britain survive the war and were still enforced, as it was not until 1954 that all rationing was at an end.

In the middle of August, 1949, Eva Turner set off once again for America, that land of milk and honey, on board a Cunard liner sailing to New York, and left Anne Ridyard in sole charge of 26 Palace Court, Bayswater, London.

September 1949

She did not stop in New York but travelled by train for three days through Philadelphia, Pittsburgh, Chicago, St. Louis, Kansas City and Tulsa before arriving at her final destination of Norman, just outside the state capital of Oklahoma City. She liked travelling by train and didn't mind being alone on the journey, as, taking her father's advice from years ago not to become easy prey because of fame or her own friendliness, she did not converse much with strangers. This gave her time to think and rest her voice, which had to be in good condition to begin her teaching post so that she could show the students what 'real singing' was.

When she stepped off the train, the scorching heat was overwhelming and she could feel the perspiration begin to gather on her brow, upper lip and even to run down her neck and back. She had worn her new mauve woollen suit to be smart, as it suited her shape since losing a little weight that summer but oh dear, she was very hot. Perhaps she needn't have worn a hat to match the suit as well as long leather gloves. The fur stole certainly should have been left in London but nothing could be done, she just had to bear it.

Her old friend Joseph Benton and Spencer Norton, Director of the School of Music, were waiting to greet her as she stepped down from the huge American train. They were sensibly dressed in rolled up shirt sleeves and lightweight trousers and Eva thought how lovely it was to see Joseph again, but hardly recognised him as the strain of looking after his mother, who had died recently from cancer, had caught up with him, but he was as jolly and cheerful as she remembered him.

The men wanted to take her to her apartment first but she wouldn't hear of that, since she wanted to see, immediately, the university campus where she would be working. The studio allotted to her was on the third floor and had a piano, a desk and several chairs and was housed in a little turret with strange little bay windows. She immediately moved the piano so that:

'I would have my back to the windows and this would provide me with good light and also a breath of fresh air, when the windows were opened. They seemed surprised at the School that I had arrived two weeks before I start teaching but I always like to be early and I will spend the time settling into my new way of life. My apartment is situated within very easy walking distance of the University but unlike some, does not have air-conditioning. This makes me think of Norman and Florence back home. Norman has set up his own engineering firm which also deals with air-conditioning and has given it the appropriate name "Turnaire Co." I am having, however, to make do with one inadequate fan, as I sit here, in my new flat, gathering my breath. I will be so glad when evening comes.'

Evening did eventually come and there was a knock at her door. On opening it she found Mary West, whom she had met earlier, standing there. Mary was the assistant to the Director of Fine Art at the University, and she insisted that Eva join her in her comfortable, air-conditioned apartment on the other side of the building, for a light supper and to cool down. Eva accepted.

Meanwhile back in London her friends, who had missed the notice in the Telegraph about her new position, were wondering what had happened to her, until one of them made inquiries as to her whereabouts, to be told: 'Eva is in Oklahoma. 'Good God' replied the other, 'which part is she singing?'

Oklahoma, October 1949

Most generally, she arose at 6.30 a.m. and began her teaching at 8 am. Some students explained to her that they could not sing so early, so:

'I told them that they had better give up singing altogether then. None of them has, so far, done so. I have both junior and senior student recitals to prepare and I am really working them very hard, putting them through their paces and preparing them.'

A local newspaper interviewed her and a day or two later, an official from the paper telephoned, in a very embarrassed state, saying that there had been a printer's error and she had been named as being the visiting Professor of Vice. She assured him that was all right, since she would now be an immediate success and ordered a few copies to send home to England. Although a little homesick and missing performing, she did not, however, look back with regret but gave of her very best in her new life.

Dawin Emanuel, one of her first students at the university remembered: 'I'll never forget my audition with her, because I went in very self-assured, literally "Mr. It" and sang a few things for her. Miss Turner closed the piano lid, looked me straight in the eye and said,

"I will accept you as a student. However, we are going to have an extreeeeemely difficult year."

After striking a chord on the piano she sang the very last few phrases of *In Questa Reggia*, she then turned to me and said,

"That's how I made my career. How do you intend to make yours?"'

At her urging, her students returned to her studio day after day to watch her teach others, hoping that they would improve their repertoire and technique, while watching fellow students. One student recalled: 'I found out that if she didn't have a student scheduled, I could go in and sing. You just went in if you had a minute. If I wasn't in there, I was outside the door listening.' This idea was not entirely popular with some of the other staff.

President Cross, who had originally proffered the invitation, said of her that he had been slightly vexed by her vitality on occasion, as she went to her studio even earlier than he went to his office. 'Watching you from the window of the President's home, where I was eating my breakfast, I was impressed with how fast you walked. It always appeared that you were leaning forward at an angle of approximately 10 degrees, from the vertical, not bent at the hips but with body straight. You floated along in such a fashion that it appeared you might be facing a strong east wind. But I found there was no wind, when I finally started to my office. It then dawned on me that your feet were moving so fast that your body had to be inclined forward, so you wouldn't walk out from under yourself.' (She clearly stopped running as she passed his window!)

Judy Bounds Coleman, a junior student, was reluctant to change teachers when Miss Turner arrived at the University but, as an outstanding student, was chosen by the faculty for this important visiting teacher's studio and said: 'I went in for my first lesson, and after I began singing, Miss Turner started making these horrible sounds accompanied by grimaces, saying:

"My God, the tone is going through me like a rapier."

Reduced to tears I left the room but Miss Turner followed me asking:

"Where are you going?"

On seeing that I was upset and offended she then said:

"I am very sorry. I didn't mean to insult you. I was telling you how you sound."

She was right. I had no basis for even understanding what she was doing, as I thought I had come into the studio to entertain her. I simply was not prepared for this sort of treatment, never having encountered it before. Miss Turner was marvellous. She opened a whole world for me. She stopped coddling me, stopped praising me and taught me a tremendous amount. I presented my junior recital in the spring of 1950 and those who were there could not believe the transformation, which had taken place in my voice and my demeanour. I shall ever be grateful to her.' Judy Coleman continued to study with Eva Turner and when Eva left Oklahoma to return England for good, in 1959, she replaced her valued mentor as the vocal professor in the University.

Dawin Emanuel, Judy's friend and fellow student at that time, said of her 'transforming recital': 'When Judy opened her mouth, out came a different voice. It was really a metamorphosis. He also said of his own lessons: 'Whenever Eva Turner felt my support sagging, her right arm would fly off the piano and collide with my abdomen. One day, I was singing for all I was worth and she was playing. She suddenly wheeled around at me without even looking, and out came that lightning fast elbow and she hit me a little lower than the diaphragm. Well, this put me half way out of the window.' He finishes this account of a lesson with: 'I literally was clinging to that window sill with both hands and the rest of me was hanging out of the window.'

Not all students reacted well to this kind of teaching and some retreated to other teachers under the strain of trying to learn to sing in this unusual teaching environment. Eva could never understand this, as she felt that if they could not cope with her, they would not cope with the singing profession itself. She did not seem to take into consideration that not all students would be thrown into the world of opera but would in fact, if enlightened, make good teachers themselves. Or indeed, that singers' personalities come in all shapes and sizes, which perhaps were not the same as hers. Her best intentions sometimes ended in tears and divisions.

Eva Turner

Most students, being young and resilient, however, responded with delight to her methods, liked her and drew her into their social lives. She was one of them, eating at the little restaurant called the 'Copper Kettle', where students could afford to celebrate on special occasions. They invited her to go to football matches, of which she knew very little but went anyway and enjoyed their company. She was young at heart and perhaps, if we think about it, had somehow missed out on youthful delights at the appropriate time.

There were many reports, from the students, of her performing in the studio, or of her taking them down to the Holmberg Hall to demonstrate the virtues of her projected sounds. She used *Ho-yo-to-ho* and *In Questa Reggia* for these purposes and she and the students, together with admirers who heard the sounds from a distance and came into the hall to listen, seem to have enjoyed these moments, which faded, as she became better at and more involved in, the nitty gritty of everyday teaching.

She was persuaded to give a recital at the University in December that first year, in which she would be accompanied by the Oklahoma City Orchestra. Eva wanted to wear the Adelina Patti jewels for the occasion but they were back in London and so Anne Ridyard, after trying to persuade her against the idea, retrieved them from the bank vault and sent them to America. It has to be acknowledged that the Patti jewels are made of paste but Eva Turner cherished them because of their association with the great lady and so they had become legendary in her mind and she felt a sense of responsibility towards their previous owner, Patti herself. While the jewels were in the post, she worried:

'O how I wish I had taken Anne's advice and not had the Patti jewels posted to me here. What if they are lost in transit? My God I can only pray. Everyone assures me that they will arrive safely but it has been five days now and no sign of them. I will have failed in my duty to look after them if, through vanity, they are lost. My new friends are sick of me, as I ask them repeatedly for reassurances but I cannot seem to stop and in fact, I can barely concentrate on preparing the recital for fear that the jewels will be lost forever.'

She was right: her new friends were really fed up with her going on about the jewels and were also relying on deep silent prayers for their safe arrival.

On December 13th 1949 Eva Turner's recital took place in the Holmberg Hall Auditorium with an eager, capacity crowd. She wore a white dress and the Patti jewels, and sang *Ritorna Vincitor* and the *Liebestod*. No one was disappointed. Local critics tell us:

'The conductor led the orchestra with a sincere desire to show off one of the greatest assets Oklahoma music scene has acquired in many years... After the first two measures of "Ritorna Vincitor", all fears were dispelled. Miss Turner's voice still has a wealth and beauty and her innate nobility of character was a revelation to the listener... Tremendous feelings went back and forth between the audience and the listener.'

Eva Turner

1949-1959 Oklahoma 255

It seems that an added motivation for giving this recital may have been to help her consider an invitation to sing *Turandot* at the Metropolitan the following year. *Ritorna Vincitor* apart from one isolated B flat lies no higher than A flats, as does the *Liebestod*. Since she did not sing *In Questa Reggia* at the concert, with its tone higher tessitura, I think we may assume that during rehearsals, she had already made up her mind on that one. A series of *Turandots* at the Metropolitan would have been a fine way to end her career but it was not to be. Dale Vliet, law professor at the University and one of Eva's closest friends in Oklahoma says: 'One of the greatest demonstrations of Eva as the artist came when she made the decision not to sing *Turandot* at the Met, because she would not appear if she were less than at her prime.'

Eva Turner merely said:

'They asked me if I would go to the Metropolitan, but after consideration, I decided against it.'

Eva Turner spent a happy Christmas with her new friends in Oklahoma once she had decided against the Metropolitan performances.

Eva tried to find outlets for her students as there was little performing going on inside the University. There was no opera programme, so she taught the students duets and trios along with their arias and contacted local clubs and organizations, where they could perform and gain valuable experience from the occasion. She also helped them enter and often win competitions. Eva Turner felt that performing, and feedback from it, was a vital part in the development of all singers and made herself fully available to the students out of hours, as the attention she wanted to devote to their development was not possible in a rigid curriculum. Since she lived near the campus the students were able to visit her apartment and report every detail of any performance they gave, no matter how small the detail or the performance.

As we have perhaps witnessed, Eva Turner was somewhat larger than life, even in America which is the home of larger than life people. The milkman, who served the flats near the university, being provided with a key, was accustomed to going into people's apartments during his early morning rounds, when people were still asleep, and placing the milk in their fridges.

He was, however, thrown into a state of confusion, on hearing Eva's vocal warming up sounds at 6.30 in the morning, as part of her preparations for the day ahead. He did not want to leave the milk outside in the heat, but was concerned as to what these noises meant, so he left the apartments in her block without delivering anyone's milk because he was so frightened. After reassurances from the other residents, who presumably also would have liked a bit of quiet at 6.30 in the morning, but wanted their milk more and knew that Eva could not refrain from singing at the top of her voice, he eventually braved the sounds and entered, at which point she made him sit down on her couch and listen to her singing. They became best of friends. The students' perceived lack of a basic vocal foundation really bugged her and she had no patience with those who ignored her demands upon them, expecting them to practise until perfection was achieved. She said of one such occasion:

'Why only yesterday I had to summon a teaching colleague to my room, to witness the insubordination of a young man who had not practised. That he wanted to be a lawyer was no excuse. Mildred merely left the room after I explained the situation. It seems to me that she too needs to rethink her ideas. If my students work hard, they have my complete devotion, if not, woe betide them.'

Mildred Andrews, the colleague in question, said later that when her phone rang and she lifted it to hear Eva's irate voice, she had imagined she was having a heart attack and raced up the stairs, almost giving herself one, to find Eva towering over a petrified, seated student. He was later to become a lawyer of some renown and whenever Mildred met him, they relived the occasion with gleeful laughter, rather than the terror the occasion had initially evoked. In my personal experience, woe did betide her students from time to time as terror struck to their very hearts but there was, perhaps because of this tension, a part of me that was always ready to laugh. Judy Coleman tells us of a similar situation to one which I experienced years later and could barely control my hysterical laughter, as a young person of around twenty years of age. I am relieved to be able to tell the story in the words of someone else, as it saves me from disclosing a similar happening.

Judy Coleman: 'Eva had, like many singers, taken great care of her teeth but had eventually succumbed to a sizeable bridge at the front of her upper teeth. If my voice became the slightest bit plummy or back, she immediately began to shout,

"Forward dear. Forward."

She would then place her thumb into her mouth, just behind her front teeth, flicking the thumb forward. From time to time, she flicked so hard, that the bridge would be dislodged. On one such occasion she clapped her hand over her mouth and went to retrieve the teeth exclaiming:

"No one must see me like this,"

but continued to teach with one hand over her mouth and the other playing the piano. Another time, I went in for a lesson and clearly the same thing had happened but this time the solution had been to tie a scarf over her face like a bandit and continue the lesson, with the scarf flopping about induced by the air she was producing, when singing or talking.'

Eva's first year in Oklahoma passed, as the students and she bonded and she began to really enjoy life in this new country and settle down with new friends. Dudley Scholte, a great friend and follower of her career, said of her when he wrote in the Gramophone Magazine a few years later:

'America had a distinct effect on her. She acquired a poise hitherto lacking and also became clothes conscious, returning home with smarter dresses than she had boasted of previously. Indeed in her heyday, she often did not seem to care about, or even be aware of, what she wore – frequently distressing her many "fans" by looking very ordinary. Very often she would arrive at whatever opera house she was due to sing in, by tram or bus – not even by taxi, let alone car!'

April 1950

She was enjoying her teaching in Oklahoma and being with all her new, generous friends gave her a new lease of life as far as her wardrobe was concerned. Americans are so good at that side of life and their foundation garments, although very expensive, do marvels for one's figure. She may, however, just have overstepped the boundaries at a party where Dale and Genevieve Vliet were also guests.

Dale explains: 'I had never seen Eva present herself with such a striking figure. Her outfit did a wonderful job of shaping her bosom and it pulled in her waist and hips as you couldn't imagine. There was just no bulge where one shouldn't have been. Eva went to a chair and went down slowly as could be, taking up no more than the front two

Eva Turner teaching in Oklahoma

258   Dame Eva Turner A Life on the High Cs

inches of it, until she was just balancing on the edge. Finally we were invited into the dining table and she couldn't get up, so pretended to linger a while, talking to us, until all the other guests had gone in. Then Genevieve and I helped her up and escorted her to the table. At the table she once again had to sit on the edge of her chair and did not eat at all heartily, as was usual for her, since there was just no room for the food inside her foundation garment. She turned quietly to Genevieve and said,

"My God, if I can just get out of this corset, I will never try to look shapely again in my life."'

Eva was always too hot in Oklahoma's summer and in late spring mused:

'I had almost forgotten the day I arrived here and nearly died from heat. I am so looking forward to England and of course Junesca. It has seemed a very long time, in many, many ways, since I left them so far behind. Only another month to go and I will be leaving here but not forever, as they have warmly invited me back for another year, in fact permanently, if I want. President Cross says that as far as university officials are concerned, my performance as a teacher was so exceptional, that I can be employed for life on the music faculty if I want it. I am also to have an increase in salary to $5000, so I have assured him I will return but as before, just for the nine months. I hope my copy of "Opera Magazine" arrives soon as it always cheers me up and gives news of home.'

Eva Turner taught her students more than singing: she took them to museums, to hear symphony concerts and to see plays. She suggested reading matter and recommended recordings to listen to as well as lending them scores to study as they were listening. Dallas hosted the Metropolitan Opera Touring Company each year and Eva, leaving her possible inner grievance with this company to the side, took students to Dallas to listen and learn, saying:

'I am most grateful that Dallas affords us the opportunity to glory in the opera in this way.'

Dawin Emanuel remembers: 'I went with Eva Turner to Dallas to a production of *Samson and Delilah* with the lovely Rise Stevens as Delilah. I was watching the performance through my opera glasses, which had accidentally focused on Miss Steven's scantily clad mid-section, when I felt Eva's elbow in my ribs followed by a stage whisper, which carried for rows:

"Dawin dear you did say those were naval glasses, didn't you?"'

On her long train journey back to New York, she wrote thank you letters to all her new friends who had welcomed her with open hearts and arms to Oklahoma, and posted the letters en-route, so that they were able to follow her journey home. Eva stopped over in Illinois, with Nursing Sister, Mary Louise Williams, who had nursed her, when she contracted typhoid fever in Milan, and had sat with her for hours, holding her hand in her own and willing her better. Eva wanted to thank her again for her kindness and dedication which Eva thought had saved her life saying:

'Even the great Prince Albert died from the Typhoid fever, despite his special nursing, so I think Sister Mary Louise really did save my life with her dedicated attitude.'

She then stayed with Victoria Rubenfeld, who had sent her packages during the war. They were hoping to go and see Pinza in *South Pacific* but Vickie told her the shows were sold out. Eva thought:

'I am sure we can do something about that. I will see to it personally.'

Pinza gave them his guest tickets and an 'enchanted evening' was shared by all. Eva and Victoria also shared many visits to the Metropolitan Opera when Eva dropped in on her way to and from Oklahoma and by way of thanking her for those treasured occasions, Victoria Rubenfeld endowed a seat at the Metropolitan Opera House, with Eva Turner's name on it, on October 1st 1965.

She wished flying was more accessible as she was always so sick on the ship and was usually glad to get off it. This time Anne was there to greet her but only for a short time, as she had to have her annual holiday but dear Sally Beacon, their daily, made sure supplies were provided and that everything was kept in order until Anne's return. When Anne came home, Eva set off, on her own, to Junesca, as the house in Bayswater, with all the tenants, could not be left unattended.

Amy Shuard sang the part of Eva in the quintet from the *Mastersingers* on August 14th and *Ocean, thou mighty monster* on August 16th in the Promenade Concerts at the Royal Albert Hall in 1950 and Eva Turner was pleased to be able to be there to be part of Amy's success. Another great learning curve for singing teachers is to be able to rejoice when a student is successful singing the teacher's own cherished repertoire, in places they themselves, once walked. Eva was at this time fifty-eight years old and many of the other singers in the Proms that year had been her colleagues and were her age or older, so what were her thoughts? She was now earning a good living as a teacher but her longing for performance never ceased throughout her life and in her own words, she never retired. She did not know Amy Shuard very well at this point but nevertheless gave generously of her time and knowledge to help her, giving her lessons on the run up to these concerts.

During that summer in London after Anne Ridyard had returned from holiday and before Eva set off once more for Oklahoma the following took place and was told to me years later by Anne. 'Eva was apt to walk about with no money in her pockets, like Royalty, which she thought she almost was, and one day having set out for a walk in Kensington Gardens, she was very soon back, asking for half a crown. She wanted it because a cat was stranded up a tree and Eva thought that if she gave a nearby workman with a ladder some money, he could be persuaded to get the cat down from the tree. I gave her the money but she was back within a short time to ask for ten shillings. When I asked her why, she said that the cat had gone right up to the top and felt that she had to offer a bigger sum of money, so I gave it to her but being Lancashire, I made her give me back my half a crown first. She was quite grand in those days you know, but we soon helped that': said Anne with a huge wink.

Oklahoma, September 1950

Eva was very pleased to have moved to a flat on the south side of Logan Apartments because the breeze there kept the flat a little cooler. But was outraged by Joseph McCarthy, who:

'seems to accuse me of being a political radical and suggests that I sign an oath of allegiance? I am British Subject and will do no such thing.'

Eva Turner did not have to sign anything and life at Oklahoma became a second home to her until 1959. She was given a full time staff accompanist which made teaching much easier as, although she liked to play for the students when they were vocalising at the beginning of their lesson, it meant that she did not have to practise the, sometimes difficult, accompaniment to their repertoire in the second part of the lesson and so could give her whole attention to their performance. She was also given a telephone in her room, which she loved, as it saved her time, as she could lift it during the lessons and answer the caller's quick question, or she could arrange to have a sudden thought, regarding the development of the student with her at the moment, fulfilled. In time air-conditioning was installed in all the rooms and so the hot weather was a little less taxing for her as the years passed.

Friends came to visit or she made huge efforts to meet them if they were anywhere nearby. Humphrey Proctor-Gregg tells us, in his book on Sir Thomas Beecham, how Eva went to meet Sir Thomas in Dallas. Eva recalled:

'A young harpist on our staff had been to Dallas to play for him and when she told him that she knew me, he called out: "Get her over here". When on her return she told me of this, I persuaded a fellow professor to drive me there for Sir Thomas' very last concert. When we went to see Sir Thomas after his fine performance, he was spread-eagled in his chair and talking to no one. When he saw me, the old smile broke out and he exclaimed, "Gentlemen, I would have you know this is Eva Turner, the greatest Aida and Turandot of her generation."'

On January 7th, 1951 Eva received a very detailed letter from Bernard Miles, in reply to her letter asking about his forthcoming production of Purcell's *Dido and Aeneas*. She had inquired about his ideas for this performance and asked if she could have a copy of the libretto and score.

With his reply, he included the cuts in the libretto which he wanted to make and also his ideas for the sets and how the action would take place on stage.

Was she having thoughts about a production for her students in America? Perhaps she was interested in performing Dido for Bernard, who was a very good friend and had at one time rented a flat from her, when he and his wife Josephine were first married. In the end however, this production, which opened the Mermaid Theatre in September, 1951, was to become famous, not least for Kirsten Flagstad's performance of Dido. Maggie Teyte, Thomas Hemsley, Edith Coates and Murray Dickie were also in the cast.

In 1951 Eva Turner was aged fifty-nine. This is not young for a prima donna but it is still young enough to be able to sing less demanding roles. This is a difficult area of dispute among singers; some think that they should retire at the height of their fame and ability, while others slide gracefully into the smaller roles and enjoy having a career, money and the delight of being among likeminded people in a world which is their home: the stage. It is undoubtedly easier for men to adopt the second approach but it is also possible for women.

The second approach means that the great singer has to leave the concerns of her adoring fans to one side, as she turns her, once special voice, into a jobbing instrument and uses it to sing roles, which need skill and great performing but less voice, especially at the top of the range. The roles I am thinking of for women of Eva Turner's vocal stature are, for example: Fricka, which she once sang, Herodias, Kabanicha, Kostelnička, Klytemnestra and even Ortrud. These roles are often sung by fine mezzos but can also be taken by great sopranos who understand their own voices and can adapt them as they become older. This presumes that the middle and bottom are in good nick and comfortable.

We have to remember that Eva's pride and joy was the top of her voice and she refused to countenance singing Kundry, which is often sung by sopranos, but does lie low. Dido is one of these roles often sung by mezzos, which commands great stage presence and vocal command but could quite easily be sung by an older soprano, and we see exactly that situation, when Kirsten Flagstad sang it. Flagstad had no great pride in her top, as her speciality was her wonderful evenness throughout the voice. So I think we can see here examples of the opposing ideas.

Flagstad was not ever interested in teaching, as she said that she knew nothing about her technique that she could pass on to others, only the use of the 'ng', through which the air must filter. She was also very rich, so she did not need to make a living, but still chose to sing this wonderful role for her close friend Bernard Miles, the fee for which was a glass of stout. Dido was just outside her usual repertoire but she enjoyed singing it and could comfortably embrace its lower tessitura. She also sang Gluck's *Orfeo* and Fricka in that tessitura.

Was Eva also thinking along these lines but, because she had always been employed for the top of her voice, was this journey a step too far? She had enough ambition and connections, which she could have put into action to restart her career, not necessarily on the occasion of *Dido and Aeneas*, but perhaps through her Italian connections, since the war was now well behind her. But, she now had her teaching and had launched into it with a will, and could depend on it for a good income, a thought which always pursued her.

Anne Ridyard left London in late spring of 1951 to visit Eva in Oklahoma, sailing the Atlantic to New York and then taking a bus through America to Oklahoma. On arrival she was entertained by Dale and Genevieve, who served each guest a huge three-quarter pound T-bone steak. Anne shook her head saying: 'You know, there must be at least three week's meat rationing on this plate,

Two-thirds of Bayreuth had been destroyed by Allied bombing in the final days of World War II, though the theatre itself was undamaged. Following the war, Winifred Wagner was sentenced to probation by a war court for her support of the Nazi party although to her credit, the theatre itself was spared and avoided destruction, as she refused to allow its use for any military purposes whatsoever.

not to mention these wonderful Idaho potatoes and fresh, lovely vegetables.'

That summer, in August, Eva went to the reopening of the Wagnerian Festival in Bayreuth. After many years of discussion and different uses of the building the Wagner Festival reopened with a performance of Beethoven's *Ninth Symphony* on July 29th, 1951, followed by the first post war performance of Wagner's *Parsifal*, conducted by Knappertsbusch with George London singing Amfortas, an interpretation which Eva greatly admired.

Eva said of George London,

'To find a true bass-baritone is a somewhat rare experience and even less common are singers of his calibre and as a result of his talent, training and experience, he is able to forget technique and give himself over wholly to interpretation.'

Martha Mödl was Kundry and Windgassen, Parsifal in this production. Eva does not mention Martha Mödl's performance but perhaps this was another example of her having inner thoughts and ideas about considering changing her own repertoire. When she heard the low tessitura, did she once more decide against the idea or was there never an obvious opportunity to grasp?

During her years in Oklahoma, Eva did not lose touch with old friends and colleagues and in 1952 travelled to Montagnana, Padua with Martinelli, whose birthplace this small town in Italy, was. Martinelli was to perform the unveiling of a plaque on the house where another great tenor Aureliano Pertile was born, also in that small Italian town. What are the chances of two such great tenors being born in a small village with a population of only a few hundred? Eva Turner said of the occasion:

'His great contemporary, Giovanni Martinelli, was to perform the ceremony and it seemed that all the elite of the Italian Opera World, past and present, had gathered to do honour to their colleague. I had been invited to come from London and I gladly accepted. The whole small town was en fête and the central square packed, when at one point of the proceedings I was asked to say a few words over the microphone. Of course I complied. And then, as I finished, the whole concourse rose as one person when the Italian brass band struck up the British National Anthem, "God Save the Queen." That was a moment of deep emotion.'

Again with Martinelli, Eva was invited to discuss, during the interval of a broadcast of *Il Trovatore* from the Metropolitan Opera House, the performance which would be listened to throughout

America. Eva sang Leonora with, among others: Masini, Pertile and Merli but not with Martinelli but he and Eva both had great experience of this opera and their constructive comments were applauded and enjoyed by all who listened. Her mezzos in this opera had included Minghini Cattaneo, Ebe Stignani, Aurora Buades and Bruna Castagna and her baritones Richard Bonelli and Formichi.

On June 29th 1956, while back in London during the summer months, Eva took part in her second *Desert Island Discs* programme. This time she chose:

1. *An die Musik* by Schubert sung by Kathleen Ferrier accompanied by Phyllis Spurr.
2. *O Del Mio Amato Ben* sung by Muzio.
3. The quintet from *Die Meistersinger* sung by Elisabeth Schumann, Gladys Parr, Melchior, Schorr and Ben Williams accompanied by the L.S.O. conducted by Barbirolli.
4. *Nimrod* played by the Queen's Hall Orchestra, conducted by Sir Henry Wood.
5. *O Patria Mia* from *Aida*, sung by Zinka Milanov, accompanied by the RCA Victor Symphony, conducted by Renato Cellini.
6. *Until* sung by Elisabeth Welch, accompanied by Stanley Black.
7. *Vissi d'Arte* from *Tosca*, sung by Renata Tebaldi, accompanied by the Suisse Romande Orchestra, conducted by Albert Erede.
8. *Finale* of the *Jupiter Symphony, No.41* by Mozart, played by the RPO, conducted by Sir Thomas Beecham.

Eva Turner visiting a Texas ranch

Eva Turner relived her career during the programme with the encouragement of Roy Plomley who, after record five, comes to their present time by asking what she is doing now:

'I'm Professor of Voice at the University of Oklahoma, on the Music Faculty.'

Roy P.: 'Are you enjoying it?'

'Enjoying it very much; the students are very enthusiastic and work very well, it's a pleasure.'

Roy P.: 'But it's a great shame you're not singing yourself.'

'Oh, thank you but I do sing in studio still.'

Roy P.: 'But that's not quite the same thing. Let's have another record.' After her sixth record:

1949-1959 Oklahoma

Roy P.: 'How are you going to manage on this island; are you a handy practical person?'

'Well, I hope I'm a little practical and resourceful. They say that Lancashire people are.'

Roy P.: 'Have you any hobbies that might be useful?'

'Oh yes. I adore swimming. I swim quite a lot.'

Roy P.: 'Well enough to harpoon a fish?'

'Well I'm a little doubtful about that.'

Roy P.: 'A good cook?'

'Simple cook, yes.'

Roy P.: 'Well you'll only have simple food so you sound as if you'll be alright.'

Eva Turner chose the seventh record, because:

'I heard a performance of "Tosca" with Tebaldi singing in New York at Christmas and she really was superb.'

Roy P: 'What do you think of the standard of singing today, is it getting better or not so good?'

'Well, I know that older people always say that the standard of singing is not as it was in their day. I don't want to say that but on the other hand I do think that the standards were higher in the past. I think today there are so many interests and life is so fast that the people don't apply themselves in the same manner and they don't take the time to develop their talent as they should.'

Eva Turner chose a figurine of Dresden or Chelsea china as her luxury.

Eva Turner tells us of her east-west crossing of the Atlantic in RMS *Mauretania* on 2nd Sept 1958:

'What a wonderful crossing I have had this time – no sickness. It was a lovely honour to be invited to sit at the Captain's table again last night on the occasion of a Gala Dinner. What a menu! Seeing turtle soup on it made me think of my first "Desert Island Discs" programme in 1942, when Roy Plomley suggested that I could harness a turtle to ride around on and I replied that perhaps when the turtle I had captured became too old to ride upon, he could be cooked for soup. I shared this memory with my dinner companions and the Captain decided that I should avoid the soup lest I was eating an old friend! How we laughed. The menu had the most wonderful variety of foods and we could have any combination we wanted. I chose the 'Suggested Menu':

R.M.S. "Mauretania"

John W. Cannell
Master
Best Wishes
Best wishes!
Best for everything
Ernest W H Hammer
Lilie M. Hammer
Frederick Coopens
Bertha L. Coopens
Evelyn Hague
Cunard

Cornet de Prosciutti et Melon
*

Tortue Claire au Xerxes
*

Supreme de Turboti, Piave
*

Filet Mignon, Rossini
Pommes Garfield
Haricots Verts
*

Coeurs de Laitue
*

Coupe Neige des Alpes

Corbeille de Fruits   Café

Amy Shuard was supposed to join her for a study period but just after Eva's return to Oklahoma she received a letter from her saying that she would not after all be coming to study with her, as she had had to pay a very big tax bill and was not in a financial position to make the trip. I wonder if this huge disappointment had anything to do with Eva Turner's decision, the following year, to come home to London and not to return to teach at Oklahoma University. My guess would be that it did, since she was so very fond of Amy and enjoyed working with her and being part of her career. I think she also realised that there were a lot of very good young voices in Britain and perhaps it was time to help them, having spent ten years helping her American cousins.

She was a diplomat as far as her own teaching career prospects and the singing careers of her students were concerned, and did not let history hold her back from making new friends and letting rifts heal. Francis Robinson, an influential friend to have, was assistant manager to the Metropolitan Opera, as well as being a raconteur and a radio personality and she sent many students to sing for him, while she was teaching at Oklahoma, in the hope that he might open a door for them.

1st December 58
Metropolitan Opera

Dear Eva,
I am thrilled to have your letter which confirms your visit. I can't wait to see you. Did your ears burn last week? Noel Coward was here and he said such warm and wonderful things about you
Love Francis.

Written at the bottom by Eva is,

'Isn't this nice?? Let Dudley read this please.'

She relinquished her position in Oklahoma with sadness and always spoke of her time there with great affection. She told the people of Oklahoma, in a little speech:

'I came for nine months and stayed for ten years - I know no better way of expressing what Oklahoma University has meant to me. Or of indicating something of the inspiration which such a splendid university can be in the life of both teacher and student. And because one should pause sometimes and think of these things, I was glad to hear an English friend of mine exclaim, after I had been telling her about Oklahoma University: "Why, it's one of the great romances of university history."

It is indeed. To think that only three years after Oklahoma was opened to settlers in 1889, the university was founded. There's vision for you! And now the vision has grown to immense reality, and on every side there is proof of the fact that those, for whom this university was founded, have seized their opportunities with both hands.

Let me say a little about the music school, since this is my special province, and of some of those who have both contributed to and gained from it. First I would have to mention that fine colleague, Joseph Benton, Professor of Voice, formerly of the Metropolitan and Chicago Operas and the leading Opera Houses of Italy, to whom I owe the invitation which originally brought me to the University of Oklahoma. Then I would note with pride and congratulations, that Carlos Moseley, once Director of our Music School, has just been appointed Managing Director of the New York Philharmonic Orchestra - comment indeed on the quality of those who have gone to make up the faculty of the Oklahoma University.

Among the many graduates of the Music School, scattered all over the musical world of America and Europe, o yes, I constantly come across them on the other side of the Atlantic, upholding the fine traditions for work and good grounding, which they have learned from O.U., I must mention: Judy Coleman, who won the Katherine Turner Long Award at the Metropolitan, who is a Professor of Voice in her own right, an opera producer and a conductor.

Also Roberta Knie, who won the open scholarship at the Royal Academy of Music in London and, from Oklahoma City itself, Bill Harper, who won a Fulbright Scholarship from the O.U. to Italy and had the scholarship renewed because of his excellence. He has now landed the signal honour of a two-year contract as leading tenor at the Opera House in Karlsruhe, Germany. I thought as I listened to him a few weeks ago, making his splendid debut in "Ballo in Maschera", it's a long road from Oklahoma to Karlsruhe, but it is an even longer road from being a boy with a fine voice to a position as leading tenor at a distinguished European House. It is a proud thought that Oklahoma University put Bill Harper firmly on that road.

This then is a glimpse of what has already been done to fulfil the vision of those who founded Oklahoma University, way back in 1892. The essential vision now is that it should increase and expand. Who ever heard of a vision that remained static? To me at any rate, it seems that the expansion and the continued development of Oklahoma University should be the proud and exciting responsibility of all Oklahomans. Talent is a gift of God, which we cannot all ask to have, but training is something which, as a human responsibility, I think we should all strive to supply to those who have that talent. To my certain knowledge Oklahoma is bursting with talent, so let us see to it that the training is never lacking.'

Her teaching ideas had been formulating during her stay in Oklahoma and here are some of her thoughts taken from an article in *Scooner Magazine* – so called after the first settlers in Oklahoma.

'*Singing is very much part of our whole being and I have found that many people don't realise that and they sing from the neck up. That is what we call white singing. This is a pity because singers don't always feel comfortable when they sing on these lines. Then there are the hooty singers. This is a pity too because that kind of singing does not go out to impinge itself on the ears of the public and arrest their attention. Therefore they don't become what we term "Box Office".*

There is a certain lethargy to combat where singing is concerned... I have found that they must have vitality and resistance. The young people today love to "live it up". Well living it up does not always contribute to being a good singer. I do warn you of that. You must conserve your vitality if you want to sing. I must say that I think the singer, of all people of applied music, is involved much more in giving of himself, perhaps more than those who find the piano ready to play, the 'cello, the violin and so on, because in singing the subconscious forces are involved... Students must realise that often to bring about achievement, you must go along with blinkers. You cannot have too many diversified interests, because time - the lack of it - often defeats us.

You know, nothing is achieved without perspiration, application, dedication, scarification - well, I don't know how many other 'ations I could mention. Students, I want you to listen to that. You can't expect it to come from outside. It must be you - you yourself who achieves it.'

Eva Turner

Eva Turner, a perceptive, energetic person, no fool, had, among all her varied successes with teaching singing in Oklahoma, as we can see from above, grasped very many salient points about human nature itself. Until she started teaching she had imagined that everyone who wanted to sing was as obsessed and enthusiastic as she was and so the realisation that the gift of a great voice was sometimes given to an individual who did not have the qualities to develop this seed, was slow to dawn and rather a disappointment when she accepted that:

'*The voice you see, is just the instrument, as a piano is to a pianist. It can be judged almost on first hearing - What you cannot assess is aptitude, or inspiration or perspiration.*'

In March 1959 she wondered if she was doing the right thing, giving up her teaching post in Oklahoma:

'*I have had such a happy, productive time here despite my worst fears that I may have undertaken too wide a diversion from my life in London in 1949. However I have loved it, respecting and admiring the whole setup at the School of Music and with students with such great enthusiasm, what more could one ask for? I am also proud to go down in the annals of the history of the university here, by reason of the fact that I gave my last public singing performance here. Despite all of this, I feel I must move willingly into the next chapter in my life and bid a sad "arrivederci" to Oklahoma'.*

(See appendix for her detailed teaching ideas at that time.)

Teaching singing was the reason Eva Turner got out of bed in the morning and this had taken over from her past routine of working on her own voice to sustain standards which took her to the top of her profession. She now studied in detail the voices of others and endeavoured to aid them on the same road and was coming home to London to continue that mission.

CHAPTER 8
1959-1981 London

The world of entertainment was changing, as performances of all sorts of music, opera and plays were brought more and more into the homes of the public through the medium of radio and television. There were also improvements in technology, which enabled, among other things, the purchase of record players by individuals, allowing records of one's own choice to be played at home. People no longer had to go outside their own comfortable environment to find first class entertainment and so, live performances of opera, along with oratorio and recital concerts, were now fighting for their very survival. Even visiting the cinema was becoming less popular and so it was no surprise when the Rank Organisation, during September 1959 disclosed a disastrous downward trend in cinema attendances and at the same the BBC announced that they had bought twenty American feature films to be shown on television. Rank Organization had closed ninety-one theatres since 1956 with another fifty-seven ear-marked for the same dark fate in 1959 and it looked as if cinemas would soon follow suit.

When Eva left Britain in 1949, the word 'teenagers' did not exist but now, as Harold Macmillan was re-elected as Tory Prime Minister to form the third Tory government in a row, there were in Britain alone five million teenagers with an identity and a culture which embraced mostly, although not exclusively, the young. Part of this identity was created by the music they listened to: the under eighteens were swept off their feet by rock'n'roll and by names like Bill Haley and Elvis Presley from America and Cliff Richards, Marty Wilde, Billy Fury, Lonnie Donegan and Tommy Steele, home grown talents, while over eighteens were drawn to jazz when the 'Trad' revival began at Humphrey Littleton's Club. Among the other early jazz players at that time were: Acker Bilk, who wore a bowler hat to let his young audience know that he was promoting British jazz, not the pure type from New Orleans, John Dankworth, classically trained and mad on jazz, and Cleo Laine his wife, all of whom brought their talents to the 50s.

Britain still had teenagers who loved classical music in the great traditions of the past but it now also had a new group of young people, never before drawn into the world of music, whose interest in these new sounds brought them together, giving them a musical home. There had always been light music and entertainment but this new popular music world was something else - it was created by the young but promoted by adults with an eye for business and making money. Whatever the young person's choice of music, it could be bought in the form of a vinyl record and played over and over whenever they wished, either alone or with friends, giving a sense of togetherness which enhanced their identity and self image.

The new technology was also used by classical musicians both to make recordings and to listen to the great masters, whose live performances were now accessible to those who could afford a recording and so, for example, Furtwängler's performance of the *Ring* cycle at La Scala in 1950 could be listened to at home after the event, without the listener having made the journey to Italy. This technology was also a very great study-aid to singers who had, up till that time, relied on score-reading and individual coaching to learn a part and of course that way of study continued but recordings were now a useful tool in learning the traditions of music making.

Live opera and classical music seemed to be under threat, at least as far as attracting future audiences was concerned. It is good, then, to see that there was still a group of young people

Amy Shuard (left), Eva Turner and Lady Marion Harewood (right)

interested in making their lives in the world of classical music and in doing it to the best of their ability, seeking out distinguished and learned musicians with whom to study at conservatoires and music academies. A singer is in many ways different from an instrumental musician, not least in that the good or sometimes even great voice often appears in the body of one not previously interested in learning the language of music and when this happens, there is a lot of catching up to do. Eva Turner was already a musician as well as a singer when she was accepted by the Royal Academy of Music as a student forty years previously, when her course of study had been financed by her father. Now the government was giving financial help to young, talented singers from all walks of life and of varying abilities, to study in places of excellence with distinguished members of staff.

Anne Ridyard wrote in the page-a-day diary, which was now to become a major part of Eva Turner's life: '21st September – Commenced teaching at the Royal Academy of Music.' Her teaching duties there were much less than in Oklahoma, as she was now only teaching two days a week but the students were all first study singers and so 'very demanding.' She was a new kid on the block as far as teaching in London was concerned and had many requests for auditions from potential private students. She was now able to teach Amy Shuard on a regular basis, so, with that and her other private students, her home was becoming an important singing studio in London.

Eva Turner approved greatly of the changes which helped young musicians study without worrying about financial implications and was always looking for ways to help them on their way, including charging a very reasonable fee to her private students. Among them in this first year were: Paul Britton, Rita Hunter, Ava June, Vicky Elliot, Mariena Midgley and Patricia Payne. Others auditioned and quickly disappeared from her diary. If she felt they were wasting their own time or hers, she did not charge for the audition, sending them away after a few minutes or again if they were especially talented she did not charge for her time in the audition. If any student had been given an introduction to her by a friend or colleague, she did not charge for that either.

One of the first surprises which greeted Eva Turner on returning home to London was Eamonn Andrews clutching her *'This is Your Life'* book. She seemed to enjoy every minute of the television occasion and shared enormous gales of laughter with her longest, dearest friend Gladys Parr. They both looked a million dollars: enormously well dressed and with a poise and command of body language and gestures which only the stage could have

Eva Turner – 'This Is Your Life' with Eamonn Andrews

Gladys Parr and Eva Turner

given them. Their love for each other was obvious as they shared laughter about times past and the money they had tried to save saying that they had lived mostly on hope. Gladys told the audience: 'Eva practised and practised and practised and learned lots of principal parts in case someone happened to erhemm fall down and break their hhmm necks! (last word only barely audible followed by laughter.) Her aim was to get herself out of the chorus and in a very short time succeeded'. Walter Midgley said she was not to worry about her meal that evening as he had brought her favourite supper with him, fish and chips. A beautiful Amy Shuard said how much she owed to the teaching of Miss Turner and knelt at her side, in the collective photo call at the end, as if she was Kundry about to wash Parsifal's feet and with a reverence of which a disciple from the Bible would have been proud. Eva Turner in her turn paid huge spontaneous tribute to Amy's Turandot. Sir Thomas Beecham and Sir John Barbirolli paid tribute to her as one of the greatest British artists; Vincenzo Bellezza came from Italy, bringing affectionate greetings from the country which had claimed her as a daughter-in-art, and she embraced him warmly, calling him Maestro and conversing immediately with him in Italian. George Ivens sent warm greetings from Canada and Jo Benton spoke to her from Oklahoma while Martinelli greeted his Aida with the impetuous embrace of Radames from times past.

Perhaps while musing about this programme and happy days in the past, Eva wrote to Kirsten Flagstad asking her if they had in fact sung together. Here is the reply.

October 16th 1959

Dear Eva,
So nice to hear from you!I cannot recall having ever sung with you in Chicago. If I knew the exact date I might be able to find out.

Dorothy Hausky (?) sang for me there when I was ill. If you wrote my accompanist Edwin McArthur I am sure he would know. The address is: 350 W.57th St NY 19.

With kindest greetings.

Yours sincerely,
Kirsten Flagstad

As Britain entered the sixties, Princess Margaret, aged 29, was 'to wed a commoner', Harold Macmillan, affectionately called 'Super Mac', gave his much criticised 'Winds of Change' speech in South Africa, which opened the possibilities of black and white equality in that country, the Thames Barrier to prevent the flooding of that 'Old Father' of London was proposed at a cost of £17 million and John F Kennedy announced that he would run for the Presidency of America.

During March Eva was involved in another *'This is your Life'*, this time, the life of Gracie Fields. In answer to Eamonn Andrew's asking her if she had seen Gracie on stage, Eva Turner replied:

'Yes I saw her many times on stage and she came to hear me too. When I was at Covent Garden she came round to see me and afterwards we walked through the market together. The porters recognised her at once and were so thrilled to see her, but I, who had been singing round the corner with Gigli and Martinelli, was unrecognised.'

Eamonn Andrews: 'What did you think of her voice?'

'Remarkable. She once asked me if I thought she'd done the right thing. Should she have trained seriously as a singer? I said no, because she had a unique gift. I remember once hearing her sing Malotte's arrangement of the Lord's Prayer. There was not a sound in the vast, packed theatre. All around me I noticed people crying silently. Gracie thought they looked sad and she wanted them to be happy, so do you know what she did? Suddenly and without the slightest disrespect for what had gone before, she turned and scratched her back (demonstrates). It was like a sudden pistol shot – the house roared with delight.'

Just after her birthday that year, Miss Turner was invited to reply to Mr Cooper's toast 'To Music' at the annual dinner of the 'Critic's Circle', the influential, historic organisation of critics. Unlike Sir James Barrie, of *Peter Pan* fame, who began his speech: 'Scum. Critics to the right of him, critics to the left of him, critics upper entrance at the back leading to conservatory, critics downstage centre, into that Circle someone has blundered', Miss Turner used her opportunity thus:

'Ladies and Gentlemen, I am of the opinion that real people, artists or otherwise, catch fire and are inspired by beautiful music. To me it has always been so very worthwhile; the work, the success, some disappointments, often some tears, but much more laughter! After ten wonderful years of teaching in America, where I must confess I left a bit of my heart, I am proud and glad, that by returning to teach at the Royal Academy of Music – my Alma Mater – I have made the full circle in music.

I am thrilled by the ever-widening public knowledge and appreciation of all branches of music, especially opera. The radio, gramophone – even television have helped. But I am doubly thrilled that the state, through the Arts Council, gives greater grants to all the arts. Yet more please! It is money well spent – far better than hydrogen bombs.

I would like to make what I consider a vital appeal. The whole country is responding to the call for more civic playhouses. Right! The living actor playing before a live audience is the very meaning of the word 'Drama'. No artificial means can ever take the place of living flesh and blood contact. Now in my young days I learned more than I can ever say by singing up and down the provinces to splendid audiences with the Carl Rosa. What is needed now are real civic opera houses in the provinces – fine big theatres, modern, with big stages and big orchestral pits. Let that vital taxpaying public see and hear regularly exactly what London sees and hears at Covent Garden and the Wells – opera ideally and splendidly presented – just like Italy and Germany. 'More opera houses for the country' that is my call to state, city and town tonight. I hope they hear me! But even if they don't; thank you for listening.'

In the 1960 April edition of Music and Musicians there is a photo of Eva Turner and Joan Sutherland, sitting chatting at the Royal Opera House, with the caption: 'Memories of the past were recalled by famous former opera star Eva Turner to contemporary singer Joan Sutherland at the Opera Ball in February. The walls of the foyer were decorated with enlargements of photos of opera singers.' Behind them is an enlarged backdrop of Eva Turner as Aida in the 1920s. Music and Musicians helps to continue her story by following her in May to the record department of Cramer's in

Bond Street, where they photographed her, while she autographed copies of the Columbia re-issue of her recordings.

The National Confederation of Gramophone Societies Records and Recording Magazine reported on a talk she gave for their society, again in May, about those recordings:

'Eva Turner, with her vibrant, warm-hearted personality, captured everyone's heart with her reminiscences of her life as an international prima donna. The audience's reaction was a mixture of amusement at her delightful anecdotes and open admiration for a woman who justly became a legend in her own lifetime. That this reputation was well deserved was proved by the excerpts she played from the new transfer to LP of the recordings she made in 1928. So full of life and vitality was she, as well as conveying all her enthusiasm for her life's work, that no one would have been surprised had she turned off the gramophone and continued singing.'

Eva Turner was chair-person of the jury for the 1960 Royal Philharmonic Society Kathleen Ferrier Scholarship and the winners: Elizabeth Harwood, 21 and Lorna Elias, 23 are photographed flanking Eva, as they all take a happy curtain-call after the event. Both women won £300, half of the prize money, because Eva Turner had advised the panel that although Elizabeth was so young, she deserved to win. The money was shared because in the end the panel remained divided as to which young woman should win the out-right prize.

Later in the year, on October 4th, Eva was in the audience for the 152nd performance of *Die Walküre* conducted by Rudolf Kempe at the Royal Opera House, when Amy Shuard sang Sieglinde, Birgit Nilsson Brünnhilde, and Windgassen Siegmund. Leslie Hurry, who had designed the 1947 *Turandot*, was the designer of this production. When I found the programme for this occasion in a little music shop, the price was marked down because it had a lot of scribbles in the middle page. On closer examination, I discovered that 'the scribbles' were remarks by Eva Turner, written in the dark, about the performance taking place, as she tried to remember things she wanted to tell Amy to help improve her performance. Like Eva, with whom she shared a striking physical resemblance, Amy wanted to improve her performance and was not at all put off by Eva's zealous attention to detail.

Eva Turner with Giovanni Martinelli

During May, Giovanni Martinelli was given a plaque to commemorate his debut fifty years previously at Covent Garden on 22nd April 1912, when he sang Cavaradossi in Puccini's *Tosca*, with Edvina in the title role, and when he was hailed as the second Caruso. He also sang in *Jewels of the Madonna*, *Manon Lescaut* and *Fanciulla del West* in that season. Miss Eva Turner presented the plaque, with pride, on behalf of the Royal Opera House and the Recorded Institute of Sound, to this great man, with whom she had sung and who himself had known both Puccini and Toscanini, two of her great idols.

When asked around this time if she felt she had been too much associated with the role of Turandot, causing people to forget her other great roles such as Aida and perhaps resented that the public hadn't appreciated her true worth? She replied firmly:

'No, I don't. It is just one of those things. It is just life.'

Shortly after that interview which had taken place in February, her patience was rewarded and Miss Eva Turner collected the medal proclaiming her to be 'Dame Commander of the Order of the British Empire, DBE,' at Buckingham Palace, on 26th June 1962, having been given the honour in the Queen's Birthday list. Her very proud, loving, brother, Norman Turner, dressed in

Anne Ridyard (left), Dame Eva Turner and Norman Turner (right)

280   Dame Eva Turner A Life on the High Cs

morning suit and top hat, with a delighted, smiling Anne Ridyard complete with long gloves, accompanied her on the occasion. Dame Eva was immensely proud of this honour and although she never referred to it directly, carried the title with humility, dignity and care, as well as pride. She felt that the title came with certain duties and although she was already seventy years old, she experienced a new, energetic lease of life and her chosen mission, that of ambassador for Britain in the world of music, was refreshed, and she assumed new authority.

She was, not only as a result of her title, but also because of her enthusiasm for 'getting things done', invited on to many committees and once she joined any group, was a staunch supporter giving of her best. She was, in 1962, invited on to the council of the newly formed Friends of Covent Garden and was a lifelong loyal supporter, wielding any influence which her name might sway.

Dame Eva Turner

'For some reason or other, sometimes one has so many commitments. You know one must set aside a space of time. You have to really decide to do it and then set aside that time. If I join I give the time.'

By February 1963, Dame Eva was in full flight, fulfilling her duties which her new title had inspired:

'I'm verrrrry busy dear... I have my duties to perform, sooooo many commitments and many people who rely on my judgement to improve themselves. On Friday I shall see Amy as Turandot. I am so looking forward to it. You know dear this opera has so many memories for me. After that I shall go back to Oklahoma in April to deliver a public lecture in the Holmberg Hall Oklahoma University the title is: "Opera - from Student to Stage." This will be my first visit to Oklahoma since I left in 1959.'

While in Oklahoma in 1963, she gave an interview saying:

'At the request of the Chancellor of the Exchequer in London, the Arts Council has formed a Board of Governors to bring into being an Opera Centre in London in September next year. I am myself the only lady on that board and I am hoping that we shall collect many students of great aptitude and talent to feed the Royal Opera House, Sadler's Wells, Glyndebourne and the Edinburgh Festival.'

Her time at the Royal Academy of Music was an enjoyable teaching one but some of the staff, including English singer-colleagues from her own singing days, could, and did, make it difficult for her to bring about her own, more international ideas. It seems that the feeling around the Academy from many of the singing staff at the time was that, however great her career had been, this did not give her the right to boss them into ideas, for the opera class etc., with which they did not agree. Dame Eva would have been the first to adhere to this idea in principal but she was frustrated by their lack of vision and felt that she had greater knowledge of the international opera world and wanted to pass it on. Her impatience with their parochial attitudes sometimes led to internal unrest in the Academy and indeed head to head rows which left scars. Once again, however, she did not hold a grudge and would in later years be unwilling to criticise these same people, or engage in gossip about her adversaries, except by a small shake of the head.

There were of course notable exceptions to this on the staff at the RAM, and one of those was Roy Henderson who was eight years younger than she and had heard and admired her in his student days. He said of her: 'In a long life, with luck, one may meet a few great personalities, who without knowing it enrich life beyond measure. Such is Eva Turner who not only thrilled me as a student by her superb singing, but later when I came to know her, revitalised me as no ordinary person could have done, with the warmth of her friendship and infectious enthusiasm. I have seen at close quarters her devotion to the task of training young singers at the RAM and how her lucky students worshipped her. Her great experience, knowledge, encouragement and lovable nature, with a vital personality, got the best out of them. Eva was one of the few singing teachers who could sing and insisted on an agile voice with a smooth vocal line. On more than one occasion we have adjudicated together, and I have been impressed by her commonsense assessment of the singers, and the way she encouraged those who showed promise.'

Another ally was John Streets who was head of the opera course at that time and who also had an international approach to learning, being a superb linguist as well as a first class musician. He said of her that she was most encouraging on hearing his

Dame Eva's involvement with the London Opera Centre, whose home was the Art Deco, Grade II listed Troxy Cinema House in the East End of London, was timely and welcome and realistically a better environment in which to wield her influence than the RAM had been. Singing teachers were not members of staff and singers studied singing privately outside the Centre, being given a couple of mornings each week free from the curriculum to do so. Everything else which the singer needed to further their operatic career was given space on the timetable, including fencing, dancing, acting skills, make-up and most importantly language and singing coaching. Many of the structural ideas of the London Opera Centres curriculum had come from Dame Eva Turner. As we may remember she had asked for help regarding stage craft, movement and dress sense since this had not been part of her own training and so was particularly concerned that singers of the future should acquire these skills at an early stage in their development.

ideas for the opera course, even when he met with opposition to his ideas of repertoire and casting from other members of the staff.

Dame Eva continued to teach at the RAM while her interest in the London Opera Centre (see appendix) was growing, so there were three years of overlapping time spent in both schools of excellence.

Her travelling, which she loved, continued and in November she went back to America to attend a very special performance at the Metropolitan.

Metropolitan Opera Association, Inc
Office of the Chairman
New York 18. N.Y.
May 28, 1963.

Dear Madame Turner,

As you probably know, Giovanni Martinelli is being honoured at the Metropolitan Opera House on the night of Wednesday, November 20th. I have been talking to him at great length about just whom he would like to have invited: Needless to say, your name led all the rest. He is bringing over Madame Martinelli and his daughters etc. for the occasion. I felt that after many years of friendship with him, I should like to do something personal as far as he is concerned. Therefore, after discussing it with him, I am inviting you to come here as my guest for the week, whatever week you choose, before or after the event. I understand from Luigi Lucioni that you have a place to stay. But if you find this place does not work out, perhaps I can have you stay at a hotel during that period. We would be greatly honoured if you would accept.

I remember of having had the pleasure of meeting you on the occasion of a broadcast some years ago. So many members of your public would love to see you back in New York that I hope you can come here at the time of the Martinelli Gala.

With very best regards,
Sincerely yours,
Lauder Greenway

New York Times 21st November 1963:

'Golden Jubilee of a Star's Debut. Martinelli Is Feted by Met. Colleagues Gather for the Event by Raymond Ericson. Backstage at the Metropolitan Opera last night, gray-haired singers greeted each other affectionately as dancers in dark brown greasepaint swirled around... Miss Turner, a noted soprano with whom Mar-

tinelli had sung at Covent Garden, flew from London for the event.
(See appendix)

On her 72nd birthday Dame Eva, had a wonderful time as usual but was especially delighted to learn that Queen Elizabeth II had given birth to a baby boy, Edward, on March 10th 1964 and she now shared a date with the Royal Family whom she had admired throughout her life.

Amy Shuard was still studying with Dame Eva, who went to listen and watch as many of Amy's performances as possible, including, on September 1965, *Die Walküre* at the Royal Opera House when Amy sang Brünnhilde and Gwyneth Jones Sieglinde. Ernst Kozub was Siegmund, Hunding, Michael Langdon, Wotan, David Ward and Josephine Veasey was Fricka. The young Valkyries were women who very soon became known to the British public: Anne Edwards, Margaret Kingsley, Ann Howard, Yvonne Minton, Rae Woodland, Noreen Berry, Maureen Guy and Elizabeth Bainbridge. Solti conducted and it was produced by Hans Hotter. Once again her programme has a lot of 'scribbles' in the middle page!

Pauline Tinsley was also studying with Dame Eva at this point. Pauline had heard her sing Handel's *Largo* and Wagner's *Dich Teure Halle* at the Wigan Hippodrome when she, Pauline, was a child of about eleven and well remembers the occasion of her first lesson with Dame Eva in the early sixties: 'I wanted to improve my Aida which I had already been singing and went to ask the Dame if she would help me (she just appeared at the Dame's front door without an appointment). When I asked if she would help me, Dame Eva asked me my birth sign and I told her I was Aries and so she said she was sorry she could not help me. As I went to leave by the front steps, she asked the actual date of my birth and I told her March 27th so she caught me by the collar and pulled me back up the stairs and into the studio saying:

'that is near enough dear, you're only a week out of Pisces, my own birth sign.'

They had a happy association and Pauline told me that she never ever did any exercises with her as they both felt that she, Pauline, had a natural placement which should not be disturbed. When I interviewed Pauline, now in her eighties, I could hear from her speaking voice exactly what Dame Eva meant. Her lessons always started and ended with: *Rejoice Greatly* by Handel, *Dove Sono* by Mozart and *Jauchzet Gott* by Bach, exercises in themselves, and Dame Eva constantly reminded her that she must always keep the voice moving and never let it get heavy. Another couple of pieces of advice which Pauline recalled were that she must never pack up with breath, as one needed very little if you were singing well and 'accelerate to the top and go for it'. Together they studied some of Pauline's best roles: Aida, Lady Macbeth, Elektra and Turandot but strangely, never Santuzza which Pauline sang at the Royal Opera House with Domingo as her tenor.

Even at the age of seventy-five, Dame Eva continued to love travelling, and was on the panel for many International Competitions. She went to Canada to judge a contest, which was part of Expo '67, organised by the Institut Internationale de Musique du Canada and travelled there by jet plane from Japan. That journey from Japan to Canada was a far cry from the journeys she made to America by sea in her earlier years. The Montreal Times reported:

> 'She tells of her early days in her still powerful voice, rolling all the r-r-rs and beaming charm and kindness, so that one can almost hear the thunder of the trains carrying her from triumph to triumph, the upward swing of the curtains, the dramatic soaring of an Italian aria and the burst of applause... It is largely due to her pioneering success and her persistent refusal to change her name that today's singers can answer the curtain calls in the greatest opera houses of the world with an English name.'

After Montreal, she flew to Oklahoma: 'with but an hour to spare before the start of the Ceremony' at which she would receive the: '1967 citation for distinguished service to the University and the Nation'. During the following week she gave two master classes and a public lecture in the Holmberg Hall, scene of former triumphs, after which a public reception was held in her honour. During the lecture Dame Eva said that she hoped the US Government would do more and more in this century to underwrite the arts:

> *'Art Councils are the key. There is support of operatic performances to a great extent by the British government... they underwrite the deficits... Also, the Opera Centre in London recently held an open international competition and scholarships totalling £750 in value were given out by the sponsors.'*

She went on to express her hope for the creation of scholarship awards at Oklahoma University, for worthy students, in the name of faculty members who have contributed their time and resources to the development of the arts. At the end of the lecture:

> 'wearing a flower print dress with a white rose pinned to it, the charming Dame Eva announced she was planning to retire at the end of July 67 from her teaching position at the Royal Academy of Music in London.'

Back in London she said of her retirement:

'There are only 24 hours in the day and because I am going out of the country so much and it's not fair to the students unless you can utterly make up the lessons, time has defeated me, so I realise that I have to resign.'

Martinelli came out of semi-retirement in 1967, at the age of 81, to sing the Imperatore in *Turandot* because the scheduled tenor was indisposed, and writes the letter reproduced below to Dame Eva shortly after that event.

Recd air Mail 3.11.'67.

October 31, 1967

Eva dear:

The wonderful week in London is over, but the warm glow will linger forever in my memory. You, perhaps, more than anyone else who was there, Eva, can realize what it means to a veteran singer to be pulled from semi-retirement to again face an audience and hear the echoes again of the applause which was and is our birthright. The body may be getting old, but the spirit in us stays forever young, and when that spirit is buoyed by wonderful friends such as you, then physical age flees and youth is re-born, if only for a fleeting moment.

So many wonderful memories we have had together Eva- a colleague such as you just does not exist any more. I remember the words of Gaetano Merola in trying to explain the difference between the artists of our generation and those of today. "In my day," said Merola," they were all generals. Today they are all privates". How right he was- and what a magnificent general you were.

I am now again in my ivory tower on top of the Buckingham hotel with my thoughts which today are my treasures. One of the most important of all my treasures is your friendship- which is among the most dear of all my possessions. Would God that we lived closer so that I might see you more often. Again God bless you for all your kindnesses to me, your wonderful sweet presence, your speech , your cable for my birthday- for---- perhaps it is best said by saying- For just being Eva Turner. My cup runneth over-- Lele sends her love in which I fervently join.

Sempre Tuo

Giovanni

Gladys Parr and Eva went back to Scotland together in December 1967, where Dame Eva gave a talk in Aberdeen to a gathering of the Scottish Opera Club at the Arts Centre. In her talk Dame Eva said:

'It was here I spent many happy and hard-working days with the Carl Rosa Opera Company and I always remember how much I loved singing in His Majesty's Theatre. We always said there was something especially different about that theatre. It was so clean, and the men wore white coats and white boots. We were never afraid of getting bad throats through dust because the dust was never allowed to lie.'

She remembered too that she had sung her first Elisabeth in Wagner's *Tannhäuser* there. The two great ladies are photographed after the event and in the background, a very young, dark haired Patricia Hay, a budding Scottish soprano at the time, is captured looking at them, as if she would like to siphon from them and preserve every small grain of their experience and knowledge.

As we have seen, Dame Eva's home was not the most important part of her life and although Palace Court was beautifully furnished and clean, cared for by the ever faithful Sally three times a week with Miss Ridyard overseeing those duties, it was not a place into which Dame Eva crept to find peace, tranquillity and her inner self: she did that whilst sitting in an opera house, concert hall or church, listening to a performance, while inwardly reliving her past glories. Her house, however, was a place into which her students, her friends and people from all over the world, coming to interview this great lady were welcomed with hospitable Italian coffee, or a lunch time Italian tipple and nibbles. She was particularly fond of her near neighbours Raymond and Charlotte and often asked them across to spend some time with herself and Anne. A hand written letter of the 29th February 1968 invited them to 26 Palace Court:

Dear Charlotte and Raymond,

Today marks the 24th year and Anniversary since Anne joined me in 1944! Also Sunday March 3rd you too have an anniversary Raymond!

Will you join us for coffee etc. on Sunday morning at 11-30 a.m.

Looking forward to seeing you then.

Love and blessings

Eva

> BAYSWATER 7760
> 26, PALACE COURT,
> LONDON. W.2.
>
> 29.2.'68.
>
> Dear Charlotte & Raymond.
>
> Today marks the 24th years and Anniversary since Anne joined me in 1944! Also Sunday March 3rd you too have an Anniversary Raymond! Will you join us for Coffee etc on Sunday morning at 11.30 a.m. Looking forward to seeing you then,
>
> Love & Blessings
> Eva.

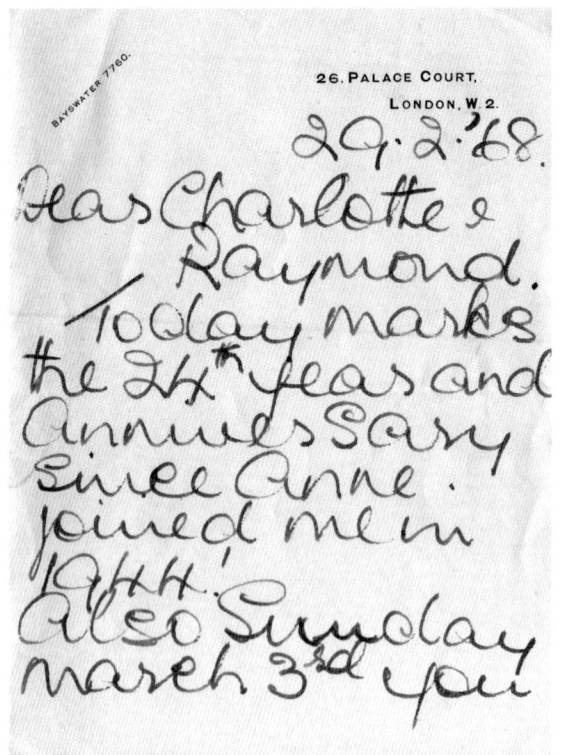

Whilst holidaying at Villa Junesca over the Easter holidays, Dame Eva was invited by Mrs Moor, the widow of Charles Moor, then living in retirement at her villa, Bella Vista, near Lugano, to come to a surprise birthday party. It was the 80th birthday, on 18th April 1968, of Frida Leider, who was staying nearby, engrossed in her second love, that of painting. The party was a great success and the two old colleagues had a wonderful time reminiscing about times past. Eva Turner:

'So vividly do I recall Frida's glorious performances in Chicago and also at Covent Garden and how she was revered by the audiences there. What a wonderful Isolde she was! She invested this role with such warmth, depth and stature. Indeed her interpretation will ever rank as among the greatest. As an artist she was supreme.'

Now in her mid-seventies the past was catching up with Eva Turner as she and her friends grew old and sometimes wiser together. Among the great highlights of this part of Dame Eva's life were the three Master Classes she gave with Martinelli during May 1968 in London. The classes were sponsored by the British Institute of Recorded Sound in association with the London Opera

Centre and took place at the Collegiate Theatre. Referring to this forthcoming event Giovanni writes in March to:

> 'Dearest Eva,
>
> I am about to depart for Rome (Via Nicotera 5) and I must write you for a two-fold reason. I have just returned from Oklahoma, where your name is still on the tongue of everyone – and I felt that if possible the whole University would pack its bags and come to London to be again with you.
>
> Secondly I must tell you of how very, very deeply I feel over my approaching joint-teaching sessions with you. I know that these were arranged by you and I can tell you that there is nothing in the world that I would rather do than be together again artistically with you. Would God that our voices could return for a week. We'd show these youngsters something again.
>
> Really, I am looking forward to this joint session as eagerly as if I was to create a new part in an opera that I had always loved but feared to sing. I anticipate and I am certain this will be one of the high water marks of my life – and as usual – it will be because of you.
>
> Lele did not want to come – she felt it would be too much, but when I told her of the close association we will have – she changed her mind in a hurry. She always admired you most greatly as an artist and loved you as a sister – so now all three will be together again. God has been good to all of us. Sometimes I wonder if I am really deserving all these marvellous happenings and the richness of the wonderful friendship I formed that has endured and grown so much in the past decades.
>
> Dear Eva – you do not have to answer this letter – it is just written as an expression of love and appreciation from the heart of your old colleague who cannot wait for May 22 when he can again join you in London.
>
> God bless and keep you
>
> Your Devoted Giovanni.'

The Stage Newspaper tells us of those classes, which took place when Eva was on the board of the Opera centre and in the year they put on *Albert Herring* as their main production:

> 'Eva Turner and Giovanni Martinelli, two of the greatest operatic artists of this century, have been giving a series of well attended Master Classes in London.

Before audiences consisting of members of the general public, these beloved veterans, in an entirely unrehearsed and spontaneous programme, hear advanced music students sing an aria from one of their famous operatic roles and then they proceed to apply constructive criticism, stressing the significance of getting enjoyment in performance and using art to conceal art, so that the audience derives the fullest possible enjoyment from the stage presentation of the opera. Public classes taken by two such past-masters of operatic art are both illuminating and entertaining and they suggest parallel presentation in the theatre at a time when one-man shows are all in vogue...

The class took the form of each of eight students singing an aria straight through. Then Dame Eva or Mr. Martinelli would do a little coaching and it was fascinating to see just what alchemy was worked by their experience and artistry. It was not merely a question of correcting intonation or breathing or pronunciation, but of showing how best to use the mechanics of singing in order to create. Great insistence was placed upon knowing everything about the opera – story, character and situation. The meaning of every word must be understood and only then, through the students own emotions, experience and imagination, can the music be brought to life. After hearing an aria from "Il Trovatore" sung very well, it was stimulating to see these superb artists exhorting the student with sung phrases, by beating time and miming the various emotions, to transform what had been a rehearsal into a performance. It made one realise that to have a voice is not enough. It also needs dedication and lot of perspiration.'

Giovanni Martinelli and Eva Turner shared many characteristics. He had a simple, honest upbringing, the oldest of 14 siblings with a father who was a cabinet maker and who encouraged Giovanni to use his naturally good voice and fine musicianship. Giovanni sang in the church from an early age and later played the oboe, when he was unable to sing between the years of eleven and seventeen as his voice broke, because he still wanted to make music. Music was the love of his life to the very end. Like Eva, he had a great generosity of spirit and an all consuming desire to sing and to give of his best to his audience. They recognised this performing, generous creature in each other and while on stage together delighted in sharing their gifts. They were healthy energetic souls which perhaps contributed to their both surviving a serious bout of typhoid fever and this abundant energy, plus their 'goodwill towards all men', seemed to create specially memorable performances. In the same year as the classes, at the age of 83, Martinelli recorded *Perché volete voi* from Zandonai's *Francesca di Rimini*, as a final lasting testament to his vocal technique which had served him well throughout his life. Shortly after this, at the age of 84, Giovanni Martinelli died quietly in his sleep in New York on the 2nd February 1969 and Dame Eva Turner, now almost 77, had lost a very dear friend and colleague.

Her generation was getting old, some of them even dying, but to be old was simply not Dame Eva Turner's mind set. She had a contained ability to imagine that death was not for her and if she worked hard enough at life, she would survive. She was somehow able to put negative thoughts of her life's ending to the back of her mind and get on with living it and so she set off once more for America to give Master Classes in Oklahoma, after which she would travel to San Francisco to be guest of honour at a performance there of *Turandot* in which the English tenor Charles Craig sang Calaf.

The Writer's Memoirs

Charles Craig had been a member of the Royal Opera House Chorus when Eva Turner had sung her last Turandots there in 1947 and had not been impressed by her singing. He did not like the quality of sound and felt that she had created a better name for herself in later life, than her singing career would have suggested she deserved but, like many people, he really had no idea what her singing career had been and had merely judged it on these final performances. He did feel, however, that they probably shared the same resentment at the lack of recognition of their talent in their own country and tried to engage her, in my hearing, on this subject. Charles felt that he had been unrecognised in Britain for the great singer which he undoubtedly was and imagined that Dame Eva felt the same way but in that he was mistaken, or that is to say, she would not have ever confessed to such a thought.

While Eva admired Charles' singing, she always thought him lacking in generosity as a performer. It might have been her attitude to give only what she could do easily and stop striving to give that little bit more if she could have found that line between enough and a little bit more, but it was not her nature to seek it or to measure it and so she always gave her all, when teaching as well as singing. Eva Turner's performance was not only of voice but was one of energetic, committed communication and this combination made her special. Charles on the other hand, with a foolproof singing technique, knew exactly where the line of vocal duty was and stopped at it with ease. His plan was to earn the good life which he had always wanted, striving to give himself and his family the material goods which his deprived childhood had not provided. He wanted to do a good job but to leave the audience wanting a little bit more, thus preserving his instrument for the next show, to be in good form to earn the next fee. Perhaps this approach of relying on vocal security related to his lesser personal confidence in the idea that life would provide. He knew from experience that life was tough and you had to look after yourself in case nobody else did.

For a singer this is a very useful idea and just goes to show that singers are also human beings with the same variety of thoughts and feelings which make up a cross section of the population. There is no blue print for being a professional singer. We are merely people who sing, some with more success than others. I think too that the word success, as well as being relative, also involves a balance of the very many complicated instincts, learned and innate, which all human beings have in different mixtures. First, one has to have a voice but after that, life itself dictates. Having known both of these singers intimately, and having been given vocal space and time by both at different stages in my singing life, I say in a considered way that they were opposite sides of the singing coin. Both knew the other side of themselves and what might have been, but neither could, nor wanted to, reach into that part, their alter ego, lest it would upset their balance. I am not sure if these were conscious thoughts but that is my interpretation of a conversation of which I was part, at Dame Eva's 98th birthday party in our home. There was recognition, each in the other, of sharing something special and private. A recognition too, that there are many roads up the mountain and not all roads lead to the top but their chosen roads had made their journeys worthwhile, as well as taking them to the summit.

Together you and I have explored the first seventy eight years of this great life, bringing us now to 1970, the year during which Dame Eva agreed to be my singing teacher. To me, she was not only a great diva, but was, more importantly to me, my friend and teacher. I was like the child who blunders blindly into her grandparents' life and grows there, accepting their nourishment and enjoying them for what life has made them without having much idea of what their former life had been. I knew Dame Eva intimately for the next twenty years, as I grew from youth to maturity, during which time she stayed maturely young.

I had always wanted to study with Eva Turner but had been advised by those who know such things, and with hindsight those know-alls knew very little, that I should have a 'safe teacher'. My teacher at the Royal Scottish Academy of Music, Muriel Dickson, concurred with this safe idea and did a little research. Before becoming a house singer at the Metropolitan Opera House in the thirties and forties, she had been a member of the D'Oyle Carte Company, which in those days did a big tour to America, where she was heard and invited to audition, successfully, for the Metropolitan. I have with hindsight an uneasy feeling that Muriel knew about Eva Turner's unsuccessful audition there, but being the noble person she was, she did not share this with me, saying only that Eva had never sung there.

George Baker had made many recordings of the Gilbert and Sullivan Operas, the 'patter' baritone roles, and was a very fine musician and Muriel Dickson, also from that world, had known him well. He was now dead but his widow, Olive Groves, his second wife, was a respected singing teacher in London and so Muriel contacted Olive and arranged for an audition for me. By this time in 1969 I was all set for the Opera Centre but needed to have a private singing teacher. Olive Groves was very kind and pleasant when I went to sing for her and so it was arranged that I would study with her when I came to London in the autumn.

At my first lesson, I was invited to sing the exercises I had learned with Muriel Dickson and then to sing an aria. I quickly realised it was better to choose something from an oratorio, as that, along with English songs, was Olive Groves' speciality, and after being told it was very good, I was asked to sing it again. This was no use at all for all sorts of reasons, one of them being that while one can learn from any repertoire really, I needed help with operatic roles, especially now that I was studying at the Opera Centre. We all know it takes two to tango and perhaps I should have been braver and more up front about what I needed from a lesson but my instinct told me that we were in polite English territory and I had absolutely no idea how to get what I wanted in that situation, so I started to be less available and to look for a way out.

I was still yearning to study with Eva Turner but my scholarship for the Opera Centre was dependent on the agreement of the Principal, James Robertson, as to how the money would be spent. Despite knowing my needs and sitting on the board of the Opera Centre with Dame Eva, he was, disloyally to both of us in my opinion, in the 'Play It Safe Team' and said that he felt I should wait awhile. I wanted him just to introduce me to her and see where that would lead but he declined.

A few weeks later Dame Eva alighted from the number 15 bus and crossed Commercial Road into the London Opera Centre, wheeling a wicker trolley basket, which had a plastic cover over it, a bit like the little plastic covers with elastic round the edges which one can buy to cover bowls. As she passed through the foyer she said 'Good Morning Dear' to the world in general in her distinctive speaking voice which I can still hear and I thought: 'this is my moment.' I approached, gathering courage, and breathed in to introduce myself, when suddenly there was an acute barking noise. Dame Eva bent down, removed the plastic cover from the wicker trolley and fished out a small, angry Pekinese dog from inside the basket which was known as Mintz's Chariot. Thrusting the little dog towards me, she asked:

'Could you take him outside to do his business dear? I will be just inside the auditorium where I will be judging.'

I hesitated in mid-refusal, since I didn't at that time know Mintz and felt it was a little too intimate for starters. I was also frightened of the little mad, barking, fluffy wriggling bundle, since I couldn't see which end was his face and which his bottom and was fearful of being bitten – I didn't know then that he had only three teeth because of his great age. As I hesitated, another dog-loving student dived between me and the yelping fluff-ball, and incidentally Dame Eva, so my moment was lost.

In the meantime, I was preparing repertoire for the various competitions held in London in the spring of 1970. Early in the year, about four months into our time together, Olive Groves became quite unwell, so I sent her flowers and used her illness as an excuse to get on with things myself with the help of the coaches at the Centre. Jeffrey Tate, then a student at the Opera Centre, having completed his medical training, is a wonderful musician and fine pianist and he said he would play for me in the Royal Over-Seas League Competition. I was in safe hands and we had a good time preparing for it.

Utu, Mintz's predessor and Eva Turner

After rehearsing with him one evening I went home to my bedsit in Hammersmith Grove and turned on the radio to hear:

'It is for the Musicians' Benevolent Fund and its new residential home at Westgate-on-Sea that I am appealing to you tonight. But first of all let me read to you a couple of sentences which distressed musicians have written: "I wouldn't wish my worst enemy to be in my present position and if you forsake me we are altogether lost, both my unfortunate self

and my poor sick wife and child..." "Truly my lot is a hard one. What is to become of me? How can I live until I am able again to earn my living by writing?" The first of those appeals was by Mozart and the second by Beethoven – at times when those composers, in the face of illness and distress were producing those works that the world of today most values. And still, at this very moment, despite the efforts of a welfare state, there are many musicians in sickness and in want. I could read you similar appeals written recently, not by Mozart or Beethoven, but by hard working and deserving singers, players and teachers who have fallen on bad times. Very, very sad appeals.

Now what do we do to help? Well I can tell you that no appeal for help from a bona-fide professional musician is ever rejected. If they meet with disaster they are assured of help. We grant pensions, we make gifts to meet immediate needs, we maintain a convalescent home for those who have been ill and we support two residential homes for older musicians, for married couples and for single men and women. It is for one of these homes which we have just opened at Westgate-on-Sea that I am especially appealing and asking for your help. We are calling this home "Elwes House" after the beloved singer, Gervase Elwes, in whose memory our fund was started fifty years ago.

We have also in this bicentenary year had Beethoven especially in our minds. Beethoven cared deeply about fellow musicians who were ill or on hard times. Almost every year he gave a charity concert and often more than one. On his death bed he said to Hummel, "We must always help our musicians." And so I am asking you most earnestly to do this very thing. We must go on helping musicians who are in want and to do this we must ask for your support. Over the years there have been many artists of high repute and popularity who have, during the course of their careers, given much pleasure to countless thousands and who have, through a variety of reasons, fallen on bitter times and would have gone under but for the timely help of the Musicians' Benevolent Fund. Just think of what the world owes to Beethoven and many other musicians. Think too of what music has meant in your own life. So please help us and send as much as you can afford. Thank you for listening to me tonight. I am indeed grateful.'

The announcer at the end declared the appeal to have been made by Dame Eva Turner.

The Musicians' Benevolent Fund and the Salvation Army were Dame Eva's main charities all her life and she had spoken from the heart. She had not merely read the piece, she meant it and I was drawn to her once again. She was my kind of person. I was now sitting down and had no idea what to do next. Why I did not just lift the phone and speak to her at this point escapes me, but the fact is, apart perhaps from not having change for the phone in the hall, I think I was lacking enough courage to face her rejection, if that had been the outcome of an audition, so I did nothing. Fate, however, took a hand in the turn of events which followed.

The Royal Over-Seas League's Music Festival, at that time headed by Audrey Strange who said of Dame Eva that she had breathed new life into the competition when she joined the panel of judges, was a hugely important event in Dame Eva's calendar. In those days, there was a mainstay of judges who sat on the jury, year after year and they all listened to all the entries for the competition; that is the string players, the wind instruments, piano and voice. There were three judges for each of these sections and so the panel was made up of 12 musicians in all, sitting behind a long table in the middle of the St Andrew's Hall, now Princess Alexandra Hall, at Over-Seas House. There was a prize for each section and an outright winner's prize. To win this outright prize all three of the judges of your own instrument section had to vote for you as well as your having to have a majority from the rest of the judges. I won my section but Marius May the 'cellist won the outright prize. I accepted this second best outcome, until Robert Easton, also on the panel, cornered me afterwards and asked what on earth I had done to offend Eva, as she had absolutely refused to agree to give me the main prize, despite my having a majority of votes from the rest of the panel.

She had behaved rather eccentrically in the early rounds of the singing competition as, when Nan Christie announced that she would sing *O luce di quest'anima*, Dame Eva asked her if it was the only aria she knew, as she had now heard her sing it four times. When Nan started the aria, Dame Eva excused herself and left the hall saying loudly that she couldn't bear to listen to it again. Nan always told that story with delighted laughter, as it was in fact her main, over-used party piece at that time and understood Dame Eva's point of view, but in fairness I think it was a bit rich coming from someone who knew the worth of a good party piece - *Ritorna Vincitor* for example!

Hearing Nan's story and with Robert Easton's information playing on my mind, I became a little annoyed at the unfairness of both situations, my inner fierceness was alerted and with that came courage. I phoned 26 Palace Court and asked to speak with Dame Eva. A kind voice asked who I was and told me that Dame Eva was not at home and asked if she might take a message. I told her I would like to sing for Dame Eva and we arranged that I should go along the very next day at 9.30 am to audition for the Dame. Help! What had I done? Peter, my soon-to-be-husband, had said to me that I must ask her why she thought I was not fit to win the main prize, as this information would help me to be a better singer and so I made up my mind to do just that. Thoughts of my Scottish uncle telling me that she was the best singer he had ever heard, and how she had completely filled the stage with her presence, came crowding in. I was nervous and in awe. My anger had died down and I focused on the opportunity to show her how good I was. I fear Peter's reasoning and mine were a little different.

Next morning I put on my very best bright green midi skirt with bronze buttons up the front, long brown leather boots and a dark purple polo neck sweater, all very modern, under my sheepskin jacket and off I went to Hammersmith Station, carrying my music case, to travel by underground to Bayswater. I can hardly believe what, in my ignorant state, I chose to sing: *Ritorna Vincitor*. I had sung it in the final of the competition and wanted her to tell me what was wrong with it or more accurately prove her wrong in her decision not to give me the prize. I think foolhardy might be an understatement.

I did not meet the owner of the kind voice from the phone call of the previous day, but was met at the front door by Dame Eva herself and ushered immediately into the studio, on the right of the entrance hall. She asked me:

'What are you going to sing dear?'

and to her everlasting credit, did not flinch one muscle as I put the score of *Aida* in front of her at the piano. She merely said that she would use her own score and stretched over the top of the piano to retrieve it from where it lay in readiness. Having shared with you the first part of this book, I am now sitting in a state of collapse at the very thought of the undercurrent which must have been in Dame Eva's studio that morning as she opened her score. How wonderful it would have been if, the history of her association with *Aida* had leapt from the covers of the score to tell its story, lifting us up and taking us, in Tardis fashion, to places where she had once reigned.

As it was, ignorance is bliss and I sang my heart out. She then asked if I knew the Nile Scene and so we performed that too. I told her I wanted to sing a bit of Wagner next and then sang

Elsa's dream from *Lohengrin*. I hope you are now smiling at this presumptuous twenty-one year old, as I am afraid it is the only kind way to deal with this committed but misguided person. That was exactly Dame Eva's reaction: she smiled and thanked me and I thanked her for playing for me. We were friends. All thoughts of challenging her about the Royal Over-Seas Prize were forgotten and it was never referred to. I left on cloud nine because she had asked me to come the next morning to begin studying with her. As I left she said she would not charge me for this consultation lesson. I thanked her and told her I was currently studying with Olive Groves, at which she gave a wry smile and said that tomorrow's lesson was on condition that I had informed Miss Groves that I would no longer be studying with her.

I went immediately to tell Olive Groves that I would be studying with Dame Eva and was greeted at the entrance to her rather lovely flat, where I had first auditioned for her, I think in the St John's Wood area, by her maid, dressed in a little black dress with a white apron and little white band on her head. Both the flat and the maid were straight out of *Poirot* television programmes set in the thirties. The maid graciously informed me that Madame Olive was very ill. When I explained my mission, she became very irate and, almost crying, told me that this news would kill her mistress, a small exaggeration I fear, but nevertheless I left without seeing Olive Groves.

I told no-one of this abortive attempt to release myself and nobody asked, but my conscience worried me for many months and then the incident faded into the wings of my busy life and didn't seem to matter anymore. About a year later, I had applied for a grant and went to an audition, where to my horror I was faced by Olive Groves and James Robertson, who had given into my wishes to study with Dame Eva but had been very cross. They were the only members of the panel. They greeted my red hot, ashamed, face warmly and I was fine in the first song but had to start the second one three times, as my concentration had gone and I kept forgetting the words. They gave me a substantial grant to be used for study purposes, which I think was a very generous gesture in the light of the circumstances and I was doubly sorry not to have said a proper goodbye to Olive Groves who died in 1974.

The working relationship between the singer and the teacher is, in my experience, a sacred one and involves great trust, understanding and patience. It also involves the forgiveness of going up the odd vocal cul-de-sac, a journey which can be brought about by either side. The language used is very important, as it has to be clear and uncomplicated, so that the singing directions are understood. I knew my own voice very well and Dame Eva recognised this and shared an understanding of the sounds I was trying to make and found no fault with the general outlines of what I was producing. I was not given a great lecture on where she came from vocally and the journey I was expected to make to match her expectations. She listened, not to what I said, which was very little, but to the voice itself and tried to pass on her ability not only to listen, but to hear in an informed way. This was the most important gift she could have bestowed. She also said very little, but guided me by giving short, clear instructions before, after and during singing. I think the ability to hear and automatically adjust the voice via the diaphragm was the most important quality we shared and through that avenue, she taught me to listen properly for the right sounds. We hardly discussed how this would be brought about technically, because, having seen and heard her pleasure or displeasure, expressed through delighted smiles or tortured grimaces accompanied by growls and grunts, at what I produced, I was able to subconsciously sift through that information and keep singing the sounds she wanted; sounds which also felt right in my body and my ears.

Without the sounds there was no information, so we started immediately with exercises which she felt would help to bring the voice into a more forward position, behind the mask. I realise now that they were the ones which she had worked on with Plum but strangely she never mentioned him in the studio. These were: Shee, Shay, Shah, each sung on a nine note upwards scale. She believed that the extra note extended your stretch. They were performed very quickly moving from key to key up a semitone each time, until you had covered the complete range of your voice and then we descended semitone by semitone. There was no rest given at any time during this exercise and she accompanied me on the piano with double octaves, in both hands, played perfectly in every key. I sometimes had the feeling that although she did not sing at all during these lessons, she was trying to show me what to do through her fingers. I swear she must have practised these scales for hours. Next we would perform extended arpeggios on the same vowel sequence and finally some quick staccato arpeggios. Again with no pause for rest. Her words were:

'Do it: quickly, properly, immediately and where are you?'

She imitated me if I pulled my mouth to the sides and the sound was too wide, and she told me to accelerate to the top and to thread if through the eye of a needle. Most importantly, she shouted: 'don't move', if she felt me coming off the voice. Her finger was often behind the top front teeth as she told me where to aim and to avoid the blunt gum sound.

As I fell on to Palace Court Road at around 12 o'clock I must have looked a bit like Sylvester the cat with stars coming out of the top of my head having been hit by a very strong implement, but I was happy. I had found the home I was looking for. I do not remember ever being invited to 'sing it again' without some suggestion as to how I could improve my singing. We had, after that first lesson, gone downstairs to meet the kind voice in the round, white-haired shape of Miss Anne Ridyard, a little like Mrs Tiggy Winkle, and I was given my first cup of the Italian coffee which I grew to love. I was completely won over. I loved everything about Dame Eva. She talked about Martinelli, Gigli, Muzio and Stignani and I hung on every word. 'This would be my life too': I thought. Miss Ridyard asked me about Scotland and with whom I had studied there and Dame Eva listened thoughtfully, seated at the top of the table. We then booked another lesson and I asked Dame Eva how much I owed her. Miss Ridyard told me each lesson would cost £3 and I would be sent a bill for a group of ten lessons, if I agreed with the arrangement, which of course I did.

Dame Eva had been horrified that I had not heard of Muzio and did not know her singing, so I was duly dispatched to the Institute of Recorded Sound, in Exhibition Road, to listen to the great voice singing Traviata. I clutched a note of introduction to the official there and was admitted to a little cubicle where I donned great big headphones. The be-suited assistant placed the record on a machine on the other side of the glass partition and in a few seconds, it crackled into life. Muzio was great but not as great, I thought, as Eva Turner, who I asked to listen to next. I was there for the rest of the day until the kindly official had to practically prise the phones from my head. This was the life. I would now settle down in London, which at that time I did not like very much, with a will, as the answers to my singing prayers lay there.

Under the Dame's tutelage I won many competitions in the next year and decided to use some of the money to study in Italy. I was young and I think I hadn't realized that I was important to her just as she was very precious to me, so without thinking, I made plans to study with Maestro Campanino, who was attached to the San Carlo in Naples. I should have asked her advice as to where to study but I was thoughtless and to be frank did not realise how deep her roots were in Italy, so off I went. She was strangely withdrawn three months later at my first lesson on my return to London and asked me nothing about my time in Naples. I was, nevertheless, invited for coffee as usual, during which Miss

Ridyard asked me how I had got on. As she asked the question, she gave me a warning look which I immediately understood and so said very little but I had been careless and can only put it down to being a young person, lacking in the confidence which would have enabled closeness in conversation. Dame Eva although kind, was very formal and in truth a little bit shy in the domestic situation, which didn't help. I didn't want her to think I was overstepping the mark by involving her in what I thought was a personal decision and so did not include her in every thought. I was also an independent little sod and felt it was my own life but I would have to be more considerate of our relationship in future. I learned nothing in Italy which I could not have learned from her. Before returning to Naples I spoke quietly and contritely to her one day and asked if she would prefer that I didn't go back. I wasn't so very keen to return anyway, as it had rained constantly from October to December and was not the weather I was expecting. I was also missing Peter to whom I was now married. She smiled at me and told me that I must finish my commitment. There was an uneasy truce.

On her 80th birthday interview by the Stage news paper, Dame Eva confessed to regretting that she had never sung Lady Macbeth in Verdi's opera, saying that she had in the past declined Glyndebourne's invitation to sing it because of an overcrowded schedule. She went on to say that the same thing happened when Giordano begged her to sing Madeleine in the opera *Andrea Chénier* which he had composed. Another of her regrets was never having sung *Traviata*, so it is interesting to see that her vocal mind was including the high notes, necessary for these roles, which she always had easily when young and never lost sight of as she grew older. They were emphasised by her as being an important box office draw, with the words: 'The Top is Box Office Dear' during every one of my lessons with her. She added that if they were not there, then one: 'Might as well shut up shop and go home.'

As a belated 80th birthday present I was able to give her tickets for a performance of *Macbeth* at Glyndebourne, although not, unfortunately, with me singing Lady Macbeth. She received the actual gift with joy unbounded. My package was: the Boy King, with three lines to sing and I was in the chorus, from whence I was extracted to sing Lady Macbeth's top D flat in the wings as she exited after her aria. Every time I sang at Glyndebourne she was, sitting proudly in the stalls and, whether I sang well or not so well, she was generous in her behaviour and made positive comments such as: good and bad performances were all 'Grist to the Mill'. Not, of course, that she approved of less than one's best but after the event, what was there to be done, except to make sure it was better the next time? She was gracious in her thanks for her ticket and never, ever gave me a hard time on the way home from such occasions: that was saved for the studio!

Dame Eva no longer drove and so had a large group of willing admirers, often past fans who had become great friends, who were more than happy to act as taxi drivers for herself and Anne. They would be included in whatever occasion was on the menu and entered into the spirit of things with great gusto. Brian Griffiths was one such friend who was very kind to 'the girls' and ferried Dame Eva to lots of concerts including the one in the photo

Linda Esther Gray, Dame Eva Turner and Brian Griffiths (right)

below where I was clearly wearing a curtain!

In November 1973 the record *Great British Sopranos* was released and there was a launch party and signing opportunity at the Army and Navy Stores in London where, left to right in the photo opposite, Gwen Catley, Dora Labette, Eva Turner, Lawrence Collingwood, Isobel Baillie and Joan Cross were at the ready with their pens.

Dame Eva absolutely adored going to performances both for the music and to meet her friends and fans and was spotted by a reporter from the Sunday Telegraph when she was at the Coliseum in November 1973, when a Royal Gala performance of *Die Fledermaus* on December 12th in aid of the Sadler's Wells Benevolent Fund was announced. The reporter told us:

> 'The production will dispense with the second act ballet and instead has several guest singers at Prince Orlofsky's party. Would Dame Eva be one of them? Well no she didn't think that would be quite on. "I don't know" said the reporter, "she'd look very distinguished sitting in state there."'

Dame Eva Turner was greatly honoured to become the President of the Wagner Society, a position she held, and of course always contributed to enthusiastically and with delight, from 1971-1985. This and her continuing interest in opera performances, led her to be on the panel which chose the winner of the Evening Standard's first opera award, in 1974, when it was given to Mr Reginald Goodall. In her speech, before the presentation by Princess Alexandra, Dame Eva made a special point of mentioning Lord Harewood, Director of English National Opera, who is: 'a worshiper of bel canto' and reminded the listeners that he was

Launching of the record 'Great British Sopranos' Left to right – Gwen Catley, Dora Labette, Eva Turner, Lawrence Collingwood, Isobel Baillie and Joan Cross

the main driving force behind Goodall's first two complete *Ring* cycles. She went on to say:

> 'This is not only Mr Goodall's wonderful achievement but the achievement of many over the space of the years.'

The next year the Evening Standard Award for Opera was presented by Dame Eva to Scottish Opera for their achievement in establishing the first new opera house in Britain for more than forty years. It was to retain its old name, Theatre Royal, Glasgow and the paper tells us:

> 'It was a night of Tartan triumph in Glasgow when, with a roar more familiar to Hampden Park, the Scots saluted the latest trophy

Dame Eva Turner

that had been taken north for a definitely home-produced victory. Repeated ovations from the 1500 capacity audience echoed late into the night for the new heroes of the highlands – Scottish Opera. This was the company that had won the Evening Standard Opera Award for 1975 and it was in their home base of Glasgow Theatre Royal that the Scots last night celebrated their new prize. It was all so appropriate. It was presented to the company on stage by that ageless prima donna, Dame Eva Turner, who first sang in that theatre more than 60 years ago and in a way it was her evening.

After a first night performance that saw the celebrated Italian, Sesto Bruscantini, making his debut in the title role of Falstaff, Dame Eva took over and the audience, including many of Scotland's leading figures, including Kenneth McKellar, took her to their hearts. She was back on the stage where she sang her first Brünnhilde, and again gave a brilliant performance in presenting the award to Alexander Gibson and Peter Hemmings, artistic director and general administrator of Scottish Opera. Dame Eva, a member of the opera award judging panel said: "We were unanimous and joyous that it should go to Scottish Opera. I do not think I have ever had so much pleasure on this stage, where I have sung so many roles for the first time, as I have had tonight." The Scots rose to her. It was a special moment.'

Gladys Parr (left), Noel Gibson and Dame Eva Turner

Dame Eva and Gladys Parr had, a couple of years before, exchanged their Valkyrie head dresses for hard hats when they visited the theatre during its renovation, after Scottish Television vacated the premises for its new building. Noel Gibson, manager of the London Opera Centre and former General Manager of the Theatre was photographed with them.

Earlier in 1975, however, it had been a sad time for Dame Eva Turner because on April 18th Amy Shuard died at the age of fifty. Amy was a very good singer and artist, and her career speaks for itself. Her relationship with the Dame had been a fruitful one of that I am certain. I met Amy Shuard on two occasions at Dame Eva's, or really just one, as the story I am about to tell, makes clear. The first meeting was over coffee after my lesson had ended and her warm-up for a performance at Covent Garden that evening was about to begin. When introducing us, Dame Eva told Amy I was married and very busy etc. and turning to me informed me that Amy too had a busy family life which included doing all her own laundry, including starching her own table linen and napkins. Why should such trivia remain in my mind I know not, but there we are, that was the mainstay of our short, somewhat uncomfortable conversation?

The next week I told Dame Eva how much I admired Amy Shuard and how I had enjoyed her Kundry very much indeed. Dame Eva looked at me astutely and then said in a whisper:

'I would love you to hear her warm up with me but I don't think it is fair to burden Amy with that on the day of a performance, although I know she would not mind, so dear, I want you to come here before her next lesson and I will hide you in my bedroom so that you can listen. Don't let's tell Anne because she would not understand.'

I agreed and even now I can't believe that we plotted in such a way together. I fear that Anne would not only 'not have understood' but would have been a mite angry with us. I did not ring the door bell but arrived at the appointed time and stood outside 26 Palace Court and waited for Dame Eva to let me in. It was like something straight out of *The Marriage of Figaro*. She came to the door and I crept into her bedroom, she ushered me inside her wardrobe and as she retreated, locked the bedroom door, not an unusual occurrence since all the doors on this floor had locks because it was a shared hallway with her tenants. As I snuggled down inside the wardrobe, with the Dame's clothes dangling around me, although this did seem a step too far since the bedroom door was locked, I heard muffled voices approaching on the stairway leading to the hall. They passed the bedroom door and I could hardly breathe for excitement. Into the studio they went and Amy's warm up began. I came out of the wardrobe very carefully, as I could hear very little from inside. The great voice sounded forth and I was thrilled to be under the same roof as such singing. The lesson was only a warm up, so quite short, say about three quarters of an hour and I was completely in awe of the wonderful sounds Amy Shuard was making for every single one of those forty-five minutes. The lesson ended and the voices retreated and in due course I was set free and ushered discreetly out of the front door by a delighted, very pleased Dame Eva. Our only excuse was a shared obsession with the human voice.

Covent Garden gave a wonderful memorial service for Amy Shuard in St. Paul's Covent Garden, the actors' church to which I went with Dame Eva, Anne Ridyard and Sally Beacon, Dame Eva's wonderful daily, and we were all extremely moved by some great singing, including John Vickers' *If With All Your Hearts* from *Elijah* by Mendelssohn. As I sat there with Sally aged about sixty, Miss Ridyard, aged seventy-two and Dame Eva now in her eighty-third year, the thought passed through my mind that if life was orderly, she would be the next to die of this little group and in that moment I prayed fervently that that would not be for a very long time. I was wrong, within the year, dear Sally had died.

Dame Eva never forgot to stretch out the hand of empathy and thoughtfulness when sympathy was required and received these letters of reply. The first was from Benjamin Britten when he was very ill:

23rd July 1976
The Red House

Dear Dame Eva,
Thank you very much indeed for your kind message
Love Ben.

The second from Peter Pears who wrote to her after Benjamin Britten's death a few months later on December 4th 1976:

Dear Eva,
Thank you very much indeed for your most kind message. It was so good of you to write.
Love Peter.

Gladys Parr had known both of those great artists, as she had sung the first Florence Pike in *Albert Herring* at Glyndebourne in 1947 when Peter Pears had been Albert and Benjamin Britten, the composer had conducted. Eva Turner shared her friend's sad feelings of loss for a great man and the passing of an era.

1976 was also the year her own beloved brother Norman passed away, causing her great heartache as the memories of their happy childhood flooded over her. They had always been very close and when Albert Broad died Norman had tried his very best to fulfil a small part of his duties as best he could. Florence his wife survived him.

As well as sharing grief, she never failed to share the joy in someone else's life. As I have written in my autobiography, I was hesitant to tell the Dame that I was expecting a baby in October 1976 but as with all news, she took it in her stride, saying:

'You have to do your duty by your husband'

and continued to teach me, sometimes with Kirsty sleeping downstairs under Anne's watchful eye. They were not however used to small children in their lives and so this was only on rare occasions but as Kirsty grew up she admired Dame Eva and looked forward to putting on her party dress, sometimes with her red wellington boots and tinsel wrapped round her arms, legs and on top of her head, whenever Dame Eva came to visit, or when they were at performances together. Kirsty sensed that there was something very special about this lady and in fact, thinking about it now, took on board some of the aspects of that grandness, including the loud projected tones when speaking. This voice has been very useful in Kirsty's chosen career of primary school teaching!

Dame Eva always retained her loyalty towards and interest in the north of England and was a staunch supporter of Fanny Waterman, visiting Leeds to lend her name to the cause and on many occasions to be at their International Pianoforte Competition. In 1977, Dame Eva wrote a letter to the Yorkshire Post to help promote the Leeds National Musician's Platform, which said:

'Sir, At the Purcell Room in London I have been assisting, along with my musical colleagues, Dame Janet Baker, Lady Barbirolli, Eleanor Warren, Richard Lewis, William Pleeth and others at the preliminary auditions of the Leeds National Musicians' Platform. I cannot help reflecting on what extremely fine talent in all forms of applied music this event has brought to life.

How fortunate Leeds is to have one of its citizens, the celebrated and inspired piano teacher, Fanny Waterman. Not only does this lady devote a great deal of her life to her own specialised art but she is one of the prime instigators in affording young musicians the opportunity to launch their talent. I must also express my admiration for Lord Boyle, the Vice Chancellor of the University of Leeds. What a great musician he is and how unstinting in his time, employed as the Chairman of the Adjudicating panel.

When the finals of the Leeds National Musicians' Platform takes place, I imagine there will be capacity audiences and that the citizens of Leeds and surrounding districts will be very anxious to hear the talent which has been brought to light by this most enterprising event.'

This cutting had been sent to Dame Eva with thanks and the following inscription written on the photo copy:

'With much love and looking forward to seeing you very soon.
Yours ever,
Fanny.'

Even as she moved into her mid-eighties Dame Eva was to be seen often at the Royal Opera House and loved going backstage to greet the performers. The Opera House was very kind to her and made a couple of tickets available to her whenever she wanted to go. As I got to know her better she often took me with her on these occasions, which was a great treat. We went together to see *Tristan and Isolde* with Jon Vickers, whom she knew very well and loved, singing Tristan. She took me round to his dressing room after the performance and it was simply lovely to see her first of all tell him what a wonderful performance he had given and then, discreetly, give a few small hints as to where he could improve. He was kind to her, listening to every word and not for a moment suggesting that he was too special to take advice.

During the first interval of that performance I wanted to buy Dame Eva a drink and she said:

> 'No thank you dear, you must save your money for study and for the future, but please could you find us two empty glasses? I have made our own special arrangement for drinks.'

During the seventies in London because of bomb scares, we were not allowed to carry brief cases or any such thing into the theatre and our hand bags were thoroughly searched. I had, however, noticed a small umbrella carrier hanging from Dame Eva's wrist earlier. With difficulty, braving raised eyebrows and a rather snooty bar man, I procured a couple of empty glasses. On returning, I found a small crowd of admirers gathered round her and, on seeing the glasses, Dame Eva politely excused herself and whispered to me that we should find a secluded corner, which we did. She then removed the umbrella holder from her wrist and produced from within a Schweppes tonic water bottle of

24th May 1977

Dear Dame Eva

I want you to know how much I appreciate your giving so much of your time yesterday to the cause of Live Music Now – I know how busy you are in your 'retirement'! I think we found some real talent among the candidates, and I now hope that during the next few months the scheme will begin to prove its worth, both to the young artists we have selected and their audiences.

With my most grateful thanks for your interest and support,
Very sincerely,
Yehudi Menuhin.

25th May 1977

It was delightful of you to turn up – in so delightfully ebullient form as ever – at the Sunday Times yesterday and extremely kind of you to think of giving me such an agreeable attractive and highly practical present. I put the hankies to very good use as I have now caught a summer cold.

Desmond.
(Desmond Shaw Taylor)

exactly the right dimensions to fit the make-shift holder and from it poured us a wonderful, somewhat lethal cocktail, saying with a little laugh:

'Something I prepared earlier for our pleasure.'

Around this time, she took the three young relatives in her life, children of Katherine Morgan her closest living relative, on their annual Christmas treat. The performance was Humperdinck's *Hansel and Gretel*, extremely appropriate for a Christmas gift to the children. The youngest child Mark was aged about ten at the time and as they were seated in the taxi on the way home, dressed in their best for the occasion, this observant child, having noted the rather hooty, sexless tones of the Sandman asked a little naughtily: 'Aunt Eva, was the part of the Sandman played by a hermaphrodite?' Without a pause for breath she replied:

'No dear she was a mezzo-soprano.'

This story for me sums up Dame Eva's innocence and perhaps her wiliness.

And while on the subject of *Hansel and Gretel* I will tell a little story of my own: While at the Opera Centre all of us singers studied with various teachers in London and we were always interested in which teacher was producing the best students. After engaging me on this subject Dame Eva, who was not usually at all gossipy, asked me if there was any teacher who was attracting good students at that time. I mentioned a few and she listened without comment. When I mentioned Audrey Langford, however, she looked beyond me into the far distance and from the great heights of Princess Turandot's throne said:

'I believe she was a very good Dew Fairy.'

This has to be among the best put-downs in history.

Dame Eva was also in the audience at the Royal Opera House for a performance of *Il Trovatore*, with Arroyo and Bergonzi. As was her usual custom she went back stage to greet and congratulate the singers. Ava Gardner and the actor from *Bonanza* were also there, along with a singer from Las Palmas, Marie Isabel Toron. Marie Isabel was congratulating Carlo Bergonzi on his superb performance and chatting to him in Italian when Dame Eva approached to kiss Carlo and then turned to congratulate Marie Isabel on her perfect Italian pronunciation, asking her where in Italy she came from. She replied that in fact she was not Italian and came from the Canary Islands, at which point Dame Eva became very excited and told her that she knew the Islands well and had very pleasant memories of them. Marie Isabel asked this charming, unknown to her, lady, 'Who are you?' and when telling the story back home in Las Palmas to a delighted audience said: 'the lady then stepped forward as if to return to the stage where the audience was anxiously waiting to hear her and said: 'I am Eva Turner''. Marie Isabel went home, thrilled to have met the great lady who was still remembered in Las Palmas for her legendary performances of 1928.

Dame Eva was to return to Las Palmas in person in a couple of years' time but before then she was very busy giving after dinner talks, among them, one to the Royal Society of Medicine, when she spoke of wondering:

'What on earth can I, a singer and musician, have to say to a gathering of medical people? Then there came to my mind something I had read in the press some little while ago, in the days of strikes, sit-ins and demonstrations among university students: there was less dissention among medical and music students than any other body. That gave me my first link. Then it came to my mind that I personally have a very close link with the medical profession and one which gives me great joy: I am the vice-president of Council for Music in Hospitals. Some of you may know of the work of this society and so, those of you who do, will forgive me if I give those who do not, a brief outline of our functions. We organise concerts to be given in hospital wards by young musicians who are starting their careers. We take music to the wards and to those people who are confined to their beds. Through the years we have learned that this is a marvellous therapy which gives so much pleasure to so many people who would otherwise be deprived of hearing live performances and it is a very welcome change from the television box! We receive letters of appreciation from doctors and nurses as well as patients, telling us what great pleasure is derived from our work.

It is always a great pleasure to me, when I am at the Royal Opera House, Covent Garden, to meet many doctor friends and one in particular, whom I think I may be forgiven in mentioning by name, is Mr George Pinker. He revels, as I do, in Wagner. Notwithstanding he has to leave his seat number at the box office, he too finds music a great chance to briefly forget the vicissitudes of life and relax. From the forgoing, I think you will agree that I, a singer, really have, in the broadest sense of the word some links with you profession and that my first misgivings were groundless. After justifying my existence so to speak, may I tell you something of my own career...'

*From left to right —
Lady Barbirolli, Dame Eva Turner, The Duchess of Kent and Dame Janet Baker*

By September 1978 she was once again back in Oklahoma being given yet another honour, after which during December the Oldham Chronicle reported:

'Two former Oldhamers were among a distinguished group of music high-ups who received the honorary fellowship of the Royal Northern College of Music at the recent award ceremony. They were Dame Eva Turner, the world famous soprano, who is now 86 and Mr Sydney Coulston former Hallé Orchestra horn player, who is now senior tutor of the school of wind and percussion at the college. Also honoured at the same time were Dame Janet Baker, the country's top contralto (sic as she as actually a mezzo-soprano) and Lady Barbirolli who as Evelyn Rothwell is one of the country's finest oboe soloists. The awards were conferred by the College's president, the Duchess of Kent, and in the evening the party heard a student performance of Handel's "Orlando" in the college's magnificent opera theatre'.

In September 1979 Peter drove Dame Eva and Anne Ridyard to Cardiff to see *Tristan und Isolde* in which I and Anne Wilkens, another of her students, were singing and as always they were perfect guests, although Dame Eva maintained a safe distance between herself and Reginald Goodall, as she was not in general terms so very keen on his vocal ideas. She felt he was too slow and did not give the singers the support they needed. Miss Ridyard's comment was 'I thought the bugger had dropped off', which she

On the 29th April 1979 Dame Eva, in the Crush Bar at Covent Garden, unveiled the bust of Sir Thomas Beecham to commemorate his birth 100 years previously.

Princess Alexandra and Dame Eva Turner

apparently whispered to the Dame during the performance, as an indication that it was so slow and she was wondering if the Maestro had gone to sleep, or perhaps even died. They also came to see me sing Tosca at the Coliseum around this time and Dame Eva paid me the only real compliment she ever gave, without following it with a suggestion for improvement. She said:

'You were Tosca dear. The beginning of Vissi d'arte was superb, especially as you were lying on your front. The E flat on which it starts was perfectly in tune, not an easy feat.'

THATCHED HOUSE LODGE
RICHMOND PARK
SURREY
June 30
1979

Dear Dame Eva,

How very kind of you to think of me — and to send me that magnificent record of yours. I am so delighted to have it, with so many wonderful recordings —

All my grateful thanks for your special gift —

The Royal Overseas Final — was remarkable, and some of the prize winners so specially gifted.

Again — thank you for your kindness

With my good wishes

Alexandra

When in 1980 Dame Eva travelled to Las Palmas for its 13th Opera Festival and to celebrate the Festival's 100th performance, she could not have been more honoured or welcomed. Montserrat Caballé sang Amelia in *Ballo in Maschera*, as Dame Eva sat in a highly decorated auditorium in which the audience, 52 years previously, at the inaugural performance of the Theatre, had heard Eva Turner sing in *Aida* and, a couple of days later, *Il Trovatore*. After the performance in 1980 she appeared on stage to be presented with a commemorative plaque by the trombone player, Signor Osorio, who had been in the orchestra all those years ago when she had performed. She was given a tremendous, emotional ovation by the entire audience and, visibly moved, Dame Eva gave a little speech of thanks and affirmed her lasting memories of Las Palmas over all the years, and her long-desired wish to return there, happily realised, to celebrate the occasion.

One could only imagine how the great Caballé must have felt about her performance being shared by this Diva from yesteryears but, as we have seen, Dame Eva had a very generous attitude

(Opposite) Dame Dr. Eva Turner

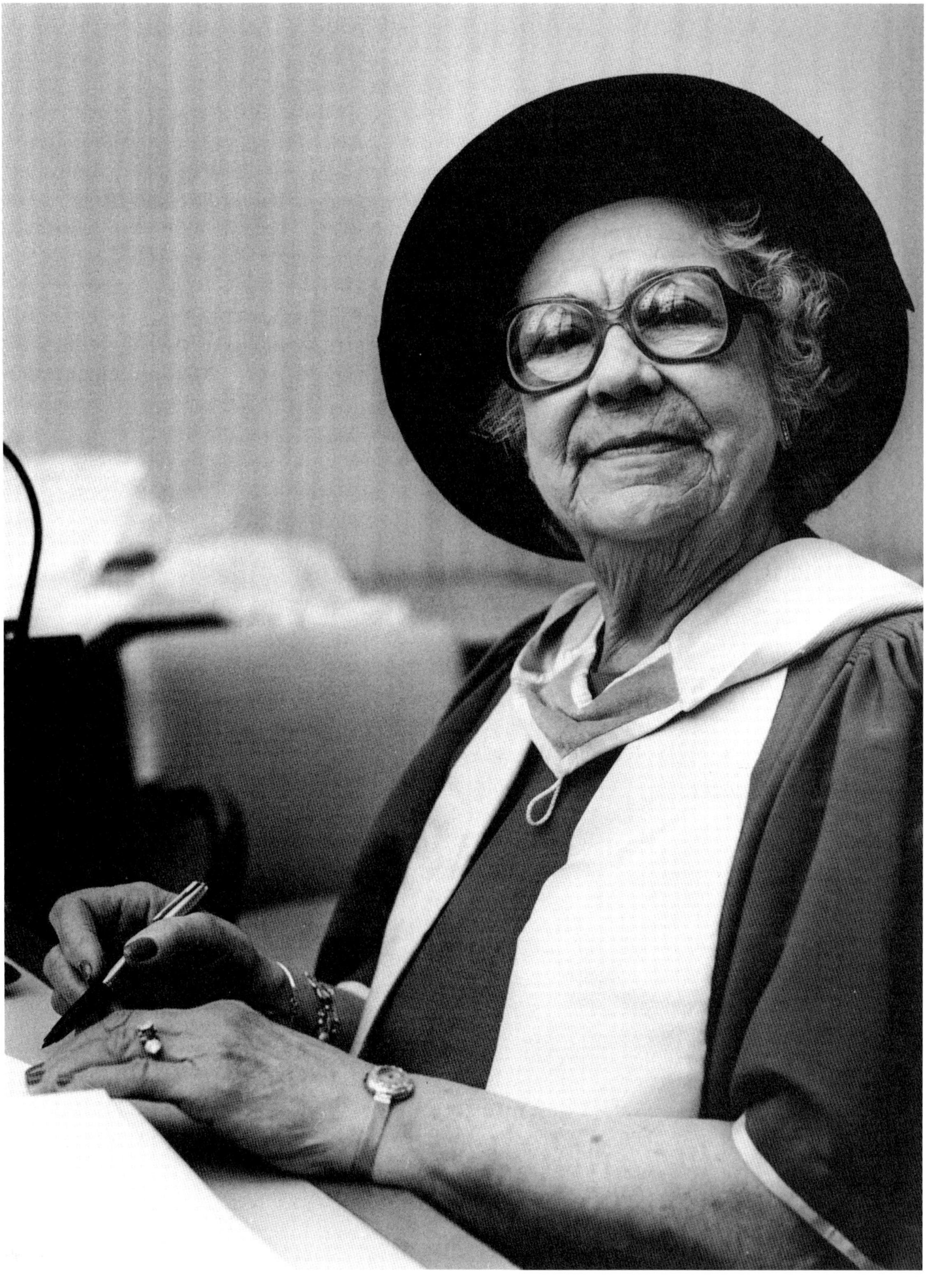

to other singers and would have handled the occasion in her usual sharing way. To be generous, when she was able, was her delight as we can see in this little article she wrote concerning an old friend:

> *'It was an absolute joy and delight to me to hear this new album of recordings just issued under the title "L'Exquise Maggie Teyte". Some of the items I have heard many times before but some others are issued for the first time. How it brought back to me so many happy memories of dear Maggie and her consummate art and again I was reminded of how her voice was so like Melba's, who was in fact her idol. You know I always found Maggie rather fey – and this shows in her voice. Few could turn a nuance or phrase as she did. She breathed a natural Gallicism – strange in an Anglo-Saxon but wholly wonderful and unique. She captures the French atmosphere so perfectly and brings to the joy of singing, an aura of innocence combined with art and an intensity which scintillated and glowed.*
>
> *From her first recording to her last, made in 1948, it is quite remarkable how little her voice has changed. She could 'float' the notes so beautifully and literally caress the words. Throughout she sings with great musicality and artistry, her diction is excellent and how wonderfully she makes the words pregnant with meaning, always maintaining a beautiful vocal line and excellent phrasing and meaning. So many times while listening to this recording, I found myself greatly moved and especially so by her exquisite treatment of Duparc's "Extase" and I loved too "L'Heure Exquise" and the "Offrande" of Renaldo Hahn. How superb too she was in the "Pelleas and Melisande." This album is certainly one of the jewels in my collection and I am most grateful to the person who has put together this marvellous collection and to the biographer who tells us so much about her career in the booklet which accompanies the album.'*

On another occasion, she sang the praises of a contemporary, Oda Slobodskaya, who although her date of birth is not certain, since she changed it to enhance her career and extend it, seems to have been born in 1888. One of Oda's students, Patricia Reakes, recalls having seen the two great ladies, dressed from top to toe in furs, approaching each other like two friendly bears and hugging accordingly. Dame Eva paid tribute to the Russian singer after her death:

> *'Oda Slobodskaya, the supreme interpreter of Russian repertoire, was a remarkable person, tall of bearing in every sense of the word, full of intensity and dramatic, even in her*

every day conversation. We are indebted and grateful to her for the privilege and pleasure of having heard much Russian music that otherwise might have been denied to us. But I also recall how she covered herself in glory in the non-Russian roles, notably during the 1935 Covent Garden season under Sir Thomas Beecham, when she interpreted the role of Palmyra in Delius's "Koanga". We became friends as I also took part in this season, having just returned from Milano to sing Amelia in "Un Ballo in Maschera". I vividly recall her numerous Promenade Concerts and the occasion that she came so generously and willingly to sing for the Royal Academy of Music Club when I was a Professor of Voice there. How can one sum up her artistry? She had the ability to make words pregnant with meaning.'

In the 1980 Proms Syllabus, we find yet another tribute to an old friend:

'I feel especially privileged to have the opportunity to pay tribute to Jessie Wood who passed away during the 1979 Promenade season on the 14th June, in her ninety-eighth year. There are many of us among the Promenaders who have reason to be grateful to her for her unswerving devotion and dedication to Sir Henry Wood, of blessed memory, during the last decade of his life, thus enabling him to carry on his wonderful work for the Promenade Concerts which he started as long ago as 1895. It can truthfully be said that she gave a second span to his career and she herself made, through him, an enormous contribution to the word of music.

After Sir Henry's death in 1944, in fact up to the time of his own passing, she maintained profound and active interest in the organising of the Promenade Concerts and she was a nightly attender at the Royal Albert Hall throughout every season until her own health began to fail and infirmity denied her the opportunity. Even after her inability to attend in person she maintained the keenest interest and was the most devoted member of the radio listening public and was, I am sure, one of the most ardent critics...'

Having sung at many performances at the Proms during my own career and having spent a wonderful summer in 2010 visiting the Proms as a proud owner of a season ticket for the arena, a birthday gift from Peter, I can only add my heartfelt thanks to Sir Henry for providing music lovers with this great institution which welcomes us all, at a verrrrry reasonable price, to be part of that wonderful imaginative, educative, enriching world of music.

Dame Eva Turner and Gladys Parr

In September 1981, in Cambridge, Dame Eva, nearly 90, christened her namesake, a lovely little Welsh cob filly by toasting her with a glass of champagne from a magnum provided by Mr Hanakamp, who owned both the filly and the 'Old Vienna' restaurant in London and who knew Dame Eva well. He named his filly after Eva as he thought it would be a lucky name when it entered competitions.

She was in December part of a distinguished group led by Dame Ninette de Valois, founder of the Royal Ballet in 1931. They were representing the Royal Ballet Circle, the ballet appreciation society, and to mark the occasion of her retirement as President of the group, Dame Ninette unveiled a plaque to commemorate Constant Lambert who was founder musical director of the Royal Ballet. Dame Eva was smiling broadly and generously in the photo, taken for the occasion and she had also taken care, I notice, to place her feet nicely.

After her own 90th birthday on January 3rd 1982, Gladys Parr sent her 'thank you letter' to Eva and Anne. She thanked them for a combined steamer and pan and joked about hoping that her cooking lived up to it adding: 'Good Morning as the diva would say' meaning: 'enough said'. Glad went on to suggest perhaps that her cooking was not up to much anymore, unless of course three-penny-worth of bones was involved! She thanked them for their kind presents over the years adding that she would probably phone soon but wanted to write.

Glad, in my experience, was kindness itself and was always willing to look on the bright side. On one occasion she came into the hall at Palace Court, as Dame Eva and I were leaving the studio and I, walking behind the Dame, must have looked a bit gloomy because she whispered into my ear: 'Don't take too much notice of Eva, she means well but sometimes gets a bit carried away with her love of the voice.' Another kindness was to the great Maggie Teyte, who confessed to Gladys after their performances together in *Die Meistersinger* that she felt the role of Eva had not been her most shining hour. Gladys Parr who had sung Magdalena with many famous sopranos in the role of Eva said she had not noticed anything untoward and in fact thought Maggie had been really rather good.

CHAPTER 9
1982-1985 Celebrations

Dame Eva's celebrations in 1982, the year of her 90th birthday began in January with a reception given at Broadcasting House to honour Roy Plomley who celebrated his 40th anniversary of presenting his programme. In the photo-call she was standing right beside him and was surrounded by many well known faces, including Michael Parkinson, the Beverley Sisters, Barry Norman and Acker Bilk to name but a few. This was closely followed, at the beginning of March, by her being cast away by Roy for a third time, this time to celebrate her 90th birthday which would fall in a few days time on March 10th. Unusually the programme was introduced by her singing *In Questa Reggia* – she did not pick the record herself so they played it for her and us.

Roy Plomley started the programme by apologising for taking her away, metaphorically speaking, from her forthcoming celebrations but she replied by saying graciously, with a little laugh:

'Oh, it will give me a little rest.'

He goes on to ask her if she had had difficulty choosing just eight records to which she replied:

'Oh I found it exceedingly difficult. Enormously difficult. Oh... so many I wanted to play.'

Her list of eight on that occasion was

1. Lotte Lehmann singing *An die Musik* by Schubert.
2. Claudia Muzio singing *Ombra di Nube* by Refice.
3. Ebe Stignani singing *O Don Fatale* by Verdi from *Don Carlos*.
4. Sixteen Singers singing *Serenade to Music* by Vaughan Williams.
5. Sir Thomas Beecham conducting the LPO in the overture to *The Silken Ladder* by Rossini.
6. Placido Domingo singing *Nessun Dorma* by Puccini from *Turandot*.
7. Part of the second movement of *Sinfonia Concertante* for Violin and Viola by Mozart, played by Isaac Stern and Pinchas Zukerman with the New York Philharmonic, recorded at the Isaac Stern Anniversary Concert which she had attended in 1980.
8. Serafin conducting the Chorus and Orchestra of the Rome Opera House performing the *Dies Irae* from Verdi's *Requiem*.

She chose Muzio's recording if she could only have one and her luxury was:

'Well as a matter of fact, I've always wanted to be able to use castanets, (Laugh) so I think I'd like a pair of castanets and if I could really use them well, I think I would perhaps come back and sing Carmen when I'm reincarnated.'

Her book was: *'The Inferno* of Dante as when I lived in Milan, I began it and I never really finished it. I'd like to have that book.'

Roy Plomley: 'And you'll have it in Italian of course.'

'In Italiano, si' was her reply.

During the interview, Roy Plomley told their audience that there would be splendid celebrations for her 90th birthday at both the Royal Opera House and the Coliseum and suggested it was a pity that the Royal Carl Rosa no longer existed as they would have given her one as well. She replied by agreeing but telling him:

'I am to have the pleasure of unveiling a tablet to Mr and Mrs Philips of the Carl Rosa in St. Paul's Covent Garden later on'

and went on to say that she was delighted about this as the company had done such sterling pioneer work for opera.

First off the starting block for the big parties was one given by the 'Friends of English National Opera', a huge happy party at the Coliseum. The 'Friends' at that time was run by Mrs Arratoon and the Arratoon family worked their socks off to give Dame Eva the party of a lifetime which, after some discussion, took place at the Coliseum. They were vigilant in their attention to detail and spent almost a year planning the great occasion which was very ably and knowledgeably chaired by Harold Rosenthal. I have already shared with you some of the highlights when, among others, Arthur Carton, Roy Henderson, Isobel Baillie, Audrey Strange of the Royal Over-Seas league, Ida Cook, Stuart Harling and Oklahoma friends, Genevieve Vliet and Margaret Swain, her accompanist there gave their best words on an evening interspersed with wonderful recorded singing from Martinelli, Amy Shuard and Eva Turner herself.

We now go to the party itself to find out more as we hear the vote of thanks:

Mrs Edith Arratoon: 'All the speakers before me have said so much about Dame Eva and the past. I can but speak only for the present... In 1974 Dame Eva opened our new season which coincided with the launching of English National Opera. She spoke to us about some of the great national singers whom she had known and with whom she had worked such as Miriam Licette and Heddle Nash. She also made warm references to Rita Hunter and Alberto Remedios, their stars at that time. Dame Eva became a member of the Opera Club as we were then and has kept up her membership for the past eight years. She has given us encouragement by attending meetings and she has helped me in adjudicating for our Opera Club prize. One of our prize winners was Marie McLaughlin who now sings at Covent Garden and English National Opera. My personal interest stems from 1928 when my mother took me to see this marvellous English soprano who was singing the part of Turandot. To this day I can see Dame Eva coming down the stairs on the stage – a magnificent regal princess. Today she still radiates the magic of her experience in opera and is passing on that magic through her pupils some of whom are with us this evening... I have longed for an opportunity to pay you a floral tribute and I now say it with flowers. Thank you for your work and help with the Friends of English National Opera and may you continue for many more years to come.'

Dame Eva celebrating her ninetieth birthday at the London Coliseum

This is followed by applause amidst thanks from Dame Eva after which Angela Arratoon and her husband brought on a huge cake with 90 candles and Angela said: 'As my husband Christopher and I stood in the wings just now, he said to me: 'We are worried about bringing a cake on to the stage. What must it be like to sing here and hit a perfect top note? I have come to know Dame Eva Turner as we have organized this evening together and she has approached it with the same interest, goodwill and whole hearted enthusiasm which she brings to everything she does. She had only one fear and she did say to me several times:

'Oh my dear, will anyone wish to come?"

Amidst laughter from the full house, Angela went on to say that they had persuaded Dame Eva that perhaps a few people would drop in as they wandered down St Martin's Lane. She then gave her a birthday card filled with signatures and told her that it came with the love of 3000 members.

Tito Gobbi led the audience in singing 'Happy Birthday to Dear Eva' and it was a very moved Eva Turner's turn to say thank you:

'What can I say? My heart is really too full to express all I feel but I would like to express my thanks to Lord Harewood

and the Board for allowing us to have this evening and to Mr Harold Rosenthal who has been so wonderful and all my friends here on stage. I am enormously moved. I don't know how to thank each one of you as I would wish, words fail me. I must also give my warm thanks to the Arratoons for arranging all this. Angela has been untiring I can't tell you and Sir Nicholas Goodison, I thank you. Will you express my thanks all over to the people behind stage, everybody who has contributed to giving this wonderful evening to me.'

The audience clapped long and loudly to help her recover from a tearful moment. She continues however with:

'I must say too my very warm thanks and appreciation to the visitors from Oklahoma my very wonderful friends there. I cannot tell you how welcome they made me always. They were wonderful to me – a home from home. Really words fail me to express all I would to all of you my friends in the audience who have come tonight. I thank you with all my heart.'

The actual day of Dame Eva's birthday was, every year, a joyous nightmare, as flowers arrived at ten minute intervals and the card attached, having been read carefully, was removed and stored in a safe place. When her own vases, and places to put them on sideboards etc., had been exhausted, the rest of the flowers were taken to the nearest hospital by one of the stoic serving chorus of friends downstairs, who had come to take it in turns to make the day a little easier for the Dame. It was not that she did not enjoy people popping in with a bottle or a lovely bit of steak, flowers arriving in a steady stream, or even the constantly ringing telephone, it was more that she needed it not to get of hand and wanted the gifts and cards to be documented in such a way that the appropriate letter of thanks could be sent to each and every donor. The letter of thanks was considered even before the gift was appreciated.

Poor Miss Ridyard, on whose shoulders, or more accurately fingers on a typewriter, most of this burden lay. All this was expected on all Dame Eva's birthdays but that it was tenfold on her 90th was almost too much to bear, not that I was in fact there on this particular birthday, as I had just, on the day before, come out of hospital after a life-threatening illness, followed by a major operation. I am still sad at not having been able to be part of any of her 90th birthday celebrations although Peter and my mother were at the Coliseum and Covent Garden for the big events and brought home, to my father, Kirsty and me, happy news of the great occasions.

I think if you and I think of the beginning of the second act of *Der Rosenkavalier*, we have a flavour of the dining room at 26 Palace Court Road on March 10th 1982. By the end of that day even she, of the endless energy, was truly exhausted but thrilled and moved by the almost three hundred cards and many personal callers; bearers of thoughtful, caring messages and gifts. All who helped and those who had lingered, were given an Italian nightcap and shared a toast to the great lady as darkness and the curtain fell on a magnificent day.

A little green folder, with a Japanese picture on the front, with the words '90th Birthday Telegrams from distinguished artists – to be preserved' boldly written across it in Dame Eva's distinctive handwriting and enfolding a great bundle of over fifty telegrams, was among her cherished mementos. Heading the list of telegrams was:

'The Royal Opera House: Warmest congratulations and best wishes on a very special occasion and many happy returns of the day from an admiring president. Charles.'

No one forgot her: George and Mary Christie sent love from Glyndebourne, Enid and Gerald Moore sent fond love, many great singers, among whom she would have wanted me to mention 'Calaf Placido', sent their love and thanks. Ruth Packer wrote that Eva Turner had been the shining light in her life and said not to think of answering as she knew she would be over-whelmed with good wishes. Many conductors among whom her friend John Pritchard sent love to one who had: 'given so much to others', all the colleges and academies and many of the competition boards and committees she had served on, sent greetings from all over the world and each one would, in time, be given a personally written thank you.

On March 12th the celebrations continued with a Welcome Party in honour of Dame Eva Turner, Sir Geraint Evans and Maestro Tito Gobbi at the Italian Institute in Belgrave Square, where 'Italian wines would be served.' I am surprised she could stand up after such a busy week but enjoy it she did, taking pleasure in the two great baritones who were also being saluted.

On March 14th came the climax of the week: a party to be held in the Royal Opera House which she knew and loved so well. It was a more formal affair but nevertheless was fun and she was thrilled to have such a fuss made of her. The programme was:

Introduction by Sir John Gielgud

La forza del destino Verdi	Overture	Sir Charles Mackerras

Patricia Routledge (former student)

Don Giovanni Mozart	Aria *Madamina il catalogo è questo*	John Tomlinson
	Recitative *In quail eccesi o numi*	Heather Harper
	Aria *Mi tradì quell'alma ingrata*	

Lord Bernard Miles

Isabeau Mascagni	Aria *Venne una vecchierella*	Valerie Masterson

Tito Gobbi

Un ballo in Maschera Verdi	Recitative *Ecco l'orrido campo*	Pauline Tinsley
	Aria *Ma dall'arido stel divulsa*	

Dame Alicia Markova

Falstaff Verdi	*L'onore! Ladri!*	Sir Geraint Evans

Interval

Hinge and Bracket

Edith Coates

Madama Butterfly Puccini	Act III trio *Io so che alle sue pene*	Josephine Veasey
	Addio fiorito asil	Dennis O'Neil
		Delme Bryn-Jones

Constance Shacklock

Aida Verdi	Aria *Ritorna Vincitor!*	Pauline Tinsley

Ljuba Welitsch

Turandot Puccini	Aria *Tu, che di gel sei cinta*	Valerie Masterson
	Aria *Nessun dorma!*	Charles Craig

Sir John Tooley

Finale

Stage Management Stella Chitty	Production Ande Anderson	Lighting Bill McGee

Orchestra of the Royal Opera House

Leader John Brown

Conducted by
Sir Charles Mackerras and John Barker

The management thanks Graham Newell for his invaluable help and advice in the mounting of this celebration and Sir Robert Mayer, The Earl of Drogheda and Alan Fluck of Youth and Music for suggesting the idea in the first instance.

Birthday Celebrations

Record Signing

    The Royal Over-Seas League held a special place in Dame Eva's life. She often met friends and entertained her American guests there as well as being heavily involved with their excellent music festival. Roderick Lakin, the present Director of Arts, and Robert Newell, its Director General, still have fond memories of Dame Eva's presence around the club and smile as they recall her visits. On one occasion Robert helped her into her mink coat at the end of the evening and waved goodbye to her as she set off in the taxi which had been ordered for her. A few moments later he was accosted by an irate member of the club saying that her mink coat had been stolen. Robert immediately realised what had happened and phoned Dame Eva at home to ask her if she would

1982-1985 Celebrations

mind sending the mink back as it was the wrong coat. Needless to say, Dame Eva had not noticed the mistake and most apologetically returned the offending animal by taxi.

At the finale of the Royal Over-Seas League Music Festival in the Queen Elizabeth Hall on 14th June 1982 special birthday tributes to Dame Eva were included and she is still unflagging in this busy year, as she receives flowers at the end of the Competition.

Thoughtful of others, as always, Dame Eva remembered, later that year in August, to send birthday greetings to the Queen Mother, who had sent her greetings to the Royal Opera House Celebration. Dame Eva, who greatly admired the Queen Mother, received a letter from the Castle of Mey in Caithness, thanking her for her kind letter and birthday wishes and confirming that the Queen Mother had had a happy day as it had also been the christening day of Prince William. The letter goes on:

'The Queen Mother is pleased to be here to enjoy a more peaceful time after some very busy and often most disturbing months.

Lady in Waiting
Ruth Fermoy.'

Celebrations for Dame Eva Turner continued all year, with every invitation to speak or to be present at an occasion accompanied by a birthday tribute, culminating in Dame Eva and Anne travelling up north on October 20th: 'Dame Eva Turner was made an Honorary Freeman of the Metropolitan Borough of Oldham as a token of the high esteem in which she was held by the townspeople of the town of her birth and in recognition of her distinguished international career and her outstanding services to opera and music.' After the official ceremony there was a concert in her honour presented by Oldham Metropolitan Music Centre.

At the end of her 90th birthday year Eamonn Andrews presented her with another red *This is Your Life* book and she was seen on television throughout Britain smiling and laughing her way through the retelling of her great life. It was a joyous happy programme with satellite relays of Placido Domingo and Dame Kiri Te Kanawa paying tribute to her from America, Dame Joan Sutherland from Australia and Tito Gobbi from Italy. Alicia Markova, Sir Geraint Evans, Sir Bernard and Lady Josephine Miles, and her old school friend Maude Thomson joined her for the occasion in person and spoke most generously of their happy relationship with Dame Eva. Also included on stage were some of her past students Pauline Tinsley, Elizabeth Vaughan, Patricia Routledge, Anna Cooper and myself among others, and Charles Craig and Dame Gwyneth Jones. Dame Eva also enjoyed the entertainment which Hinge and Bracket provided for the occasion and is seen photographed with them on another occasion.

After her own celebrations were eventually over, she sent the following taped message, in 1984, to her old friend John Streets. Her speaking voice on this tape is still very youthful and healthy, despite now being in her nineties:

'I've had the great pleasure of knowing John Streets for many years and in that time, have had many occasions to admire his work, especially as Head of the Opera Class at the Royal Academy of Music. He has always put to excellent use the knowledge and experience he acquired in that home of

METROPOLITAN BOROUGH OF OLDHAM

Conferment of the Honorary Freedom

of the

Metropolitan Borough of Oldham

upon

Dame Eva Turner DBE, Mus.D.

Queen Elizabeth Hall, Civic Centre, Oldham

20th October 1982 at 6.00 p.m.

Dame Eva Turner and Elizabeth Robson

1982-1985 Celebrations   327

Hinge and Bracket with Dame Eva Turner

Dame Eva Turner (left), Dame Gwyneth Jones as Turandot and Sir Colin Davis (right)

opera, Italy. In fact, I think all privileged to come under his tuition, have greatly benefited from this. Whenever we meet we always converse in Italian since it has such a great place in our backgrounds.

His judgement in casting the right personnel for operas has been exceedingly good. On several occasions it has even influenced my decision in awarding the bursary from the Friends of the Royal Opera House, Covent Garden, which is at my disposal to award where I hear potential. He has so many attributes that one could go on expounding these for a long, long time and of course the object of this party tonight is to have the opportunity to pay, in some measure, our respect and appreciation of those attributes.

Alas, circumstances deny me the pleasure of being with you since I shall be on the other side of the world with the Royal Opera House, Covent Garden, in Los Angeles. However, through the kindness of Nell Romano, a former student, who has very kindly arranged to tape my message, I am able to raise my voice and add a small recitative and aria, to all the other messages of good will and God speed for the future, knowing full well that whatever John undertakes, will be done with conscientiousness and loyalty and application plus.

John, you will be very sorely missed as Head of the Opera Class and always most fondly remembered. In bocca al lupo sempre. Tante tante cose, Eva.

(She pronounced her own name with the E as in the A of April).

In 1984 she was presented with an Honorary Doctorate of music by Oxford University and made a Fellow of St. Hilda's Oxford.

The reason for Dame Eva's being on the other side of the world during John Street's celebration was that she had been coaching Dame Gwyneth Jones on her first Turandot which would take place at the Olympic Arts Festival in Los Angeles, and Gwyneth had very kindly asked her to be at the performances. Dame Gwyneth tells us in a newspaper report of the time:

'Eva was the Turandot of our age, so it would have been very foolish not to seek her advice. She was there when Puccini was dying and when Alfano was writing the end – she was one of the first to sing the role. My old teacher Luigi Ricci told me to beware of Minnie and Turandot. He was Puccini's personal assistant for years, and told me that the composer himself thought of them as 'dangerous roles'. While Turner was naturally able to help in points of detail, especially with the 'attacca', that certain way of attacking phrases, it was above all a sense of tradition that she sought to pass on. When she talked about working with Toscanini or Martinelli, you had the feeling they were standing there in the room.' Dame Gwyneth went on to say that steeped, as she was, in the

more statuesque school of acting, Turner did have difficulties with this Kabuki-influenced production: 'Eva was used to a much more static portrayal and she missed the crown, the long fingernails and that famous sweeping train.'

Dame Eva said later that she grew, over the years, to like the production. Let us now read a few words from Dame Gwyneth Jones written for this book:

'When I was invited by the Royal Opera House Covent Garden to sing my first Turandot in their new production, which was planned to premier at the Los Angeles Olympic Arts Festival on the 9th July, 1984, I immediately contacted Dame Eva Turner, to ask her if she would be kind enough to work with me on the role. It would have been extremely foolish, if I hadn't taken the advantage of the incredible possibility to work with one of the greatest Turandot's of our time. She was there when Puccini died before he could finish writing the opera, making it necessary for Alfano to compose the end. To my great delight she graciously agreed and this became the beginning of a wonderful Friendship.

I had met Dame Eva in 1960, when Ruth Packer, who was my singing teacher at the Royal College of Music, took me to Dame Eva's home to ask her where I should go to study abroad, as I had won the Boise Foundation Award. She said that she had heard that Dr. Herbert Graf was opening a new Opera Studio at the Zürich Opera House. I had also heard from Sir Geraint Evans that he had studied with Maria Carpi, a very good singing teacher in Geneva, so I decided to combine both, by travelling every weekend by train from Zürich to Geneva.

The lessons with Dame Eva were an experience never to be forgotten! We usually started at 10 o'clock in the morning, in her elegant music room on the ground floor of her house in Palace Court Road. Dame Eva, full of energy, would look into the score with the occasional 'Wait a minute dear, wait a minute' and then suddenly play the chord with a loud triumphant cry 'Immediately!', which often took me so by surprise that my placement of 'In Questa Reggia' didn't come quite as I wanted it to. 'No, no my dear, that's not Rrright! You've got to get it Rrright!' Then she looked again into the score to find the chord again. Almost every morning I went over to the piano to clean her glasses for her, as they were usually covered with powder, which she always put on liberally with a large powder puff. This usually made her chuckle, because it made her realise why she couldn't see the music clearly. However, her cries of 'Immediately!' definitely helped me to find the 'Attaccca' which is vitally important for this great role. Turandot must sing, in the Second Act, with tremendous decisive thrust, which feels rather like throwing knives at Calaf, in order to give the impression of being the Cold Icy Princess, whereas, as we know she later melts with the kiss and reveals her true feminine character. Dame Eva often, proudly and lovingly recollected experiences with Martinelli and Toscanini and one almost had the feeling that they were standing at the end on the piano.

At the end of the lesson, we always went downstairs, where she lived with her dear Friend and Companion Anne Ridyard, to have a chat and her favourite drink, which was a mixture of Martini Bianca, Vermouth and lemon juice, which she kept in an old Lee & Perrin Worcester sauce bottle. I felt that she should have something nicer, so I bought her a beautiful little crystal bottle; but of course the Lee & Perrin bottle soon reappeared. The crystal bottle was 'Too nice to use!'

I visited her as often as possible, whenever I was in London and invited her to come with me to Los Angeles, as I felt that it was very important that she should be present at the performances. I arranged for her to have a suite next to ours, so that I could take care of her; but this was not so easy, because she insisted on going downstairs to the Café to have breakfast at the crack of dawn, despite the fact that I begged her to order it in her room. 'No, no my dear', she insisted, 'it's cheaper down in the cafe and there is such a nice waitress, who is so kind to me'. One morning, the elevator was not level with the floor and she had a nasty accident. I was awoken by the hotel reception, telling me that she had been taken to hospital for a check-up. Thank goodness, she was not seriously hurt and didn't miss one single event. She was really quite amazing with her 92 years. Every morning she would ring me, 'I can't hear you warming up your voice, my dear!' She couldn't understand that I preferred to go to the Theatre to do this, in order not to disturb the other guests.

My daughter Susanne who was 12 years old at the time, was playing the role of the Prince of Persia and I was very fortunate to have Placido Domingo as my Calaf, which pleased Dame Eva immensely; because she absolutely adored him. I took her to all the performances and invitations and was surprised that she seemed to remember everyone's names and sometimes, even telephone numbers. Everyone loved her and her presence made the visit even more special.

At first, Dame Eva was rather critical of Andre Serban's fabulous production; because of the lack of the staircase, head dress and long sweeping train, but eventually she got used to it and I think that she actually enjoyed the new dramatic, colourful Kabuki style, which was a great success in Los Angeles. We returned to London and the production had a further three performances there, with the Premier opening the season on September 1st, with enormous success. The following morning Dame Eva rang me in great distress, to tell me that she had lost a large diamond from her Ring, which was not insured. I told her not to worry and immediately rang Covent Garden and asked them to stop the cleaners vacuuming until I had time to look for it. My inner voice told me that I would find it! I rushed to Covent Garden and searched the area where I knew she had been sitting, without success. Then I went to look in the Ladies Room – and, there it was – on the step at the entrance! She was amazed and very delighted when I brought it to her!

Dame Eva Turner

CHAPTER 10

1985-1990 And Draw Her Home With Music

Despite my own singing life being in decline during 1984 climaxing in failing to sing Turandot in Scottish Opera's new production, I was touched to find, in a personal letter to her old friend Jack Blunden, Dame Eva asking if he would bring a string of pearls back with him from his foreign travels as she wanted to give me them for Christmas:

'If they are not too, too expensive.'

On January 21st 1985, I went to an early morning singing lesson, to find that Dame Eva had been waiting for me since shortly after breakfast at seven. She threw up the keys of the padlock on the gate, as had been her habit in recent years to save climbing the stairs and I let myself in to find that Anne had collapsed behind her bedroom door and as Dame Eva had been unable to lift her, she had covered her in a blanket and awaited my arrival. I guessed, rightly, that it was too serious for either of us to deal with and sent immediately for an ambulance.

As I sat in the ambulance with Anne and watched the doors closing behind us on Dame Eva on the pavement, I knew we were all now in another part of our lives. St Mary's Paddington was the hospital of our destination and when we arrived I was invited to help Anne into a hospital night gown while she groaned in agony. When I returned to Palace Court a few hours later to update Dame Eva, she was sitting at the top of her dining room table with her hands clasped in a similar position to the one in which she was sitting when she told me of her own father's death. She too knew that the life she had been used to was over and that she had perhaps lost her best friend but this did not prevent her from trying to deal with the situation in her own way and insisted against doctor's orders that Anne should be brought home to Palace Court. There was, however, absolutely no way she could be looked after in the Victorian house with all its stairs and lack of modern facilities, so Dame Eva eventually, after Anne was diagnosed as having had a stroke which caused severe brain damage, gave in to the inevitable and she along with Anne's own relations organised that Anne should be moved to a nursing home in Ealing.

Students and friends rallied round as Dame Eva dealt with the situation as best she could and when Anne was moved to Ealing, Dame Eva was accompanied on her visits there at least once a week by her close friend and ex-student Maureen Lefevre. This arrangement continued until the end of Dame Eva's life and thereafter Maureen continued to visit weekly until Miss Ridyard died in February 1992. This was the regular visiting routine but there were other visits with anyone who was able and willing to go with the Dame, sometimes on the spur of the moment, when Dame Eva had a sudden great longing to see Anne. She was very unwell and so the visits were not easy and made Dame Eva feel extremely helpless and depressed but they continued nevertheless, as duty and love had to be obeyed.

Maureen Lefevre had secretarial skills and so also helped Dame Eva deal with her correspondence for some time until a more permanent solution could be arranged, when Pauline Allen, an ex-member of Covent Garden chorus was employed to help with her letters. Elizabeth Robson another ex-student was very kind and, as she was now a well known local councillor, having been a singer of standing, advised Dame Eva on, and arranged for, adequate home help for her as she got older because up till this point, Dame Eva had never really recognised that she was ageing and that there were certain facilities which she could be given. I was there for her when she needed a friend to share with or a trusted ear to listen but Dame Eva was never really happy ever again although she did her best to get on with life and got used to the traumatic visits to Anne who eventually, after a few years, more or less settled into her new life. In retrospect we all realised how much of Dame Eva Turner's boat had been kept afloat by Anne Ridyard, as it now took a team to do the work she had been doing, single handed, for years.

Dame Gwyneth:

'In January 1985, I heard the sad news that Dame Eva's friend Anne had had a stroke and had been taken to hospital. She was later taken to a nursing home in Ealing, because it was impossible for Dame Eva to take care of her. I was extremely worried about Dame Eva and flew to London to visit her as often as my busy schedule allowed. In May 1987 I had two performances of Turandot at Covent Garden, followed by several weeks of rehearsals for a new production of "Die Frau Ohne Schatten" which was to have 6 performances, which meant that I could go regularly to spend quite a lot of time with Dame Eva and shop and cook for her. I often took her to visit Anne in Ealing, which was very upsetting

for her. When I had a free evening, I would ring her up and say, "Dame Eva, tonight the Dames are going out on the Town, which restaurant would you like to go to?" Sometimes the journey in the taxi was difficult, because Dame Eva insisted on instructing the driver which was the shortest way. On one occasion the driver said "Ladies, one more word from the back and you're out!" We always had a very lively time, because she chatted to all the waiters etc. and proudly told them exactly who we were. It became obvious to me that she needed help now that Anne was no longer there for her, so I asked her if I may tidy up a bit for her. I started to give her apartment a 'Spring Clean' and when I cleaned out Anne's room, I discovered, stuffed behind her bed, a 'Golden Disc' of Dame Eva. I was amazed and rushed to the next room and said to Dame Eva, "Look what I have found, this is incredible! I had no idea that you had a 'Golden Disc'. We must hang it on the wall for everyone to see! This is something to be very proud of."

"No, no my dear" she said, modestly, "it's nothing!" but I hung it on the wall.

As we know Dame Eva was born in Oldham and came from a previous generation, which probably accounts for the fact that she was extremely careful when spending money. She used the lowest possible voltage electric bulb on the steep dark staircase to the basement where she lived and always called out "Put the light out, dear!" I tried to convince her that it was very dangerous; because she could trip in the dark and so I changed the bulb. I also arranged for a woman to come in to cook and clean for her; but she told her not to come anymore as soon as I left town, in order to save money, which was truly not necessary for her. This might have been the reason for her having her fatal accident, when she probably tripped over her nightdress, when going to collect the post from the letter box at the entrance.

When cleaning out the kitchen and various cupboards, I discovered that she possessed the most beautiful china and crystal ware, all neatly wrapped up and stored; but she was using chipped and not very nice things. So I told her, "Dame Eva, I'm going to throw these old things away. You are a Dame and you should enjoy using these lovely things, whilst you are still alive and not leave them behind for someone who might not appreciate them."

One day she gave to me a small Pendant and chain, which she said had belonged to the famous Swedish singer Christine Nilsson, which had a small Pansy with tiny precious stones and the inscription in French "Je Pensée a Te" (see appendix). This was to bring me

Dame Eva Turner and Dame Gwyneth Jones

Luck and I always wore it when I sang Turandot. She also told me at a later date that she wished to bequest to me in her Testament "The Adeline Patti Jewels" and that both items should be passed on to "The soprano of my choice". I always wore Patti's necklace, when I performed a programme called "O Malvina", which was written by Klaus Geitel about the famous Diva Malvina von Carolsfeld, who was Richard Wagner's first Isolde.

Receiving these jewels from Dame Eva, inspired me to visit Patti's Castle, which is situated in the Brecon Beacons, in Wales. I found it in a dreadful state of repair. I decided to apply for Lottery Money from the Arts Council of Wales in order to restore it to its former Glory and to create an International Opera Centre for Young Artists with performances in the beautiful little Opera House and a Summer Festival in the Gardens. However, this was not meant to be; because after four years of very hard work and huge personal financial investment, the project was turned down by my own people the Arts Council of Wales. As they say "A prophet is not recognised in his own Land".

Dame Eva told me about her Villa Junesca, on the Lake of Lugano, where she used to stay during her performances in Italy, which she had been unable to visit for many years and told me that she would very much like to sell it; but didn't know how to do this. I contacted my friend André Ginesta, an Estate Agent in Kuesnacht/Zürich, Switzerland, who had helped me to buy my own house there. Then I invited Dame Eva to come to have a holiday with me at my home, so that we could then drive down to Lugano together with André, so that he could see the house and we could empty it for her. The house was, of course, in quite a state after being left for so many years. We sat Dame Eva on a chair, and she gave us instructions, which things should be disposed of and which she would like to keep. At the end, my car was full of music, letters, costumes and various bits and pieces. André and I looked like a couple of chimney sweeps and we were all very hungry, so we went, content with our days' work, to have a lovely meal in a restaurant on the side of the lake. Then I drove back to Zürich with the car packed full of her things, which I later took to The Royal Opera Museum.'

Dame Eva Turner

When Dame Eva was 95, in 1987, Sue MacGregor and she shared a relaxed interview which was really rather more of a conversation, since they both enjoyed a happy time as Dame Eva relived her life. I have already used a lot of the information from that interview in earlier chapters, but wanted to share with you again how great her love of opera and of singing had been throughout her long life.

Dame Eva: *'My father took me to a performance of 'Trovatore', in Bristol, where I lived from the age of ten and from that moment I knew that I wanted to sing in opera.'*

Sue MacGregor: 'What was it about it?

Dame Eva: *'It just was that I adored opera. I was absolutely – what can I say? I thought of nothing else really.*

Sue MacGregor: 'You had quite a long apprenticeship with the Carl Rosa Touring Opera Company.'

Dame Eva (interrupting): *'Well you see I joined them for a year in the chorus and little by little did small parts and became the prima donna as we said - PD pay on delivery'*

Sue MacGregor (smiling): 'What did that mean in practice?'

Dame Eva (laughing): *'Well give the goods.'*

After pointing out that Eva Turner had sung in both the Italian and German repertoire and noticing that not many sopranos are equally comfortable in both, Sue asked: 'so you obviously had from an early stage a remarkable voice. What do you attribute that to?'

Dame Eva (hesitantly): *'O I don't know. Just to the, well I think it was God given - possibly, I think.'*

Even at this great age Dame Eva is completely 'with it' in conversation but is clearly trying to be a little modest as well, so Sue leads her a little on to a further conversation about how singing is actually executed saying: 'But you see you have the reputation of not only having a very beautiful voice but a very big one and this implies wonderful breath control. Was there somebody who gave you advice about that from an early stage?'

Dame Eva: *'O yes, I had a manager who helped me enormously: Mr Richards Broad criticised me very much for which I was intensely grateful because I think you always know yourself what you do well. You don't always know your faults - enough well* (laughing at her own phraseology). *For instance I used to practise breathing even walking. I would take twelve steps taking the breath in, twelve steps holding it and twelve steps letting it out and that is extremely difficult. But it taught me a lot I was able to do long phrases, and so, on as a result.'*

Sue MacGregor: 'I think you built yourself a house in Italy'

Dame Eva: *'Yes I did. On the Lake of Lugano because Milano in those months was very hot.'*

Sue MacGregor: 'What was it like?'

Dame Eva: *'O it was lovely, right on the edge of the Lake of Lugano just a few miles outside Lugano.'*

Sue MacGregor:' In fact you were just therefore across the border in Switzerland.'

Dame Eva: *'Yes that's right.'*

Sue MacGregor: 'Was it quite easy to get to the opera houses from there?

Dame Eva: *'O yes, by road and of course by electric train. And then a day there would be to swim a lot and be in the garden enjoying the rest and change.'*

Sue MacGregor: 'Did you practise in the house too?'

Dame Eva: *'O yes and you know often across the lake they would ring and say: Signorina, canta ancora. Sentiamo cosi bene.'*

Sue MacGregor (for the listener): 'They enjoyed your singing.'

Dame Eva. *'Yes. They used to ask me to keep on singing because it went over the lake so I suppose it carried.'*

Sue MacGregor: 'Has anything untoward ever happened to you on stage.'

Dame Eva: *'I was once singing "The Girl of the Golden West" the Puccini opera. I had, in the second act, put the ladder up, you know after putting the tenor to hide in the loft, and I hadn't fastened it completely and it fell on my head and I really saw stars. I don't know how I kept on but luckily I was able to continue.'*

Sue MacGregor: 'You're still a very keen opera goer yourself.'

Dame Eva: *'O yes, I am going to-night.'* (Laughter from both).

Dame Eva was in great demand on television as well as on radio in 1987 and joined in each interview with great joy, telling her life stories all over again. In August a very sprightly Dame Eva Turner appeared on the Terry Wogan show when Plácido Domingo, whom she adored, paid huge tribute to her both in words and song, singing a little bit of Calaf's music to her while on his knees before her. They then engaged in a conversation about the use of sur-titles in the opera house, when both agreed that they were a good idea and that anything which could be done to bring more audiences to the opera was to be embraced.

In 1988 Dame Eva recorded a spoken introduction (see appendix) to her old recordings which were to be brought out in a compact disc and her voice has the strength and vitality of a much younger person. I think she was certainly right in one thing: her instrument was indeed God given in its strength. That is not to say that she didn't work hard to perfect her technique but without such a voice it would not have mattered how hard she worked, she could not have arrived at such a 'perfect vocal emission'; to use her own words.

Gladys Parr died on November 4th 1988. She had been less active in her declining year but never lost her sense of humour. Her memory lives on as we can still hear her on a very famous recording of the

Gladys Parr

1985-1990 And Draw Her Home With Music 339

quintet from *Die Meistersinger von Nürnberg*. Needless to say Dame Eva was deeply saddened by Glad's death and as was her custom sent a donation to the Musicians Benevolent fund in her memory.

On Sunday, the day after Dame Eva's 98th birthday in 1990, Peter collected her from Palace Court and went with her to visit Anne in her Ealing nursing home. I had asked a few close friends, about twenty opera lovers, for lunch and hoped that she would join us after the visit if she felt able. She was delighted to come and was happy to sign all the records and programmes which

Eva Turner
The National Portrait Gallery

people had brought with them in the hope that she would pen her wonderful bold signature on them. She stayed all afternoon and pointed to the spot where she thought her Blüthner grand piano would look best. I smiled and told her I would just have to make do with the old upright as she had no intention of leaving us just yet. She smiled a rather sad smile and we left it at that. I wanted to tell her I would cherish her piano, and her memory, forever but thought that was a little bold under the circumstances and truly hoped I wouldn't be the piano's proud possessor for a while yet as we were all looking forward to grand celebrations for her 100th birthday. She was tired as she left to go home and I noticed that she was a bit unsteady on her feet and that she gladly accepted a helping hand as we positioned ourselves for a photograph in the front garden.

A few weeks later she fell and when Maureen Lefevre and I went to St Mary's Hospital to visit her, we were alarmed to find that, although she recognised us, she wandered in and out of reality and thought that I was in a wedding veil. Although she went home and had a lift installed for her by Katherine Morgan, who had the unenviable task of overseeing her care, she fell again and broke her hip after which she was taken to the Devonshire Private Hospital just round the corner from Wigmore Street where Maureen lived and so she was able to pop in regularly to see her. Dame Eva faded away over a six week period and died on Saturday June 16th a couple of days after my last visit, although Maureen saw her again a few hours before the end. I heard the sad news when I turned on my radio on Sunday morning as the nation was told of the death of an English Prima Donna.

Dame Gwyneth:

'She was found, with a broken hip, lying on the cold stone floor in the hall. She was taken to St. Mary's Hospital, where she was put into a large ward with many other people. I contacted the hospital and insisted that she should be transferred to a private room, where she would have more privacy and personal care. She died shortly afterwards and I flew to London in order to attend her funeral, after which we went back to her house where Jean and Bruce, who rented apartments upstairs in Dame Eva's house, told me, as I stood looking at the disc which I had hung on the wall, "we gave the Golden Disc to Dame Eva! We thought that she deserved to have one, so we had it made for her for £5 in Petticoat Lane!" I could feel Dame Eva smiling down on us – it was so typical of her that she kept her secret and I am sure that she enjoyed the joke!

SERVICE OF THANKSGIVING

FOR THE

LIFE AND WORK OF

DAME EVA TURNER
D.B.E.

10th March, 1892 - 16th June, 1990

West Chapel
Golders Green Crematorium

Friday, 29th June, 1990
at 2 p.m.

On the 5th February, 1991 I had the honour to sing at her Memorial Service at Westminster. I was very sad to have lost such a dear Friend and will always treasure the memories of the wonderful times we shared.'

There was a simple service of thanksgiving for her life in the West Chapel at Golders Green Crematorium on Friday 29th June 1990 where we were asked not to send flowers but, if we wished, to give a donation to the Musicians' Benevolent Fund; her lifelong charity along with the Salvation Army, both remembered in her will.

She also left financial provision for Anne Ridyard until her death, and created scholarships in the name of Anne Ridyard and Dame Eva Turner at the Royal Northern College of Music. Moneys for scholarships at the Royal Opera House and the Royal Academy of Music were provided for as well as many personal gifts to family and friends. The endowments depended on the sale of her house and Katherine Morgan attended to her financial affairs enabling her wishes to be carried out.

At the end of this great life, I once again refer to the thirteen year old school girl Catherine David's interview of 1988:

Catherine: 'There are so many beautiful opera houses of today, which was your favourite?'

Dame Eva: *'Well, I loved singing at Covent Garden, this I loved and I liked La Scala and I loved the opera house at Turin and I loved the Chicago Civic Opera. I never sang at the Metropolitan, New York. They had sopranos walking about who didn't have parts and when I was interviewed I said that unless I could be guaranteed my appearances I couldn't accept, so I never sang at the Metropolitan.'*

Catherine: 'I know you are very busy in the musical world now, but how have you spent your years of retirement?'

Dame Eva: *'I have not really ever retired dear, but now in a way it is forced upon me. You see I am in my 97th year and alas it has caught up with me. I have arthritis in this arm so I cannot play, so I gave up my teaching on my 96th birthday! And I cannot do all the walking and stairs and things. Really, it is now catching up with me. The years are passing so I don't do any teaching now. I cannot play.'*

Catherine: 'Do you still go to the opera?'

Dame Eva: *'Yes. I go to Covent Garden and they are wonderful to me. They often send transport to ensure that I will be there.'*

Catherine: 'What advice would you give to a young up-and-coming singer of today?'

Dame Eva: *'Well, to hear all they can and to apply themselves. You see people often do not apply themselves enough to achieve a basic vocal foundation and to get the supremacy of control and what we call "L'impostazione d'avanti" which means a forward placement of the voice. Then you have to challenge your ear and match the tones all through the range of the pure vowels. Then people do not sing enough florid work. For instance, sopranos should sing "Rejoice Greatly" and all the agility pieces. I do not know if people do that enough today because life is at a much quicker pace you see and often I think they begin to sing major roles far too quickly.'*

Catherine: Throughout your singing career did you ever want to have a family of your own?

Dame Eva: *'I don't think I really did, dear, if I am candid. I think I was really so enveloped with the desire to sing, I loved being in the Opera and waited for each performance to do better and better.'*

Catherine: 'Thank you so much...'

Dame Eva: *'A pleasure dear... you know, now you must tell you something about yourself...'*

The first of ten performances of *Turandot* at Covent Garden which opened the new season in September 1990 was the occasion of thanks to Sir Colin Davis for: 'his unique commitment to the opera house over the past quarter of a century'. That performance was also dedicated to Dame Eva Turner and the Evening Standard said of her:

'Eva Turner was a famous Turandot of her day, and died aged 98 in June. Just before her death Dame Eva gave last night's star Dame Gwyneth Jones a pendant on condition that she passed it on *in turn to a chosen soprano from the next generation when the time came. Last night Dame Gwyneth wore it next to her heart.'*

A Service of 'Thanksgiving for the Life and Work of Dame Eva Turner' took place at Westminster Abbey on Tuesday February 5th 1991. The Lord Mayor of Westminster, the Representative of His Royal Highness The Prince of Wales and His Royal Highness The Duke of Kent were, in their turn, conducted to their seats before the Bidding began at 3pm. The Dean thanked God for the life and work of Dame Eva and brought the Bidding to a close with: 'Above all we thank God for her strong Christian faith, for those human qualities of frankness and honesty, generosity and humour which made her loved by those who knew her. *Thou shalt show me the path of life; in thy presence is the fullness of joy; at thy right hand there is pleasure for ever more.'*

Sir Geraint Evans and The Duke of Kent read the lessons and Sir John Tooley gave The Address. The congregation sang: *The Lord's My Shepherd*, *Fight the Good Fight* and *Jerusalem*.

> 'And did those feet in ancient time
> walk upon England's mountain green,
> And was the Holy Lamb of God
> on England's pleasant pasture seen,
> And did the countenance divine
> shine forth upon our clouded hills
> And was Jerusalem builded here
> among these dark satanic mills?'

Instrumental ensembles from both the Royal Academy and the Northern College of Music took part and the Chorus and Orchestra of the Royal Opera House, accompanying Dame Gwyneth Jones and Denis O'Neill, was conducted by Sir Colin Davis. The programme was: *Elisabeth's Greeting* from *Tannhäuser* by Wagner, *Easter Hymn* from *Cavalleria Rusticana* by Mascagni, *Ingemisco* from Verdi's *Requiem* and Chorus of Hebrew Slaves from *Nabucco* also by Verdi.

Eva Turner was then listened to in the crowded Abbey as her introductory spoken words on her compact disc, followed by her singing Turandot's *In Questa Reggia* were 'heard loud and clear'. The recording of the *Serenade to Music* by Vaughan Williams, sung by the original sixteen singers, was played as we left the service and allowed the Abbey to return to stillness and silence, after a truly moving and marvellous event.

A month later Katherine Morgan travelled to Standish carrying Dame Eva's ashes, and there on a bleak day in March, the month of her birthday, with daffodils bowing their sunny heads to brighten the gloom, a small procession made its way to the grave-side of Eva's mother and father, where Eva wished her ashes to be placed beside them in the family grave, not far from Oldham.

Turner family gravestone

How sweet the moonlight sleeps upon this bank!
Here will we sit and let the sounds of music
Creep in our ears: soft stillness and the night
Become the touches of sweet harmony.

William Shakespeare

APPENDIX

Eva Turner Lives On: Her Recordings

When the original seventy-eight recordings were produced, people all over the world could share Eva Turner's voice and rejoiced in doing so. Pietermaritzburg is the capital and second largest city of the province of KwaZulu-Natal in South Africa and is better known as Maritzburg. Their newspaper the Natal Witness tells us on December 11th 1928 about one of her early recordings for Columbia Records:

> 'Only one vocal record has been sent this week but it is one well worth a special place in the gramophone world for it is excellent. Eva Turner, who has made a great name for herself lately as an operatic soprano, is recorded singing "Ritorna Vincitor" the big aria from "Aida" in which she is accompanied by an orchestra, under the direction of Sir Thomas Beecham. She has a beautiful voice, which she uses with much expression and she sings with a dramatic intensity of feeling which is yet absolutely effortless. The strength and power of the voice distracts in no way from the clear, sweet quality which is one of its greatest charms and the soft lyrical passage which occurs at the beginning of the second part shows this to great advantage. A soft or at least a half-tone needle is advised for playing this record'.

Lest you think that Dame Eva lived wealthily on the sale of her recordings, which were sent as far afield as Sydney, Melbourne, Durban, Boston, South America, Johannesburg and Cape Town, here is a copy of an early recording contract:

Columbia Gramophone Company Ltd
108 Clerkenwell Road
London EC1
13th Sept 1928

Eva Turner
Piazza Susa 2
Montforte
Milan
Italy

We shall pay the artist the following royalty on the saleable records made, deducting 15% to cover records unsold or damaged:

On double-disc records containing on both sides selections recorded solely by the artist 20%

On double-disc and on single disc records containing on one side only selections recorded solely by the artist 10%

On duets, half of the above, trios, one third and quartets, one quarter.

In the little booklet produced for the re-issue of her recordings on compact disc, Richard Bebb, the actor, married to Gwen Watford, tells us a little about how the CD was conceived and made:

'Eva Turner's records were all made for the Columbia Company between 1927 and 1940. The first series was made in Milan, but so great was the success of her Turandot at Covent Garden in 1928 that the company immediately decided to remake most of the operatic titles under better recording conditions in London, and with the collaboration of her great friend Sir Thomas Beecham. This CD presents from her recordings, one version of every aria and song published on 78s; the only exceptions are the Turandot extracts recorded live at the 1927 Coronation Season at Covent Garden and her brief solo contribution to Vaughan Williams's "Serenade to Music" (not included on the disc). In addition Dame Eva has given permission for three hitherto unpublished recordings to be included. These are of the greatest possible interest and importance. Because we have so far had a recorded evidence of the Italian side only of her career, her tremendous success as a singer of German music has largely been forgotten. The arias from "Tannhäuser" and "Lohengrin" are the only two arias she ever recorded. Both are sung in English and are therefore excellent momentos of the early days of her career when she sang with the Carl Rosa, when she sang the roles of Elisabeth and Elsa countless times up and down – and across – the length and breadth of the British Isles. The third of the hitherto unpublished recordings, "Love and Music" from "Tosca", has the added attraction of being, in my opinion, the loveliest of all recordings of her voice (even though the excellence of her diction cruelly exposes the banality of the English translation). In addition, her account of "One Fine Day" from "Madama Butterfly" has previously been published only on the long-deleted LP compilation "Great British Sopranos."

That we have been able to include the "Tannhäuser" aria at all is an extraordinary story. The only surviving copy had been broken into three quite separate pieces. Thanks to the brilliant skill of John R.T. Davies, who volunteered his services to save this unique recording, a tape was produced without a single needle-jump, but, of course, with multiple ticks every second. What has been achieved with the latest computer-aided noise-reduction techniques is nothing short of miraculous. The dedication and skill of everyone who laboured to preserve this recording has put all vocal collectors greatly in their debt.'

Edward Greenfield writing in the Guardian at the time of the release:

'One of the most exciting developments in the CD age has been the astonishing vividness with which historic recordings have been transferred to the new medium. Now with the arrival of CEDAR, the process of cleaning off the sound varnish of clicks, crackle and hiss takes a computerised leap forward with spectacular results.

The most fascinating so far involves Dame Eva Turner's broken record. When EMI was planning a CD collection of the recordings that this most masterful of British sopranos made for Columbia in the inter-war period, she – now in her late nineties – showed them a test record she made in 1933 of "Elisabeth's Greeting" from Wagner's "Tannhäuser". It had got broken into three pieces, the only surviving copy.

First it was lovingly glued together. When it was played there was no jumping of grooves, but naturally the persistent click was intolerable. That was until CEDAR took them all out, automatically filling in each microscopic gap with surrounding material. The finished result is among the most thrilling, rich and intense recordings of Dame Eva's voice ever made. Not only that that "Tannhäuser" aria but "Elsa's Dream" from "Lohengrin" and "Vissi d'arte" from Puccini's "Tosca" are among the recordings never published before, along with "Turandot", "Aida" and "Trovatore" recordings and much else that amply confirm what legend told us – that Dame Eva was a dramatic soprano unmatched in this country and not just in her own generation.

I also cherish her own spoken introduction, lustily emphatic and recorded only last year when she was a mere 97. Walter Legge used to say that her top Cs projected right through the back wall of Covent Garden out into Bow Street, and even her speaking voice today makes you believe it.'

'1988 is the centenary of the gramophone and it is a great thrill for me that all my most important old recordings should be coming out in the new form of compact disc. The extracts from the 1937 Coronation Season performances of "Turandot" at Covent Garden have already appeared after having

been buried for so many years in the archives of EMI and it is a great delight to me that these preserve my association with the great Sir John Barbirolli and that Prince of Italian tenors Giovanni Martinelli. Giovanni was such a wonderful colleague, so marvellous an artist and so loving a friend and I count the days when we did master classes together in London as being among the happiest in my life. I remember very little about my first recordings in Italy in 1926 but I do have a vivid recollection of the making of the very first of them. The finale of Act 2 of "Aida" and "La Gioconda". The engineers had great difficulty in matching my voice with that of the other soloists and eventually, they placed me right at the back behind the chorus. Even then, I am happy to say I don't think that you will have any difficulty in hearing me. I am so very pleased that among my later records made in London are several which commemorate my long association with Sir Thomas Beecham. I sang with him so many times and to sing under his baton was always an inspiration to me. Our musical collaboration was strengthened by the fact that we were both Lancastrians and shared exactly the same sense of humour. All my life, I can honestly say I have been fiercely critical of my own work. Throughout my career I really was always striving to improve my standards in every way that was within my power and I truly never failed to have a daily singing lesson with my manager and teacher Professor Albert Richards Broad. In listening to my old records now there are some details I wish I could improve on but on the other hand I am also very happy that I can hear then again in such excellent sound and in this marvellous new form. I am now in my 97th year and I send you all my loving greetings. Bless you. Eva Turner. June the twenty first 1988.'

I asked David Nice one of the foremost, erudite music critics of today, with enormous interest in the voice, to listen to the cd and to write a few words for this book:

'First to strike the listener are the diction and the essential core colour, in a speech and then an aria. How grateful we ought to be that EMI saw fit to record an introduction from Dame Eva in 1988, and then to jump straight back 60 years to a piece of legato singing that will surprise anyone who only knows her implacable Turandot. In Leonora's "D'amor sull'ali rose" from Verdi's "Il Trovatore", the crystal-clear Italian joins perfect portamenti and trills like pearls on a line. And Turner has the instinct for the right forward *movement here – you sense it's Beecham who wants to hold her back (he redeems himself by getting the strings to sing their hearts out along with Santuzza's lament). And it's a reminder of how seriously sopranos took tone colour to move on to the darker dilemma of Aida's "Ritorna vincitor" and realise with some surprise that it comes from the same Westminster session of July 1928.*

Play the sequence to a keen listener without supplying the dates, and the guess might be that the later recordings represent an early freshness in the voice. Certainly, once past the 1926 debut appearances in the "Aida" and "Gioconda" ensembles where the Turner trumpet was famously placed way behind the other singers, the 'Suicidio' is expressive but rather wild, like a voice over stretched in lyric-dramatic territory that's about to implode (the less than happy circumstances recorded in this biography go some way to explaining why). Yet only two years later, we hear a perfect security – and an ever brighter, warmer sound in the Puccini arias from 1933 sung in English, though Turner's Cio-Cio San is no 'baby-wife', as the infelicitous translation has it.

Here, as in the "Trovatore" recording, the purely human expression of the characters' dilemma may surprise anyone who thinks of Turner as the archetypal ice princess. Inevitably, perhaps, the "In questa reggia' of 1928 presents first the limitations and then the supreme strengths of the Turner approach. Where, we might ask, are the 'yielding', the piano 'cosa lontana', the dolce con dolore that Puccini asks for to inscape the woman within the vengeful icon? But all that is forgotten with the sheer radiant energy of 'Ma nessun m'avrà', the rock-solid top As, Bs and Cs with which this Turandot, taking over Calaf's protest to her own declarations, rises to the opera's great climax. And there, too, is the amazing thing about these 78 recordings: that while those of us who never caught her live can have no idea of how the laser-like projection hit the back of an opera house, the penetrating but never unpleasant brightness of the sound still comes across with incomparable vividness.

As indeed it does in her only two Wagner recordings, rightly ecstatic in Elisabeth's greeting and presenting us with an Elsa dressed not in a simple white shift but armed in a golden breastplate of tone every inch as dazzling and transfixing as her rescuer knight's. The narratives may not tell the whole story about these characters, but the dramatic-soprano sound is unquestionably the most secure any of us will ever experience."

Lyceum Theatre, Edinburgh

A complete list of Eva Turner's performances at the Lyceum Theatre, Edinburgh 1916-24, with relevant critiques from The Scotsman.

1916

2nd March *The Magic Flute* by Mozart. 2nd and 3rd Genii sung by Eva Turner and Gladys Parr.

6th March Although not a direct review of this performance, it gives a little of the flavour of the times:

'On Saturday evening the Carl Rosa Opera Co. concluded a successful fortnight at the Royal Lyceum Theatre with the ever popular "Maritana".

Darkened streets and stormy nights were much in evidence during the engagement, but despite these and the many other claims on the public at this time the company received a gratifying measure of patronage from the lovers of high-class opera.'

These were the prices at The Lyceum with a rough equivalent in today's money to give you an idea of their worth; Boxes 22/- (£170), Orchestral Stalls and Dress Circle 5/- (£20), Amphitheatre Stalls 3/- (£12), Pit 2/- (£8), Amphitheatre 1/- (£4), Gallery 6d (£2). Government entertainment Tax extra. Prices held until 1920.

1917

20th March *Faust* by Gounod. Siebel sung by Gladys Parr.

21st March *Butterfly* by Puccini. Kate sung by Eva Turner.

22nd March 'Miss Eva Turner did very well as Kate.'

22nd March *Carmen* by Bizet. Mercedes sung by Gladys Parr.

26th March *Rigoletto* by Verdi. Magdalene sung by Gladys Parr.

27th March 'Special praise is due to the delightful Magdalena of Miss Gladys Parr. Her acting was graceful and the rich smoothness of her voice and the artistic intelligence of her singing were among the most enjoyable features of the opera.'

30th March *Maritana* by Vincent Wallace. Maritana sung by Eva Turner. Lazarillo sung by Gladys Parr.

31st March *Carmen* by Bizet. Mercedes sung by Gladys Parr.

2nd April 'Miss Turner made an admirable Maritana. The singing of Miss Gladys Parr, particularly in the fortress scene was strikingly effective.'

1918

18th February   *Tannhäuser* by Wagner. Venus sung by Eva Turner.

19th February 'Eva Turner's fine rendering of the small part of Venus was full of promise of greater things.'

22nd July   *Carmen* by Bizet. Micaela sung by Eva Turner.

23rd July 'Miss Eva Turner, one of the best of the recent acquisitions to the company was a very successful Micaela. She improves in every new role in which she is heard and while her voice is at once brilliant and sympathetic, her acting is excellent in the combination which it presents of spontaneity and a perfect balance with the vocal demands of the character.'

26th July   *Don Giovanni* by Mozart. Donna Anna sung by Eva Turner.

27th July 'As Donna Anna, Miss Eva Turner sang with facility and expression and acted artistically.'

27th July   *Maritana* by V. Wallace. Maritana sung by Eva Turner.

1919

12th March *Faust* by Gounod. Siebel sung by Gladys Parr.

15th March *Maritana* by V. Wallace. Maritana sung by Eva Turner. Lazarillo sung by Gladys Parr.

17th March 'In "Maritana," Miss Eva Turner gave a real dramatic significance to the title role.' 'Miss Gladys Parr was an excellent Lazarillo.'

18th March *The Tales of Hoffmann* by Offenbach. Giulietta & The Countess sung by Eva Turner.

19th March *Tannhäuser* by Wagner. Venus sung by Eva Turner.

20th March *La Bohème* by Puccini. Musetta sung by Eva Turner.

21st March 'The Musetta of Miss Eva Turner was a fine performance musically, while on its dramatic side it was also a very convincing study of a temperament.'

21st March *Carmen* by Bizet. Mercedes sung by Gladys Parr.

22nd March *Mignon* by Ambroise Thomas. Frederick sung by Gladys Parr.

1920

12th April   *Cavalleria Rusticana* by Mascagni. Santuzza sung by Eva Turner.

13th April 'Miss Eva Turner, one of the most promising of The Carl Rosa artists, made her first Edinburgh appearance as Santuzza. It was an excellent rendering, vocally and dramatically of a part which affords great opportunities.'

13th April   *Tales of Hoffmann* by Offenbach. Nicklaus sung by Gladys Parr.

15th April   *Tannhäuser* by Wagner. Venus sung by Eva Turner

16th April   *The Miracle or The Story of Antoine* by Reginald Sommerville. Thérèse sung by Eva Turner, Jean Marie sung by Gladys Parr.

17th April 'Opera by Mr Reginald Sommerville' 'As Thérèse, Miss Eva Turner gave an excellent account of a part in which she had to contend with a good deal that is merely conventional' '...and Miss Gladys Parr as the mother of Antoine, Jeanne Marie, was artistic in her study of a pathetic character.' 'In view of the fact that the opera was new to Edinburgh, there were too many empty seats in the theatre. Under such circumstances an impresario can hardly be expected to display much eagerness to produce new operas.'

17th April   *Carmen* by Bizet. Lilias Pastia performed by Albert Broad

17th April   *Merry Wives of Windsor* by Nicolai. Mine Host of Garter Inn performed by Albert Broad. Mrs Page sung by Gladys Parr.

19th April 'Miss Beatrice Miranda as Mrs Ford and Miss Gladys Parr as Mrs Page gave full value to the humour of the various situations in which they became involved or in which they involve those against whom they are in league.'

20th April   *Mignon* by A. Thomas. Antonio sung by Albert Broad. Frederick sung by Gladys Parr.

22nd April   *Faust* by Gounod. Siebel sung by Gladys Parr.

24th April   (Matinee) *Il Trovatore* by Verdi. Leonora sung by Eva Turner. Azucena sung by Gladys Parr.

26th April 'Miss Eva Turner adorned the role of Leonora by the purity and high range of her voice, while Miss Gladys Parr, as Azucena, the gipsy woman, was fully equal to the demands, dramatic as well as vocal, which the part entailed.'

24th April   *The Bohemian Girl* by Michael W. Balfe. Captain of the Guard performed by Albert Broad.

27th April   *Faust* by Gounod. Siebel sung by Gladys Parr.

1921

Boxes 2.8/-, Orchestral Stalls and Dress Circle 7/-, Amphitheatre Stalls 4/- 6d, Pit 3/-, Amphitheatre 1/- 6d, Gallery 1s.

13th April   *The Mastersingers* by Wagner. Magdalena sung by Gladys Parr. Hans Foltz performed by Richards Broad

14th April 'The Magdalena of Miss Gladys Parr supplied an admirable contrast: she sang delightfully and the humour of the part was realised with quiet effectiveness which was very artistic.'

14th April   *Lohengrin* by Wagner. Ortrud sung by Gladys Parr.

15th April 'As Ortrud, Miss Gladys Parr appeared in a character of a different type from that with which she has hitherto been associated, and made a wonderful and dramatic figure as the evil influence in the drama.'

15th April   *Madama Butterfly* by Puccini. Suzuki sung by Gladys Parr.

16th April   *Carmen* by Bizet. Lilias Pastia sung by Albert Broad.

16th April   *Il Trovatore* by Verdi. Leonora sung by Eva Turner. Azucena sung by Gladys Parr.

18th April 'Vocally delightful as were Miss Eva Turner's Leonora and the Azucena of Miss Gladys Parr, they were not less fine as dramatic conceptions, the charm and the dignity of the one and the sombre intensity of the other being well brought out.

The rage of Azucena, where she is captured and the tragedy of Leonore in the prison scenes were much in advance of the conventional transports ordinarily indulged in by a prima donna.'

18th April   *The Tales of Hoffmann* by Offenbach. Nicklaus sung by Gladys Parr.

20th April   *Faust* by Gounod. Siebel sung by Gladys Parr

21st April '...there was the convincing feeling which she imparts to all her work in the Siebel of Miss Gladys Parr.'

21st April   *The Valkyrie* by Wagner. Brünnhilde sung by Eva Turner.

22nd April 'In the second act, Miss Eva Turner, as Brunnhilde from her first appearance, held the attention of the audience. Brünnhildes are not always as youthful in effect as Wagner intended that his warrior maidens should be, but Miss Turner was youthful and intensely dramatic as well. Her voice rang out like a trumpet in the passionate declamatory music of the part, while every word could be heard distinctly.'

22nd April   *Cavalleria Rusticana* by Mascagni. Santuzza sung by Eva Turner.

23rd April 'Miss Eva Turner the Brünnhilde of the previous night was Santuzza. Comparison with the previous appearances in the same role displayed the striking advance which Miss Turner has made within the past year or so, both as a singer and an actress. It is a genuinely dramatic conception of the character.'

23rd April   *David Garrick* by R. Sommerville. Mrs Smith sung by Gladys Parr.

23rd April   *Maritana* by V. Wallace. Alcada performed by Albert Broad. Maritana sung by Eva Turner.

16th May   *Carmen* by Bizet. Lilias Pastia performed by Albert Broad

1922

11th April   *Cavalleria Rusticana* by Mascagni. Santuzza sung by Eva Turner.

13th April   *Faust* by Gounod. Marguerite sung by Eva Turner. Siebel sung by Gladys Parr.

14th April   *Rigoletto* by Verdi. Magdalena sung by Gladys Parr.

15th April   *Mignon* by A. Thomas. Antonio performed by Albert Broad.

15th April   *Il Trovatore* by Verdi. Leonora sung by Eva Turner. Azucena sung by Gladys Parr.

16th April   A Grand Concert for The Actors' Benevolent Fund.

17th April   *Tannhäuser* by Wagner. Elisabeth sung by Eva Turner.

18th April   *Butterfly* by Puccini. Butterfly sung by Eva Turner. Suzuki sung by Gladys Parr.

19th April   *Lohengrin* by Wagner. Elsa sung by Eva Turner

20th April 'The Elsa of Miss Eva Turner was one of the best interpretations of a character that she has given in Edinburgh. She caught the right note of girlish exaltation and the singing of the dream music in the first act in particular was full of charm.

20th April   *The Tales of Hoffmann* by Offenbach. Antonia sung by Eva Turner. Nicklaus - Gladys Parr.

22nd April   *Maritana* by Somerville. The Alcada performed by Albert Broad. Lazarillo - Gladys Parr.

1923

Children in arms not permitted. Ladies occupying boxes or seats in stalls and four front rows of dress circle must remove their hats at evening performances.

10th April	*Masked Ball* by Verdi. Amelia sung by Eva Turner. Ulrica sung by Gladys Parr.
13th April	*Mignon* by A. Thomas. Antonio performed by Alfred Broad. Frederick sung by Gladys Parr.
14th April	*The Tales of Hoffmann* by Offenbach. Antonia sung by Eva Turner. Nicklaus - Gladys Parr.
14th April	*The Bohemian Girl* by M.W.Balfe. Captain of the Guard performed by Albert Broad.

1924

7th April	*Fidelio* by Beethoven. Leonore sung by Eva Turner.

8th April 'The Leonora or Fidelio, last night was Miss Eva Turner. Within the last few years she has given many fine performances in Edinburgh, but, so far, she has done nothing so fine as her Leonora. In the great aria in the first act, "Thou Monstrous Fiend" and in the music of the prison scene, she displayed an impressive dramatic quality, while her voice has gained greatly in beauty since she was last in Edinburgh.'

8th April	*Faust* by Gounod. Siebel sung by Gladys Parr.
9th April	*Aida* by Verdi. Aida sung by Eva Turner.

10th April 'Miss Turner's Aida was brilliantly successful. There are great histrionic opportunities in the role and her presentation of the captive Princess, torn between submissiveness and pride, affection for her own race and her for its enemy Radames, was very convincing. The beautiful music assigned to the character was also delightfully rendered, and in this respect Miss Turner's interpretation had many fine moments.'

11th April	*Butterfly* by Puccini. Butterfly sung by Eva Turner. Suzuki sung by Gladys Parr
12th April	*Il Trovatore* by Verdi. Azucena sung by Gladys Parr
14th April	*The Marriage of Figaro* by Mozart. Cherubino sung by Gladys Parr.

15th April 'Miss Gladys Parr was a fine Cherubino. She sang the music of the part with just the smooth perfection which it demands, while her portrayal of the demurely impudent page, with roguery and romantic sentiment struggling for mastery, was as artistic a piece of comedy as has been seen in opera in Edinburgh for many years.'

15th April   *Samson and Delilah* by Saint-Saëns. Delilah sung by Gladys Parr.

16th April   *Fidelio* by Beethoven. Leonore sung by Eva Turner.

17th April   *Lohengrin* by Wagner. Ortrud sung by Gladys Parr.

18th April 'Ortrud is a character which can be made either merely melodramatic, or something more. Last night, Miss Gladys Parr achieved something more. Dramatically, her interpretation of the character was excellent. There was no exaggeration, but it was always vital and significant, while her singing was delightful.'

18th April   *Cavalleria Rusticana* by Mascagni. Santuzza sung by Eva Turner.

19th April 'Miss Eva Turner has appeared in Edinburgh before as Santuzza, with excellent effect. In every respect, however, her impersonation has greatly improved, and the impression that she created in London last summer when she sang the role with the British National Opera Company can be easily understood. It is a powerful and moving interpretation, vocally full of warmth and emotion.

19th April   *Mignon* by A. Thomas. Antonio performed by Albert Broad. Mignon sung by Gladys Parr.

Greenock

Greenock, one of the provincial towns visited in Scotland, was the fifth largest town in Scotland. It is situated twenty-five miles south west of Glasgow, on the shores of the River Clyde which was its primary transport artery, providing an outlet to the world for imports and exports, and so ship building, rope and sail making, along with the export from its sugar refineries, were its main industries. One of the events at that time in the 1920s, showing that these industries were growing rapidly, was the purchase of the West Highland Churchyard, with the idea of building more industrial sites on it. When the grave of Highland Mary, one of Robert Burns' sweethearts who was buried there, was opened, they found beside her body buried there for almost one hundred and forty years the bottom board of an infant's coffin. This brought to the surface again the idea that she died, not of typhoid fever, but in giving premature birth to one of Burns' illegitimate children, of which he had many. The town, who gave the first Burns' Supper in 1804, was shocked at this misdemeanour but nevertheless built on the land where her grave had once been situated.

The owners of these industries would be powerful, wealthy men and able to buy tickets for the opera, sitting in the best seats but the workers, many living in cramped accommodation without even running water, would also be able to see these performances from 'the gods', at affordable prices, in the Alexandra Theatre (later the King's Theatre) Greenock, built 1905 and demolished in 1973 after becoming a picture house. It was always Carl Rosa's intention that everyone should be able to afford a ticket to attend his opera company's performances and to share and understand the joys of opera in English. He wanted the ordinary man to be part of this audience and so it was in Greenock.

The local paper bought for one penny, or borrowed if funds were low, would confirm or not the reader's feelings of the previous night's performance and so his interest was quickened and encouraged. One of those men born in Greenock at the turn of the century, my Uncle James Maclean, a riveter in the shipyards, still remembered performances given by the Royal Carl Rosa Opera Company in the twenties and said to me, before his death in 1963, that he had never heard another voice like Eva Turner's. He remembered not only her special voice but her huge stage presence, and reflected: 'She seemed to fill the stage.'

Covent Garden

There was no resident opera company at Covent Garden during the war years as the building had been a furniture depository. The King and Queen came to Covent Garden, on May 13th, 1919, to celebrate its re-opening when *La Bohème* was chosen by the King for the occasion it is said, because of its short length. Sir Thomas Beecham conducted with the great Nellie Melba singing Mimi. Melba had first sung at Covent Garden thirty years before and had another triumph at this performance, despite her advancing years of fifty eight. She had not enjoyed working with Beecham, however, as she was not interested in stagecraft nor did she like his conductor-orientated performances and so did not return for the revival the following year.

Opera at Covent Garden, at this point in its history, was in a state of disarray: Sir Thomas's own British artists rescued a performance of *Madama Butterfly* on May 26th, 1919, conducted by Percy Pitt. They sang in English while the chorus sang in Italian and the other soloists in French. A month later on June 18th, Sir Thomas conducted a performance of *Ballo in Maschera* with

Martinelli and Destinnova (better known as Destinn) in the cast, where it was reported that the prompter was as audible as the singers! Sir Thomas fell out so badly with Destinn on this occasion that she slapped his face and walked out of Covent Garden never to return, despite having been loved by its audiences since the beginning of the 20th century.

Before the war, Covent Garden had relied on great, adored stars to boost its summer season of opera and raise standards. Now it could no longer depend on their appearance, as they were singing in America where they could earn more money. It would seem too that Sir Thomas Beecham, who was a demanding and sometimes verbally abusive conductor, was changing the balance of power away from singers towards conductors and big singing names did not like this.

Inside Britain there was a great debate and struggle as to how best to establish a National Opera Company. Strategies changed from year to year and so no permanent British company was formed, the lack of which created an environment where there was no platform, of a good consistent standard, from which singers could spring from London to the international opera scene.

The struggle to obtain money for a permanent company continued and in 1919 Lady Maud Cunard, (one of Sir Thomas Beecham's many mistresses), organised a Christmas Opera Ball and explained in the Observer on November 23rd:

> *'I am anxious that people should understand the reason why I am forced – yes forced to give this ball. It is because the state refuses to support opera in any shape or form in this century.'*

A list of those attending included: the Duke of Argyll, librettist for Hamish McCunn's *Diarmid*, Lord Beaverbrook, the Duke and Duchess of Sutherland, the Aga Khan and the Princess of Monaco. A double box would have cost £210 and the sum to be raised was to be £10,000.

La Scala Milan

A plan to replace the old theatre Teatro Ducale, which had burned down in 1776, was accepted the same year by Maria Theresa and the building of the new theatre on the deconsecrated ground was completed within two years. It was to be known as Nuovo Regio Ducal Teatro alla Scala but very soon became known as La Scala. In the tradition of that time, the main floor had no chairs and these spectators would have stood to watch the performance and would have been on the same level as the orchestra which was in full view. (As we know it took till Toscanini's time for a pit to be installed and lights in the auditorium to be dimmed during performances.)

Puccini's Death

Puccini had travelled from his beloved Italy to Brussels a short time before his death in search of recommended, innovative treatment for throat cancer. He had been a chain-smoker of cigars all his life so the cancer surprised no one. Elvira his wife accompanied him on the journey. The recommended treatment at that time was extremely uncomfortable and painful: the climax was radium treatment administered through seven glass needles. To enable Puccini to breathe during this operation, a hole was pierced in his throat: nourishment would be given in liquid form through his nose and the procedures were performed while he was under a local anaesthetic, because his heart was too weak to survive a full anaesthetic. At first, the operation seemed to go well and Puccini was allowed out of bed after four days but at that point he collapsed and died quietly in bed. Just before his death, his hands had moved slowly over the coverlet as if he was playing the piano, or perhaps beating time, while his lips moved as in humming. The cause of the collapse was uncontrolled bleeding, causing a heart attack which killed him on November 29th, 1924.

On December 1st, before nine o'clock in the morning, the nursing home, Place de la Couronne, where Puccini had died, was crowded with people. The coffin containing his body, covered in the Italian flag and surrounded by wreaths, was placed on the funeral carriage. One wreath composed of orchids was from King Victor Emmanuel, while a similar one was sent by the King and Queen of the Belgians. A third, of white lilies, came from Mussolini. At ten-thirty the coffin, covered with flowers, followed a procession formed by a delegation from the Italian societies in Brussels. The Italian Ambassador, Puccini's son, representatives from the Brussels Conservatoire and delegates from the Italian Senate followed the hearse. The route to Sainte Marie Church was lined by crowds and the church was full an hour before the funeral service began. Artists from the Theatre de la Monnaie sang: Gounod's Ave Maria, Franck's Panis Angelicus and Niedrmeyer's Paternostra during the service. Afterwards, the procession was re-formed and the coffin taken to the Gare du Nord to await transportation to Italy that evening.

Turandot

Turandot, pronounced in those days without the final t, was to be the role with which Eva Turner later became most associated and she was often invited to talk about the opera. Among her papers was the text of a talk about the story of *Turandot* in her own words:

'It is more than likely that 90% of you already know the story of the opera "Turandot" but for the other 10% I want to commence my talk by reading the story and I hope you who already know it, will bear with me:- The Princess Turandot, wonderfully beautiful, fabulously cruel and cold as an icicle, wishes to enslave all men but to give her heart to none. To all who come to woo she gives three riddles. He who dares to try to solve them declares his readiness to do so by beating upon a great gong. Invariably the suitors fail and the punishment is death at the hand of the Public Executioner. The young Prince of Persia has come as the latest pretender to the hand of the Princess and the populace is furious that another young life is to be sacrificed to the capriciousness of Turandot. However when she appears, radiantly beautiful, on the balcony, the crowd is at once subdued and cowed. One young man alone stands upright and although he had just been shouting vengeance on her, he now becomes deeply enamoured and cries her name aloud. His old father and Liu, his faithful slave, try to dissuade him but he insists on offering to solve the riddles and win Turandot in marriage. Ping, Pang and Pong, three ministers of Turandot who have already tried in vain to dissuade against the suitor, enter and bewail the dull type of entertainment that now exists: three riddles, three failures and a head off! Bells announce that the guessing is about to commence.

Outside the palace the crowd is assembled. Centuries before, a maiden of Turandot's race had suffered shame and the Princess Turandot has resolved that the shame from the past shall be washed out in blood. Turandot gives the three riddles again and one by one they are rightly guessed by the unknown suitor. The Princess is dismayed and humiliated. The Prince offers her an alternative. If she can find out his name by day break, he is prepared to die.

The city has been forbidden to sleep and all are commanded to aid in finding out the name of the young man. Police seize the old man and the slave girl Liu and they are dragged before Turandot to be tortured if they will not reveal the secret. Suddenly the girl calls out that she alone knows the name but as she loves the young man and wishes him to be happy, she is determined to die rather than divulge the name. She seizes a dagger from a soldier's belt and to escape torture, stabs herself. Turandot and the young man stand before the body of the faithful Liu. The Princess realises what love can accomplish but does not want to yield to its power. To prove that he loves her, the suitor says that he will voluntarily tell his name. He declares that he is Calaf, son of Timur. Turandot, however, cannot resist her love for him and the assembled people applaud the lovers' first kiss.

That briefly is the outline of the story... The story is based on a fairy tale by Count Carlo Gozzi. The same story was developed by Goethe and Schiller and the scene of the story is laid in Peking and its surroundings. I myself was at the very first performance conducted by Toscanini, where the cast was; Rosa Raisa, Miguel Fleta, and Maria Zamboni. When it came to the point in the opera where Puccini had laid down his pen for the last time, Toscanini turned to the audience and said, 'A questo punto, moriva il Maestro'.

Throughout Italy wherever we did "Turandot" for the first time, the conductor would put down his baton and turn to the audience saying again 'A questo punto, moriva il maestro.' When this happens Turandot is quite alone on the stage, veiled. I must tell you always when this happened, I was so deeply and profoundly moved, that I was intensely grateful for the refuge of the veil and also for the fact that when the opera continues after this point, it is the tenor who sings first. From this point on Franco Alfano is responsible for the score. He was requested by Toscanini to finish the opera from rough sketches left by Puccini. Alfano was considered by Toscanini to be the most fitting for the task and Toscanini's choice of him was surely the best that could have been made. I have always noted a little difference in the style, however, when singing the role of Turandot.

It was, of course, particularly unfortunate that the pen fell from the Maestro's hand before the final love scene between the Princess and her successful suitor, as I feel quite sure that it would have been there that Puccini's peculiar power of raising the temperature by a lyrical outburst might have been expected.

The Second Act, first part, the difficult ensemble music of Ping, Pang and Pong, is itself some of the most original in the opera. Undoubtedly the action of the opera is delayed in order that the caperings of the courtiers may diversify the interest and spin out the entertainment. The characters of Ping, Pang and Pong undergo quite a transformation from Gozzi's original fable to those we see in the opera. They now become grotesquely sinister figures with a sadistic streak in them and they indulge in macabre humour. As Mosco Carner writes in his excellent book, "Puccini, A Critical Biography" - "they are capable of a poetic mood wholly unknown to Gozzi's prosaic Masks."

In my opinion the most dramatic part of the opera is in the second scene of the second act, often called "The Riddle Scene". Here it is that Turandot meets her challenger and poses him the riddles. The answers to the riddles are: HOPE, BLOOD, TURANDOT. Very short answers, you may think, but it is really very exciting and tense from the moment that the trumpets sound their perfect fifth and Turandot sings "Straniero, ascolta" and Calaf succeeds in answering. If he didn't, I suppose the opera would have ended here. Following this Turandot pleads with her father and says that she will not be his - Calaf's that is, of course. However, her father says "Her sacred oath is binding" and she must fulfil her promise. At this point as I have already told you, Calaf throws down his challenge and tells Turandot he is prepared to die, if she can guess his name.

The last act opens with the tenor (Calaf) singing almost at once that beautiful aria "Nessun Dorma". The interest then moves to the slave girl, Liu, singing her beautiful aria "Tu che di gel sei cinta" (Thou who with ice are girdled) - after which she stabs herself. Now comes the last duet for Calaf and Turandot. I have done this duet with many and various cuts. I was always sorry, I recall, when the pages given to Turandot in the "Del primo pianto" were cut, because here the womanliness of Turandot comes into evidence and her complete softening and dissolving, conquered by the power of love, gives the spiritual transformation of Turandot. I am very glad to tell you that this cut is not being made in the new production, for which I rejoice. We come now to the last big scene, where Turandot declares to her father and to all assembled, "I know the name of the stranger - it is LOVE". I have always thought it is very wonderful when a woman realises she has met her affinity.'

The casting for the Vienna tour

Ballo in Maschera – (Amelia) Eva Turner, (Riccardo) Oreste de Bernardi, (Renato) Luigi Montesanto, (Ulrica) Marie Szücs-Velmar and (Oscar) Elizabeth Gero.

Aida – (Aida) Eva Turner, (Amneris) Eugenia Besalla, (Radames) Giuseppe Taccani and (Amonasro) Luigi Montesanto.

Trovatore – (Leonora) Eva Turner, (di Luna) Giulio Fergosi, (Manrico) Francesco Battaglia, (Azucena) Schlosshauer-Reynolds and (Ferrando) Leopold Stöger.

Cavalleria Rusticana – (Santuzza) Eva Turner, (Turridu) Battaglia and (Alfio) Ernst Taber.

Tosca – (Tosca) Eva Turner, (Cavaradossi) Battaglia, (Scarpia) Montesanto.

The dates were: 12th and 14th August *Ballo in Maschera*, 17th and 27th *Aida*, 22nd *Trovatore*, 25th and 29th *Cavalleria Rusticana* and 31st *Tosca*.

Claudia Muzio

Born, on February 7th, 1889 in Pavia, 20 miles south of Milan and was registered at birth as Claudina Versati of unknown parentage. Her father was a stage director at Covent Garden and the Metropolitan and her mother, Marchese Gino Monaldi, a chorus singer. They were not married when Claudia was born but did get married at a later date. She travelled with her parents to London when she was two years old and went to school there, becoming fluent in English. She returned to Turin at the age of 16 to study with Annetta Casaloni, a piano teacher and former operatic mezzo-soprano who had created the role of Maddalena in the world première of Verdi's *Rigoletto* and then continued her vocal studies in Milan with Elettra Callery-Viviani.

Critics wrote of her: 'Her voice, talent, schooling, style, feeling and the most refined taste had revealed themselves to a high degree' when she debuted in Italy in Arezzo on January 15th, 1910 in the title role of Massenet's *Manon*. Despite her youth, she made rapid progress in the opera houses of Italy, sang Manon Lescaut with Martinelli at the Teatro Dal Verme in Milan in 1912 and debuted at La Scala Milan in 1913, as Desdemona in Verdi's *Otello*. She first sang in London at Covent Garden in Puccini's *Manon Lescaut* in 1914 and stayed on to sing other roles including Mimi and Tosca both with Caruso. She triumphantly faced her Metropolitan audience in New York in December, 1916 as Tosca and was so successful that she continued to appear there during six successive years. She fell out with the management at the Met in 1922, and henceforth, made the Chicago Opera House her artistic home in America.

In her later years, Muzio had experienced some financial anxiety after losing money through the extravagance of a manager, rumoured to be her lover and then again in the Wall Street crash. In 1929 she married Renato Liberati, seventeen years her junior and in 1930 started to experience some health problems, but continued singing and recording. She died in a Rome hotel of what was officially described as heart failure but there was much speculation about other possible causes of death, including suicide. She is buried in the Cimitero del Verano in Rome. Adriano Belli, a critic for the press in Roman of the time, agrees with Eva Turner's thoughts about Muzio's singing:

> 'Muzio in this opera, ("Traviata"), which she lives in a really startling way, shines with a vocal and dramatic sincerity that intensifies the expressiveness of both singing and acting. And the suffering character leaps out of the stage picture with a reality so life-like and convincing that we can only wonder if we are hearing a performance of a singer or the interpretation of a great dramatic actress. A glow of poetry and human truth radiates from this distinguished artist. Her voice produced with flexible spontaneity varies between the softness of velvet and the penetrating vibrancy... She possesses above all that fascinating inner and deep intensity which enables her to captivate her audiences.'

Chicago Season

The information about dates and cast in all Eva Turner's Chicago Seasons is partly culled from the day-by-day chronology developed by the late Charles Jahant.

1928/9

Aida – 3rd (matinee), 19th, 29th November, Conductor Roberto Moranzoni, Eva Turner (Aida), Cyrena Van Gordon (Amneris), Ulysses Lappas (Radames), Cesar Formichi (Amonasro)3rd. Montesanto (Amonasro) 19th and Bonelli (Amonasro) 29th. Conductors Moranzoni 3rd, 29th and Polacco 19th.

Un Ballo in Maschera – 7th November Broadcast, 17th, Conductor Henry Weber, Eva Turner (Amelia), Van Gordon (Ulrica), Alice Mock (Oscar), Charles Marshall (Riccardo), Richard Bonelli (Renato).

Cavalleria Rusticana – 15th November, 1st, 11th, 30th December, Conductor Moranzoni, Eva Turner (Santuzza), Ada Paggi (Lola), Forest Lamont (Turiddu), Luigi Montesanto (Alfio).

Il Trovatore – 4th, 22nd December, Conductor Polacco, Eva Turner (Leonora), Van Gordon (Azucena), Marshall (Manrico) 4th, Cortis (Manrico) 22nd, Bonelli (Di Luna) Lazzari (Ferrando).

Die Walküre – 8th, 24th December, Frida Leider made her debut at Chicago singing Brünnhilde. Forest Lamont was their Siegmund, Olszewska (Fricka), Kipnis (Wotan) and Coutreil (Hunding) with Polacco conducted. 15th December Schipper for Kipnis 31st January Chicago Opera on Tour Boston Opera House Schipper for Kipnis

Le Nozze di Figaro – was broadcast on 3rd January and was followed by performances on 9th, 20th, and 25th. Henry Weber – Conductor, Eva Turner (La Contessa), Edith Mason (Susanna), Claire (Cherubino), Lazzari (Figaro), Bonelli (Count). Moranzoni conducted it on February 4th when they went to the Boston Opera House on tour.

1929/30

Die Walküre – 21st, 30th November, 29th January 1930 Chicago and 3rd February 1930 in Boston. Frida Leider (Brünnhilde), Eva Turner (Sieglinde), Olszsewska (Fricka) Theo Strack (Siegmund), Kipnis (Wotan), Baromeo (Hunding) 21st and Coutreil (Hunding) last three performances.

Tannhäuser – 7th, 15th, 23rd December. Eva Turner (Elisabeth), Leider (Venus) 7th and 15th Van Gordon (Venus) 23rd, Strack (Tannhäuser), Bonelli (Wolfram) and Kipnis (Heinrich). Polack was the conductor.

Eva Turner also sang in a Gala performance of *Aida*, Act II on 10th January. The programme included *Romeo and Juliette*, with Hilda Burke, *Rigoletto* with Margherita Salvi and *Trovatore* with her beloved Muzio.

1938

Turandot – 19th November Masini (Calaf), Garrotto (Liu). 9th December Tokatyan as Calaf. Conductor Leo Kopp

Aida – 26th November Gigli (Radames) and Maranzoni conducting. 17th December Martinelli (Radames)

Walküre – 27th November Eva Turner (Sieglinde) with Manski (Brünnhilde), Rene Maison, (Siegmund), Kipnis (Wotan) and Weber conducted.

Manzoni Requiem

The requiem is referred to in Eva Turner's contract by its original name the *Manzoni Requiem* because: when Rossini died in 1868, Verdi suggested that a number of Italian composers should collaborate on a Requiem in Rossini's honour, and he began the effort by submitting *Libera me*. During the next year a Mass was compiled by 13 composers, of whom the only one well known today is Verdi himself. The premiere was scheduled for 13th November, 1869, the first anniversary of Rossini's death. However, on 4th November, nine days before the premiere, the organising committee abandoned it. Verdi blamed the scheduled conductor, Angelo Mariani, for this, pointing to Mariani's lack of enthusiasm for the project, even though he had been part of the organising committee from the start. This row marked the beginning of the end of their long-term friendship, as Verdi never forgave him, although Mariani pleaded with him to repair their friendship. (The piece fell into oblivion until 1988, when Helmuth Rilling premiered the complete *Messa per Rossini* in Stuttgart.

In the meantime, Verdi kept toying with his *Libera me*, frustrated that the combined commemoration for Rossini's life would not be performed in his, Verdi's, lifetime. In May, 1873, the Italian writer and humanist Alessandro Manzoni, whom Verdi had admired all his adult life and met in 1868, died. Upon hearing of his death, Verdi resolved to complete a Requiem, this time entirely of his own writing, for Manzoni and travelled to Paris in June, where he began work on the Requiem, giving it the form we know today. It included a revised version of the *Libera me*, originally composed for Rossini and was first performed the following May in the church of San Marco in Milan, on the first anniversary of Manzoni's death, with Verdi conducting. Teresa Stolz, the soprano at this first performance, went on to have a brilliant career. She had been engaged to Mariani in 1869, but later left him amid rumours, never substantiated, that she was having an affair with Verdi, this probably being the real reason for the fallout between the two composers.

The Imperial League of Opera 1935

London – 24th September and 2nd October *Siegfried*, 26th September *Freischütz*, 30th September and 4th October *Ballo*. (A performance on the 5th Oct of *Der Freischütz* was later added.)

Birmingham – 10th October *Siegfried*.

Liverpool – 14th and 23rd October *Freischütz*, 16th and 25th October *Siegfried*. (19th October – Matinee of *Der Freischutz* was added)

Manchester – 30th October and 6th November Matinee *Siegfried*, 1st November *Freischütz* and 4th November *Ballo*. (These dates were revised – 31st October *Siegfried*, 1st and 6th November *Der Freischütz* and 4th November *Ballo*)

Bradford – 13th November *Freischütz* and 15th *Siegfried*.

Leeds – 18th November *Siegfried*, 22nd *Ballo*.

Ballo in Maschera 1935

The cast: Eva Turner (Amelia), Arthur Fear (Manrico), Dino Borgioli (Riccardo), Stella Andreva (Oscar) and Constance Willis (Ulrica).

About the work itself, a little historical piece included in a review of the time is quite interesting:

'Masked Ball performed in Italian, and argument for it being in English, was originally called Gustave III based on the historic fact of the assassination of the King of Sweden at a masked ball. Verdi's opera, with the libretto by Somma after Scribe, should have been produced in Naples in 1858 but was banned because of the attempted murder of Napoleon III by a man named Orsini about that time. This was in the period of unrest before the Italian War of Independence and the authorities saw in the fate of Gustave III the seed of popular trouble.

After a lot of argument a new version was prepared for a performance in Rome, the scene being transferred to Boston Massachusetts, Gustave was replaced by Richard, Earl of Warwick and founder of the city. The chief conspirators were two Negroes Sam and Tom and the sorceress Ulrica was an Indian Squaw. The locale of the tragedy as it was performed last night was placed in Naples in the 17th century another variant of the original theme and altogether a more plausible one, lending great scope for a picturesque production. This work of three quarters of a century old seems to a modern audience stilted and full of obsolete conventions but it can never be ridiculous because of the music.'

Covent Garden season in 1935

The London press tell us a little more about the short season at Covent Garden in 1935:

'Sir Thomas Beecham, let me say at once, has justified his bold step by the excellence of the performances of his London and Provincial Opera Society (which is linked up in some way with the Imperial League of Opera, an organization almost as mysterious as the Holy Roman Empire) and by his originality of choice of what was a necessarily small repertoire. At Covent Garden the audiences have been adequate but not superlatively large. This may be because of the ancient and snobbish prejudice against British singers, who are here in the majority, or because for some inscrutable reason people regard Wagner in converse fashion to an oyster, that is to say that it should not be consumed when there is an r in the month, that "Siegfried" etc. slip down the gullet of the musically succulently and harmlessly in June and July but are distasteful and even dangerous in September and October. I can only say I enjoyed my autumnal taste of "Siegfried" just as fully as I ever did at Covent Garden in June or at Bayreuth in August and that I am at this moment still alive whatever may happen before these lines appear in print. Mr. Walter Widdop in the title role was better than many a foreign "Siegfried" – a fine performance – and Miss Eva Turner is among the great Brünnhildes. It is a pity that in spite of the 'cuts' we did not hear her until about 11pm. Why not the old plan of starting at five o'clock with a dinner interval?

Why Weber's "Der Freischütz" was dragged from the shelf after years I cannot imagine. There are flashes of music in it which seem to pave the way to Wagner and a good aria or two but on the whole this is a specimen of early German romanticism is insufferably tedious when it is not unintentionally comic. Mr. Walter Widdop, Miss Eva Turner, Mr. Percy Hemming, Mr. Frank Sale, Mr. Arthur Fear and others performed conscientiously and well the difficult task of saying and singing a lot of utterly preposterous things and Sir Thomas Beecham saw that everything and everybody was good – except of course the composer who died in 1826.'

(Weber had, in 1824, been the Musical Director at Covent Garden and his *Oberon* from which comes *Ocean, Thy Mighty Monster*, given its debut there in 1826).

1936

Cast for London Provincial Opera Company was: Walter Widdop (Tristan), Eva Turner (Isolde), Constance Willis (Brangaene), Norman Allin (King Mark) and Booth Hitchen Kurwenal.

1937

Cast for *Ballo* was: Borgioli (Ricardo), Brownlee (Renato), Constance Willis (Ulrica) and Barbara Lane (Oscar).

Sir Henry Joseph Wood

Sir Henry, with whom Eva Turner had a long association, was born on March 3rd 1869. He founded the Proms in 1895 and had an enormous influence on musical life in Britain, improving access for the ordinary person to concert music and raising the standard of orchestral playing. He had been a church organist from the age of ten and also played both the violin and piano. When he went to the Royal Academy of Music at the age of 16 to begin his formal musical education, he studied singing with Manuel Garcia, as at that time his ambition was to become a teacher of singing, and so he attended classes of as many singing teachers as he could, both as a singer and as an accompanist and gave singing lessons throughout his life. When he left the RAM, he found work as a singing teacher and as an orchestral and choral conductor and gained experience by working for several opera companies, including the Carl Rosa Opera Company in 1891. He collaborated with Arthur Sullivan on the preparation of *The Yeomen of the Guard* and *Ivanhoe* and published a manual *The Gentle Art of Singing*.

In 1893, Robert Newman, the manager of the Queen's Hall, a beautiful building, with exquisite acoustics, in Langham Square in central London, round the corner from Henry's home, proposed holding a series of promenade concerts there, with Henry Wood as conductor. The term promenade concert, at that time, referred to concerts in London parks, where the audience could walk about as they listened and Newman's aim was to improve the musical taste of the British public who were not used to listening to serious classical music unless it was presented in small doses with plenty of other popular items in between. Henry Wood shared those ideals. Dr George Cathcart, a wealthy ear, nose and throat specialist, offered to sponsor the project on condition that Wood took charge of every concert. He also insisted that the pitch of the instruments, which in England was nearly a semitone higher than the pitch used on the continent, should be brought down to a normal concert pitched A.

All of the above being agreed, on August 10th 1895, the first of the Queen's Hall Promenade Concerts took place with an orchestra of about 80 members playing the Overture to *Rienzi* by Wagner as its very first piece.

British conductors were not highly thought of at that time and certainly not thought capable of conducting the great Wagner works but Henry Wood changed all that and for many years Monday night was 'Wagner Night' at the proms. He was meticulous and thorough in his preparation, and built up a large library of scores, which were carefully marked up in coloured pencil. The Jubilee Concert in 1938 was given:

> 'because of the brilliant services which he has rendered during the last fifty years this country is now ranked among the most musical nations of the world.'

In 1898 Henry Wood married Princess Olga Ourousoff, a Russian noblewoman, and became greatly interested in Russian music, which he performed frequently. He adopted a Russian pseudonym, Paul Klenovsky, for his compositions and arrangements, and supplied an imaginary biography of his alter ego for use in programme notes. Klenovsky was a real person, a recently deceased young musician friend of Alexander Glazunov's, and Henry Wood thought a foreign name would secure a more favourable reception to his compositions, than his own. His famous medley *Fantasia on British Sea Songs*, prepared for the 1905 centenary celebrations of the Battle of Trafalgar, is now an indispensable item at the Last Night of the Proms.

In 1904, after a rehearsal in which he was faced with a sea of entirely unfamiliar faces in his own orchestra, he, at one stroke, abolished the deputy system, in which players had been free to send in a deputy whenever they wished. Forty players resigned and formed their own orchestra: the London Symphony Orchestra.

His beloved Olga Ourousoff died in 1909 and Henry married Muriel Ellen Greatrex in 1911 with whom he had two daughters. Despite an unhappy marriage he continued with his career and went on fighting for improved pay for musicians, and introduced women into the orchestra in 1911. The following year, continuing his pursuit of new works, he conducted Arnold Schoenberg's *Five Orchestral Pieces*, saying to the orchestra: 'Stick to it, gentlemen, this is nothing to what you'll have to play in 25 years' time'.

A little more than 25 year later Sir Henry was to conduct a *Serenade to Music* which Vaughan Williams wrote especially for him, not of the atonal type he was talking about above, but also a great work: one of great harmonic, lyrical and poetic sensitivity. By this time he was much happier in his private life. As we know there are always two sides to a story but it seems that Lady Muriel was discontented and unkind to her husband and despite trying to continue the situation in a seemly manner, Sir Henry was forced to leave her.

He never spoke of this in public but it was obvious to his friends that the recent re-entry of a singing friend from years before, into his life was making him happy and more able to concentrate on his music. This friend, the widow Jessie Linton née Goldsack, was to become known as Lady Jessie Wood, when she changed her name by deed poll, after repeated unsuccessful attempts on Sir Henry's behalf to obtain a divorce from Lady Muriel Wood.

Dame Isobel Baillie

A sprightly Dame Isobel, whose birthday falls on the 9th of March, the day before Eva's, was also at the ENO 90th party and told the audience on that occasion that she had never met Eva before they sang together in *Serenade to Music*, as they had inhabited different performing worlds, because she sang only oratorio and recitals. They had, however, shared Lancashire where Dame Isobel, although born in Scotland, had had her beginnings and this had bonded them in an unspoken way and Isobel said that she had admired Eva from afar.

As Dame Isobel wished Dame Eva a 'Happy 90th Birthday' it was obvious that although they had not shared a stage often, they shared the feelings of what it took to get out there and perform, and Dame Isobel's voice filled with emotional and truthful best wishes from a great old lady who understood how important friendship was as one got older. Her time ran out the very next year when she died at the age of 88 and Dame Eva represented the Lancastrian Society at Dame Isobel's Memorial Service, at St. Sepulchre's Church, Holborn, on 15th November 1983. Sir Henry Wood had been a boy organist at that church and his widow Lady Jessie Wood had created the Musicians' Chapel there, with a most beautiful stained glass window, in his memory. Dame Eva remained to chat with people after Isobel's service until the church was empty, remembering a colleague and a friend. Eva chose the original recording of the *Serenade to Music*, as one of her records to be cast away with, when she took part in her first *Desert Island Discs* in 1942 and spoke with affection of all her colleagues.

Mary Jarred and Roy Henderson

Roy Henderson, the youngest in the *Serenade* group was the last to die and he revelled somewhat in this small victory. John Steane in the Gramophone of June 2000 remembered visiting them in later life when only they and Eva were alive and that Roy: 'recalled quite cheerfully that the tenors went first, among them Frank Titterton, who always carried around a little apothecary's bag with medical remedies for any emergency.' John Steane also said that Mary Jarred had told him that the sixteen of them were a very happy company, adding darkly 'on the whole'. 'Eva Turner', he says, 'was of course magnificent and remembered everything. She particularly recalled looking out into the hall during the rehearsal and noticing that Vaughan Williams had come in 'looking like... an old farmer really'.'Sadly, Mary Jarred was not well enough to attend Dame Eva's 90th Birthday Celebrations at the Coliseum, given to her by the Friends of ENO, but Roy Henderson who was able to go was at his most humorous and clearly enjoyed telling tales from the past. When talking of this famous performance, he implied that the ladies in the group of singers were all rather large and he wouldn't have minded cuddling up to a couple of them on a cold night, if he had met them at King's Cross Station. He told the receptive audience that Eva's great gift to the world, as well as her marvellous natural voice, was her very generous big heart. His resonant voice was wreathed in smiles as he wished Eva a 'Happy Birthday' expressing the wish that they should both be back in 10 years for her 100th.

Queen's Hall

The night fire watchers had heard the clattering of the bomb on the roof and went to work with their hose putting the fire out. They then went to turn off the hose pipe but the water supply had already stopped and so they looked for another source of water which was not available, as the main water mains had been broken by high explosive bombs. During that delay, the fire broke out again and the London Fire Service, stretched to its limits as they were needed at the House of Commons, Westminster Abbey, the British Museum and the Royal Mint, to name but a few, was not able to help the poor old Queen's Hall, which was far down their list of priorities and so by morning she was a smouldering ruin. The lovely hall was mourned, as if it had been a very close personal friend, by all who knew her.

Ourselves as Teachers
Fundamental steps towards fuller vocal achievement

It is a great pleasure to be here with all of you and I feel very honoured to have the privilege of talking with you. The deepest sincerity and humility impel me to bring to you today some of my observations and conclusions about ourselves as teachers – our own techniques, our goals, our obligations to our students and their obligations to us. I think I can conclude that the art of singing is very near to the heart of each one of us here. And it has also been our life's work in various phases. Real musical talent is obvious. And how so many long to sing! But all this effort put forth in striving for vocal perfection will not compensate for God given talent. Many voices, as we teachers know, are not worth the cultivation, and that means time and opportunity lost. On the other hand, the most beautiful voice will be as nothing unless it is enriched by years of study devoted to proper projection and brought to the peak of sensitive interpretation. Proper projection and sensitive interpretation and feeling constitute the foundation stones of full vocal achievement. This is the critical area where many young people should be intelligently enlightened. Student's own laziness or training by incompetent teachers cause many to fall down and never reach the top.

I thought it might be well to discuss the various productions we hear, which must be remedied at the outset, such as:

1. *Breathy Tone – caused by the cords being a little open when singing.*
2. *Hooty Tone – caused by the placement being too far back.*
3. *White Bleating Tone – which is, of course, a lack of quality*
4. *Wobbly Tone, or Tremolo, – caused by lack of support or lazy attacks*

With your permission let us investigate these aforementioned productions.

1. *In my own experience, I have found that the breathy tone is caused by the individual's being very lethargic and unable to effect a proper attack, thus enabling the cords to function in their right relationship. It has always appealed to me as being of the utmost urgency to warn students about attack. There is so much confusion about attack and shock of the glottis. The right attack is constructive; the shock of*

the glottis destructive and harms the student. Many people trying to avoid shock of the glottis avoid attacking the tone altogether, or very greatly, very much to the detriment of the individual's singing. You know that when the breath disturbs the cords and functions in this manner, it must never be like that and so on. How does one bring about the proper attack. (Demonstrate)

2. The hooty tone I have found to be brought about by the placement not being forward enough and hence directed to the soft palate. (Give the example of throwing the ball against a curtain, or against a wall - the teeth as a sounding board.) In my own experience, when I have coordinated such placement with the brilliance and frontal placement, I have found that it can become a very beautiful, full tone and reaches the audience in every part of the concert hall or the opera house, instead of being locked up on the platform or the stage. The sensations the students experience when they bring about the necessary placement, they can recapture.

3. The white bleating tone, I find is caused by a frontal placement without any support of the body at all and devoid of quality. How do you bring about the proper body support? (Demonstrate)

4. In many cases the wobbly tone is caused by the person's breathing wrongly; in some cases, in trying to take too much breath and thus causing a restriction; a lack of command of the organ and wrong breathing, sometimes raising the shoulders and causing neck restriction; and again, the failure to command their instrument or have it developed that it will respond to their every command. Their stance in the studio must be taken into account; breathing from only the top of the lungs avoided, etc.etc. Deep breathing from the diaphragm is the necessity. (Demonstrate.) Volume is one of the reasons, when acquired at the wrong cost, the singer loses all he gives the vocal cords, too much noise results and harm begins.

People who cultivate the voice have widely different ideas as to what constitutes the best method of development and its preservation. Sometimes we hear, 'How high can you sing?' quotes. But what about the foundation part of the voice, that is, the middle notes? The tremulo, one of the most objectionable and unbearable vocal faults, is often brought about by the spreading of the vocal cords through straining.

A splendid means of developing vocal essentials and furthering vocal agility is to give time to study of such things as "Rejoice Greatly" from the Messiah, "Nymphs and Shepherds" of Purcell, "O Thou that Tellest" from the Messiah - indeed, more of Handel and Bach. Here I may say that if only the students will remember that they have to plow before they can plant and that when they are given life and opportunity! To my mind man's purpose is unfulfilled unless he has the creative urge and so many have the mistaken idea of substituting activity for purpose. How many times I tell my students that the most important motive for work in the school and in life is the pleasure in work, pleasure in its result and the achievement and the knowledge of its value to the community and the state. For this thought I have to thank Albert Einstein.

I am asked repeatedly when a person should begin studying voice. I think it is difficult to give a set rule for this. Some people are more mature at certain ages than others; and as we know, the male voice changes radically at puberty. Many successful singers begin at an early age. I myself began when I was 13 years of age. This brings us to the question of how long does a good voice need training. Lamperti said he needed seven years to develop a voice.

I have often been asked whether singers are given enough technique before assuming repertoire. I am often of the opinion that they are not. But prevailing and individual circumstances determine so many things. For instance, if students have to meet certain requirements within a given time, one has to try to combine everything for that eventual result, regardless of whether the necessary time is forthcoming for the necessary study. In line with this necessity, I would like to see five years substituted for four in the University for voice.

In my opinion, in this present day, as I observe it, I feel that too little importance is attached to the question of technique. I am a most enthusiastic upholder of technique in singing - because I well know its value when invading such operas as "Turandot", "The Ring", Leonora in "Il Trovatore" and Donna Anna in "Don Giovanni" The student is most interested in singing songs and is rather bored by vocal exercises as such, or any of the ground work needed to establish a control of the muscles. I have heard countless auditions throughout my years as an artist. Pitiably few performers had the goods to offer, or were worth listening to.

I think more attention should be paid to extended arpeggios to develop a range, quick scales to bring about an even quality, sustained notes for steady tone, chromatic scales to help intonation, staccato to further a good attack, crescendi and decrescendi on sustained notes without tonal discrepancy, to mention but a few of the fundamentals requiring our attention. Evenness of tone in all registers must be achieved. VOWEL law must govern.

There are some people, perhaps, who will not agree with me when I say that our first attention must be directed to bringing about these foundations before we invade music literature and effect the necessary interpretation. Teachers would profit by pausing to think of the great privilege and of course, at the same time, the tremendous responsibilities teachers have in being the moulders of these young people in their formative years. Also, when we come upon splendid gifts and aptitudes, how we are in duty bound to try with all our might and main to develop them to the best of our ability. I never cease asking myself how I can impress upon the students, that application and perspiration are the necessary qualities, that knowledge is power when all else fails, and that God helps those who help themselves. It is true that once the correct fundamentals are established, practise goes a long way towards making perfect.

I have often asked myself whether the students are enthusiastic enough to apply themselves in this way and whether the enthusiasm and incentive can survive in them long enough to accomplish these things. I have questioned myself many times, again, as to whether the student has been inquiring enough within himself or herself as to what are the essentials for vocal standards or a career; whether their ears are discerning enough for them to make the comparisons in what they hear in relation to what they hear from others, and also from themselves. The question of success or failure as a singer is simplified by self-judgement and discrimination. This is quite a work, to bring the student to the understanding of the essentials for public performance as compared with what they hear themselves. What the individual hears from himself can be very misleading for the individual, since the ear is posited behind where he emits the tone. And at that time, when rightly produced, travels out to the public ear much more effectively than the tone which the student hears for himself.

Are students with potentialities made aware of the facts and limitations in the music profession? Were this done more, there would be fewer young people labouring in a Fool's Paradise, and suffering such keen disappointment and sadness that they do not reach their goal or ideal.

When a singer is about to enter upon a public career, there is one point to be considered, that of fitness for concert or opera. I think if you can sing in concert, if you have feeling and discernment, you can also sing in opera, providing you have the necessary range, etc., etc., though it is a well known fact that some who are good in concert are by no means fitted for opera. The operatic stage demands so much of everything – voice, judgement of singing, acting, ease of movement, dramatic instinct and feeling – these are all so absolutely necessary to the operatic singer. Here I should say that I have heard many people discuss voice theoretically and in a splendid manner, but I must also observe that I have also known that when it comes to the practical aspect and the arousing of the individual to the sensations and placement, and the remedial steps for his or her peculiar vocal faults, that is something else.

There are those with a name at the top of their profession who have published articles regarding singing, diction, written word etc. There is likelihood and some danger that each individual will put a different construction or a different tonal result on that written word. (The danger is for the teacher). Are we not as teachers made more aware day by day that one can lead a horse to water, but one cannot make it drink, and how in consequence we at times really suffer from our efforts being so frustrated. No matter how the teacher succeeds in propounding and getting some result, without the intent and enthusiasm of the student to recapture such, our efforts go for nothing. Our efforts may be sometimes substituted for receptivity on the part of the student, how well we know. Here let me say, I know of no avenue more demanding or more exhausting than this field of vocalism- of vocal teaching.

There is nothing to prevent anyone's putting out a shingle to say he is a teacher of singing! We have many teachers who are good coaches, but do not know the foundations which should be established. I am inundated from all over asking for advice etc. I often wonder if I have courage enough to be frank with a lot of these people who have no aptitude or talent.

It is certainly true that a great number of musicians become music teachers in one of its fields at sometime in their lives, although here let me mention that Flagstad always declared she would never teach, as I did also until I reaped some success with fellow artists who told me it was my duty to teach. The sad, deplorable state of affairs is how too frequently so few of them really know how to teach when they enter that field. It is only too obvious in some cases that teaching becomes a substitution as a result of a frustrated career. As a result the field is far too greatly populated with poor and mediocre teachers. I know of no avenue more demanding or exhausting – I repeat, than that of vocalism. Potential singers seem to put up a resistance to using their 'person' – one of our plans of action when trying to rouse an individual out of lethargy. Also, persons coming from the Southwest do not have the same opportunities in so many ways. They do not hear as much music etc.

If some of my outlines seem in another world than that which perhaps you might have known, it might be well to outline a little of my own background.

The London Opera Centre

The coaching at the London Opera Centre came in three types and taught the singer how most usefully to work with and learn from a good coach. There was the main repetiteur who worked at one of the big houses and who came to the Opera Centre once a week to give the student thoughts on the inner meaning of the role, ideas about the character, and how to put the finished polish on a part which they had already studied with the staff repetiteur. Their knowledge of how an orchestra sounded and their ability to convey this through there playing was valuable to the inexperienced singer who perhaps had never as yet sung with an orchestra. They understood how the voice worked and how the involvement of precise language could help a singer. Then there were coaches who were resident members of staff, with whom the student studied three times a week, learning the roles which they were going to perform at the end of term. Finally there were the student coaches, who aspired to be on the staff at the opera houses or even in some cases, to become conductors. These young students were eager to work with singers as much as possible and each learned from the other how this relationship could be built into something which served them both. The singers studied their part in a relaxed environment, sometimes knowing as much as the young coach and the more talented coaches learned how best and most quickly to help the singer. If this partnership flourished, the singer was helped to achieve a more creative, artistic performance, based on the composer's ideas and on shared thoughts about how to bring the character to life. If a singer enjoys working with a certain coach then they use them throughout their lives, employing them behind the scenes to help with the role learning which has to be achieved in their career.

Martinelli

New York Times 21st November 1963:

'Golden Jubilee of a Star's Debut. Martinelli Is Feted by Met. Colleagues Gather for the Event by Raymond Ericson.

Backstage at the Metropolitan Opera last night, gray-haired singers greeted each other affectionately as dancers in dark brown greasepaint swirled around. "It is like old home week," Nina Morgana said to Ruth Miller, wife of Mario Chamlee. And it was. The retired singers were there to help the opera company celebrate the 50th anniversary of Giovanni Martinelli's debut, which took place on Nov 20th 1913. The dancers were waiting to go on in "Aida" which would bring the Gala Evening to a close.

Two sessions of music, during which current members of the Metropolitan sang arias, led to the high point of the event in which Lauder Greenway, chairman of the board of the Metropolitan Opera, presented a gift to Mr Martinelli on behalf of the company. Seated and standing on stage were former colleagues of the tenor. They included: Licia Albanese, Rose Bampton, Karin Branzell, Anna Case, Rita de la Porte, Miss Miller, Miss Morgana, Carmella Ponselle, Jessie Rogge, Bidu Sayao, Eva Turner, Giuseppe Bamboschek, John Brownlee, Thomas Chalmers, Mario Chamlee, Frederick Jagel and Alexander Sved.

Miss Turner, a noted soprano with whom Martinelli had sung at Covent Garden, flew from London for the event. Mr and Mrs Chamlee journeyed from their present home in Los Angeles. Maria Jeritza, who was present in the audience, was also introduced to the audience by Mr Greenway.

When Mr Martinelli strode on stage for the presentation, looking vigorous, handsome, white-haired and belying his 78 years, they gave him a standing ovation. After his spoken tribute, Mr Greenway presented the tenor with a leather-bound, gold stamped album containing Metropolitan programmes for each of the 36 roles that he had sung with the company. In his reply, Mr Martinelli remarked that: "I was not so nervous that November night 50 years ago. Oh for the recklessness of youth!" A little later he said, "I understand when this evening's programme was being planned there was some fear that I might want to sing. Please dissipate that thought but if ever they find that Verdi did write a "King Lear," and the score is discovered, I might consider making myself available." Mr Martinelli was, perhaps, referring to the fact that at the age of 53 he had tackled for the first time the title role of Verdi's "Othello", making it one of his biggest successes of his career that established a record for its 33 seasons with the Metropolitan.

During the first part of the gala, Mr Martinelli sat quietly in Mr Greenway's box, accompanied by his wife and two daughters. He listened attentively to the singers, many of them young, as he still listens today in his constant attendance at opera performances. The program was devoted to music from operas in which Mr Martinelli had sung for the Metropolitan. Among the singers, only Zinka Milanov, who sang beautifully two arias from Otello, went back to the tenor's era with the company. Others who took part were: Cornell MacNeil, Gianna d'Angelo, Barry Morell, Lucine Amara, Enzio Flagello, Raina Kabaivanska, John Alexander, Robert Merrill, Anna Moffo, Giorgio Tozzi, Rita Gorr and Cesare Siepi. In the Aida scene were Mary Curtis-Verna, Irene Dalis, Carlo Bergonzi, Mario Sereni, Bonaldo Gisiotti and John Macurdy. Conductors included Fausto Cleve, Joseph Rosenstock, George Schick and Kurst Adler.

Telegrams congratulating the tenor arrived from many artists who could not be present: Edith Mason, Stella Roman, Rosa Ponselle, Gertrude Wittergren, Leontyne Price, Gladys Swathout and her husband Frank Chapman; Vincenzo Belezza, Lauritz Melchior, Charles Kullman, Salvatore Baccaloni and many others. Geraldine Farrar sent a laurel wreath in which were entwined ribbons representing the colors of the Italian and the American flags.

The audience included many socially and culturally prominent people, including Rudolf Bing, general manager of the Metropolitan, and Sergio Fenoaltea, Italian Ambassador to the United States who came from Washington. Mr Martinelli, incidentally, was wearing the decoration that symbolised his title Knight Commander of the Order of Merit of the Republic of Italy. The gala, a benefit for the Metropolitan, brought in $55,000 at the box office. A reception at the Metropolitan Opera Club followed the performance, at which Mr Martinelli was presented with another gift by the Metropolitan Opera Guild.'

The Pendant

When Dame Eva gave Gwyneth the pendant she wrote this accompanying letter:

'In 1927 I was singing at the Politeama Florentina in Florence (which later became Teatro Comunale) with Maestro Gui, the conductor. After the performance, there came into my dressing room the Baroness Pauline de Bush with a party of her guests from her villa in Santa Margherita. In 1928 I came to the Royal Opera House, Covent Garden to sing in the International season the role of Turandot. During that time the Baroness gave a wonderful party for me at the famous Bath Club. Among the guests was Madame Kirkby Lunn and Madame Adeline Genee, the famous ballet dancer. The Baroness became a wonderful dear friend of mine and through her I came to know Dame Adeline, as she became, who I often met at various banquets. Through the years, after a lapse of time, she lived at the Hyde Park Hotel. It was there when lunching with her one day she presented to me this pendant and chain which is quite historic as it belonged to the famous Swedish singer, Christine Nilsson who was a relation of Dame Adeline's husband. In view of this association with this famous singer, Dame Adeline was most anxious that I became its possessor. The writing on the pendant is in French.

I am sure, dear Gwyneth, no doubt you will have heard of this lady. As a souvenir of your first Turandot, I am presenting it to you with the hope it will signal many more outstanding successes for you and prove a "Porte Bonheur" for all time. It has been a dear and prized possession of mine and I now give it into your care as a token of my love and affection.'

Oh John

The song which Eva sang to entertain her student friends was probably a popular song, words by Andrew B. Stirling, music composed by Jimmie V. Monaco and sung by Miss Hanid Alexander (among others) who appeared at the Liverpool Empire in 1905.

I heard about him Sunday;
by chance I met him Monday; I was captur'd.
Arranged to meet on Friday,
'cause he knew that was my day – Heart enraptured.
Now, I was there at eight, and say,
I had a lovely wait about an hour – In a shower.
I felt just like the last rose of summer,
it's a shame! But I love him just the same.

Chorus

Oh, John! Oh, John!
You're the sweetest man I ever laid my eyes upon
You've got a loving way, that's why I say –
I'd let you break appointments with me every day.
And oh, John! Oh John!
You've got me going, going, now I'm gone!
For my heart keeps thumping, pumping,
jumping, jumping. When you kiss me –

Oh, John!

Index

Aberdeen, 50, 124, 173, 197, 287
Adeline Patti jewels, 254, 336
Aeolian Hall, 39
Agathe, *Der Freischütz*, 9, 186
Aida, *Aida*, 8, 26, 49-50, 54, 57-8, 62, 64, 66, 68-9, 73, 79-83, 88, 93-4, 96-7, 99-103, 113, 115-18, 121, 130, 134, 136, 141-3, 147, 152, 155, 157-8, 161, 168, 170-1, 194, 197, 199, 203-5, 209, 212-3, 225, 227, 232-3, 236-7, 240, 246, 262, 265, 276, 278, 280, 284-5, 297, 314, 324, 347, 349-50, 357, 365-7, 381-2
Albanese, Licia, 198, 218, 381
Albani, Dame Emma, 62, 98-9
Albert Herring, 289, 307
Alexandra Theatre, Hull, 68, 359
Alfano, Franco, 91-2, 102, 235, 329-30, 363
Allen, Lillian Stiles, 208, 228
Allen, Pauline, 334
Allin, Norman, 121, 208, 370
Amelia, *Un Ballo in Maschera*, 49, 58, 97, 142, 144, 187, 196-7, 314, 317, 365-6, 369
Amonasro, *Aida*, 68, 94, 97, 100, 116, 136, 157, 197, 199, 232, 365, 366
Anderson, Ande, 324
Andrea Chenier, 18
Andresen, Ivar, 116
Andrews, Eamonn, 275, 277, 327
Andrews Mildred, 257
Anello del Nibelungo, L', 82
Angelis, Nazzareno De, 89, 115
Ansseau, Fernand, 116
Antonia, *The Tales of Hoffmann*, 67, 356, 357
Archibald, Phyllis, 19
Armistice Day, 42-3

Arratoon, Angela, 29, 320-1
Arroyo, Martina, 310
Ashton-in-Makerfield, 161, 181
Athenian, (Newspaper), 65
Attack on the Mill, The, 39-40
Austral, Florence, 178, 225
Australia, 41, 77, 132, 177-8, 181, 247, 327
Austria, 46, 98
Azucena, *Il Trovatore*, 19, 52, 95, 354–7, 365, 367

Bach, Johan Sebastian, 284, 377
Baillie, Dame Isobel, 208, 228, 302, 320, 373
Bainbridge, Elizabeth, 284
Baker, Dame Janet, 308, 312
Baker, George, 223, 293
Baker, Richard, 188
Balfe, Michael W., 40, 354, 357
Balfour, Margaret, 208
Ballo in Maschera, Un, 50, 97, 188, 196, 227, 270, 314, 317, 359, 365-6, 369
Bampton, Rose, 199, 381
Barbirolli, Lady Evelyn, 308, 312
Barbirolli, Sir John, 26, 157, 198, 213, 238, 265, 276
Barker, John, 324
Barrie, Sir James, 277
Barron, Florence, 38
Bassi, Anna Massetti, 177
Bath, Hubert, 186
Battaglia, Franco, 95, 161, 171, 365
Baylis, Lillian, 186, 194
Bayreuth Festival, 116
Bayswater, London, 1, 27, 195, 249, 260, 297

BBC, 52, 76, 185, 216
Beacon, Sally, 260, 306
Beecham, Sir Thomas, 9, 70, 166, 171, 173, 184, 186, 191, 194, 200, 208, 212, 226, 232, 262, 265, 276, 313, 317, 319, 347-8, 350, 359-60, 370
Beer, Sidney, 202
Beethoven, Ludwig van, 103, 109, 177, 190, 206, 227, 233, 264, 295, 357-8
Beethoven's Ninth Symphony, 227, 264
Beggar's Opera, The, 224
Belfast, 121, 166, 174
Bellezza, Vincenzo, 113, 122-3, 130, 135, 150, 156-7, 276
Benthall, Michael, 235
Benton, Joseph, 246-7, 250, 269, 276
Bergamaschi, Ettore, 103
Bergonzi, Carlo, 310, 382
Berlin, 93, 116, 154, 241
Berlioz, Hector, 34-5, 61, 228
Bernardi, Oreste de, 97, 365
Berry, Noreen, 284
Besalla, Eugene, 97, 365
Beverley Sisters, 319
Bevin, Teleri, 83-4
Bilk, Acker, 273, 319
Birmingham, 42, 165-6, 174, 188, 236, 238, 241, 368
Birmingham Post, 125, 187
Blake, William, 12
Blois, Colonel, 113, 125, 154, 155-7, 170
Blunden, Jack, 191, 333
Bohème, La, 35, 42, 47, 64, 79, 92, 212, 353, 359
Bohemian Girl, The, 33, 39-40, 354, 357
Boland, William, 41, 57, 65, 68, 70
Bolivar, Simon, 158
Bonelli, Richard, 145, 265, 366-7

Borgioli, Dino, 177, 179, 186, 196-7, 213, 221, 369, 371
Borough Theatre, Stratford, 61
Boult, Sir Adrian, 177, 220, 228, 233
Bournemouth, 40, 173-4, 220
Bournemouth Symphony Orchestra, 220
Bowdon, Alice, 21
Brangwyn Hall, 228
Braunschweig, 93, 95
Brazil, 109
Breathy Tone, 375
Bremer, 93
Breslau, 93, 96
Brighton, 69, 186
Bristol, 16-17, 19, 21, 24, 26, 35, 57, 98-9, 116, 124, 133, 177, 181, 196, 220, 224
Bristol Evening News, 57, 98
British Institute of Recorded Sound, 288
British National Opera Company, 119, 241, 358
Britten, Sir Benjamin, 234, 307
Britton, Paul, 275
Broad, Ada, 171, 220-1, 224
Broad, Albert Richards (see also Plum), 46-7, 51, 71, 78, 86, 106, 110, 112, 127, 130, 136, 163, 200, 204, 221-2, 307, 338, 350, 354-8
Brown, John, 324
Brownlee, John, 157, 181, 196, 371, 381
Brunazzi, Lina, 161
Brünnhilde, *The Ring* cycle, 49, 52-3, 62, 66, 68, 90, 105, 144, 152, 156, 175-6, 180, 183, 188, 191, 194-5, 209, 279, 284, 305, 355, 367
Brunskill, Muriel, 177, 195, 208, 228, 232
Bruscantini, Sesto, 305
Brusino, 105, 145, 159, 167-8, 171-2, 174, 180, 214-5, 218, 220
Bryn-Jones, Delme, 324
Buades, 265

386   Dame Eva Turner A Life on the High Cs

Buenos Aires, 5, 107-8, 113, 235
Burck, Lotte, 183
Busch, Fritz, 177, 183
Butt, Dame Clara, 21, 26
Butterfly, *Madama Butterfly*, 3-8, 36, 45-6, 49, 54, 61-2, 64-6, 68-9, 71, 73, 78, 88, 90-2, 123, 175, 212, 324, 348, 352, 355-7, 359

Caballé, Montserrat, 314
Cadbury, George, 76
Calaf, *Turandot*, 91, 102, 113, 122-3, 161, 199, 209, 238, 291, 323, 331, 363-4, 367
Callas, Maria, 91
Campion, Miss Kate, 5
Caniglia, Maria, 210, 212
Capuano, Maestro, 116-8
Caracas, 158-9
Carlisle, 39, 45
Carmen, 25, 39, 64, 240, 320, 352-6
Carron, Arthur, 233
Carton, Arthur, 46, 320
Carton, Ida, 40, 46
Caruso, Enrico, 18, 76, 80, 280, 365
Castagna, Bruna, 265
Catalani, Alfredo, 107, 175
Catley, Gwen, 302
Cattaneo, Minghini, 157, 265
Cavalleria Rusticana, 35-6, 42, 48, 64, 94, 115, 130, 141, 224, 233, 344, 353, 356, 358, 365, 367
Cavaradossi, *Tosca*, 7, 280, 365
Cenerentola, 179
Chabrier, Emmanuel, 226
Chant Fatale, Le, 66
Chaplin, Charlie, 75
Chicago Civic Opera, 105, 130, 139-41, 143, 148, 150, 152-4, 246, 249, 342
Chicago Daily Journal, 144

Chicago Daily Tribune, 152
Chicago Evening Post, 142, 144
Chitty, Stella, 324
Christie, Dame Agatha, 1
Christie, Nan, 296
Christie, Sir George and Mary, 323
Cigna, Gina, 197-8, 246
Cimarosa, Domenico, 65
Cio Cio San, *Madama Butterfly*, 4
Clandestine Marriage, The, 65
Coates, Albert, 167, 186, 194-5, 200-1, 205, 208, 262
Coates, Edith, 235, 324
Cobelli, 235
Coleman, Judy Bounds, 252, 257, 270
Coliseum, 29, 40, 61, 302, 313, 320, 322, 374
Collegiate Theatre, 289
Colman, Ronald, 205
Cologne, 241
Colomba, 23-5
Colón, 107-9, 113, 159
Colston Hall, 17, 24, 196
Columbia Graphophone Company, 60, 128
Columbia Records, 181, 347
Concorde, 2, 3, 9
Contessa, La, 141, 142, 144-5, 367
Cook, Ida, 113, 115, 130, 320
Cooper, Anna, 327
Cooper, Emil, 99-100
Cooper, Gladys, 171
Cooper, Sir Edward, 26
Copenhagen, 145, 149
Corder, Frederick, 24, 35
Cortol, 177
Coulston, Sydney, 312
Covent Garden, 5, 9, 19, 25, 29, 40-1, 45-7, 54-5, 62-6, 68, 70-2, 78, 105, 113, 115–7, 119,

Index 387

122, 124-8, 130-1, 133-7, 139, 141, 147-9, 153-8, 170-1, 184-6, 188-9, 194, 197, 199-202, 208, 211-3, 226, 234-7, 239, 241-2, 244, 246-7, 249, 277-9, 281, 283, 288, 305-6, 311, 313, 317, 320-2, 329-30, 332, 342-3, 348-9, 359-60, 365, 369, 370, 381, 383
Covent Garden Syndicate, 116, 170
Craig, Charles, 63, 291, 324, 327
Cricket on the Hearth, The, 25, 40
Crighton, Ronald, 195
Cross, Joan, 26, 218, 220, 241, 247, 252, 259, 302, 374

Daily Dispatch, 134
Daily Mail, 41, 56, 65, 103, 116, 124, 130, 137, 150
Daily Sketch, 124, 126, 221
Daily Telegraph, 66, 122, 149, 197, 212
Dallas, 259, 262
Daly's Theatre, 35
Damnation of Faust, The, 34-5
Daniani, 100
Dankworth, John, 273
Dante and Beatrice, 64
Darmstadt, 241
David, Catherine, 17, 41, 62, 64-5, 284, 342, 356
David Garrick, 64, 65, 356
Davies, Ben, 19, 25, 63
Davis, Sir Colin, 328, 343-4
Davis Theatre, Croydon, 237
Delius, Frederick, 317
Denmark, 116
Denmark, King and Queen of, 147
Desert Island Discs, 39, 47, 68, 71, 87, 108, 225, 265-6, 373
Desmond, Astra, 121, 191, 208, 228
Destinn, Emmy, 18, 360

Devonshire Private Hospital, The, 341
Dickie, Murray, 262
Dickson, Muriel, 293
Dido and Aeneas, 262-3
Domingo, Placido, 285, 319, 327, 331, 339
Don Carlos, 101, 107, 237, 319
Donegan, Lonnie, 273
Don Giovanni, *Don Giovanni*, 33, 196, 324, 353, 377
Donna Anna, *Don Giovanni*, 196, 353, 377
Dream of Gerontius, 224
Dresden, 93, 119, 266
Dresden Opera, 116
Drogheda, Earl of, 324
Drury Lane Theatre, 34
Dublin, 42-4, 62, 166, 174, 232
Duchess of Kent, 312
Duchess of York, 137
Duke of Kent, 181, 344
Dundee, 41, 164-5, 173

Eadie, Noel, 241
Eames, Emma, 152
Easton, Florence, 113
Easton, Robert, 208, 296
Edgar, 90
Edinburgh, 31, 35, 41, 50-2, 105, 165, 173, 191, 194, 281, 352, 354, 356-8
Edinburgh Festival, 281
Edwards, Anne, 284
Elder Dempster Line, 117
Elena, *Mefistofile*, 46, 115
Elgar, Sir Edward, 76, 224, 226
Elias, Lorna, 279
Elijah, Mendelssohn, 223, 241, 307
Elisabeth, *Tannhäuser*, 2, 41, 49, 50, 65-6, 105, 150, 152-3, 156, 178, 181-2, 197, 202,

211, 222, 224, 265, 287, 348-9, 367
Elliot, Vicky, 275
Elsa, *Lohengrin*, 49, 54, 56, 66, 68, 105, 168, 298, 348-9, 356
Emanuel, Dawin, 46, 251, 253, 259
Empire Stadium, Wembley, 237
English Nation Opera, 303
English Opera Society, 208
Ernani, 32, 101, 107
Evans, Sir Geraint, 323-4, 327, 330, 344
Eva Pogner, *Die Meistersinger,* 57
Evening News, 16, 57, 98, 101, 126-7, 153, 199
Evening Standard, 64, 124-5, 303-5, 343
Evening Standard Award, 304

Fabroni, 172
Fagoada, Isadora, 183
Falstaff, 79, 305, 324
Fanciulla del West, La, 90, 99-100, 280
Faust, 33-5, 61-2, 64, 69, 246, 352-7
Faverò, Mafaldo, 198, 211
Fear, Arthur, 186, 369, 370
Fergosi, Guilio, 365
Ferone, 140, 150, 168, 172
Ferrier, Kathleen, 230, 265, 279
Fidelio, *Fidelio*, 3, 49, 69, 70-1, 73-4, 78, 88, 103, 106, 108-9, 113, 142, 155-6, 179, 196, 210, 233, 235, 357-8
Fields, Gracie, 179, 211-3, 218, 224, 277
Figaro, *Le Nozze di Figaro*, 33, 72-3, 141-2, 145, 306, 357, 367
First Lady, *The Magic Flute*, 39-40
Flagstad, Kirsten, 194, 201, 209-10, 237, 262-3, 276-7, 380
Fledermaus, Die, 303
Fleta, Miguel, 91, 107, 363
Florence, Evangeline, 25

Fluck, Alan, 324
Fonteyn, Margot, 212
Formichi, Cesare, 171, 197, 265, 366
Forza del Destino, La, 141, 147, 152
Foster, Hebden, 19, 41
Francesca di Rimini, 134, 291
Franci, Benvenuto, 108, 109
Frankfurt, 93, 95, 155-6, 161
Freeman's Journal, 42, 43
Freia, *Die Rheingold*, 82, 89-90
Freischütz, Der, 8-9, 188, 368-9
Fricka, *The Ring* cycle, 66, 68, 156, 263, 284, 367
Friends of English National Opera, 115, 320-1
Furmedge, Edith, 201
Furtwängler, Wilhelm, 274
Fury, Billy, 273

Gaiety Theatre, Dublin, 42-3, 232
Galli-Curci, Amelita, 80, 144
Gardner, Ava, 310
Garrick Theatre, 63
Garrotto, 209, 367
Genii, *The Magic Flute*, 38, 352
Genoa, 33, 103, 107, 141, 152, 175
Germany, 34, 69, 77, 93, 95-6, 98, 103, 105, 109, 134, 153, 155, 157-8, 162, 200, 214, 241, 270, 278
Gershwin, George, 76
Gibson, Sir Alexander, 305
Gielgud, Sir John, 324
Gigli, Beniamino, 80, 97, 178, 209-10, 213, 277, 300, 367
Gilbert and Sullivan, 293
Gioconda, La, 101-3, 136, 350
Girl of the Golden West, The, 339

Index   389

Giulietta, *Tales of Hoffmann*, 42,-3, 65-6, 353
Giurana, 179
Glasgow, 50-3, 69-70, 101, 124-5, 157, 164-5, 173, 191, 194, 200, 220, 224, 227, 236, 304-5, 358
Glasgow News, 157
Glasgow Weekly Herald, 69
Globe, 64
Gloucestershire, 37
Gluck, Christopher, 237, 263
Glyndebourne, 281, 301, 307, 323
Gobbi, Tito, 321, 323-4, 327
Golders Green Crematorium, 342
Goldsack, Jessie, Lady Wood, 225, 233, 373
Goodall, Sir Reginald, 303-4, 312
Goossens, Sir Eugene, 66, 186
Götterdämmerung, 79, 167, 203, 205, 224
Greenock, 48, 58-9, 358-9
Greenway, Lauder, 283, 381-2
Grove, Sir George, 34
Grove, Olive, 223, 293-4, 298
Guardian, 5, 19, 33, 38, 54, 68, 124, 349
Gui, Vittorio, 80, 89, 156, 383
Gurney, Ivor, 37
Guy, Maureen, 284

Hackett, Charles, 210
Hackett, Karleton, 142, 144
Hafgren, Lily, 90
Haley, Bill, 273
Hamburg, 93, 215
Handel, G F, 284, 312, 377
Hansel and Gretel, 35, 310
Harewood, Lord George, 235, 303, 322
Harper, Heather, 270, 324
Harty, Sir Hamilton, 25, 177, 219
Harwood, Elizabeth, 279

Hay, Patricia, 287
Hedmont, E C, 40, 46
Hedmont, Maria, née Kacerovsky, 46
Heldy, Fanny, 116
Hemmings, Peter, 305
Hemsley, Thomas, 262
Henderson, Roy, 208, 227-8, 282, 320, 374
Herodias, *Salome*, 263
Hersee, Rose, 33, 72-3
Hill, Carmen, 25
Hill, Ina, 19, 133
Hinge and Bracket, 324, 327-8
Hippodrome, London, 181, 284
His Majesty's Theatre, Aberdeen, 287
Hitchen, Booth, 68, 370
Hitler, 86, 214
Holmberg Hall, 254, 281, 285
Holt, Harold, 131, 164-5, 167, 172, 180-1, 184-5, 189, 191, 195, 200, 202, 204, 211, 223-4, 237
Hooty Tone, 375
Hotter, Hans, 284
Howard, Ann, 284
Huddersfield, 61, 119, 197, 233
Huddersfield Choral Society, 197, 233
Huddersfield Town Hall, 197
Hull, 30, 40, 55-7, 68, 153
Hull Daily Mail, 56
Hull Evening News, 153
Humperdinck, Engelbert, 35
Hunter, Rita, 275, 321
Hurry, Leslie, 235, 238, 279
Hutchings, Elizabeth, 84

Ibbs and Tillett, 60, 61, 180, 222
Imperial League of Opera, 186, 201, 368, 370
Irving, Sir Henry, 34

Isaacs, Jeremy, 343
Isabeau, 150-2, 154-6, 159, 324
Isolde, *Tristan and Isolde*, 68
Italian Institute, 323
Italy, 28, 50, 69, 71-2, 75, 77-9, 82, 85-7, 90, 92, 98, 101, 103, 106-7, 109, 113, 115-6, 119, 122, 127, 130, 139, 141-2, 145, 149, 151, 153-4, 157-9, 161, 168, 175, 177, 181, 183, 196-7, 204, 211, 214, 216-8, 221, 227, 234-5, 240, 246, 264, 269-70, 274, 276, 278, 300-1, 310, 327-8, 347, 350, 361, 363, 365, 382
Ivens, George Washington, 19, 20, 276
Iwa, Princess, 53, 171

Japan, 4, 7, 8, 16, 285
Jarred, Mary, 208, 228, 230, 374
Jeanette, *Le Chant Fatale*, 66
Jeanne D'Arc, 172
Jeannie Deans, 35
Jeritza, Maria, 113, 124-5, 134, 381
Jewels of the Madonna, 64, 280
Johnson, Herbert M, 142, 149-50, 203-4
Jones, Dame Gwyneth, 86, 284, 327–30, 334, 336, 341, 344
Jones, Keith, 13
Jones, Parry, 64, 182, 197, 208, 228, 232-3
June, Ava, 275
Jung, Carl, 22

Kabanicha, *Kat'a Kabanova*, 263
Kalter, Sabine, 196-7
Karlsruhe, 93, 270
Kassel, 93
Kate Pinkerton, *Madama Butterfly*, 4, 36
Kathleen Ferrier Scholarship, 279
Kavanagh, J W, 64, 72
Kempe, Rudolf, 279
Kennedy, John F, 277

King and Queen of Denmark, 147
King George V, 25, 178
Kingsley, Margaret, 57, 284
King's Theatre, Greenock, 48, 58, 359
King's Theatre, Hammersmith, 88
Kipnis, Alexander, 152, 195, 209, 367
Knappertsbush, Hans, 264
Koanga, 317
Koerner, Zoe (also known as Corner), 25
Kopp, Leo, 209, 367
Kostelnička, Jenufa, 263
Kozub, Ernst, 284
Kundry, *Parsifal*, 179-80, 263-4, 276, 306
Kurwenal, *Parsifal*, 201, 370

Labette, Dora (also known as Lisa Perli), 241, 302
Lady Macbeth, *Macbeth*, 285, 301
L'Africana, 203-4, 209
Laine, Cleo, 273
Lake Lugano, 145, 196, 219
Lakin, Roderick, 325
Lambert, Constant, 211, 233, 235, 238, 318
Lamperti, Francsco, 7, 377
Lancashire, 8, 10-2, 62, 82, 116, 119, 121, 124-7, 134, 136-7, 158, 173, 191, 197, 212-3, 221, 228, 230-1, 261, 266, 373
Langdon, Michael, 284
Langford, Audrey, 310
Lappas, Ulysses, 142-4, 366
Lark, Kingsley, 57
La Scala, 342
Las Palmas, 116-7, 310-1, 314
Laurenti, 115
Lazaro, Hipolito, 150-1
Lazzari, Sylvio, 145, 367
Leeds, 39, 115, 241, 308, 369

Index   391

Leeds National Musician's Platform, 308
Lefevre, Maureen, 334, 341
Legge, Walter, 208, 211, 232, 349
Lehman, Lotte, 116
Leicester, 35, 166, 174, 225, 236-7
Leider, Frida, 72, 116, 144, 152-4, 156, 288, 367
Leonora, *Il Trovatore*, 19, 49, 52, 65-6, 92-3, 95, 103, 119, 133, 142, 354-8, 365, 367, 377
Leonore, *Fidelio*, 3, 49, 74, 88, 96, 355, 357
Levi, Edgardo, 16, 25, 39, 121, 132-3
Levin, Bernard, 242
Lewis, Richard, 308
Licette, Miriam, 186, 321
Lindi, Aroldo, 94, 100-1, 122-3
Littleton, Humphrey, 273
Liu, *Turandot*, 91, 113, 122-3, 150, 161, 198, 209, 211, 362-4, 367
Liverpool, 117, 125, 166-8, 172, 174, 188, 200, 220, 227, 236, 369
Lloyd, Roderick, 232
Lohengrin, 49, 61, 64, 158-9, 171, 298, 348-9, 355-6, 358
Loki, Loge, *The Ring* cycle, 68
Lola, *Cavalleria Rusticano*, 64, 365, 367
London Broadcasting Radio, 85
London, George, 264
London Lyceum Theatre, 34
London Opera Centre, 197, 282-3, 288, 293, 305, 380
London Philharmonic, 226, 232, 237
London Symphony Orchestra, 22, 148, 177, 194, 237, 372
Lord Mayor of Westminster, The, 344
Loreley, 107
Louise, 47, 115, 134, 260
Luccioni, José, 211
Luonnotar, 208

Macfarren, George Alexander, 35
MacGregor, Sue, 85, 337-8, 339
Mackenzie, Sir Alexander Campbell, 23, 25-6, 35
Mackerras, Sir Charles, 324
Macklin, Hughes, 40, 121
Macmillan, Harold, 273, 277
Madama Butterfly, 3-5, 7, 36, 69, 90-2, 324
Magdalena, *Die Meistersinger*, 318, 352, 355-6
Magic Flute, The, 38-40, 352
Mailänder Opern Stagione, Der, 93
Maine, Basil, 126
Maison, Rene, 209, 367
Malandri, Antonio, 109
Malta, 32-4
Manchester, 5, 16, 19, 34-5, 38, 54, 98, 124-5, 165-7, 173, 195, 236, 241, 369
Manchester Guardian, 5, 19, 38, 54, 124
Mannheim, 93
Manoel Theatre, Malta, 33
Manon Lescaut, 92, 280, 365
Manski, Dorothee, 209, 367
Manzoni's Requiem, 177
Maranzoni, Maestro, 209, 367
Marguerita, *Faust*, 62
Marini, Luigi, 115
Marinuzzi, Gino, 103, 108-9, 113, 175, 178
Maritana, 38, 42, 57, 63, 352-3, 356
Mark, King, 370
Markova, Dame Alicia, 324, 327
Marriage of Figaro, The, 33, 306, 357
Martin, Riccardo, 246
Martinelli, Giovanni, 134, 197-9, 201, 203, 209, 264-5, 276-7, 279, 283, 286, 288-91, 300, 320, 329, 331, 350, 360, 365, 367, 381-3
Mascagni, Pietro, 43, 64, 151-2, 154-6, 324, 344, 353, 356, 358

Masini, Galliano, 209, 218, 265, 367
Masked Ball, The, 49, 58, 197, 220, 357, 369
Mason, Edith, 145, 367, 382
Mastersingers, The, 66, 260, 355
Masterson, Valerie, 324
Matrimonio Segreto, Il, 65
Mayer, Sir Robert, 324
May, Marius, 296
Mazzonis, Barone Paolo, 179
McCampbell, C, 68
McCormack, John, 191, 205, 232
McCrorie, Peter, 297, 301, 312, 317, 322, 340
McCunn, Hamish, 35, 360
McGee, Bill, 324
McKellar, Kenneth, 305
McLaughlin, Marie, 321
Mefistofele, 115
Meistersinger, Die, 50, 265, 318, 340
Melandri, Antonio, 108, 147
Melba, Dame Nellie, 46-7, 75, 126, 178, 226, 316, 359
Melchior, Lauritz, 116, 171, 194, 265, 382
Menuhin, Yehudi, 309
Mephistopheles, 99
Mercedes, *Carmen*, 39, 352-3
Merli, Francesco, 113, 147, 150, 157, 181, 265
Mermaid Theatre, 262
Messiah, 224, 230, 241, 377
Metropolitan Opera House, 1, 141, 202-3, 260, 264, 283, 293, 342
Micaela, *Carmen*, 39
Midgley, Marierra, 275
Midgley, Walter, 238, 276
Mignon, 58, 268, 353-4, 356-8
Milan, 5, 71-2, 75, 78-9, 85, 89-90, 93, 101-3, 106, 108-9, 113, 116, 119, 140-1, 147, 149-50, 153, 155, 157-8, 167-8, 172, 174-5, 179-80, 183, 217, 260, 320, 347-8, 360, 365, 368
Milanese Opera Company, The, 93
Milanov, Zinca, 233, 265, 382
Miles, Lady Josephine, 327
Miles, Lord Bernhard, 262-3, 324, 327
Mimi, *La Bohème*, 43, 359, 365
Minnie, *La Fanciulla del West*, 99-101, 329
Minns, Flora, 233
Minton, Yvonne, 284
Miracle, The (*The Story Of Antoine*), 52, 354
Miranda, Beatrice, 40-1, 354
Miranda, Lalla, 41
Missa Solemnis, 177
Mödl, Martha, 264
Molajoli, Maestro, 101
Montagnana, Padua, 134, 264
Monte, Albertina dal, 84, 95, 100, 103, 107, 113
Montesanto, Luigi, 97, 365-7
Monthly Musical Record, 157
Montreal, 91-2, 285
Montreal Times, 91, 285
Moor, Charles, 71, 105-7, 109-10, 145, 154-5, 179, 198, 213, 288
Moore, Gerald and Enid, 323
Morgan, Katherine, 310, 341-42, 345
Morning Advertiser, 64
Moseley, Carlos, 269
Mozart, Wolfgang Amadeus, 265, 284, 295, 319, 324, 352-3, 357
Mrs Smith, *David Garrick*, 65, 179, 356
Munich, 241
Musetta, *La Bohème*, 42-3, 64-6, 68, 353
Musical Times, 24-5, 29, 70-1, 139
Music and Musicians, 278
Musicians' Benevolent Fund, 191, 296, 342
Mussolini, 78-9, 85, 91, 155, 217, 227, 361

Muzio, Claudia, 92, 105, 107-9, 141, 154, 194, 246, 265, 300, 319-20, 365,-7

Nagasaki, 91
Naples, 33, 110, 112, 141, 149, 161, 300-1, 369
Nash, Heddle, 208, 228, 321
National Confederation of Gramophone Societies, 279
Nedda, *Pagliaci*, 54
Newcastle, 166, 174
Newell, Graham, 324-5
New Mirandola Theatre, 141
New Orleans, 273
Newton, Ivor, 196, 222
New York Philharmonic, 269, 319
New York Times, 283, 381
Nicklaus, *Tales of Hoffmann*, 64, 354-5, 357
Nilsson, Birgit, 279, 383
Nilsson, Christine, 335
Noble, Dennis, 199, 232
Noorden, Alfred van, 35-6, 63-4
Noorden, Walter van, 19, 35-6, 45
Nordisa, 24
Norman, Barry, 319
North America, 79
Northern College of Music, 312, 342
Nottingham, 39, 174, 235
Novello, Ivor, 134
Nozze di Figaro, Le, 141, 142, 145, 367
Nürnberg, 93-4

Oberon, 21, 136, 220, 370
Observer, 45, 63, 125, 360
Oklahoma, 230, 243, 246-7, 249, 251-2, 254, 256, 258-61, 263-5, 268-72, 275-6, 281, 285, 289, 291, 312, 320, 322

Oklahoma City Orchestra, 254
Oklahoma University, 246-7, 268-70, 281, 285
Oldham, 10, 12, 15-6, 54, 125, 127, 167, 191, 212-3, 218, 224, 233, 312, 327, 335, 345
Oldham Chronicle, 312
Olszewska, Maria, 154, 367
Olympic Games, 22, 77, 237
O'Neil, Dennis, 324, 344
Opera Comique, Paris, 116
Orchestra of the Royal Opera House, 324
Orfeo, 263
Orlando, 312
Ortrud, *Lohengrin*, 56, 263, 355, 358
Otello, 79, 365, 382

Packer, Ruth, 323, 330
Pagliacci, 64, 79, 130, 134, 204
Palace Court, 2-3, 8, 12, 195, 236, 249, 287, 297, 300, 306, 318, 323, 330, 333, 340
Palermo, 33, 183, 227
Palmyra, *Koanga*, 317
Pampanini, Rosetta, 122-3, 171
Panizza, Ettore, 5, 71, 78, 80, 89, 92, 105, 147, 210
Papagena, *The Magic Flute*, 36
Parenti, Mario, 103
Parepa, Euphrosyne or Eufrasina, 31-4, 72
Paris, 77, 157, 169, 171-2, 177, 189, 215–7, 240, 368
Paris Opera, 41, 116
Parkinson, Michael, 319
Parr, Gladys, Glad, 5, 11, 27, 29-30, 38-9, 47, 51-2, 57-8, 64, 68, 87, 121, 173, 186, 216, 222-3, 228, 234, 246, 265, 275, 287, 305, 307, 318, 339, 352-8
Parsifal, 170, 180, 227, 264, 276
Pasero, Tancredi, 108
Passadoro, 181

Patti, Adelina, 63, 254
Payne, Patricia, 275
Perez Galdos Theatre, 116-7
Perli, 241
Perry, John, 66
Pertile, Aureliano, 103, 116, 130, 134, 264-5
Peter Grimes, 234
Philharmonic Orchestra, 164, 167, 174, 186, 202, 226, 233, 237, 269
Phillips, H B, 61, 71
Picture Post, 228
Pinker, Sir George, 311
Pinza, Ezio, 108-9, 157, 210, 213, 260
Pisa, 115
Pitt, Percy, 71, 127, 359
Pleeth, William, 308
Plomley, Roy, 39, 63, 69, 226-7, 265-6, 319-20
Plum, See also Albert Richards Broad, 46-7, 49, 55, 71-2, 77-8, 82, 87-8, 90, 98-9, 106, 125, 139, 141, 145, 153-4, 159, 162-3, 168, 171, 175, 177-82, 186, 200, 202-5, 208-12, 214, 216-8, 220-1, 223-4, 228, 245-6, 299
Plymouth, 42, 205, 210
Portugal, 99-101, 105
Powell, Lionel, 131-2, 148, 159
Presley, Elvis, 273
Prince Albert, 260
Prince Arthur of Connaught, 23-4
Princess Alexandra Hall, 296
Princess Alice, 76
Princess Helena Victoria, 131, 134
Princess Margaret, 277
Princess Marina, 181
Princes Theatre, Bristol, 17
Pritchard, Sir John, 323
Proctor-Gregg, Humphrey, 262
Promenade Concerts, 76, 182, 205, 222, 224, 227, 233, 260, 317, 371

Pro Patria, 48
Puccini, 4, 5-7, 35, 79, 90-2, 102, 111, 113, 122, 124, 126, 135, 149-50, 210, 220-1, 238, 242, 280, 319, 324, 329-30, 349, 352-3, 355-7, 361, 363-5
Purcell, Henry, 262, 308, 377

Queen Elizabeth Hall, 326
Queen Elizabeth II, 284
Queen Elizabeth the Queen Mother, 326
Queen Mary, 25, 178, 203-4
Queen of Italy, 183
Queen's Hall, 26, 77, 164-7, 172, 174, 181, 190, 194-5, 205, 222, 224, 265, 371, 374
Queen Victoria, 15, 35, 41, 75
Quilter, Roger, 231

Rachmaninoff, Sergei, 76, 181, 205-6, 226, 230, 373
Radames, *Aida*, 81, 94, 97, 100, 103, 134, 143, 157, 197, 232, 276, 357, 365-7
Radio Four, 85
Raisa, Rosa, 91, 134, 141, 154, 171, 363
Rankl, Karl, 232, 237
Rank Organisation, 273
Rasponi, Lanfranco, 84
Raybould, Clarence, 194
Records and Recording Magazine, 279
Reeves, Wynn, 212
Referee, 136, 244
Regent's Theatre, Chemlsford, 235
Rendle, Frank, 63, 66
Rentur, 203
Resurrection, Tolstoy, 235
Rheingold, Das, 89, 227
Rhinegold, The, 68
Richards, Cliff, 273
Ridyard, Anne, 2-3, 228-9, 231, 233, 236, 245,

Index 395

249, 254, 261, 263, 275, 280, 287, 300-1, 306-7, 312, 322, 331, 333-4, 342
Rimsky Korsakov, 108
Ring cycle, The, 82, 92, 156, 179, 182-3, 274
Rio de Janeiro, 3, 79, 108
Robertson, James, 42, 293, 298
Robinson, Stanford, 225, 238, 268
Robson, Elizabeth, 327, 334
Rome, 33, 97, 106, 152, 154-6, 159, 175, 289, 320, 366, 369
Romeo and Juliet, 47, 226
Rome Opera House, 320
Ronald, Landon, 164, 195, 205, 242
Rootham, Daniel, 21, 26
Rosa, The Second Mrs, 34, 36
Rose Bowl Pasadena, 205
Rose, Carl August Nicholas, 31
Roselle, 178
Rosenkavalier, Der, 323
Rosenthal, Harold, 240-1, 320, 322
Rossini, 178, 268, 319, 368
Routledge, Patricia, 324, 327
Royal Academy of Music, 21-4, 27, 29, 35, 38, 40, 69, 75, 98, 137, 270, 275, 278, 281, 285, 317, 327, 342, 344, 371
Royal Albert Hall, 178, 191, 205, 224-6, 230, 237, 260, 317
Royal Ballet, 318
Royal Carl Rosa Opera, 17, 26, 30, 34, 40, 47, 49, 58, 63, 122, 169, 359
Royal College of Music, 22, 330
Royal Festival Hall, 5, 8, 28
Royal Lyceum Theatre, Edinburgh, 51, 352
Royal National Eisteddfod, 236
Royal Northern College of Music, 312
Royal Opera House, 9, 29, 49, 68, 102, 113, 117, 128, 154, 183-4, 188, 198, 212-3, 235, 237, 278-81, 284-5, 291, 309-11, 320, 323-4, 326, 329-30, 342, 344, 383
Royal Over-Seas League's Music Festival, 296
Royal Over-Seas League, The, 294, 296, 325-6
Royal Philharmonic Society, 279
Royal Scottish Academy of Music, 293
Royal Society of Medicine, 311
Rubenfeld, Victoria, 260
Russian Revolution, 75

Sadler's Wells, 234, 241, 303
Salfi, Francesco, 197
Salvation Army, 296
Salvatore, *Allegra*, 183, 382
Samson and Delilah, 61, 64, 259, 358
San Carlo, 110, 112, 115, 147, 161, 300
Santley, Sir Charles, 33, 73
Santuzza, *Cavalleria Rusticana*, 42-3, 58, 61, 64, 66, 68, 73, 93, 95-6, 115, 139, 142, 144, 285, 353-4, 356, 358, 365, 367
Sao Luis Theatre, 99
São Paolo, 108
Sargent, Sir Malcolm, 197, 224-5, 232, 237
Sassoon, Siegfried, 37
Scala, La, Milan, 71-2, 89, 93, 103, 360, 365
Scala Theatre, The, 5, 70-1, 79, 85, 90
Scandiani, Maestro, 80
Schipa, Tito, 107-8
Scholte, Dudley, 258
Schorr, Friedrich, 265
Schubert, Franz, 265, 319
Scotsman, 52, 68, 191, 352
Scottish National Opera, 41
Scottish Opera, 41, 287, 304-5, 333
Seager, Gladys, 65
Seligman, Sybil, 7
Serafin, Tullio, 320
Serban, Andre, 332

Serenade to Music, 205-6, 228, 319, 348, 372-3
Sereno, Bianca, 100
Shaftesbury Theatre, 63
Shakespeare, William, 79, 207, 242, 345
Sharpless, *Madama Butterfly*, 68
Sheffield, 39, 61, 124, 166, 173, 195
Sheridan, Margarita, also known as Peggy, 232
Shuard, Amy, 246, 260-1, 268, 275-6, 279, 284, 305-6, 320
Sibelius, 208
Siebel, *Faust*, 64, 352-7
Siegfried, 180, 188, 191, 194, 204, 233, 268-70
Siegfried, *The Ring* cycle, 66, 69, 115, 183, 189, 195
Sieglinde, *Die Walküre*, 82, 89-90, 141-2, 144, 152, 155-7, 179, 182-3, 203, 209, 279, 284, 367
Siegmund, *Die Walküre*, 183, 209, 279, 284, 367
Silken Ladder, The, 319
Simon Boccanegra, 210
Slobodskaya, Oda, 186, 232, 316
Snowden, Ethel, 134
Snowman, Daniel, 33, 48, 49
Solti, Sir Georg, 284
Somerville, Reginald, 121, 356
Sonderhausen Orchestra, 23
Sonnambula, La, 32-3
South American, 105, 108-9, 158
Southampton, 202, 204
South Pacific, 260
Stage Newspaper, The, 289
Standish, 10, 167, 190, 345
St Andrew's Hall, 165, 173, 296
Star, 68, 125, 222, 225, 283, 381

Steele, Tommy, 273
Stefano, Giuseppe, 91
Stern, Isaac, 319
Stevens, Rise, 259
Stignani, Ebe, 197, 213, 265, 300, 319
St James Palace, 8
St Martin's Lane, 321
St Mary's Hospital, 333, 341
Stockholm, 22
Stockport, 233, 237
Strange, Audrey, 296, 320
Strauss, Richard, 179, 228, 232
Streets, John, 202, 282, 327
Suddaby, Elsie, 208, 228
Suez, Ina, 150
Suffragette Movement, 22
Sullivan, Sir Arthur, 31, 34, 206, 293, 371
Supervia, Conchita, 178
Susanna, *Le Nozze di Figaro*, 33, 64, 73, 145, 367
Susanna's Secret, 64
Susanne (Dame Gwyneth's daughter), 331
Sutherland, Dame Joan, 40, 278, 327, 360
Suzuki, *Madama Butterfly*, 4-5, 46, 68, 355-7
Swansea, 63, 211, 220, 227-8, 234
Swindon, Wiltshire, 29, 39-40
Switzerland, 105, 145, 215, 219

Taccani, Giuseppe, 97, 365
Tales of Hoffmann, The, 42, 45, 61, 64, 353-7
Tango, Egisto, 93-4, 96-7, 145
Tannhäuser, 2, 36, 41-2, 50, 61, 64-5, 150, 152, 168, 171, 178, 181, 195, 224, 227, 287, 344, 348-9, 353-6, 367
Tate, Jeffrey, 294
Tauber, Richard, 178
Taylor, Desmond Shaw, 48, 86, 168, 310

Tchaikovsky, 172, 226-7
Teatro Colón, 107-8, 113
Teatro Reale, Rome, 156
Teatro Regio, 79, 175, 182
Teatro Verdi, Pisa, 115
Tebaldi, Renata, 265-6
Te Kanawa, Dame Kiri, 327
Telegraph, 58, 64, 66, 122, 124, 149, 157, 197, 199, 212, 249, 251, 302
Tetrazzini, Luisa, 82
Teyte, Maggie, 217, 241, 246, 262, 316, 318
Thais, 68
Thais and Thalmae, 68
Theatre Royal, Glasgow, 52
Theatre Royal Lyceum, 34
Theatre Royal, Manchester, 19
The Page, *Tannhäuser*, 36, 41
Thérèse, *The Miracle*, 52, 354
Thill, Georges, 116
This is Your Life, 20, 47, 275, 327
Thomas, Goring, 35
Tibbett, Lawrence, 210
Times, The, 9, 66-8, 72, 134, 156, 171, 177, 199, 242, 285, 310
Tinsley, Pauline, 284, 324, 327
Titanic, The, 22, 24, 239
Titterton, Frank, 177, 208, 228, 374
Toini, Antonietta, 116, 118
Tokatyan, Armand, 209, 367
Tomasini, Alfredo, 197
Tomei, Giulio, 177, 213
Tomlinson, Sir John, 324
Tooley, Sir John, 324, 344
Toron, Marie Isabel, 310
Torri, Rosina, 113
Tosca, *Tosca*, 7, 57, 64, 68, 92-3, 95-6, 134, 136, 138, 147, 171, 265-6, 280, 313, 348-9, 365
Tosca, La, 7,
Toscanini, Arturo, 71-2, 75, 78-84, 86, 89-92, 105, 134, 154, 215, 226, 280, 329, 331, 361, 363
Toye, Frances, 178
Toye, Geoffrey, 165, 184-5
Traviata, 108-9, 194, 220, 300-1, 366
Tremolo, 375
Treviso, 103
Trial by Jury, 34
Trieste, 101-3
Tristan and Isolde, 64, 226-8, 309
Trouble, *Madama Butterfly*, 45-6
Trovatore, Il, 17-9, 35, 49-50, 52, 56-7, 61, 64-6, 73, 88, 92-3, 95, 117-8, 133, 142, 264, 290, 310, 314, 349, 354-7, 365-7, 377
Troxy Cinema House, 282
Troyens, Les, 167
Tsar Sultan, 108
Turandot, *Turandot*, 45, 91-2, 102-3, 105-7, 110-6, 119, 122-6, 130-1, 134-9, 141, 147, 149-50, 155, 157-8, 161, 178-9, 181-2, 184, 198-200, 203-4, 209-12, 218, 229, 235-9, 241-2, 246, 256, 262, 276, 279-81, 285-6, 291, 310, 319, 321, 324, 329-31, 333-4, 336, 343-4, 348-51, 362-4, 367, 377, 383
Turin, 35, 79, 92, 102-3, 106, 113, 175, 177, 179, 182-3, 196-7, 235, 365
Turin Conservatory, 92
Turner, Charles (father), 9-10, 13, 20, 23, 45, 101, 161-2, 186-7, 190, 223, 337, 345
Turner, Elizabeth, née Park (mother), 10-11, 15-16, 77, 90, 345
Turner, Florence (sister-in-law), 169-70, 177-8, 214, 225, 228, 233, 250, 307
Turner, John (uncle), 190
Turner, Norman (brother), 9-10, 13, 15, 18, 161, 164, 169, 177-8, 181, 202-3, 214, 220,

222-5, 228, 233, 250, 280, 307
Turridu, *Cavalleria Rusticana*, 43, 134
Twilight of the Gods, 228, 233
Typhoid fever, 260

Usher Hall, Edinburgh, 50, 165

Valkyrie, The, 49, 66, 157, 305, 355
Valois, Dame Ninette de, 318
Vaughan, Elizabeth, 7
Vaughan Williams, Ralph, 205-7, 319, 344, 348, 372, 374
V.E. Day, 232
Venus, *Tannhäuser*, 41-3, 54, 61, 65, 152-3, 353-4, 367
Verdi, 26, 32, 35, 57, 68, 79, 81-2, 92, 97, 115, 135, 141, 147, 157, 171, 177, 195-7, 227, 233-4, 237, 301, 319-20, 324, 344, 352, 354-7, 365, 368-9, 382
Verdi's Requiem, 26, 32, 35, 57, 68, 79, 81-2, 92, 97, 115, 135, 141, 147, 157, 171, 177, 188, 195-7, 227, 233-4, 237, 301, 319-20, 324, 344, 352, 354-77, 365, 368-9, 382
Verona, 103, 150-1, 172, 246
Vickers, Jon, 307, 309
Vienna, 72, 96-7, 116, 154, 157, 318, 365
Vienna Volksoper, 96
Villa Junesca, 86, 147, 166-7, 184, 196, 200, 219, 288, 337
Villa Marina, Douglas, Isle of Man, 236
Villi, Le, 90
Vliet, Genevieve, 256, 258, 320
Voltolini, Ismaele, 100-1, 118-9
Votto, Antonino, 218

Wagner, 17, 36, 68, 73, 152, 168, 194-5, 226-7, 264, 284, 287, 297, 303, 311, 336, 344, 349, 353-6, 358, 370, 372

Wakefield, Elsbeth, 64
Walker, Norman, 201, 222, 228
Walküre, Die, 53, 89, 141-2, 152, 154, 175, 180, 183, 194-5, 279, 367
Wally, La, 136, 175
Walton, William, 76, 126
Ward, David, 284
Warren, Eleanor, 308
Waterman, Dame Fanny, 308
Webber, Charles, 171-2, 174
Weber, Carl Maria von, 9, 21, 136, 370
Weber, Henry, 142, 145, 209, 366-7
Webster, Sir David, 237
Weekly Dispatch, 119, 128, 130
Welch, Elisabeth, 222, 265
Welitsch, Ljuba, 324
Wendon, Henry, 235
Werneth Council School, 15
Westminster Abbey, 344, 374
Weston-super-Mare, 40
White Bleating Tone, 375
Whitley Bay, 213
Widdop, Walter, 115-6, 188-9, 191, 194-5, 208, 216, 224, 370
Wiesbaden, 93, 241
Wigan Hippodrome, 284
Wigan Observer, 45
Wilde, Marty, 273
Wilkens, Anne, 312
Williams, Ben, 43, 265
Williams, Harold, 177, 195, 208
Williams, Mary Louise, 260
Williams, Tom, 235
Willis, Constance, 197, 369, 370-1
Wilson, Kirsty, née McCrorie, 307-8, 323
Wilson, Mary, 24, 178
Wimbledon Theatre, 49, 88

Index 399

Windgassen, 264, 279
Winkworth, Arthur, 99
Wobbly Tone, 375
Woman's Hour, 76
Woodland, Rae, 284
Wood, Sir Henry, 77, 180-2, 190, 195, 205-6, 208, 222-6, 228, 230, 233, 265, 298, 317, 371-3
Wotan, *The Ring* cycle, 89, 152, 195, 209, 284, 367
Wright, Sheila, 188-9, 210, 222, 224, 237

Yorkshire, 116, 206
Yorkshire Post, 308

Zamboni, Maria, 91, 363
Zandonai, Riccardo, 291
Zeeti, Aldo, 161
Zerlina, *Don Giovanni*, 33
Zukerman, Pinchas, 319

COMPACT DISC
The Opera World of Dame Eva Turner

Eva Turner

1 Turandot, Puccini, In Questa Reggia — 5.43
   Conductor: Stanford Robinson
   Rec: 17 June 1928 Matrix AX 7636-2 & 7637-3 Col D1631

2 Aida, Verdi, Ritorna Vincitor — 6.34
   Conductor: Sir Thomas Beecham, Bart., C.H.
   Rec: 19 July 1928 Matrix AX 3931-3 & 3932-2 Col L2150

3 Aida, Verdi, O Patria Mia — 3.53
   Conductor: Stanford Robinson
   Rec: 17 June 1928 Matrix AX 3925-1 Col L2156

4 Il Trovatore, Verdi, D'Amor Sull'Ali Rosee — 3.51
   Conductor: Sir Thomas Beecham, Bart., C.H.
   Rec: 19 July 1928 Matrix AX 3933-1 Col L2156

Walter Widdop

5 Maritana, Wallace, Yes Let Me Like A Soldier Fall — 3.03
   Conductor: Lawrence Collingwood
   Rec: 23 January 1930 Matrix Cc 17998-3 Gram D 1887

Elisabeth Schumann

6 Die Meistersinger von Nürnberg, Wagner, Quintet: Selig, wie
   die Sonne meines Glückes lacht — 4.42
   With Gladys Parr, Lauritz Melchior, Friedrich Schorr, Ben Williams
   London Symphony Orchestra Conductor: Sir John Barbirolli, C.H.,
   Rec: 16 May 1931 Matrix 2B543 Gram D2002

Alexander Kipnis

7 Der Wildschutz, Lortzing, Funflausend Taler — 4.32
   Conductor: Erich Orthmann
   Rec: 17 April 1931 Matrix 2D330-2 Gram EJ696

Lotte Schöne

8 Die Zauberflöte, Mozart, Ach Ich Fühl's — 4.28
   Conductor: Fritz Zweig
   Rec: 8 April 1931 Matrix 2D257-2 Gram EJ262

Frida Leider
9 Don Giovanni, Mozart, Or sai che l'onore 3.56
   Conductor: Sir John Barbirolli, C.H.
   Rec: 11 May 1928 Matrix CR2010-1 Gram 2-053325

Tito Schipa
10 Orfeo ed Euridice, Gluck, Che Farò 4.24
    Conductor: Carlo Sabajno
    Rec: 9 May 1932 Matrix 2M482-3 Gram DB1723

Claudia Muzio
11 Ombra di Nube, Refice 3.23
    Conductor: Licinio Refice.
    Rec: 6 June 1935 Matrix CBX 1365-1 Col BQX2502

Beniamino Gigli
12 Aida, Verdi, Celeste Aida 4.33
    Conductor: Walter Goehr
    Rec: 28 May 1937 Matrix 2EA5255-1 Gram DB3225

Ebe Stignani
13 La Favorita, Donizetti, O Mio Fernando 7.13
    Conductor: Vincenzo Bellezza
    Rec: 10 December 1946 Matrix CBX 1594-1 & 1595-1 Col LX1106

Aureliano Pertile
14 Luisa Miller, Verdi, Quando le Sere 3.44
    Conductor: Carlo Sabajno
    Rec: 17 October 1927 Matrix CD4759-1 Gram DB1111

Giacomo Lauri-Volpi
15 L'Africana, Meyerbeer, O paradiso 3.33
    Conductor: Franco Ghione
    Rec: 28 May 1934 Matrix 2W2532-2 Gram DB2263

Giovanni Martinelli
16 La Forza del Destino, Verdi, Io Muoio! Confessione! 8.02
    Conductor: Rosario Bourdon
    Rec: 18 January 1928 Matrix CVE 41625/6 Victor 8104

Playing time 76.34

CD produced by Nimbus Records, Monmouth U.K.
© & ℗ 2011 Wyastone Estate Ltd
Compilation and transfers from original source material by Norman White

ACKNOWLEDGEMENTS

The publishers are grateful to the following individuals and organisations for providing photographs and for permission to reproduce copyright material. Every effort has been made to trace and acknowledge copyright holders.

p.340 – Eyeglasses and Spectacles – Making music, Lucinda Douglas-Menzies (National Portrait Gallery)

p.207 – Henry Wood surrounded by his chosen singers for 'Serenade to Music' (The Tully Potter Collection)

Back Cover – Portrait of Dame Eva Turner by June Mendoza

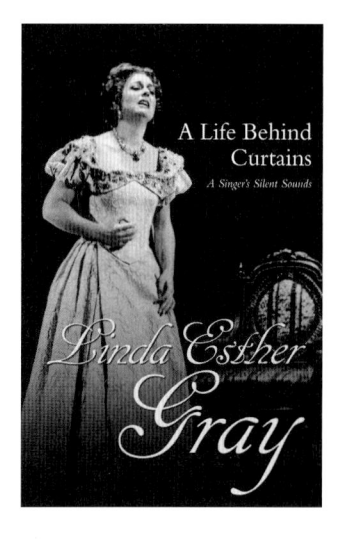

OTHER BOOKS BY GREEN OAK PUBLISHING

A Life Behind Curtains

A Singers Silent Sounds – Linda Esther Gray

A Life Behind Curtains tells the human story of loss and recovery.

Linda Esther Gray lost her voice just as she was about to reach the height of a singer's aspirations and sing at the Metropolitan Opera House. The story spans her childhood and her early life, through her singing career into disaster, how she struggles to survive without her voice and then returns to being able to sing again.

Linda tells the story with truth and the imagination that she once employed to communicate and move her audiences throughout the world.

'Few performers are naturally 'stars', that is those that dominate the stage by the merest twinkle in their eye. I have no doubt whatsoever that Linda is one of such. Those who never saw her on stage missed something very special indeed.'
TONY PALMER

'To see and hear Linda in performance is to be thrilled and moved by her wonderful voice and commitment to the composers' wishes. Communication is the essence of great singing. These gifts are mirrored in her unswerving devotion to family and friends.'
ELIZABETH GALE

'Glyndebourne has always prided itself on its discovery of vocal talent on the verge of International recognition. To the role of Mimi, Linda brought a depth of pathos which wrung a deluge of tears from the audience. Her career leaves a lasting impression of a singer of exceptional talent with an innate ability to hold centre stage without artifice or apparent effort - a true artist.'
SIR GEORGE CHRISTIE

'Few artists are able to combine such warmth of personality with a truly heroic scale of singing. Working with Linda was always a joy and I can easily imagine, with all its ups and downs, her life will make an engrossing book.'
MARK ELDER

OTHER BOOKS BY GREEN OAK PUBLISHING

Can We All Sing?

A Handbook for Singers – Linda Esther Gray

Can We All Sing? is a little handbook for singers and also for those who would like to try. Linda Esther Gray has spent her life in the singing world. She sees life through the prism of sound and in this handbook hopes to pass on some of her singing thoughts and ideas.

Contents

Discovery and Research
What is natural singing?
Where and What is our Instrument?
How Can We Improve On Nature?
How Should We Exercise Our Voice?
Are We In Balance
Anatomy
Research
Interpretation
Repertoire
Performing
Preparing our Mind and Body
Communicating with our Audience and Colleagues
Winding Down After a Performance
Dealing with Feed Back
Learning from Performing

Illustrated by Caroline Finlayson

Available from Green Oak Publishing.

www.greenoakpublishing.com
www.singbelcanto.com